A sociology of

mental health and illness

Third edition

A sociology of
mental health and illness

Third edition

Anne Rogers
and
David Pilgrim

Open University Press

Open University Press
McGraw-Hill Education
McGraw-Hill House
Shoppenhangers Road
Maidenhead
Berkshire
England
SL6 2QL

email: enquiries@openup.co.uk
world wide web: www.openup.co.uk

and Two Penn Plaza, New York, NY 10121-2289, USA

First published 2005

Reprinted 2006, 2007

A catalogue record of this book is available from the British Library

ISBN-13:   978 0335 21583 6 (pb)   978 0335 21584 3 (hb)
ISBN-10:   0335 21583 1 (pb)   0335 21584 X (hb)

Library of Congress Cataloging-in-Publication Data
CIP data applied for

Typeset by RefineCatch Ltd, Bungay, Suffolk
Printed in the UK by Bell & Bain Ltd, Glasgow

For Steven and Jack (Again!)

Contents

Preface to the third edition

Our first preface in 1993 emphasized that this book was *A*, not, *The Sociology of Mental Health and Illness*. Today, more than ever, it is quite a risk to write 'The Sociology' of anything. Moreover, as the wide-ranging references listed at the end of the book indicate, we continue to draw our material from sociology but also many other sources, including psychology and psychiatry. Sociological analyses of our topic are not offered only by sociologists. Since the previous edition was published in 1999, good examples of this point from other disciplines have appeared, including Richard Bentall's *Madness Explained* (2003) and Christopher Dowrick's *Beyond Depression* (2004) (from psychology and medicine respectively). Both of these provide illuminating ways of exploring psychological abnormality in its social context by emphasizing historical analysis and a close attention to the meaning of the personal accounts of people with mental health problems.

Our development of sociological reasoning is helped by the examination and incorporation of work in these other disciplines. Sometimes this involves using the empirical findings of their studies to build up an argument. Sometimes it is about applying a sociological approach to their production. A further complication is that some sociologists now co-author their work with collaborators from other disciplines and this joint work may appear in non-sociology journals. Although disciplinary silos are still often jealously protected in the academy, research in an applied and broad area like mental health invariably leads to a range of inter-disciplinary outcomes.

As a consequence of these considerations, we cannot write a sociology book which *only* refers to sociology titles (or if we did the product would be much the poorer). However, this broad engagement with our topic means that boundary lines have to be drawn at times. For example, our partial and partisan summary of the field means that we focus on some native concerns in detail. This is exemplified in the chapter on race in which we overwhelmingly dwell on the post-colonial British picture, although in many other chapters the material would be relevant to any Anglophone audience.

We wrote the first edition of the book at the end of the 1980s when sociological debates about mental health and psychiatry were not as salient as they had been during the 1960s and 1970s. During those earlier decades, mental illness had been subject to considerable scrutiny and was used as an exemplar in mainstream sociological theorizing on deviance and social control. The popularity of sociological work about psychiatry during that 'counter-cultural' period was also fuelled by radical critiques from some mental health professionals, who questioned their own traditional theory and practice. While a sociological interest in mental health continued in North America, in Britain the 1980s witnessed sociological interest in health and illness turning more and more to mainstream topics of physical and chronic illness. Sociology's reputation for being an intellectual fellow traveller of, or contributor to, 'anti-psychiatry' had diminished. (Note: sociology was a fellow traveller but the main drivers of 'anti-psychiatry' were psychiatrists.)

The sociological imagination of anti-psychiatric writers was challenged. First there was the appearance of Anthony Clare's urbane and reformist *Psychiatry in Dissent* (1976), which defused the libertarian and Marxian resonances of psychiatry's critics and then by a more aggressive return to psychiatric tradition in John Wing's *Reasoning About Madness* (1978). This contained a contemptuous attack upon the ideas of Michel Foucault. Wing's defence of his profession involved a dismissal of lay views of madness and an appeal for more robust medical conceptualizations of mental disorder. This sort of critique from those like Wing, who until then had worked collaboratively with sociologists, helped to deflate sociological confidence in the study of mental health and illness. Goodwill between sociology and psychiatry was also lost in these cross-disciplinary spats. The legacy of this loss is still evident today, with psychiatric texts expressing doubts about the worth of sociological contributions to an understanding of mental health (Gelder *et al.* 2001).

By the late 1990s, when our second edition appeared, several contradictions seemed to have emerged in: mental health service practices; civil society's interest in mental health; and the analyses sociologists deploy in understanding these social relationships. During the mid-1990s the topics of mental health and illness enjoyed some rekindled sociological attention. Consumerism and user participation within the NHS and wider society found a particularly strong voice within mental health campaigns.

Sociological work on the problematic history of institutionalization and deinstitutionalization and women's mental health were re-invigorated by a series of government social policy considerations, as well as by the rise of feminist ideas within community care debates. At the same time, within psychiatry, biological ideas had found a fresh vigour, with a renewed interest and enthusiasm for psychopharmacology, hi-tech brain photography and behavioural genetics.

Reflecting on the 'decade of the brain', an academic champion of biological psychiatry, Samuel Guze (1989) had asked the rhetorical question, 'biological psychiatry: is there any other kind?'. If this sort of triumphalist conclusion had been genuinely warranted by evidence, then, it would seem, decades of socially informed correctives to bio-reductionism had all been in vain. After its professional dismissal as a therapeutic abomination, psychosurgery, which involves the destruction of healthy brain tissue, returned to respectability within NHS medical practice. Despite recurrent hostile user campaigns ECT remained the 'treatment of choice' for severe and intractable depression. These were powerful signals that the cognitive interests of the psychiatric profession were still driving a bio-medical orthodoxy.

While pharmaceutical research and marketing stabilized this trend, the continuing zeal of many psychiatrists for electricity and even the scalpel showed that drug company profit alone could not explain the position championed and enjoyed by Guze and others. The latter included psychiatric historians, like Edward Shorter (1998: vii), who argued that:

> . . . if there is one central intellectual reality (sic) at the end of the twentieth century, it is that the biological approach to psychiatry – treating mental illness as a genetically influenced disorder of brain chemistry – has been a smashing success.

Shorter's confident claim begs the question: 'smashing success for whom?'. Has it been a 'smashing success' according to patients or psychiatrists or politicians or the majority of us, who are sane by mutual consent, or the pharmaceutical industry? These are both common-sense and sociological questions because they indicate communities of interest with potentially competing aims and views of reality. But scientism and bio-reductionism within psychiatry have not gone unchallenged in mental health debates in recent years. Some critical psychiatrists have argued that we have come to live in a post-psychiatric society and that their own profession can 'no longer claim any privileged understanding of madness, alienation or distress' (Bracken and Thomas 1998). 'Post-psychiatry', rather than 'anti-psychiatry', now coexists in tension with mainstream bio-medical views.

Additionally, a further trend we noted at the time of writing the second edition was the increasing integration of sociological ideas about mental health and illness with those from other disciplines concerned with mental health. For example, feminist psychologists have drawn on social history and social constructionism to analyse gender and mental health. In mental health nursing there was, and continues to be, evidence of the integration of key concepts associated with the sociological analysis of mental health.

The increasing salience of the 'psy complex' and the popularity of sociological analyses, which focus on the ontological status of emotions and intimacy in everyday life, currently sit alongside evidence of the increasing social exclusion and stereotyping of people with severe and enduring mental health problems. The rise in popularity of counselling, psychological therapies and psychoanalytical ideas and the 'regulatory systems' in contemporary society, which promote rather than crush subjectivity (Miller and Rose 1988), have extended into the arenas of primary care and self management. And yet, the old 'anti-psychiatric' targets (including for the early Foucault) are still evident about coercive control and surveillance, in new service developments, such as 'assertive outreach' and the 'care programme approach', 'early intervention for psychosis' and the extension of legal measures of control to community settings. A concern with risk, which pervades sociological and cultural analysis generally, has found a peculiar expression in the mental health field.

Research has consistently demonstrated the importance of social support networks and employment in the community and the *risk to* mental health when these are absent. However, as work we summarize in Chapters 2 and 10 shows, public, media and politician concerns have focused unduly on the actual or assumed *risk from* psychiatric patients.

This prejudicially narrow focus on risky patients by several powerful interest groups contributes to the stigmatization and social exclusion of all people with mental health problems. An ethical imperative then arises for students of mental health and illness to generate a knowledge-based corrective. The latter points up the evidence we have that people with mental health problems are at risk of victimization in their childhood, in the patient role during service contact, and when living in open community settings. It also highlights that mental status is not a particularly good predictor of violence.

In his *Unhealthy Societies*, Richard Wilkinson (1996) has demonstrated many aspects of the relationship between agency and structure in understanding health inequalities. Social analyses of this type can provide a rich conceptual basis for understanding the inter-play between self-identity, personal experience and the social circumstances which generate variations in well-being. They provide us with some confidence both to avoid the seduction of common stereotypes of decontextualized risky individuals and to understand how patients survive as precarious agents in risky life circumstances. In the final chapter of the book, we draw attention to what Bernard Williams, the moral philosopher, called an 'effort at identification', when trying to understand the lives of psychiatric patients. It is only through that effort that a proper sociological analysis of mental health problems can be furnished.

Moving from patient narratives to their wider social context, since the mid-1990s, globalization has been of increasing interest to sociologists (and many others). Definitions of it vary but, broadly, it includes *both* an economic trend of trans-national domination by a limited number of capitalist organizations *and* a cultural trend of international convergence and homogenization ('the global village') – enabled by changes in technology such as the World Wide Web and the speed and availability of air transport. The emergence of the 'anti-globalization' movement largely reflects provoked opposition to the first of these. The second trend has found its advocates and critics on both the political left and right.

Of particular interest for the topic of this book is the World Health Organization's Report on mental health (WHO 2001). This strongly advocates the universalization of key features of mental health provision irrespective of cultural, social or economic context.

> The World Health Report 2001 provides a new understanding of mental disorders that offers new hope to the mentally ill and their families in all countries and all societies . . . It examines the scope of prevention and the availability of, and obstacles to, treatment. It deals in detail with service provision and planning; and it concludes with a set of far-reaching recommendations that can be adapted by every country according to its needs and its resources.

In suggesting a universally applicable list of recommendations, the WHO Report represents a development, which has the powerful potential to affect polices on mental health and illness across the globe. In the USA, President Bush has already endorsed those referring to mass community screening for mental health problems and increases in psychotropic drug availability. Other recommendations relate to providing treatment in primary care, providing care in the community, educating the public about mental health, involving communities, families and consumers, developing national policies, programmes and legislation, developing human resources (training), linking with other agencies, monitoring treatment and prevention and undertaking more research.

The WHO document excludes culturally specific ways of managing mental distress and consolidates a medicalized approach to mental health, which prioritizes the use of psychotropic drugs as the first line of treatment. It reproduces an ideology of progress based upon the greater availability for all of medical solutions to complex psycho-social problems. Its emphasis on legislation for all implies that laws enabling professionals to lock up others without trial and interfere with their bodies without fear of prosecution for common assault are unquestionably a sign of social advancement. The concurrent emphasis in the document on the involvement of users and carers also mirrors the contradictions in current mental health policies of more developed societies.

This 'more of the same' position contains important silences about psychological distress as a pathway into social understanding and to the power struggle between professional tribes and between professionals and mental health service users. The pharmaceutical industry is presented as a neutral supplier of much-needed products, as if its profit seeking has had no role in shaping the landscape of mental health services. The emphasis on screening is consistent with an old public health ideology of state surveillance. Within the WHO model there is no consideration of the peculiar ethical and political role of psychiatry in its normal routines.

Finally, we note the recent trend of re-examining an old and unresolved problem for the human sciences – the relationship between psyche and soma. Questions about the legitimacy of mental and physical illness have been revitalized by recent debates about the problematic nature of so called 'medically unexplained symptoms'. The split between mind and body fits uneasily with the way in which problems are articulated and expressed by patients.

The preference from many patients for the presentation of distress as neither simply physical nor simply mental is clearly shown by explorations of 'depression'. The latter has been found to be grounded *both* in the materiality of the body *and* immersed in subjective experiences and the social contexts of women's lives (Burt and Chapman 2004). (We explore this point further in Chapter 4.) Also, descriptions of essentially physical complaints, such as musculoskeletal problems, suggest a lack of clear demarcation between pain located in specific parts of the body and broader social and personal concerns. At the same time, people with these conditions may be unwilling to recognize these concerns as 'depression' or 'psychological distress' (Rogers and Allison 2004).

The failure to be commensurate with the Western Cartesean dualism or the 'mind/body split' poses a problem for disciplinary knowledge within medicine. It also creates health service challenges about 'condition management'. Those who are unable to articulate their problem as *either* a physical *or* a mental one are caught in an existential limbo. They then experience an extra vulnerability when faced with forms of professional knowledge and service organization, which are ill equipped to respond helpfully. The primary care system is left to contain biopsychosocial distress, often without recourse to the quantity and quality of palliation available to those designated with clear physical problems on the one hand or psychiatric problems on the other (May *et al.* 2004).

We hope that the updated text in this new edition reflects and records the implications of these changes in various chapters. The chapter topics, with some slight rewording of some titles, are the same as in the previous edition, with one exception. In recognition of the rekindled sociological interest in stigma and social exclusion, we have introduced a new dedicated chapter.

Anne Rogers
David Pilgrim

Acknowledgements

We are grateful for the many sources of feedback, from course tutors and published reviews, passed on to us by Open University Press about the previous edition of this book. The extensive and constructive advice offered to us from Mick Carpenter at the University of Warwick and two other anonymous reviewers to improve the text has been particularly appreciated. Thanks are also offered to our colleagues at the Universities of Liverpool and Manchester and, of course, the many students who have bought the book over the past decade and justified the production of this new edition.

Anne Rogers
David Pilgrim

Chapter 1

Perspectives on mental health and illness

Chapter overview

This chapter will make some necessary conceptual clarifications about the question of terminology. Our assumption at the outset is that terminology remains such a controversial issue for the sociology of mental health and illness because there are markedly differing ways of speaking about mental normality and abnormality in contemporary society. Rather than assuming that there are competing claims about the same issue, or set of issues, we need to take a step back and check on different frameworks of understanding. In other words, what perspectives or discourses do we need to understand at the outset about normal and abnormal mental life?

The chapter will cover the following four perspectives outwith sociology:

- psychiatry;
- psychoanalysis;
- psychology;
- the legal framework.

The lay view is dealt with in the next chapter because of its importance to understanding public responses to mental health problems. Labelling theory (societal reaction theory) will also be dealt with in the next chapter.

This chapter will then cover the following four-perspectives within sociology:

- social causation;
- critical theory;
- social constructivism;
- social realism.

The perspectives outwith sociology

Psychiatry

We start with psychiatry because it has been the dominant discourse. Accordingly, it has shaped the views of others or has provoked alternative or opposing perspectives. While psychiatric patients (Rogers, Pilgrim and Lacey 1993) and those in multi-disciplinary mental health teams (Colombo *et al.* 2003) evince a complex range of views about the nature of mental disorder, each of these models competes for recognition and authority alongside the traditional and dominant medical approach deployed by psychiatry

Psychiatry is a speciality within medicine. Its practitioners, as in other specialties, are trained to see their role as identifying sick individuals (diagnosis), predicting the future course of their illness (prognosis), speculating about its cause (aetiology) and prescribing a response to the condition, to cure it or ameliorate its symptoms (treatment). Consequently, it would be surprising if psychiatrists did not think in terms of illness when they encounter variations in conduct which are troublesome to people (be they the identified patient or those upset by them). Those psychiatrists who have rejected this illness framework, in whole or in part, tend to have been exposed to, and have accepted, an alternative view derived from another discourse (psychology, philosophy or sociology).

As with other branches of medicine, psychiatrists vary in their assumptions about diagnosis, prognosis, aetiology and treatment. This does not imply, though, that views are evenly spread throughout the profession, and as we will see later in the book, modern Western psychiatry is an eclectic enterprise. It does, however, have dominant features. In particular, diagnosis is considered to be a worthy ritual for the bulk of the profession and biological causes are favoured along with biological treatments.

This biological emphasis has a particular social history, which is summarized in Chapter 8. However, this should not deflect our attention from the capacity of an illness framework to accommodate multiple aetiological factors. For instance, a psychiatrist treating a patient with antidepressant drugs may recognize fully that living in a high-rise flat and being unemployed have been the main causes of the depressive illness, and may assume that the stress this induces has triggered biochemical changes in the brain, which can be corrected by using medication.

The illness framework is the dominant framework in mental health services because psychiatry is the dominant profession within those services (see Chapter 8). However, its dominance should not be confused with its conceptual superiority. The illness framework has its strengths in terms of its logical and empirical status, but it also has many weaknesses. Its strengths lie in the neurological evidence about madness: bacteria and viruses have been demonstrably associated with madness (syphilis and encephalitis). Such a neurological theory might be supported further by the experience and behaviour of people with temporal lobe epilepsy, who may present with anxiety and sometimes florid psychotic states. The induction of abnormal mental states by brain lesions, drugs, toxins, low blood sugar and fever might all point to the sense in regarding mental illness as a predominantly biological condition.

The question begged is: what has medicine to do with that wide range of mental problems that elude a biological explanation? Indeed, the great bulk of what psychiatrists call 'mental illness' has no proven bodily cause, despite substantial research efforts to solve the riddle of a purported or assumed biological aetiology. These illnesses include anxiety neuroses, reactive depression and functional psychoses (the schizophrenias and the affective conditions of mania and severe or endogenous depression). While there is some evidence that we may inherit a vague predisposition to nervousness or madness, there are no clear-cut laws evident to biological researchers as yet. Both broad dispositions run in families, but not in such a way as to satisfy us that they are biologically caused. Upbringing in such families might equally point to learned behaviour and the genetic evidence from twin studies remains contested (Marshall 1990).

It may be argued that biological treatments that bring about symptom relief themselves point to biological aetiology (such as the lifting of depression by ECT or the diminution of auditory hallucination by major tranquillizers). However, this may not follow: thieving can be prevented quite effectively by chopping off the hands of perpetrators, but hands do not cause theft. Likewise, a person shocked following a car crash may feel better by taking a minor tranquillizer, but their state is clearly environmentally induced. The thief's hands and the car crash victim's brain are merely biological mediators in a wider set of personal, economic and social relationships. Thus, effective biological treatments cannot be invoked as necessary proof of biological causation.

A fundamental problem with the illness framework in psychiatry is that it deals, in the main, with symptoms, not signs. That is, the judgements made about whether or not a person is mentally ill or healthy focus mainly (and often singularly) on the person's communications. This is certainly the case in the diagnosis of neurosis and the functional psychoses. Even in organic conditions, such as dementia, brain damage is not always detectable post-mortem (see Chapter 6). In the diagnosis of physical illness the diagnosis can often be confirmed using physical signs of changes in the body (e.g. the visible inflammation of tissue as well as the patient reporting pain).

However, it is possible to overdraw the distinctions between physical and mental illness. For example, an internal critic of psychiatry, Thomas Szasz (1961), has argued that mental illness is a myth. He says that only bodies can be ill in a literal sense and that minds can only be sick metaphorically (like economies). And yet, as we noted earlier, physical disturbances can sometimes produce profound psychological disturbances. Given that emotional distress has a well-established causative role in a variety of psychosomatic illnesses, like gastric ulcers and cardiovascular disease, the mutual inter-play of mind and body seems to be indicated on reasonable grounds.

It is true (following Szasz 1961) that the validity of mental diagnosis is undermined more by its over-reliance on symptoms and by the absence of detectable bodily signs, but this can apply at times even in physical medicine. For instance, a person may feel very ill with a headache but it may be impossible to appeal to signs to check whether or not this is because of a toxic reaction, for instance a 'hangover', or a brain tumour. Also, people with chronic physical problems have much in common, in terms of their social role, with psychiatric patients – both are disabled and usually not valued by their non-disabled fellows. Finally, the absence of a firm biological aetiology is true of a number of physical illnesses, such as multiple sclerosis. Thus, the conceptual and empirical uncertainties that Szasz draws our attention to, legitimately, about mental illnesses, can apply also to what he considers to be 'true illnesses'.

A final point to note about the biological emphasis in psychiatry is that it has been repeatedly challenged by a minority of psychiatrists, including but not only Szasz. For example, some retain diagnosis but reject narrow biological explanations. They prefer to offer a biopsychosocial model which takes into account social circumstances and biographical nuances (Engel 1980; Pilgrim 2002a). Others have argued that madness is intelligible provided that the patient's social context is fully understood (Laing and Esterson 1964). More recently some psychiatrists have embraced social constructivism and argued that their profession has no privileged understanding of mental disorder. This emerging 'post-psychiatry' 'emphasizes social and cultural contexts, places ethics before technology and works to minimize medical control of coercive interventions' (Bracken and Thomas 2001: 725).

Psychoanalysis

Psychoanalysis was the invention of Sigmund Freud. It has modern adherents who are loyal to his original theories but there are other trained analysts who adopt the views of Melanie Klein; others take a mixed position, borrowing from each theory. Thus, psychoanalysis is an eclectic or fragmented discipline. Its emphasis on personal history places it in the domain of biographical psychology. Indeed, Freud's work is sometimes called depth or psychodynamic psychology, along with the legacies of his dissenting early group such as Jung, Adler and Reich. Depth psychology proposes that the mind is divided between conscious and unconscious parts and that the dynamic relationship between these gives rise to psychopathology.

Like other forms of psychology, psychoanalysis works on a continuum principle – abnormality and normality are connected, not disconnected and separate. To the psychoanalyst we are all ill to some degree. However, the medical roots of psychoanalysis and the continued dominance of medical analysts within its culture have, arguably, left it within a psychiatric, not psychological, discourse. It still uses the terminology of pathology ('psychopathology' and its 'symptoms'); assessments are 'diagnostic' and its clients 'patients'; people do not merely have ways of avoiding human contact, they have 'schizoid defences' and they do not simply get into the habit of angrily blaming others all of the time, instead they are 'fixated in the paranoid position'. The language of psychoanalysis is saturated with psychiatric terms. Thus, the discipline of psychoanalysis stands somewhere between psychiatry and psychology.

Psychoanalysis, arguably, has two strengths. First, it offers a comprehensive conceptual framework about mental abnormality. Once a devotee accepts its strictures, it offers the comfort of explaining, or potentially explaining, every aspect of human conduct. Second, there is a symmetry between its causal theory and its corrective programme. That which has been rendered unconscious by past relationships can be rendered conscious by a current relationship with a therapist.

Its first weakness is the obverse of biological psychiatry. The latter tends to reduce psychological phenomena to biology, whereas psychoanalysis tends to psychologize everything (i.e. the biological and the social as well as the personal). A person with temporal lobe epilepsy or a brain tumour would be helped little by a psychoanalyst. The brain-damaged patient would certainly give the analyst plenty to interpret, but the analyst would be wrong to attribute a psychological, rather than a neurological, cause. Likewise, socially determined deviance (like prostitution emerging in poor or drug-using cultures) may be explained away psychoanalytically purely in terms of individual history (Pilgrim 1992; 1998). A second weakness of psychoanalysis as a frame of reference is that it can do no more than be wise after the event. It has never reached the status of a predictive science.

Psychology

Psychoanalysis has competed with other psychological accounts of mental abnormality. Moreover, because psychology, as a broad and eclectic discipline, focuses, in the main, on 'normal' conduct and experience it has offered concepts of normality as well as abnormality. Buss (1966) suggests that psychologists have put forward four conceptions of normality/abnormality:

1 the statistical notion;
2 the ideal notion;
3 the presence of specific behaviours;
4 distorted cognitions.

The statistical notion

The statistical notion simply says that frequently occurring behaviours in a population are normal – so infrequent behaviours are not normal. This is akin to the notion of norms in sociology. Take as an example the tempo at which people speak. Up to a certain speed, speech would be called normal. If someone speaks above a certain speed they might be considered to be 'high' in ordinary parlance or 'hypomanic' or suffering from 'pressure of thought' in psychiatric language. If someone speaks below a certain speed they might be described as depressed. Most people would speak at a pace between these upper and lower points of frequency.

A question begged, of course, is who decides on the cut offs at each end of the frequency distribution of speech speed and how are those decisions made? In other words, the notion of frequency in itself tells us nothing about when a behaviour is to be adjudged normal or abnormal. Value judgements are required on the part of lay people or professionals when punctuating the difference between normality and abnormality. Also, a statistical notion may not hold good across cultures, even within the same country: for example, slow speech might be the norm in one culture, say in rural areas, but not in another, such as the inner city.

The statistical notion of normality tells us nothing in itself about why some deviations are noted when they are unidirectional rather than bidirectional. The example of speech speed referred to bidirectional judgements. Take, in contrast, the notion of intelligence. Brightness is valued at one end of the distribution but not at the other. Being bright will not lead, in itself, to a person entering the patient role, but being dim may well do so.

In spite of these conceptual weaknesses, the statistical approach within abnormal psychology remains strong. Clinical psychologists are trained to accept that characteristics in any population follow a normal distribution and so the statistical notion has a strong legitimacy for them. This acceptance of the normal distribution of a characteristic in a population means that in psychological models there is usually assumed to be an unbroken relationship between the normal and abnormal. However, this notion of continuity of, say, everybody being more or less neurotic, may also assume a discontinuity from other variables. For instance, in Eysenck's (1955) personality theory neurosis and psychosis are considered to be personality characteristics that are both normally distributed but separate from one another.

The ideal notion

There are two versions of this notion: one from psychoanalysis and the other from humanistic psychology. In the former case, normality is defined by a predominance of conscious over unconscious characteristics in the person (Kubie 1954). In the latter case, the ideal person is one who fulfils their human potential (or 'self-actualizes'). Jahoda (1958) drew together six criteria for positive mental health to elaborate and aggregate these two psychological traditions:

1 balance of psychic forces;
2 self-actualization;
3 resistance to stress;
4 autonomy;
5 competence;
6 perception of reality.

The problem is that each of these notions is problematic as a definition of normality (and, by implication, abnormality). The first and second are only meaningful to those in a culture who subscribe to their theoretical premises (such as psychoanalytical or humanistic psychotherapists).

The resistance-to-stress notion is superficially appealing but what of people who fail to be affected by stress at all? We can all think of situations in which anxiety is quite normal and we would wonder in such circumstances why a person fails to react in an anxious manner. Indeed, the absence of anxiety under high-stress conditions has been one defining characteristic of 'primary psychopathy' by psychiatrists. Likewise, those who are excessively autonomous (i.e. avoid human contact) might be deemed to be 'schizoid' or be suffering from 'simple schizophrenia'.

As for competence, this cannot be judged as an invariant quality. As we will see when discussing young adults and mental health in Chapter 6, norms of competence vary over time and place. Likewise with perceptions of reality. In some cultures, seeing visions or hearing voices is highly valued, and yet it would be out of sync with the reality perceived by most in that culture. In other cultures the hallucinators may be deemed to be suffering from alcoholic psychosis or schizophrenia.

The presence of specific behaviours

The emergence of psychology as a scientific academic discipline was closely linked to its attention to specifiable aspects of conduct. It emerged and separated from speculative philosophy on the basis of these objectivist credentials. Behaviourism, the theory that tried to limit the purview of psychology to behaviour and eliminate subjective experience as data, no longer dominates psychology but it has left a lasting impression. Within clinical psychology, behaviour therapy and its modified versions are still common practices. Consequently, many psychologists are concerned to operationalize in behavioural terms what they mean by abnormality.

The term 'maladaptive behaviour' is part of this psychological discourse, as is 'unwanted' or 'unacceptable' behaviour. The strength of this position is that it makes explicit its criteria for what constitutes abnormality. The weakness is that it leaves values and norms implicit. The terminology of specific behaviours still begs questions about what constitutes 'maladaptive'. Who decides what is 'unwanted' or 'unacceptable'? One party may want a behaviour to occur or find it acceptable but another may not. In these circumstances, those who have more power will tend to be the definers of reality. Thus, what constitutes unwanted behaviour is not self-evident but socially negotiated. Consequently, it reflects both the power relationships and the value system operating in a culture at a point in time.

Distorted cognitions

The final approach suggested by Buss emerged at a time when behaviourism was becoming the dominant force within the academic discipline. However, during the 1970s this behavioural emphasis declined and was eventually displaced by cognitivism. As a result, psychologists began to treat inner events as if they were behaviours (forming the apparently incongruous hybrid of a 'cognitive-behavioural' approach to mental health problems) or they increasingly incorporated constructivist, systemic and even psychoanalytical views (e.g. Bannister and Fransella 1970; Guidano 1987; Ryle 1990). It is not clear even now whether the ascendancy of 'cognitive therapy' within clinical psychology during the 1980s was driven by cognitivism or was merely legitimized by it. So much of the seminal writing on cognitive therapy came not from academic psychology but from clinicians, some of whom were psychiatrists, not psychologists, offering a pragmatic and a-theoretical approach to symptom reduction (e.g. Beck 1970; Ellis 1970).

The legal framework

Mental disorder represents the main point of contact between psychiatry and the law. The early days of psychiatry in the nineteenth century were heavily influenced by eugenic considerations – it was assumed that a variety of deviant conducts could be explained by a tainted gene pool in the lower social classes. This degeneracy theory, which characterized early biological psychiatry, linked together the mad, the bad and the dim. However, during the First World War and its aftermath such an underlying assumption began to falter. In the forensic field, there emerged a resistance to the old eugenic ideas of degeneracy, which accounted for criminality in terms of an inherited disposition to bad conduct (Forsythe 1990). This was replaced by an increasing interest in environmental or psychological explanations for lawbreaking. Since that time, psychiatric experts have played a major role in identifying and explaining criminal conduct.

Currently, in British law the notion of 'mental disorder' includes four separate conditions: 'mental illness', 'mental impairment', 'severe mental impairment', and 'psychopathic disorder'. The first of these is not defined; the second and third are references to people with learning difficulties, who are additionally deemed to be dangerous; the fourth refers to antisocial individuals who are 'abnormally aggressive' or who manifest 'seriously irresponsible conduct'. At the time of writing, the British government has offered a single definition of mental disorder in its Draft Mental Health Bill (Department of Health 2004), which might displace the descriptions of four separate conditions:

> 'Mental disorder' means an impairment of or a disturbance in the functioning of the mind or brain resulting from any disability or disorder of the mind or brain . . .
>
> (p. 3, S5)

Superficially this reads like a coherent English sentence. However, it poses a number of problems for the reader:

- the inter-dependent constituent parts of 'impairment', 'disturbance', 'disability' and 'disorder' are not explained or defined;
- the word 'disorder' is used to mean both the whole and a part, with no clear logical distinction between the two roles in the definition;
- the inclusion of the word 'brain' suggests that any patient suffering from a neurological disease affecting the central nervous system could potentially be framed as being mentally disordered;
- the word 'functioning' is used to connote functional criteria, apparently dealing with the difficulty that most mental health problems are of unknown or contested origins. Confusingly though, the words 'resulting from' are inserted, implying causal reasoning to the reader. This offer is then immediately retracted. The antecedents suggested are simply a restatement of dysfunction in the mind or brain (the use of the words 'disability' and 'disorder').

The legal framework thus tends to deploy tautological definitions or accepts that mental disorder is what mental health experts say it is. In particular cases tried in court, psychiatric opinion is offered as an expert view on the presence or absence of mental disorder. Because mental illness is not legally defined, judges have sometimes resorted to the lay discourse. In 1974, Judge Lawton said that the words 'mental illness' are 'ordinary words of the English language. They have no particular medical significance. They have no particular legal significance'. Lawton refers to the dictum of Lord Reid in a case where the defendant's mental state was being considered:

> I ask myself what would the ordinary sensible person have said about the patient's condition in this case if he had been informed of his behaviour? In my judgment such a person would have said 'Well the fellow is obviously mentally ill'. (cited in Jones 1991: 15).

This lay conception of legal insanity has been called 'the-man-must-be mad' test (Hoggett 1990).

In one sense, therefore, the legal framework accepts a psychiatric framework, but when the latter is found lacking then ordinary language definitions are invoked. It also raises the question about whether mental disorder is simply, for legal and lay purposes, incomprehensible conduct. 'Normal' criminal acts are clearly goal directed. 'Mentally disordered' criminal acts are not directed towards obvious personal gain. The boundary between these is not easy to maintain though, especially when making judgments about sex offenders. The latter seek personal gratification even if this is not financial. Under different circumstance, they may or may not be diagnosed as mentally disordered. Sex offenders may end up either in prison or in secure psychiatric units, showing that sexual gratification as a criminal motive confuses those prescribing a judicial response.

Also, some murderers are adjudged in commonsensical terms to be sane, despite the contrary view of expert witnesses. If the legal framework looks to lay people through a jury system to clarify the presence or absence of mental abnormality, then this ambivalence is likely to be reflected in their judgements. Lay people may argue that, on the one hand, a person must be 'sick' to perpetrate heinous acts but, on the other, that the acts warrant severe punishment or even death.

Whatever the logical strengths and weaknesses of the legal framework and the varied outcomes generated by the interaction of legal, psychiatric and lay opinion, it is practically and politically very important for two key reasons. First it defines the conditions under which mental health professionals can and cannot detain patients and compulsorily treat them, even when they have not broken the criminal law. These conditions will be dealt with in more detail in Chapter 10. Second it makes decisions about those who have broken the criminal law and who provisionally are deemed to be mentally disordered. In criminal law, for a person to be judged guilty, the court must be satisfied that there was malicious intent. Unintended but reckless or negligent acts are lesser crimes than those where 'malice aforethought' or *'mens rea'* is evident. For this reason, they tend to lead to less severe sentencing. In the case of British mentally disordered offenders, these judgments about culpability may be modified further in a legal setting, when the defendant's mental state is considered:

- The perpetrator may not be deemed fit to stand trial – they lack a 'fitness to plead'. In these circumstances, they may be sent to a secure hospital without trial, provided that their role in the offence is clear to the court. If their mental disorder is treatable or recovery emerges naturally with time, then they may be recalled at a later date to face trial;
- Whether or not the patient is deemed fit to plead, they may be judged to be 'not guilty by reason of insanity'. When this is the case, then the court, having taken psychiatric advice, decides that the person was sufficiently mentally disordered at the time of the offence that they were unaware that their actions were wrong. The insanity defence is more common in some countries than others. It is rare in Britain, where the next contingency is more likely to operate;
- The defence of 'diminished responsibility' can be invoked, when mentally disordered offenders commit murder, but not in the case of other crimes in current English law. The legal term used in this context is suffering from 'abnormality of mind', which does not map neatly on to diagnostic categories preferred by psychiatrists;
- The most contentious decision is in relation to temporary loss of reason and intention. This might apply to automatism (crimes committed while sleep-walking) and more commonly but also, more controversially, crimes committed while under the influence of drugs or alcohol. Substance abuse is particularly contentious. On the one hand it is deemed to be a mental disorder. On the other hand in some crimes, such as dangerous driving, the intoxicated driver is typically treated much more harshly, by the courts, than the sober one. When this happens, the presence of a mental disorder, where the offender can demonstrate their long-term substance dependence, does not mitigate the action but the reverse occurs.

Conclusion about the perspectives outwith sociology

The expert perspectives on mental health and illness all have a certain persuasiveness. Equally, we have noted some credibility problems that each encounters. The illness and legal frameworks emphasize discontinuity (people are ill/disordered or they are not) whereas the other perspectives tend to emphasize continuity. It is a matter of opinion whether a continuous or discontinuous model of normality and abnormality fits our knowledge of people's conduct and whether one or the other is morally preferable. Traditional psychiatrists might argue that, unlike psychoanalysts, they do not see abnormality everywhere. Psychoanalysts might argue that the pervasive condition of mental pain connects us all in a common humanity.

Our concern here is not to resolve these questions but to record them in order to demonstrate that the topic of mental health and illness is highly contested. There are no benchmarks that experts from different camps can agree on and discuss. Thus 'mental disorder' or 'mental illness' or 'maladaptive behaviour' or simply being 'loony' do not necessarily have a single referent. It is not only a matter of terminology, although it is in part. It is not simply like the difference between speaking of motor cars and automobiles. In our discussion, each perspective may be warranting certain types of reality but not others. What we have is a fragmented set of perspectives, divided internally and from one another, which occasionally overlap and enter the same world of discourse.

A final comment on the four perspectives is that all of them have difficulty in sustaining notions of mental health and illness which are stable, certain or invariant. In each case, the caveat of social relativism has to be registered. Judgements about health and illness (physical as well as mental) are value laden and reflect specific norms in time and place.

The perspectives within sociology

Having discussed perspectives about mental health and illness from outside of sociology, we now turn to contributions within the latter academic discipline. Four major sociological perspectives will be outlined: social causation, critical theory, social constructivism and social realism. A fifth perspective (societal reaction or labelling theory) will be considered separately in Chapter 2. These five perspectives bear the respective imprints of major contributions from Durkheim, Weber, Freud, Foucault and Marx. These influences are not linear but cross-cut and are mediated by the work of later contributors such as Sartre and Mead. Different theoretical perspectives have been popular and influential at different times. However, it is important to acknowledge that there is no set of boundaries to neatly periodize disciplinary trends. Rather, there are sedimented layers of knowledge which overlap unevenly in time and across disciplinary boundaries and professional preoccupations. The social causation thesis arguably peaked in the 1950s when a number of large-scale community surveys of the social causes of mental health problems and of the large psychiatric institutions were undertaken.

However, one of its most quoted exemplars appeared in the late 1970s and early 1980s (Brown and Harris 1978) and studies in the social causation tradition were set to proliferate in the late 1990s with an explicit government policy agenda designed to tackle the social, economic and environmental causes of mental health problems (Department of Health 1998). Similarly, there is no absolute distinction between sociological knowledge and other forms of knowledge. In relation to lay knowledge/perspective some sociological perspectives (such as symbolic interactionism) in large part draw on the meaning and understandings of lay people. More recently, and in line with a refound enthusiasm for psychoanalytical approaches applied to sociology, the sociological perspective of 'social constructionism' within sociology has been treated 'as if it were a client presenting itself for psychoanalysis' (Craib 1997). According to Craib social contructionism (discussed in more detail later):

> . . . can be seen as a manic psychosis – a defense against entering the depressive position . . . Sociologists find it difficult to recognise the limitations of their discipline – the depressive position – one reason being that we do not actually exercise power over anybody; social constructionism enables us to convince ourselves that the opposite is true, that we know everything about how people become what they are, that we do not have

to take account of other disciplines or sciences, but we can explain every-thing . . . a non-psychotic theory is one which knows its own limitations.

(p. 1)

The four sociological perspectives will now be considered.

Social causation

This response from sociologists essentially accepts contructs such as 'schizo-phrenia' or 'depression' as legitimate diagnoses. They are given the status of facts in themselves. Once these diagnoses are accepted, questions are then asked about the role of socially derived stress in their aetiology.

The emphasis within a social causation approach is upon tracing the rela-tionship between social disadvantage and mental illness. Given that many sociologists have considered the main indicator of disadvantage to be low social class and/or poverty, it is not surprising that studies investigating this relationship have been a strong current within social studies of psychiatric populations (see Chapter 3). Social class has not been the only variable investi-gated within this social causation perspective. Disadvantages of other sorts, related to race, gender and age have also been of interest. These studies will be picked up in Chapters 3, 4, 5 and 6.

The advantage of this psychiatric epidemiological perspective is that it pro-vides the sort of scientific confidence associated with objectivism and empiri-cism (methodological assurances of representativeness and pointers towards causal relationships). Four main disadvantage of the approach can be identi-fied. First, pre-empirical conceptual problems associated with psychiatric knowledge are either not acknowledged or are evaded (see for example Brown and Harris 1978). Second, psychiatric epidemiology investigates correlations between mental illness and antecedent variables. However, correlations are not necessarily indicative of causal relationships. Third, the investigation of large subpopulations cannot illuminate the lived experience of mental health problems or the variety of meanings attributed to them by patients and sig-nificant others. Fourth, medical epidemiology attempts to map the distribu-tions of causes of diseases, not merely the cases of disease. Because most of psychiatric illness is described as 'functional' (i.e. it has no known biological marker and its cause or causes are either not known or contested), then psychiatric epidemiology cannot fulfill the general expectation of mapping causes.

Critical theory

During the twentieth century, a number of writers attempted to account for the relationship between socio-economic structures and the inner lives of individuals. One example was the work of Sartre (1963) when he developed his 'progressive-regressive method'. This method was an attempt to understand biography in relation to its social context and understand social context via the accounts of people's lives. This existential development of humanistic Marxism competed with another and more elaborate set of discussions about the relationship between unconscious mental life and societal determinants and constraints.

Within Freud's early circle, a number of analysts took an interest in using their psychological insights in order to illuminate societal processes. This set a trend for later analysts, some of whom tended to reduce social phenomena to the aggregate impact of psychopathology (e.g. Bion 1959). The dangers of psychological reductionism were inevitable in a tradition (psychoanalysis) which had a starting focus of methodological individualism. Moreover, the individuals studied by psychoanalysis were from a peculiar social group (white, middle-class, European neurotics).

Out of this tradition emerged a group of Freudo-Marxists who came to be known as 'critical theorists', most of whom were associated with the Frankfurt Institute of Social Research which was founded in 1923 and led after 1930 by Horkheimer (Slater 1977). This group accordingly came to be known as the 'Frankfurt School'. The difference between the work of the Frankfurt School and most of clinical psychoanalysis was the focus on the inter-relationship between psyche and society. In an early address to the Institute, Horkheimer (1931: 14) set out its mission as follows:

> What connections can be established, in a specific social group, in a specific period in time, in specific countries, between the group, the changes in the psychic structures of its individual members and the thoughts and institutions that are a product of that society, and that have, as a whole, a formative effect upon the group under consideration?

These inter-relationships between the material environment of individuals and their cultural life and inner lives were subsequently explored by a number of writers in the Institute, including Marcuse, Adorno and Fromm. In addition, there were contributions from Benjamin (who was a marginal and ambivalent Institute member) and Reich, a Marxist psychoanalyst and outsider. These explorations had an explicit emancipatory intent and were characterized by anti-Stalinist as well as anti-fascist themes. Within the Frankfurt School, Freudianism was accepted as the only legitimate form of psychology which was, potentially at least, philosophically compatible with Marxism. (Both Freud and Marx were atheists and materialists, although Freud's materialism was barely historical.) The compatibility was explored and affirmed, though, by one member in particular who was a psychoanalyst – Fromm. The integration of Freudianism was selective and critical, filtering out or querying elements such as the death instinct (a revision of classical psychoanalytical theory by Freud himself (Freud 1920)) and questioning the mechanistic aspect of instinctual drive-theory.

The role of this group of critical theorists in social science has been important and seemingly paradoxical. For a theory which drew heavily, if selectively, upon clinical psychoanalysis, the raft of work associated with the Frankfurt School (which was largely relocated in the USA with the rise of Nazism) focused not on mental illness but instead upon what Fromm called the 'pathology of normalcy'. It was only seemingly paradoxical because psychoanalysis was (and still is) concerned with the notion that we are all ill – psychopathology for Freud and his followers was ubiquitous, varying between individuals only in degree and type. Accordingly, the concerns of this group of

Freudo-Marxists were about life-negating cultural norms associated with authoritarianism and the capitalist economy and the ambiguous role of the super-ego as a source of conformity and mutuality. These norms were said to be mediated by the intra-psychic mechanism (especially the repression) highlighted in Freud's theory of a dynamic unconscious.

Critical theory is exemplified in studies of the authoritarian personality (Adorno *et al.* 1950), the mass psychology of fascism (Reich 1933/1975; Fromm 1942) and the psychological blocks attending the transitions from capitalist to socialist democracy (Fromm, 1955). When Habermas (1989) came to review the project of the early Frankfurt School, he suggested a six-part programme of topic focus: forms of integration in post-liberal societies; family socialization and ego development; mass media and culture; the social psychology behind the cessation of protest; the theory of art; and the critique of positivism and science.

The work of the Frankfurt School eventually fragmented, with Horkheimer recanting his younger Marxism, and Fromm and Marcuse in post-war USA taking divergent and mutually critical paths about the programme summarized in Horkheimer's mission statement cited above (Marcuse 1964; Fromm 1970). The continuation of a project to examine a 'critical theory of society' was maintained by Habermas and Offe in the 1970s and 1980s (Habermas 1972; 1975; 1987; Offe 1984). Moreover, resonances of critical theory can be found in a variety of leftist Freudian projects which continued to explore the relationship between economics, culture and the psychopathology of the individual (Sennett and Cobb 1973; Jacoby 1975; Holland 1978; Lasch 1978; Richards 1984; Kovel 1988), as well as 'anti-psychiatry' (Cooper 1968; Laing 1967).

There is a continuing body of work which examines the way in which contemporary western society is developing in a pathological direction – through the culture of narcissism or the fragmented self represented in the metaphor of schizophrenia (Harvey 1989). Thus, critical theory is included here as an important sociological current of relevance to this book because it has been an influential framework for connecting the psyche and society.

The problems of critical theory have been twofold. First, as was indicated earlier, the theoretical centre of gravity of this project (the Frankfurt School) fragmented. Second, the meaningfulness of any hybrid of dialectical materialism and psychoanalysis requires social scientists to accept the legitimacy of both of its component parts and their conceptual and practical integration. This requires a triple act of faith or theoretical commitment which leaves many unconvinced, dubious or even hostile to the expectation.

The German version of Freudo-Marxism (the Frankfurt School) emerged in the first half of the twentieth century and its traces in social science, with the exception of Habermas and Offe, tend recently to be faint and influenced by other theoretical positions. For example, the long list of post-war American and British writers cited above have been part of a theoretical tradition which is still psychoanalytically orientated but reflects changes such as the impact of Klein and later object-relations theorists. Another Freudo-Marxian hybrid can be found, more recently, in French intellectual life, especially following the work of Althusser and Lacan (Elliot 1992). This current moved in a different direction from the Frankfurt School and contributed to the emergence in the 1970s of post-structuralism; a variant of the next perspective we summarize.

Social constructivism

One of the most influential theoretical positions evident in the sociology of health and illness over the past 20 years has been social constructivism – as mentioned earlier, it sometimes appears as 'social constructionism', especially, though not only, in psychological literature. A central assumption within this broad approach is that reality is not self-evident, stable and waiting to be discovered, but instead it is a product of human activity. In this broad sense all versions of social constructivism can be identified as a reaction against positivism and naïve realism. Brown (1995) suggests three main currents within social constructivism:

1 The first approach is not concerned with demonstrating the reality or otherwise of a social phenomenon but with the social forces which define it. The approach is mainly traceable to sociological work on *social problems* (Spector and Kitsuse 1977). To investigate a social problem, such as drug misuse or mental illness, is to select a particular aspect of reality and thus, implicitly, concede the factual status of reality in general (Woolgar and Pawluch 1985). In particular, the lived experience of social actors, those inside deviant communities or those working with and labelling them, are the focus of sociological investigation. The social problems emphasis, which gave rise to this version of social constructivism, has been associated, like societal reaction theory, with methodologies linked to symbolic interactionism and ethnomethodology;

2 The second approach is tied more closely to the post-structuralism of Foucault and is concerned with *deconstruction* – the critical examination of language and symbols in order to illuminate the creation of knowledge, its relationship to power and the unstable varieties of reality which attend human activity ('discursive practices'). Foucault's early work on madness, however, was not about such discursive concerns (Foucault 1965). The latter have been the focus of interest of later post-structuralists (see below);

3 The third approach is associated neither with the micro-sociology of social problem definition nor with deconstruction but with understanding *the production of scientific knowledge* and the pursuit of individual and collective professional interests (Latour 1987). This science-in-action version of sociology is concerned with the illumination of interest work. This version of social constructivism examines the ways in which scientists and other interested parties develop, debate and use facts. It is thus interested in the networks of people involved in these activities. Unlike the post-structuralist version of social constructivism noted earlier, it places less emphasis upon ideas and more upon action and negotiation (e.g. Bartley *et al.* 1997). This approach is thus compatible with both symbolic interactionism and social realism (see next section).

These three versions of constructivism are not neatly divided within many studies within medical sociology. Bury (1986) notes that the notion of social constructivism subsumes many elements, some of which are contradictory. However, certain core themes can be detected across the three main types described by Brown. The first is that if reality is not rejected as an epiphenomenon of human activity (as in very strict constructivism) it is nonetheless problematized to some degree – hence the break with positivism. The second relates to the importance of reality being viewed, in whole or part, as a product of human activity. What constructivists vary in is whether this activity is narrowly about the cognitive aspects of human life (thought and talk), or it is conceived in a broader sense in relation to the actions of individuals and collectivities. The third is that power relationships are inextricably bound up with reality definition. Whether it is the power to define or the power to influence or the power to advance some interests at the expense of others, this political dimension to constructivism is consistent.

When we come to examine sociological work on mental health and illness these three core elements are evident. Constructivists problematize the factual status of mental illness (e.g. Szasz 1961). They analyse the ways in which mental health work has been linked to the production of psychiatric knowledge and the production of mental health problems (e.g. Parker *et al.* 1995). Also, they establish the links which exist in modern society with the coercive control of social deviance by psychiatry on the one hand and the production of selfhood by mental health expertise on the other (e.g. Miller and Rose 1988).

The final point to be made about social constructivism is that it does not necessarily have to be set in opposition to social realism (the view that there is an independent existing reality) or social causationism (the view that social forces cause measurable phenomena to really exist). It is certainly true that strong social constructivism challenges both of these positions (see e.g. Gergen 1985). However, a number of writers who accept some constructivist arguments point out that, strictly, it is not reality which is socially constructed but our *theories of reality* (Greenwood 1994; Brown 1995; Pilgrim 2000). So much of the apparent opposition between constructivist and realist or causationist arguments in social science results from a failure to make this distinction. This brings us to our next perspective.

Social realism

The final perspective to be discussed in this chapter is that of social realism – a perspective held by the authors (Pilgrim and Rogers 1994) as well as others working in the field of mental health and the social psychology of emotions (Greenwood 1994). Bhaskar (1978; 1989) outlines the philosophical basis of realism and we will draw out, briefly, the implications of his work for a sociology of mental health and illness. His version is called 'critical realism'.

As the name implies, critical realism accepts that reality really does exist (contra strict constructivism). However, the 'critical' prefix suggests that it diverges from social causationism. The latter follows the Durkheimian view that external social reality impinges on human action and shapes human consciousness. The Weberian view emphasizes the opposite process – that human action inter-subjectively constructs reality. Critical theory, following Freud, emphasizes the role of unconscious processes, especially repression, and is rooted in methodological individualism (clinical psychoanalysis). By contrast to all of these, critical realism attends to conscious action or agency and is critical of methodological individualism.

Bhaskar argues, following Marx, that human action is neither mechanically determined by social reality nor does intentionality (voluntary human action) simply construct social reality. Instead, society exists prior to the lives of agents but they become agents who reproduce or transform that society. Material reality (the biological substrate of actors and the material conditions of their social context) constrains action but does not simply determine it. Social science and natural science warrant different methodologies and social phenomena cannot be reduced to natural phenomena, even though the latter may exert an influence on the former and are a precondition of their existence.

Bhaskar (1989: 79) highlights the difference between natural and social science in the light of this basic starting point. Here we quote three major differences between natural and social structures and then draw out the implications for the topic of this book:

> 1. social structures, unlike natural structures, do not exist independently of the activity they govern; 2. social structures, unlike natural structures, do not exist independently of the agents' conceptions of what they are doing in their activity; 3. social structures, unlike natural structures, may be only relatively enduring so that the tendencies they ground may not be universal in the sense of a space-time invariant.

The implication of point 1 is that mental health work is part of a social structural set up so that objective or disinterested descriptions and action within that work are untenable. Point 2 follows closely in its implication – the professional knowledge perspectives we rehearsed earlier in the chapter contribute to the constitution of mental health work and the health and welfare structures they inhabit. Point 3 implies that mental health work must be understood within its specific context of time and place – it is historically and geographically situated. As a consequence of points 2 and 3 social psychiatric investigations should be accepted tentatively. They may supply useful information about the relationship between social variables such as gender or class (see later chapters) but they cannot be credited with the same scientific status as, for example, knowledge claims from biochemistry or physiology.

Because critical realism is a materialist, rather than idealist, basis for social science (cf. the Kantian idealism underlying the work of Weber and Foucault and their followers) it can accommodate material causation (e.g. temporal lobe epilepsy) alongside a critical analysis of the interests being served by the way mental health problems are described and conceptualized in a society at a point in time (e.g. a critique of the interests served by psychiatric knowledge). Such a critical reading comes near to the deconstruction emphasis of post-structuralism and the critiques of interest work found in critical studies of the production of scientific knowledge, but differs in its position during the exercise about the factual status of reality.

As will become clear, we consider that evidence of social structural influences on mental health can be furnished by methodologies rooted in Durkheimian sociology. Equally, the concerns of social constructivists can furnish critical readings which give insights into the interests being served by discourses (what Bhaskar calls the 'agents' conceptions'). In other words, all sorts of methodologies used by sociologists to study mental health and illness can furnish illuminative information and, potentially, can be subjected to a critical reading (Pilgrim and Rogers 1999).

The relevance and applicability of sociological theory are themselves influenced by the particular time and social context in which they are used. More and more sociologists are employed in applied research contexts which lie outside their core disciplines. Sociology has also influenced generations of health workers including medical practitioners, nurses, psychologists and social workers. In comparison, 'pure' sociologists are a small minority of those who have had access to sociological knowledge through their socialization and education as health and social welfare professionals. Additionally, working in the field of mental health and health services research is a largely inter-disciplinary endeavour. Thus, social realism allows coexisting explanations about mental health.

Discussion

With the exception of social causationism, sociological perspectives problem-atize the notion of mental disorder. The force of these arguments can be seen in the continuing debates both within sociology and across other disciplines. Various forms of ambivalence are evident on all sides. Social realists can still 'do business' with psychiatry, particularly if a biopsychosocial model is deployed and investigated in a spirit of genuine inter-disciplinary collabor-ation. The inter-disciplinary project of 'social psychiatry' describes this con-vergence of disciplinary interests. We also mentioned the tendency for some critical psychiatrists to embrace social constructivism.

Some sociologists have gone some way to legitimize the core business of psychiatry by accepting that the psychoses are true illnesses, while designating 'common mental disorders' as being forms of social deviance (not illnesses). Horwitz argues that 'a valid definition of mental disorder should be narrow and should not encompass many of the presumed mental disorders of diag-nostic psychiatry, especially appropriate reactions to stressful social condition and many culturally patterned forms of deviant behaviour' (2002:15). A prob-lem with this partial validation of psychiatric diagnosis is that it relies too readily on immediate social intelligibility. That is, stress reactions and cultural context warrant attributions of non-pathology, whereas psychosis does not. We return to this point in Chapter 5.

Some medical practitioners have recently rejected the concept of mental illness but not in the way that was evident in the Szaszian critique noted earlier. Baker and Menken (2001) suggest that the term 'mental illness' must be abandoned because it is an erroneous label for true brain disorder. They are dismissive of the countless critiques and ambiguities previously identified by dissenting psychiatrists and sociological critics. Instead they argue for a clear philosophical assertion that *all* mental illnesses are brain disorders as 'an essential step to promote the improvement of human health' from within clinical medicine:

We suggest that it is unscientific, misleading and harmful to millions of people world wide to declare that some brain disorders are not physical ailments. Neurology and psychiatry must end the twentieth century schism that has divided their fields.

(2001: 937)

This resort to dogmatic assertion, about biodeterminism, in one fell swoop discards all of the sociological theorizing about mental disorder in favour of medical jurisdiction and paternalism, purportedly in service of the common good. However, this medical confidence simply evades an obvious point: the bulk of what are called 'mental disorders' still have no *definitive proven* biological cause. The only aspects of the social this medical dogmatism leaves intact are the environmental factors, which might putatively contribute to the aetiology of illness. However, this stance is one reflection of a deeper problem for *both* medicine and sociology; the problem of mind/body dualism.

Baker and Menken create a unity between mind and body by asserting the single centrality of the skin-encapsulated body out of which each and every form of human ill emerges. Radical social constructivism generates another unitary position by arguing instead that 'everything is socially constructed'. In this view, reality, truth claims and causes are all dismissed just as readily as Baker and Menken dismiss the conceptual objections facing the concept of mental illness. This goes further than labelling theory, which left the ontological status of primary deviance intact. It ascribed to it a basic reality and permitted a variety of causes. Radical social constructivism does not make this concession, and primary not just secondary deviance is examined critically. The constructivist position is not consistent though. For example, Szasz deconstructed the representations of mental illness in order to render it a 'myth'. At the same time he accepted uncritically the reality of physical illness.

Carpenter (2000) notes the proliferation of diagnostic categories after the appearance of the third edition of the American Psychiatric Association's Diagnostic and Statistical Manual (*DSMIII*). Various sociological commentators have pointed to how interests, agencies and technology have promoted the medicalization and institutionalization of certain diagnostic categories, such as post-traumatic stress disorder, depression and eating disorders. Lyons (1996) points to activities of the drug companies in promoting Prozac as an acceptable drug to make life better for all – almost a recreational drug. Such a trend is reinforced in primary care, where depression has come to be accepted as a legitimate condition amenable to a technical fix. Identifying technologies (e.g. anti-depressant medication and counselling) as a means of management located within primary care is likely to have contributed to increasing medicalization (May *et al.* 2004).

In response to this proliferation of diagnostic categories and the medicalization of everyday suffering Horwitz argues that only symptoms that reflect psychological dysfunctions, considered to be universally inappropriate, should warrant being labelled as true mental diseases. The advantage of this approach is that it is an attempt to overcome the void left by the relativistic nihilism characteristic of some post-modernist approaches to the conceptualization of mental health problems.

On the face of things, Horwitz is following those sociologists of mental health and illness who have aligned themselves with a critical realist position (i.e. presenting a weak social constructivist argument without abandoning the notion of mental illness and undermining the notion that mental distress exists). However, he may precariously be introducing another essentialist view of psychiatric disorder. He is implying some self-evident and natural distinction between true mental illness and varieties of socially generated mental distress. This is akin to some older psychiatric classifications which distinguished mental illness from distressing environmental reactions (Fish 1967).

From a critical realist perspective it is clearly the case that pressure groups and drug companies also do much to promote and maintain *all* diagnostic categories. Profit makes none of the distinctions considered or asserted by Horwitz. Moreover the criteria of 'universal inappropriateness' is difficult to sustain for any diagnostic category. For example 'hearing voices' has been associated with the diagnostic category of 'schizophrenia' but it would fail to fit the categorization of 'universally inappropriate'. Not only is voice hearing evident in the general population – it is continuously distributed like most symptoms – in some cultures it provides evidence of spiritual superiority.

Another difficulty for sociology trying to define the unique and troublesome features of mental illness is the tendency to leave physical illness non-problematized (the Szaszian error). The focus on mental disorder means that sociologists have at times claimed for mental health what applies more generically. For example Horwitz's key argument about the proliferation of psychological categories clearly includes examples which are considered to be essentially physical (even though they may also be identified with certain psychological tendencies). In accepting mind/body dualism sociologists, like those in other disciplines, may disregard or dismiss physical health problems as unproblematic and fail to consider the common social processes shaping the definition and causes of all illness behaviour and experience.

The ontological status of musculoskeletal disease, as an essentially physical entity, provides an interesting point of comparison of the way in which the mind/body dualism has overridden the experience and conceptualizations of peoples' pain and distress provided in a recent study in which:

> . . . . respondents' conceptualisations of the physical body emphasised fragility and paralysis. This view of the body resonates with an understanding of incapacity, or of not being able to act as desired, which emerges from a sense of ineptness, weakness and pain. . . . Descriptions of an amorphous sense of pain which accompanied this sense of precariousness seemed to suggest a lack of demarcation between pain located in specific parts of the body and concerns in broader social and personal worlds and in this respect pain and suffering transcended the commonly understood notion of the physical body and extended to include other personal disappointments.
>
> (Rogers and Allison 2004: 81)

Ironically, in failing to construct alternative models of illness *in general* both sociologists and medical practitioners may remain trapped in forms of mind/body dualism or offer implausible assertions to impose a unity, such as medical naturalism or radical social constructivism.

Finally, it may seem, at first reading, that sociology is somehow a separate and recent commentator on mental health and illness. This is only partially true. Over the past 50 years newly trained sociologists have contributed to knowledge about psychiatry and the mental patient, but this may give the false impression that sociology is merely responding to the dominant discourse on health and illness, coming from health professionals.

However, social science existed at the beginnings of medicine. Before the latter settled down to become preoccupied with individual bodies and their parts, social medicine emerged in the eighteenth century as a programme of political intervention to prevent ill health (Rosen 1979). Indeed, Foucault (1980) argues that medical surveys of society in the early nineteenth century were the true roots of modern sociology, not its reputed fathers like Comte, Marx, Durkheim and Weber. (For a wider discussion of this topic see Kleinman (1986) and Turner (1990).)

In the particular case of mental health, so much research of the epidemiological variety was intertwined with medical research. The discipline of social psychiatry demonstrates this overlap (Goldberg and Morrison 1963; Warner 1985). Also, some of the ground-breaking epidemiological work of the 1950s and 1960s involved the collaboration of sociologists (e.g. Hollingshead and Brown) with psychiatrists (e.g. Redlich and Wing).

However, it is also true that the more recent response of sociologists has been seen as oppositional by those inside clinical psychiatry. During the late 1960s, sociologists became part of 'anti-psychiatry' or 'critics of psychiatry', according to leaders of the offended profession, such as Roth (1973). Thus, sociologists are in an ambivalent relationship to psychiatry. On the one hand, they have contributed to an expanded theory of aetiology, in tracing the social causes of mental illness; on the other, they have set up competing ways of conceptualizing mental abnormality.

The bulk of the work we have reviewed in this chapter reflects a dominant sociological interest in mental abnormality and in psychiatry. By comparison, over the past 100 years, there has been much less sociological (and for that matter general social scientific) interest in ordinary emotional life, non-deviant conduct and professional knowledge outside of the governance of psychiatric experts. However, this is changing. One major shift about this became evident in the work of post-structuralists (e.g. Rose 1986; 1990). Although this had mental health experts as a central focus (the 'psy complex'), it did demonstrate, under the prompt of Foucault, the diffused and widespread influence of 'the confessional' and other personalizing discourses in everyday life.

Outside of post-structuralist frameworks we find a more pluralistic sociological interest in ordinary emotions (Elias 1978; Hochschild 1983; Freund 1988; James 1989; Giddens 1992; Beck and Beck-Gersheim 1995; Bendelow and Williams 1998). This range itself may reflect an aspect of post-modernity – diverse commentaries on personal life are becoming increasingly legitimate and demanded. We also find commentaries with resonances of psychoanalytical ideas about ordinary emotional life (Craib 1998) and those which bridge psychoanalysis and social constructionism (Lupton 1998).

Within this shift in social science, there has developed a sociological interest in the ways in which society has followed the trend of the fast food chain McDonald's in a whole range of cultural process (including sexual activity, health care 'delivery', and dying). This 'McDonaldization thesis' (Ritzer 1995;

1997) reflects a shift in society towards consumerism. Within this thesis, it is suggested that the emotions, like food, have become subject to both commercial prepackaging and increasing everyday interest to ordinary people.

This chapter has rehearsed and summarized a set of perspectives about mental health and illness both inside and outside of sociology. The very existence of such a wide range of viewpoints highlights that the field of mental health and illness is highly contested. As a result, any discussion of the topic cannot take anything for granted – one's own assumptions, and those of others, need to be checked at the outset and at each stage of a dialogue or analysis thereafter.

Questions

1 What are the strengths and weaknesses of the legal perspective on mental illness?

2 Compare and contrast two approaches to mental health and illness within sociology.

3 Discuss the relevance of the Frankfurt School to contemporary discussions about mental health.

4 Compare and contrast social constructivism with social realism when conducting sociological studies of mental health and illness.

5 Discuss recent developments in the sociology of the emotions.

6 How have sociology and psychiatry dealt with the mind/body dualism?

For discussion

Consider your own views about mental health and illness. How do they relate to the range of perspectives offered in this chapter?

Further reading

Giddens, A. (1992) *The Transformation of Intimacy*. Cambridge: Polity Press.

Horwitz, A. (2002) *Creating Mental Illness*. Chicago: University of Chicago Press.

Kleinman, A. (1988) *Rethinking Psychiatry*. New York: Free Press.

MacLachlan, M. (1997) *Culture and Health*. New York: Free Press.

Tyrer, P. and Sternberg, D. (1987) *Models for Mental Disorder*. Chichester: Wiley.

Chapter **2**

Stigma revisited and lay representations of mental health problems

Chapter overview

While the previous chapter dealt with expert, or disciplinary, knowledge about mental health and illness, this one extends a sociological understanding of the processes of stereotyping, stigmatization and social exclusion of people with mental health problems. Approaches to these topics have varied from a social psychological emphasis on prejudice to structural critiques emphasizing a social disability model.

This chapter considers:

- lay views of psychological differences;
- stereotyping and stigma;
- labelling or social reaction theory and its modification;
- the role of the mass media;
- social exclusion.

Lay views of psychological differences

In every culture there is some notion of emotional or psychological difference. Not all cultures identify these differences in exactly the same way, nor do they use identical terms. Equally, however, no culture is indifferent to those who are sad, frightened or unintelligible in their conduct (Horwitz 1983). It is a well-rehearsed argument that in Europe, from the seventeenth to the twentieth century, such differences were accounted for decreasingly by demonic possession and increasingly by medical notions. This is sometimes known as the period when madness became 'medicalized' (Scull 1979) or when psychiatry became 'possible' (Foucault 1965).

With or without an expertise in the field of mental abnormality, most people know madness when they see it. Equally, most of us can identify for ourselves when we are sad or anxious. This has become more salient with individualism and resonates with the discussion on self surveillance which is seen as intrinsic to the psy complex (see discussion in Chapter 1)

Any of us might be directly involved in invoking a medical diagnosis for a friend, a relative or even a stranger in the street acting in a way we find perplexing or distressing. Any of us might reach a point where we decide that our own distress warrants a visit to the doctor or other expert for help. Everyday notions of 'nervousness' suggest that a concept does prefigure a psychiatric label of phobic anxiety or some other version of neurosis. Likewise, if people act in a way others cannot readily understand they run the risk of being dismissed as a 'nutter', a 'loony', 'crazy', 'mad' or even 'mental'. Again, these prefigure notions of psychosis within a professional discourse.

Users of mental health services rejecting psychiatric notions of mental illness have often opted instead for 'mental distress'. A problem with this term is that it alludes only to the pain of the patient and it gives no notion that they can be distressing, frustrating or frightening to others at times. Indeed, from the lay but non-patient perspective, the latter is often the preoccupying concern.

There is considerable overlap between lay and psychiatric notions of mental health and illness. For example, in psychiatric disease categories, such as anorexia nervosa, where there is uncertainty about the cause and a large cultural component to the diagnosis, lay and psychiatric epistemologies have been found to be similar (Lees 1997). However, there are also differences between lay perspectives and disciplinary and formal knowledge. Notions about antisocial behaviour sometimes appear to be less readily accommodated within the lay discourse of distress and oddity.

Two examples of this appeared in Britain in the early 1980s when juries were asked to consider the states of mind of two mass murderers and rejected expert psychiatric views that the men were mentally disordered. Peter Sutcliffe (the so called Yorkshire Ripper) murdered several women on the pretext of being on a mission from God. Jurors were not prepared to allow him the excuse of mental ill health and found him guilty of malice aforethought. What confirmed the difference in this case between lay and expert views of mental abnormality was that the expert witnesses for *both* the defence *and* the prosecution were of the view that he was schizophrenic.

A similar discrepancy between lay and psychiatric discourses about antisocial behaviour emerged in the trial of Denis Nilsen, who killed, dismembered and stored the remains of 15 young men in his home in London. The jury found him guilty of murder. Forensic psychiatrists acting as defence witnesses failed to persuade ordinary people that Nilsen was a psychopathic personality.

The lay discourse contains a contradiction about mental abnormality and antisocial conduct. As Rosen (1968) points out, in Ancient Rome and Athens madness was defined in pre-psychiatric times by two characteristics: aimless wandering and violence. In Laos, 'crazy' people are called 'baa'. Westermeyer and Kroll (1978) studied villagers' perceptions of the 'baa' people at a time when the country had no mental hospital or mental health professionals. They found that non-'baa' people adjudged their deviant fellows to be violent in 11 per cent of the cases, before their change of character, but, this attribution went up to 54 per cent after 'baa' was identified.

In France, a 'family colony' has existed at Ainay-le-Chateau since 1900. These psychiatric patients are fostered by families in the community instead of being inside an institution. Jodelet (1991) studied the ways in which citizens construed the patients in their midst. She found that the patients were segregated not by walls but by personal constructions – mainly based on fear of contamination by the illness and fear of unpredictable danger. This fear is so great that a taboo has emerged in the colony about patients marrying non-patients. When sexual relationships of this type have developed over the years, which are rare, this has led to the couple being banished from the locality.

As we will see in Chapter 10 the relationship between 'mental illness' and dangerous acts is not large. However, public views tend to exaggerate the extent and link between violence and schizophrenia. This is a cross-cultural phenomenon. In the US, which has been called a 'psychiatric society' by Castel *et al.* (1979), the public has mixed views about the association of mental disorder and violence. Research on public opinion undertaken some time ago has shown that most people considered that a person diagnosed as schizophrenic is more likely to commit a violent crime than other people (Field Institute 1984) but more recent research suggests that violent imagery is less pronounced (DYG Corporation 1990), with only 24 per cent of 1000 respondents viewing mentally ill people as more dangerous than others.

Lay people tend to spontaneously view 'mental illness' as being about psychotic or unintelligible behaviour with violent behavior seen as reflecting mental illness or disorder. This is why, as we noted earlier, defence lawyers can appeal to lay jurors to consider mental abnormality as an exculpating factor when judging the source of violent acts. However, the commonest diagnosis in psychiatry is actually depression. This particular diagnosis is not the lay stereotype of a mentally ill person. Moreover, depression and the distress linked to stressful personal circumstances now occupy an ambiguous space in the minds of lay people. Terms such as 'stress' (as an internal subjective state not as an external objective pressure) and 'depression' are now part of the vernacular in Western societies. They are seen as an extension of normal existence and are not necessarily seen as mental illness (Pilgrim and Bentall 1998).

What this points to is a recurring theme across disciplinary and lay perspectives. For example, early traditional psychiatric accounts of mental illness focus overwhelmingly on madness (the functional diagnostic categories of 'schizophrenia' and 'manic-depression') and depict anxiety and depression as stress reactions and not true mental illnesses (Fish 1968). This old psychiatric dichotomy has been reinstated in some recent sociological accounts. For example, as we noted in Chapter 1, Horwitz (2002) argues that there are true mental diseases (the psychoses including extreme depression) and there is an extensive range of diagnostic categories, which are merely psychiatric codifications of variations in normal mental states, which vary in quality, prevalence and style of evaluation from culture to culture.

Thus we can see a degree of convergence between lay attributions about mental abnormality, traditional psychiatric accounts and some sociological accounts (see more discussion about this in the previous chapter). This does not imply though that a fixed consensus exists across these three communities of thought. Currently, most Western psychiatrists *do* see anxiety and depression as being mental illnesses. By contrast, many mental health service users, even those with diagnoses of 'major' or 'severe' mental illness, do not depict their problems in illness terms. Also, many sociologists frame mental illness either as a form of 'residual deviance' or as a cognitive by-product of professional activity (a 'discourse' of the 'psy complex').

Stereotyping and stigma

We have already begun to draw attention to the micro-sociological phenomenon of stereotyping. This refers to the tendency of human beings to attribute fixed and common characteristics to whole social groups. Stereotyping can be thought of as a form of social typing. It is not always negative but it is always narrow and potentially misleading, because it ignores individual variability within social groups and the overlap of characteristics across them. The shift from stereotyping to stigmatization involves an enlargement of prejudicial social typing (an error of reasoning). Two other processes are added to this cognitive error. The first is emotional and entails any combination, depending on the personal target of the stereotype, of anxious avoidance, hostility or pity. A second feature of stigmatization, which goes beyond the cognitive error of stereotyping, is moral. Those stigmatizing others can show caring paternalism or moral outrage and revulsion, depending on the deviance involved. The stigmatized person is thus set apart from their fellows in these additive ways culminating in increased social distance, between the labeller and the labelled. The latter suffers consequent depersonalization, rejection and disempowerment (Jones *et al.* 1984; Braithwaite 1989; Hayward and Bright 1997). According to labelling theory stigmatized people become isolated and demoralized and develop, what Goffman (1963) called, a 'spoiled identity' (see Box 2.1).

The negative stereotypes underlying the stigmatization of people with mental health problems contain three recurring elements about: intelligibility; social competence and credibility; and violence. Although we will now discuss these elements separately, a single personal image may capture or embody all three at once. The strongest negative attributions seem to focus on the spectre of a homicidal madman – a deranged being who explodes violently, erratically and inexplicably (Foucault 1978). However, because stereotypes are characterized by false generalizations and inaccurate claims about social groups, and

---

Box 2.1 **Accounts from Erving Goffman and Bruce Link about stigma**

Erving Goffman, in his book *Stigma: Notes on the Management of Spoiled Identity* (1963), describes stigma as a

> special kind of relationship between attribute and stereotype . . . [an] attribute that is deeply discrediting . . . that reduces the bearer . . . from a whole and usual person to a tainted, discounted one . . . We believe that a person with a stigma is not quite human . . . We tend to impute a wide range of imperfections on the basis of the original one . . . We may perceive his (sic) defensive response to his situation as a direct expression of his defect . . .
>
> (pp. 14–16)

Goffman goes on to point out that stigma is generated in a social situation. It is a reaction by society that spoils a person's identity by a set of imposed norms that are bought to bear on an encounter. According to Goffman these norms

> concern identity or being . . . Failure or success at maintaining such norms have a very direct effect on the psychological integrity of the individual. At the same time, the mere desire to abide by the norm – mere good will – is not enough, for in many cases the individual has no immediate control over his (sic) level of sustaining the norm. It is a question of the individual's condition, not his will; it is a question of conformance not compliance . . .
>
> (pp. 52–3)

Bruce Link extends this focus on social psychological aspects of *conformity* to wider social processes about *power* in his conference paper to the American Public Health Association in 2000 *The Stigma Process: Re-conceiving the Definition of Stigma*:

> We conceptualize stigma as a process. It begins when dominant groups distinguish human differences – whether 'real' or not. It continues if the observed difference is believed to connote unfavorable information about the designated persons. As this occurs, social labeling of the observed difference is achieved. Labeled persons are set apart in a distinct category that separates 'us' from 'them.' The culmination of the stigma process occurs when designated differences lead to various forms of disapproval, rejection, exclusion and discrimination. The stigma process is entirely contingent on access to social, economic and political power that allows the identification of differentness, the construction of stereotypes, the labeling of persons as different and the execution of disapproval and discrimination . . .

because the stereotyping associated with mental illness is so powerful, the empirical validity of the main constituent elements described earlier invites particular scrutiny. In Chapter 10 we will be looking at the evidence about psychiatric patients and dangerousness. Here we will focus on questions of intelligibility, competence and credibility.

Intelligibility

An implicit 'meta-rule', in any social context, is that participants have an obligation, if called upon, to render their speech and conduct intelligible, about any rule transgression or role failure (Goffman 1955; 1971). If rules are followed and role expectations delivered by a person, then this obligation about intelligibility is not demanded of them. Generally, we only want to know why things have gone wrong or why our expectations in a social situation are not being fulfilled. With the peculiar therapeutic exception of psychoanalysis and the peculiar sociological exception of ethnomethodology, which, in different, ways interrogate normality or hold it to account, people are very rarely asked to explain or justify their compliance with role-rule expectations. This would be a tiresome disruption of everyday social interactions and incompatible with the free flow of social activity. However, when and if a rule infraction or role failure occurs, while others may ignore it for a while, at some point they usually expect and demand an explanation or an 'account' (Scott and Lyman 1968). The sane transgressor then will offer this account persuasively (e.g. the apology offered by someone making an honest mistake) or unpersuasively (e.g. the vacuous or dishonest explanation offered by the caught out criminal) (Tedeschi and Reiss 1981).

This is where the first attribution then arises about madness: sane fellows cannot elicit or recognize an intelligible account or excuse from the transgressor. A person living in a world of their own is not in the social world observing the meta-rule of required mutual intelligibility. The mad person or incipient 'schizophrenic' offers no account to others for their deviant conduct or offers one that does not make sense. They are said, therefore, to 'lack insight' into their conduct. The term 'lack insight', in this context, refers to the breakdown in an implicit social contract about our obligation to account to others, if required, for our transgressions.

Coulter (1973) points out that the most powerful ascriptions about madness do not come from psychiatrists. The latter only rubber stamp decisions and evaluations already made on commonsense grounds by others. Most typically, this will be the relatives of the patients, but it may come from others, such as strangers in the street. Here for example, Jonathan Miller, the playwright, gives his account of the implicit social contract of mutual accountability studied by Coulter and its role in defining madness (then codified as mental illness by psychiatry). Miller (1991: 31) calls it a 'very complicated constitution of conduct':

It appears in the family first of all and then of course it appears in public places, there's a vast, very complicated constitution of conduct, which allows us to move with confidence through public spaces, and we can instantly and by a very subtle process recognize someone who is breaking that constitution. They're talking to themselves; they're not moving at the same rate; they're not avoiding other people with skill that pedestrians do in the street. The speed with which normal users of public places can recognize someone else as not being a normal user of it is where madness appears.

Goffman (1971) analysed the social obligations we have for one another in public places, such as respecting personal space and reciprocating communications. Failed obligations require some form of remedial action, such as an apology or explanation. Miller suggests in his description above that mad people have abandoned, or they are incompetent at, what Goffman (1959) called 'impression management'. The latter refers to the subtle and dynamic range of communications we give out to others to indicate that we are conducting ourselves well and appropriately in a particular social situation.

A sociological rather than psychiatric account defines madness not by an objective decontextualized checklist of peculiar behaviours only recognized by experts. Instead, it takes a step before diagnosis and examines those actions, which are described and evaluated by others in a particular social context. For example, take Miller's point about people talking to themselves in public. He does not mention a public place where this rule does not apply – church. People may speak to themselves in this context with no negative evaluation. He also does not mention a very common street scenario of talking to oneself without inviting an attribution of madness – the use of mobile phones.

These give examples of how the ascription of sanity or insanity requires the sort of subtle situation-specific judgments which Miller and Goffman are keen to identify. The praying person in Church, or the mobile phone user, operate in a context in which others can decode the nature of their speech behaviour. By contrast, praying in the 'wrong place' or speaking out loud with no mobile phone in the hand invites ascriptions of madness. Madness is thus an ordinary social judgment awaiting medical codification. In a society without psychiatrists, the latter would never arrive but the social judgments would remain (Westermeyer and Kroll 1978). In the family, deviance may be noted but ignored (Lemert 1974). This suggests that identifying residual deviance, and doing something about it, are separate processes.

The point made by Coulter and Miller about a general meta-rule implies a global and trans-historical quality about human interaction. However, the application of this meta-rule can vary over time and place; another reason why judgments about madness need to be qualified by social and cultural relativism. For example, cross-cultural studies show how some peculiar actions, such as those linked to hallucinations, may be valued as mystical powers in one culture but dismissed as symptoms of mental illness in another. This shows that the same deviant action may be positively connoted in one context but negatively in another.

Thus unintelligibility, as a building block of stereotyping and stigma, is only applicable in those social contexts in which it is disvalued. Nonetheless, there is some empirical validity for the stereotype that psychiatric patients are unintelligible. After all, whether we use the term 'madness' or technicalize it as 'schizophrenia' or 'bi-polar disorder', conduct which baffles others is the core basis for the attribution madness. While these are social judgments made in context (not scientific descriptions) they are still practically justified by the meta-rule about intelligibility.

However, psychotic patients are not *invariably* unpredictable. Mental health workers and significant others who get to know patients over months and years will describe their predictability (including cues of an imminent period of acute psychosis). Thus single or episodic attributions of unintelligibility do not imply constant unpredictability. The stereotype of the wild and unpredictable lunatic may still exist, but the typical manifestations of mental health problems are more complicated but also more mundane.

The legacy of the term 'maniac' still haunts the public imagination, even though psychiatric texts now depict a much less dramatic version of the manic pole of bi-polar disorder (Healy 2000). During the stereotyping of psychiatric patients, an encounter with unintelligible conduct elides quickly and unreasonably into expectations of unpredictability and violence. Most patients, most of the time, are neither unpredictable nor violent. The frenzied and deranged lunatic can rarely be found anywhere in practice. By contrast, most of the lives of psychotic patients are characterized by low-grade depression or anomie, an experience shaped by their social exclusion.

Competence and credibility

To summarize some relevant connecting points made earlier, the first element of stereotyping about mental illness is actually quite persuasive for some patients, some of the time. It is not only reasonable to claim that some people diagnosed as being mentally ill lack intelligibility, this empirical claim has actually been the main sociological rationale for understanding 'major' mental illness, as a form of residual deviance, rather than individual pathology. However, there are also three important caveats here.

First, only some psychiatric patients (those deemed to be psychotic) speak and act in ways that others cannot readily comprehend. Most patients (those who are depressed or anxious) not only obey the meta-rule of mutual intelligibility, they may actually use their distress as part of this obligation. For example, the agoraphobic patient may argue that they stay in all of the time because they are fearful of leaving their home. They do meet the social obligation of intelligibility and they use their symptoms as a cognitive resource for this purpose.

Second, some psychotic patients are largely intelligible all of the time. For example, there are patients with circumscribed delusions, who only speak and act oddly when these are discussed or prompted. Third, most psychotic patients are rarely persistently mad. Madness tends to be episodic, with varying time periods of conformity to norms and evidence of a normal commitment to intelligibility in between crazy episodes. Moreover, social niches may exist in which these deviant qualities are functional or are attributed to social value. Here are some examples of these social situations and the value-frame they provide about mental abnormality:

- The first example is in relation to creativity. The latter, like madness, involves transgression. To create something original or to think in an original way requires a suspension of conformity and the production of something which is out of the ordinary. There is some evidence of both forms of transgression overlapping in the same individuals but this is not the same as saying that madness is intrinsically creative. We can neither conclude that all people with a diagnosis of mental illness are creative nor that all creative people are mentally ill. However, the incidence of mental health problems does seem to be higher in creative artists, novelists, poets and musical composers (Chadwick 1997). There is also some evidence that bi-polar disorder has a higher incidence in unusually successful people. This group manifests periods of excessive energy and industriousness and the grandiosity they experience ensures that innovative thought experiments are attempted in practice during manic phases (Jamison 1998).

• A second example of social niches in which mental abnormality enables better performance is in relation to obsessionality. Patients with a diagnosis of obsessive-compulsive disorder are preoccupied with orderliness and rule following to a point that they even construct new rules for themselves to comply with (compulsive rituals). If they are not allowed access to this rule following then they become very distressed. Those with a diagnosis of obsessive compulsive personality disorder are conformist, hygienic, pedantic and moralistic in their outlook. In the nineteenth century, these types of problems were viewed as a form of insanity, whereas now they are framed by psychiatrists as neurotic or personality problems (Berrios 1985). What psychotic and obsessive compulsive problems highlight in different ways is that mental health is defined implicitly by a capacity to conform to role-rule relationships. When patients are mad and they act or speak unintelligibly, then they underconform. By contrast, obsessional patients over conform. Tasks which require close attention to detail and are repetitive are done exceptionally well by obsessional people. The latter are well suited to any occupation involved in counting money carefully or in slowly checking details in a task. Societies which are organized around mechanical rationality would place more of a value in careful rule compliance than those which were more laisser faire. The obsessive-compulsive personality seems to be an exaggerated version of North American materialistic individualism (a preoccupation with individual work responsibilities defining the person's identity and an emphasis on a person's unique material possessions). In a British context, Marks (1987) notes that the features of an obsessional personality read like a 'list of Victorian virtues'.

• A third example is in relation to spirituality and religious leadership. The close relationship between religion and mental abnormality can be found in psychiatric texts, which, since the mid-nineteenth century have focused on 'religiosity' or have distinguished between healthy and pathological religious commitment (e.g. Donat 1988; Tseng 2003). Between 10 to 15 per cent of people with a diagnosis of schizophrenia are described as having religious delusions (Koenig *et al.* 1998). Also, as an indication of the importance of cultural context, the content of these delusions is closely linked to prevalent religious beliefs in a patient's particular time and place (Wilson 1998). Thus, generally, religious commitment and experience can be a focus of diagnostic interest for psychiatrists. This interest may discredit the patient's right to be taken seriously by others. On the other hand, the charismatic seminal leaders of the main world religions could be diagnosed retrospectively as suffering from some form of psychosis. With the exception of Judaism, the major religions have placed a positive value on poverty, social isolation and even begging. Christ wandered in the desert and knew that he was the son of God (any other person making this claim now would be called 'deluded'). Siddhartha, who became known as the Buddha, abandoned his comfortable aristocratic existence and went into the forest, isolating himself from the world and putting himself in jeopardy. This type of incorrigible social withdrawal has traditionally been associated with madness – the aimless wandering described in antiquity. The prophet Mohammed craved isolation and sought refuge in a cave near Mecca, where he experienced a frequent command hallucination, telling him to cry. These three famous individuals rejected the constraints of daily living and the norms of their host society and acted in a way that would now invite a diagnosis of 'schizophrenia'. However, eventually, their actions yielded not less, but more, social credibility. Together, Jesus Christ, the Buddha and the prophet Mohammed are now worshipped by the majority of the world's population – they have what could be called a form of global and trans-historical 'hyper-credibility'. They also reflect and reinforce a tradition, which pre-dates their existence, in Hinduism of a mendicant tradition of holy men, who put themselves outside of society, with no direct means of support. This lifestyle overlaps strongly with that of madness. Holy mendicants, venerated religious leaders and mad patients are separated only by whether their conduct in common is deemed by others to be a product of spiritual choice and duty or of involuntary psychological incompetence.

It may seem, on common sense grounds, that mental abnormality intrinsically signals social incompetence. However, the above three points challenge this idea. Mental abnormality is not inherently creative but it does seem to be linked, in some people, to enhanced creativity. Also, some symptoms may be linked to enhanced industriousness (in mania) or attention to detail (in obsessionality). These can find positive social expression. Indeed, the various ways in which actions are socially valued or disvalued leads to a highly ambiguous picture, in which those who are deemed to be psychologically normal may be judged to be superior to the abnormal, most of the time, but in some circumstances the reverse may apply. Much depends on a particular social situation placing a value on, and continuing to support, what the identified patient is expressing.

The most dramatic example given above is in relation to individual claims of extraordinary spiritual status. Most of the time, such claims are dismissed as symptoms of mental illness but the logical implication of this routine dismissal is that the world's major religions venerate people who were mad. The ambiguity highlights again that the same abnormality of thought and action may be praised or pathologized in different social contexts.

To summarize the theme of this section, is it fair to stereotype people with mental health problems as being continuously irrational in thought and action and so undeserving of social credibility? The answer is clearly in the negative. People manifesting symptoms of mental illness can be highly goal directed, creative, reliable and even inspirational across many generations. Despite this, the powerful stereotype that they should be denied credibility because of their irrationality leads to stigma and discrimination in most modern societies.

Does labelling matter?

The above discussion questioned whether or not there was any evidence to provide legitimacy for negative attributions about people with mental health problems. Our conclusion was that little exists about violence and that competence (warranting social credibility) can be affected positively, as well as negatively, by the experience of mental health problems. We emphasized, though, that the question of evidence for lack of intelligibility was more complicated. On the one hand, the absence of intelligibility is a sociological rationale to account for madness in non-medical terms. This rationale is supported by studies of the processes of lay ascriptions about unintelligibility (prior to formal diagnosis by professionals of psychosis). On the other hand, most psychiatric patients are not mad and those that are, are not mad all of the time. Thus, for most of the time, most people with a psychiatric diagnosis, like most other people, comply with the 'meta-rule' of mutual intelligibility.

We now address a different empirical question. If negative stereotyping is unreasonable but still occurs, does any prejudicial action flowing from it matter? Put differently, what evidence is there that negative social reactions have any detrimental effect on people with mental health problems? When labelling theory first emerged (Scheff 1966) it was faced with an empirical critique and consequently lost its popularity within sociology. Studies emerged which did not seem to confirm the detrimental impact of negative social reactions on people with mental health problems (e.g. Crocetti *et al.* 1974; Kirk 1974). These studies were complemented by a strong counter-claim to social reaction theory; that labelling actually gave patients the positive opportunity of access to effective pharmacological and psychological treatments to ameliorate their problems. Gove (1982) suggests that labelling is driven, in the main, not by social contingencies but more by the patient's symptoms. He emphasized that patient behaviour, not the prejudices of others, determines labelling. Primary not secondary deviance is highlighted in this view. In Chapter 8 we address the difficulty with this 'positive access to treatment' argument, when we examine the negative effects of both drug and talking therapies.

Link and Phelan (1999) revisited the empirical status of labelling theory and drew attention to a number of studies, which, *contra* the critique of Gove, clearly demonstrate the negative impact of labelling. These studies indicate that disvalued social statuses, such as prostitution, epilepsy, alcoholism, convict status and drug abuse form a hierarchy of stigma, with mental illness being near to the bottom (Albrecht *et al.* 1982; Skinner *et al.* 1995). Some experimental studies also show that knowledge of a person's psychiatric history predicts social rejection (Link and Cullen 1983; Sibicky and Dovidio 1986; Harris *et al.* 1990). To confirm this, surveys of the general public show that fear of violence and the need to keep a social distance diminish with increasing contact with people with a psychiatric diagnosis (Alexander and Link 2003). Also, some naturalistic studies, even at the time that labelling theory was losing its popularity in sociology, demonstrated that a psychiatric history reduced a person's access to housing and employment (e.g. Farina and Felner 1973).

These types of finding have led Link and his colleagues to offer a 'modified labelling theory', which has empirical support in a series of studies they

conducted and are summarized in Link and Phelan (1999). These studies demonstrate two main findings. First, provided that best practice is offered in mental health services, people with mental health problems can derive positive
benefits to their quality of life (in a qualified way, thus supporting Gove's
claim about the positive impact of labelling). Second, whether or not specialist
mental health services have positive or negative effects (a function of their
range of quality) independent stigma effects persist from, and are embedded
in, social processes in the community.

The theory Link and colleagues have developed to account for this second
finding, which is supported by their additional experimental investigation of
lay views of mental illness, relates not to direct prejudicial action by others but
by a shared cultural expectation. The latter is that mental illness will lead to
suspicion, loss of credibility and social rejection. All parties, including and
especially the person who develops a mental health problem, share this
assumption from childhood. Consequently, the diagnosed person enters, or
considers entering, interactions with others operating this assumption. For
their part, the non-patient also expects the diagnosed person to be expecting
social distance.

This shared field of assumptions then leads to a disruption in confidence to
engage in both parties and a self-fulfilling prophecy ensues – the patient keeps
their distance and the non-patient expects and lets this occur. Subsequently,
this creates social disability and isolation in the patient. Thus, this modified
labelling theory is not about the unidirectional impact of the prejudicial
actions of one party on another but an interaction that creates social rejection,
based upon shared acculturated assumptions.

The modified labelling theory of Link and colleagues is also supported by the
work of Thoits (1985), who drew upon studies in the sociology of emotions
(Hochschild 1979), which emphasises shared internal assumptions, rather
than social reaction *per se*. Thoits noted that labelling theory was preoccupied
with involuntary relationships (as was much of this tradition including that of
Goffman (1961)); whereas we know that most consultations for mental health
problems occur voluntarily, mainly in primary care services. Thoits's view is
that we learn from a young age to self monitor emotional deviance. For
example, we begin to learn when it is appropriate to be happy, angry, sad or
fearful. Consequently, we also can identify in ourselves when our emotionally
driven actions will be considered inappropriate by others.

Thoits, following Hochschild, describes this as people being aware that they
are transgressing 'feeling rules'. For example, the phobic patient knows that
their fear is irrational but they also feel as though their actions are not in their
control. The depressed adult knows that their low mood and lack of confidence disables them from carrying out normal family and work obligations
expected of them, and this knowledge may fuel their depression further.

The implication from the work of Thoits, Link and colleagues that labelling
is incorporated into a negative view of self has been challenged by some. For
example, Camp, Finlay and Lyons (2002) studied women with chronic mental
health problems and found that such a negative acceptance of stigma is 'neither straightforward nor inevitable'. However, confirming the view of Thoits,
the respondents were aware of their symptoms and their social implications.
Badesha and Horley (2002) also found that positive and negative views about
psychiatric diagnosis varied between patients. Of these different groups,

women with a diagnosis of schizophrenia had the most negative view of themselves. By contrast, another study by Wright, Gronfein and Owens (2000) found a more consistent internalization of negative views from others in psychiatric patients. In the group studied the stress of chronic social rejection was a key feature in their biographical accounts.

Thus the notion of 'feeling rules' is a useful conceptual adjunct to that of the meta-rule of intelligibility, discussed earlier in relation to madness. Those breaking 'feeling rules' may well be capable of complying with the meta-rule of intelligibility, but they still receive a psychiatric diagnosis. Indeed, the latter may be negotiated with their full cooperation, once they have self labelled their rule breaking or role failure. The diagnosis is a professional codification of the person's own view that they have transgressed a 'feeling rule', just as one of 'schizophrenia' reflects the lay judgment of others that the patient has acted unintelligibly. What all patients then have in common is that they accept that others now will harbour changed expectations about rights of citizenship, personal credibility and social distance.

Once a person has lost their reason or fails to act competently as an adult in situation-specific ways, and others know this, then he or she is held in permanent suspicion. For this reason, people with a psychiatric diagnosis are ambivalent about disclosing their problems to others, though once this step is taken some benefits (such as increased self esteem) as well as costs (such as more prejudicial responses from others) may accrue. These mixed outcomes suggest that any ambivalence from a patient about 'coming out' is reasonably warranted (Corrigan and Mathews 2003). In the section on social exclusion we will extend this discussion of the social consequences of stigmatization and discrimination.

The role of the mass media

Studies of media representations of mental illness have recorded consistent findings about negative images. There has been a recurring emphasis within these media portrayals upon psychosis and its assumed link to violence. This negative image seems to have a transglobal consistency. A focus on violence and madness can be found in the mass media of the USA (Sieff 2003), Canada (Day and Page 1986), Germany (Angermeyer and Schulze 2001), New Zealand (Nairn *et al.* 2001) and Britain (Philo *et al.* 1996; Rose 1998). The style (e.g. dramatic camera work) or mood (e.g. menacing music) in radio and TV accounts of mental illness shape fear in the audience and exaggerate the violent propensity of patients (Wilson *et al.* 1999). Olstead (2002) provides a content analysis of two Canadian newspapers over a ten-year period and their depiction of mental illness and violence. He notes that the journalistic strategy throughout was to depict the 'otherness' of mentally ill people. (We endorse this analytical point in the discussion of race at the end of Chapter 5).

The link portrayed between mental illness and violence is all the more significant because of the lack of empirical evidence that mental state is a good predictor of dangerousness. Moreover, it is common to find stories and headlines which would not be tolerated about other minority social groups. Even when non-psychotic patients are described, these do not accurately match the symptom profile of patients with the diagnosis. For example, Wahl (2000) examined media depictions of obsessive-compulsive disorder and found that less than one third concurred with psychiatric descriptions. Wahl (1995) emphasizes that accuracy of information is relevant because the mass media are the most common source of understanding for the general public about mental illness. It can be noted though that the notion of 'accuracy of information' is problematic, given that psychiatric knowledge is contested. It may be more valid to simply record that media depictions do not always concur with psychiatric ones. Sieff (2003) has noted that the mass media may now be lagging behind the general public. The latter are more likely to have a broader and more subtle view about types of mental health problem than the mass media they encounter. At the same time, the link made between violence and psychosis in the public imagination has hardened (and remains empirically unfounded) over the last 50 years.

Less attention has been given by the newsprint media to depression than other diagnoses but a content analysis of the Australian press in one year (2000) (Rowe *et al.* 2003) revealed three discourses (the bio-medical, the psycho-social and the administrative/managerial). A consistent message was the need for protection of these patients (rather than the protection of others) and depression as individual pathology. Apart from violence, the other negative image found in the mass media is that of pathetic dependency or silliness (Corrigan 1998). Patients may be depicted as being naïvely cheerful, childlike and quirky, leading to their social incompetence. Their assumed immaturity and social incompetence readily becomes the butt of humour. For example, people with mental health problems form easy targets for TV programmes, such as Frasier and the Bob Newhart Show (Sieff 2003).

This point can also be found in cartoon depictions and even in advertising, where the notion of 'nuts' is used to make a moral or humorous point about human failings (Wahl 1995). Cinematic portrayals of mental health problems have also been dominated by negative imagery but Sieff (2003) points to some counter-examples recently, where films have been more sensitive about the seriousness of the patient's distress or have emphasized positive human attributes (e.g. the Oscar-winning *A Beautiful Mind*). Wahl (1995) historically analysed cinematic depictions of mental illness and found that these more sensitive and less stigmatizing portrayals have increased since the mid-1980s.

The literature summarized here suggests two processes in tension. The first is a self-reinforcing tradition of negative framing of mental health problems. Journalists and story tellers play upon existing public prejudices (to entertain or to create a dramatic effect). They also use their own tried and tested frames of analysis and depiction from past stories. This first process is therefore a conservative vicious circle, with the assumed link between mental illness being rehearsed and reinforced by new events or story lines. The second process is about changing to more accurate and sensitive narratives or reporting. The depth of the inertia about negative media imagery is emphasized by the study of children's media. The latter provide negative stereotypes, which both anticipate and reinforce adult media representations (Wahl 2003). And yet, some shifts into more balanced or sensitive reporting and narratives have occurred. Sieff (2003) suggests that sociological research in this area should concentrate on the cognitive sets of media producers in order to identify how these two processes in tension arise and are resolved.

Social exclusion and discrimination

Earlier we examined stereotyping and stigma. The literature about these has tended to focus on the personal and interpersonal aspects of creating a depersonalized and 'spoiled' identity. This emphasis has been criticized for being reductionist (reducing the field of inquiry to that of the characteristics and plight of the stigmatized individual). Critics have shifted the focus of attention away from those with a psychiatric diagnosis and towards the collective discriminatory response of others. This alters the field of sociological enquiry from the concept of stigma to that of social exclusion. Efforts to utilize an equivalent of 'racism' or 'sexism', such as 'sanism' or 'mentalism' have not been very successful (Sayce 2000) suggesting a failure of the required internal cognitive shift in individuals, who constitute the 'sane' majority.

The fear and distrust of madness historically is deeply ingrained. Also modern societies place a high value on rationality and so demonstrable irrationality may be used as a warranted basis for social rejection and invalidation. In most modern liberal democracies, racism and sexism are not seen as either rational or fair grounds for the distrust and dismissal of others and a universal human rights framework is conceded by a majority of people about race and gender. This assumes that black people and women should have the same rights as white people and men. This can be contrasted with the fact that loss of reason is retained as an undeclared societal judgment for not allotting equal rights to the group we are discussing. If this conclusion is correct, then it would imply that psychiatric patients are still not viewed as deserving equal civil rights by most people in society. A universal corroborating factor supporting this interpretation is that some form of 'mental health' law exists in most societies, which permits the involuntary detention and coercive treatment of people who have committed no crime. This common legal feature points to a wide-spread legitimation (from voters and politicians) of the discriminatory treatment of people with mental health problems.

Sayce (2000) points out that although the frame of individual stereotyping needs to be widened to look at collective responses, the cognitive features of the latter are still an important starting point to understand a range of stances in society about the social inclusion or exclusion of people with mental health problems. She notes that different interest groups manifest different assumptions about three inter-related aspects of discrimination towards people with mental health problems:

- the nature of mental health problems;
- the causes of mental health problems;
- what should be done about discrimination.

If a psychiatrist or the relative of a patient considers that the latter is suffering from a genetically caused disturbance of brain biochemistry, then they will argue that discrimination will be reduced by campaigning for us all to accept mental illness to be like any other illness. Moreover, they would also demand more research into the (putative) genetic causes of mental illness, now framed as a brain disease, in order to reduce the prevalence of future 'sufferers'. The latter term is common within this approach because patients are seen as diseased victims of biological misfortune (being born with the wrong genes). By contrast, a service user who argues that psychological difference is caused by a variety of oppressive factors will argue for social change and the right to full citizenship and so the reduction or abolition of compulsory psychiatric treatment.

The first position about mental illness being a brain disease was taken up as an active campaign in the wake of 'anti-psychiatry' being accused of blaming parents for their children's madness. During the 1990s in the USA the National Alliance for the Mentally Ill led a campaign with a title that captures their assumptions about causation and anti-discrimination: 'Open your minds: mental illnesses are brain diseases'. The second position is more prevalent in the new social movement of disaffected patients (see the discussion in Chapter 11 about the mental health service users' movement).

There are overlaps between these contrasting positions about anti-discrimination (for example both argue for a greater public acceptance of people with a psychiatric diagnosis). However, apart from different assumptions operating about causality, there are also differences about the social policy demands. The relative lack of beds and inpatient treatment facilities have been pointed up by those committed to a bio-deterministic model of madness as evidence that 'sufferers' of 'schizophrenia' are being discriminated against by health services. This is the opposite of the demands of those focusing on citizenship who want to minimize hospitalization and maximize community support and social inclusion. The latter refers to equal access to ordinary opportunities to work, housing and leisure facilities.

Thus the way in which mental health problems are represented shapes social policy preferences. For example, a biological view of depression might lead to an educational campaign to encourage patients to seek anti-depressant treatment. For this reason the drug companies in some of their marketing strategies depict depression in a matter of fact way as a biological illness. Social inclusion in this context would be limited to an equal right to medical treatment. By contrast an environmental etiological view would lead to calls for reductions in social stressors (like poverty, work stress and so on) (Goldstein and Rosselli 2003). Social inclusion in this context would be about people with mental health problems having access to benign and supportive living environments and to satisfying work roles.

The representations of different diagnostic groups by others can also affect degrees of treatment equity within mental health services. For example, mental health workers tend to be paternalistic towards psychotic patients but distrusting and rejecting of those with a diagnosis of personality disorder (Markham 2003). Both are stigmatized groups but different attributions about personal 'fault' from professionals lead to differential levels of personal acceptance and support.

The micro-sociological emphasis upon labelling and prejudicial action perspective limits the debate about stigma and social disadvantage to empirical considerations about one-to-one interactions or the immediate social obligations of a social actor in a group of people directly around them (see earlier). The shift of emphasis by Sayce about the collective impact of acculturated assumptions about mental illness allows us to examine a different set of questions, which may be easier to answer. This is similar to the analytical advantage of shifting from a study of racial prejudice or the racism of an individual to that of studying institutional racism. Whether or not individuals reacted negatively to mental illness and whether or not the latter feels rejected by this reaction, we can ask:

- what is their experience of life?
- what evidence is there about their role in the labour market?
- to what extent are psychiatric patients allowed to enjoy full citizenship?

With regard to the life experience of psychiatric patients, their principle concerns are in relation to various aspects of their social status (Rogers, Pilgrim and Lacey 1993). They focus on oppressive and discriminatory features of community living, including poor physical health care, little informed choice about treatment, loss of employment, inability to return to paid work, poor community support services and poverty. The evidence on labour market disadvantage is unambiguous. Patients with a diagnosis of psychosis have only a one in four chance of being employed (Jenkins and Singh 2001). People with mental health problems are nearly three times as likely as physically disabled people of being unemployed (Labour Force Survey 1997–8). Moreover being employed reduces the chances of relapse in psychotic patients (Warner 1984).

Although there is clear evidence that people with mental health problems suffer labour market disadvantage, for some problems cause and effect are ambiguous. For example depression and anxiety may disable a person from coping at work but stress at work is an increasingly commonly cited cause of depression (Rogers and Pilgrim 2003). Evidence of a diverse range of discriminatory processes other than labour market disadvantage is also evident.

People with mental health problems are the target in most societies of a dedicated legal framework to remove their liberty without trial and to permit involuntary interference with their bodies and solitary confinement. This humiliating and degrading experience may be compounded by vulnerability to sexual assault during periods of detention of female patients. Mental patients have more limited social networks than others and these are more likely to be confined to those of mental health professionals and other patients (Pescosolido and Wright 2004). They are also more likely to be poor and housed in stressful, socially disorganized neighbourhoods. It is this cumulative list that demonstrates unequivocally that a person with a mental health problem experiences multiple disadvantages, which culminates recurrently in their social exclusion. The evidence discussed by those either supporting or criticizing labelling theory can be contrasted with this unambiguous picture of institutional discrimination against people with mental health problems.

Social capital, social disability and social exclusion

Social capital is often used in the social science literature to refer to social participation in the activities of the formal and informal networks of civil society and/or as generalized trust. Social participation and trust are two aspects of social capital that mutually affect each other. In this regard as we have seen earlier mental health users tend to have different ties as a result of their contact with services. Their social class position and marginalization in local communities means that they are unlikely to have the advantages of 'weak ties' (Granovetter 1973).

'Strong ties' refer to kinship and peer group contacts. These are small in number and, although strong, generally have little instrumental value to the individual. 'Weak ties' refer to personal connections which are personally superficial but may be instrumentally powerful. For example, they might create employment opportunities and career progression. They may also create a general sense of safe civility and neighbourliness in a locality. Strong ties cannot easily serve larger community purposes, whereas weak ties can. For this reason Granovetter refers to the 'strength of weak ties'. This point applies to psychiatric patients in the community in particular because they are often both poor and socially avoided by non-patients. Indeed, psychiatric patients may, as a result of their primary psychological disability and the avoidance of others, lack *both* strong and weak ties.

Thus, while the concept of social capital has gained much popularity (particularly in social policy reforms), the distinction between weak and strong ties is important to place it in context. Those with multiple weak ties (i.e. those already financially and psychologically robust in a community), may be the very people who find it easier to contribute to, and gain from, social capital in a locality.

Sociologists of deviance introduced relevant concepts such as primary and secondary deviance in drawing attention to the social processes which lead to the creation of stigmatized identities. A criticism of labelling theory from those like Walter Gove was that it was overly-focused on secondary deviance (or 'deviance amplification') and that it denied the positive value of labelling. 'Disability' refers to the disadvantage and restriction of activity of people with impairments created by contemporary forms of social organization. Social disability theory traces the oppressive consequences of these restrictive and excluding forms of organization. A similar criticism to that about secondary deviance from Gove could also be levelled at the social model of disability because impairment (primary deviance) is downplayed. Nonetheless, it is a model which is popular with disabled people themselves; whether they are activists or academics (Barnes and Mercer 2004). It has also found some favour with mental health service users (Beresford 2005) and within academic analyses of the relationship between a psychiatric diagnosis and oppressive experiences (Mulvany 2000).

Conclusion

This chapter has explored the ways in which people with mental health problems are understood, depicted and reacted to by others. With the loss of popularity of labelling theory in the 1970s, this type of sociological interest diminished. Sociological debate about the role of lay views of mental health problems and their links to prejudicial action has now been revitalized in a number of ways:

• First, there has been a successful reassertion of the labelling theory approach (especially that associated with Bruce Link and his colleagues). This encourages us to revisit the work on stigma and mental health started by Erving Goffman in the 1950s and 1960s. Moreover, the tension with the competing body of knowledge created by Walter Gove and his colleagues, which emphasizes primary psychiatric disability, rather than social reactions to it, is useful to explore. Those who emphasize primary deviance (the patient is deemed to fail socially because they are mentally ill) will see labelling, especially that done diagnostically by professionals, as being positive not negative, as it warrants access to care and treatment. Labelling can be framed as a human right which gives the labelled person access to restorative interventions provided by others. By contrast, those who emphasize deviance amplification arising from labelling, will view psychiatric diagnosis as a potential social disadvantage to its targets.

- Second, the role of the mass media in responding to and reinforcing public prejudices has now been well researched and has exposed important social processes, which maintain prejudice and stigma. A sociological research programme around media depictions and the thought processes of writers and journalists has been established.
- Third, it is now clear that there is no firm epistemological starting point about the nature of mental health problems and so any sociological inquiry must examine the ways in which different social groups depict this nature. Stigma and discrimination allow one way into this inquiry, because they encourage us to examine the interests being expressed by this rather than that way of depicting mental health problems. The study of social representations of mental health and illness then becomes an important area of sociological inquiry in its own right.
- Fourth, it may be that an individualistic focus on stigma is a necessary but not a sufficient way of understanding collective discrimination. Even if labelling theory in its modified or original form were proved to be empirically unfounded, what is not in doubt is the evidence about social disadvantage. The evidence about the social exclusion of people with mental health problems is unambiguous. They are more likely to live in poor localities and suffer the ecological consequences of this vulnerability. They encounter labour market disadvantage. They die early. They are shunned by others. They are detained without trial. They are lawfully assaulted, isolated and they are subjected to the imposition of life-diminishing interventions. This list (some of which we explore further in later chapters) provides a wide range of topics for sociological inquiry. Moreover, an emphasis on social exclusion can accept either of the positions described in the first point above, about the tension in emphasis between primary and secondary deviance. An emphasis on social exclusion is concerned less with the sources or causes of mental illness or residual deviance and more with the politics of discrimination and the constraints upon citizenship imposed upon people with a psychiatric diagnosis.

Questions

1 What are the similarities and differences between labelling theory and modified labelling theory?

2 What contribution did Erving Goffman make to our understanding of mental abnormality?

3 Does labelling affect the lives of people with mental health problems?

4 What evidence is there that those with a diagnosis of mental illness are unintelligible?

5 How does an emphasis on social exclusion differ from one on stigmatization?

6 Can a social model of disability be applied to people with mental health problems?

For discussion

Consider the various ways in which people with mental health problems are affected by the individual and collective reactions of others.

Further reading

Goffman, E. (1971) *Relations in Public*. Harmondsworth: Penguin.

Mulvany, J. (2000) Disability, impairment or illness? The relevance of the social model of disability to the study of mental disorder. *Sociology of Health and Illness*, 22(5): 582–601.

Sayce, L. (2000) *From Psychiatric Patient to Citizen: Overcoming Discrimination and Social Exclusion*. Basingstoke: Macmillan.

Thoits, P.A. (1985) Self-labeling processes in mental illness: the role of emotional deviance. *American Journal of Sociology*, 91: 221–49.

Wahl, O.F. (1995) *Media Madness: Public Images of Mental Illness*. New Brunswick, NJ: Rutgers University Press.

Chapter 3

Social class and mental health

Chapter overview

This chapter will cover:

- the general relationship between social class and health status;
- the relationship between social class and diagnosed mental illness;
- the relationship between poverty and mental health status;
- social capital, neighbourhood and mental health;
- social class and mental health professionalism;
- lay views about mental health and social class.

The general relationship between social class and health status

Establishing the relationship between social class, social and economic conditions and poor mental health has been a dominant trend in both social psychiatry and sociology. A close association between sociology and medicine is evident within this tradition traceable to nineteenth-century social medicine (Kleinman 1986). One of the earliest studies in psychiatric epidemiology, which sought to establish a link between schizophrenia and social class (Faris and Dunham 1939) was carried out in the context of the development of 'human ecology' as a theoretical trend within the Chicago School of Sociology (Park 1936) and since then some sociologists have continued to collaborate with psychiatrists. There are other ways in which a link between social conditions and milieu has been made. Some theorists have made a link between social conditions and the collective psychological well-being of a society. This was a feature of the work of Fromm, a member of the Frankfurt School (discussed in Chapter 1).

This focus also appears in the developing area of the 'sociology of emotions' and the analytical links being made between the unconscious dimensions of human experience and identity in post-modern societies (discussed at the end of Chapter 1). Mental health is part of a wider topic (health). Before we examine mental health this wider relationship between social class and ill health will be summarized.

In Chapter 1 we noted the social causation position in medical sociology. The empirical case for this position is at its strongest in relation to the correlations which have been established between social class and ill health. Link and Phelan (1995: 81) summarized 40 years of work in medical sociology which has supported the social causation of disease by noting that:

> Lower SES [socio-economic status] is associated with lower life expectancy, higher overall mortality rates and higher rates of infant and perinatal mortality. Moreover, low SES is associated with each of the 14 major cause-of-death categories in the International Classification of Diseases as well as many other health outcomes including major mental disorders.

However, the authors go on to note that the social causation case is not limited to considerations of class. Other social variables are implicated such as gender. Men have higher mortality rates at all ages, higher rates of coronary heart disease, respiratory disease and ulcers. Women have higher rates of diagnosed mental illness (see Chapter 4) and hypertension (the raised prevalence reflecting greater longevity in women). In relation to race, African Americans have higher rates of mortality at all ages, renal failure and stroke but lower rates than whites of coronary heart disease. In Britain, Irish people and those who emigrated from the Caribbean and their British-born offspring have significantly higher rates of diagnosed major mental illness (see Chapter 5).

A British study comparing community samples of 15, 35 and 55-year-olds found a class gradient on a number of health indicators throughout the life span. However, class differences were not found in the youngest group in relation to chronic physical illness and mental health (Ford *et al.* 1994). Another study focusing on lower-class adolescents – 1000 young, unemployed people (15–21 years) in Scotland – found that a third of the males and two-fifths of the females were exhibiting evidence of 'psychological morbidity' by 18 years of age (Sweeting and West 1995).

The importance of the life course perspective in understanding the determinants of inequalities in mental and physical health is succinctly put by Bartley and her colleagues (1998: 573):

> The more data we have which show how early circumstances contribute to health in later life, the clearer it becomes that 'social class' at any given point is but a very partial indicator of a whole sequence, a 'probabilistic cascade' of events which need to be seen in combination if the effects of social environment on health are to be understood. Different individuals have arrived at any particular level of income, occupational advantage or prestige which have different life histories behind them. Variables such as height, education and ownership of additional consumer goods act as indicators of these past histories.

Traditionally, inequalities in both physical and mental health have been explained with reference to four main factors which were originally identified in the Black Report (DHSS 1980).

- *Artefact explanations* suggest that inequalities are an artefact of the way in which official statistics have been collated (Illsley 1986). By implication the artefact explanation attacks the assumption that health inequalities exist at all and that there is a causal relationship between social conditions and health. However, new methods available for validating the existence of class inequalities, using longitudinal Census data on health inequalities and linking these to death certification and cancer registration, have confirmed that health inequalities are not likely to be due to statistical bias (Bartley *et al.* 1998);
- *Selection explanations* suggest that long-term illness or 'health capital' in early life constrains social mobility and continued inequalities in illness in adulthood (Power *et al.* 1996). In other words health status determines socio-economic position (Illsley 1986) (as in the 'social drift' hypothesis discussed in more detail later);
- *Cultural/behavioural explanations* suggest that lifestyle and health-related behaviours (such as cigarette smoking, diet and lack of exercise among manual groups) lead to health inequalities;
- *Materialist explanations* emphasize the differential exposure to health threats inherent in society over which people have little control. Thus, this explanation suggests that a person's socio-economic position, and material deprivation in particular, leads to poorer health among people in lower social classes.

Over the last two decades there have been extensions elaborating on this four-fold typology. The debates about the causes of inequalities in health and illness have moved beyond simplistic unitary explanations and have incorporated more complex theories and concepts from mainstream sociology and the sub-discipline of the sociology of health and illness. The use of other indicators and proxies for social class (e.g. the use of housing tenure and car ownership), which have produced similar socio-economic gradients in health, has lessened the strength of the artefact explanation (Davey Smith *et al.* 1990). The importance of time, biography and longitudinal lifecourse research (Mheen *et al.* 1998; Shaw *et al.* 1998) and of 'place' (e.g. the types of spatial effects which may impact on health status (Macintyre *et al.* 1993; Curtis and Jones 1998)) may act to reinforce inequalities in health status and health care operating within a locality.

There is a greater emphasis too on the relationship between social structure and human agency in gaining insights into the nature of health inequalities. Recent sociological analyses have made use of the notions of social capital, personal identity and the situated actions and decisions made by individuals, when exploring health inequalities. The lack of 'social capital', which refers to 'features of social life-networks, norms and trust that enable participants to act together more effectively to pursue shared objectives' (Putnam, cited in Wilkinson 1996: 221), implies that the quality of social relationships and, most importantly, our perceptions of where we are relatively to others in the social structure, are likely to be important psycho-social mediators in the cause of inequalities in health (Wilkinson 1996).

Informed by this approach, Nettleton and Burrows (1998) have explored the experience of mortgage debt and insecure home ownership: They point to the way in which people's notion of home and home ownership are part of their sense of identity and aspirations, which provide a basis for what Laing (1959) called 'ontological security'. A threat to the latter may occur when, for example, mortgage arrears impact negatively on an individual's mental health.

As part of this transition in theorizing about health inequalities more generally, greater importance has been attributed to social-psychological factors as mediators in health inequalities (Williams 1998) and emotions have come to be seen as central to the relationship between social structure and health.

> . . . the fact that socio-economic factors now primarily affect health through psycho-social rather than material pathways, places emotions centre-stage in the social patterning of disease and disorder in advanced Western societies. In this sense, emotions, as existentially embodied modes of being in the world and the *sine qua non* of causal reciprocity and exchange, provide the 'missing link' between 'personal troubles' and broader 'public issues' of social structure.
>
> (Williams 1998: 133)

One final point with regard to the broader research agenda about health inequalities and ill health is the politicized context within which social and medical research has been undertaken. During the 1980s, ideological pressure, intended perhaps to gloss over the persistent and growing inequalities between rich and poor, found expression in a change of official terminology. There was also a seeming imbalance between work, which prioritized cultural individual and artefact explanations, compared to work which focused on material deprivation (Davey Smith *et al.* 1990). During this period, the term 'inequalities' was replaced by the preferred official (Conservative) government term 'variations' in health. With an incoming Labour health administration in

1997, not only was there a reversal to the previous terminology, but there was the appointment of a public health minister and a Green Paper with the aim of tackling inequalities and unmet need (Department of Health 1998). More recently a White Paper on public health has appeared extending this work (Department of Health 2004).

The relationship between social class and diagnosed mental illness

Class remains a predictable correlate of mental ill health. Basically the poorer a person is the more likely they are to have a mental health problem. A class gradient is evident in mental health status across the bulk of the diagnostic groups but it is not a neat inverse relationship. For example, affective disorders are diagnosed fairly evenly in all social classes, whereas a very strong correlation exists between low social class and the diagnosis of schizophrenia.

Faris and Dunham (1939) studied the intake of patients to hospital from different parts of Chicago. They found higher rates of illness for schizophrenia, alcoholism and organic psychosis in those groups from poor areas. The greatest difference was in the diagnosis of schizophrenia. There was seven times the rate of schizophrenic diagnosis for people from poor inner city districts compared with middle-class suburban areas. The investigators concluded that the combination of poverty plus a lack of social cohesion in a locality precipitated schizophrenic breakdown. They argued that those vulnerable to breakdown are those who, for developmental reasons, became socially isolated during childhood. The stress of poverty and social disorganization then pushes these vulnerable individuals into psychosis. Faris (1944) then elaborated this 'social isolation' theory of schizophrenia.

After the Second World War, Dunham (1957) drew attention to several studies that confirmed the role of social isolation in the aetiology of schizophrenia; there were exceptions though. Clausen and Kohn (1959) did not find the relationship between isolation and psychosis in the small city of Hagerstown, Maryland. Also, Weinberg (1960), studying the histories of patients with a diagnosis of schizophrenia, did not find a pattern of social isolation. Gerard and Houston (1953) found that divorced and single people who already had a diagnosis of schizophrenia moved to inner city areas. At this stage the controversy over 'social drift' emerged. Its proponents argued that mentally ill people drift into poverty. Its opponents argued that poverty precipitates illness.

Lapouse et al. (1956) and Hollingshead and Redlich (1958) did not find in their surveys that people diagnosed as schizophrenic drifted into poor areas, but they confirmed the class gradient in the diagnosis of schizophrenia. Overall, the early epidemiological evidence strongly pointed to an over-representation of patients considered to have schizophrenia in lower-class samples (e.g. Tietze et al. 1941; Stein 1957; Goldberg and Morrison 1963). These patients were particularly over-represented at the bottom of the social scale (Dunham 1964). The question is, why does this class gradient exist?

Broadly, there have been two competing hypotheses about why mental illness is diagnosed more in poorer populations. The first is the 'drift' hypothesis and the other is the 'opportunity and stress' hypothesis. The 'drift' hypothesis, which suggests that illness incapacitates social competence, has two aspects. One has already been mentioned – that psychotic patients perhaps drift into poorer urban areas. The other is that patients drift down the social scale. Here the assumption is that patients from all classes above that of the lowest stratum (the unskilled and the unemployed) who become mentally ill cannot maintain their class position and they sink to the bottom of society, in class terms.

Empirical work suggests that the different causal explanations vary according to the type of mental health problem under investigation. A large-scale epidemiological study in Israel (Dohrenwend *et al*. 1992) concluded that social causation was stronger than social selection in producing the inverse association of socio-economic status to severe depression in women, substance abuse and antisocial personality in men. However, in relation to those who carried a diagnosis of schizophrenia the epidemiological evidence was more supportive of the social selection explanation.

Investigations to date have not resolved the drift versus stress debate. Given the mixed evidence for both, there have been some attempts to integrate elements of each of them. For example, the mixed model of Kohn is assessed by Cochrane (1983). The hypothesis relating to stress and opportunities suggests that these differentially affect lower-class people compared with those from the middle and upper classes.

Srole *et al*. (1962) and Langer and Michael (1963) in their large-scale community surveys of mental health in the US found that lower-class people were more likely to have psychotic symptoms and middle-class people were more likely to have neurotic symptoms. They accounted for this difference in part by suggesting that middle-class children are over-inhibited compared with their lower-class equivalents. Their sexual and aggressive impulses were considered to be more controlled. This was thought to lead to problems of anxiety and guilt appearing more often in non-lower-class groups. Also, the emphasis on self and identity was found to be a stronger preoccupation during upbringing in non-lower-class families. This may mean that a sense of identity is stronger in these groups. By contrast, identity strength may be lower, on average, in lower-class groups. Lower-class people may be more readily vulnerable to the loss and fragmentation of their sense of self and thus may become psychotic.

These speculations about psychological differences in upbringing and their consequences can be added to much stronger evidence about the material differences between classes. Poor people have to struggle with the personal consequences of material deprivation. In their locality they must endure higher stress from crime, traffic and dirt and their home conditions are more likely to be cramped. Their diet and physical health will be inferior to those further up the class scale. They will be vulnerable to unemployment more often and the jobs they obtain will lack a sense of personal control. All these factors will contribute to lower levels of self worth and esteem. When they enter the patient role lower class patients are more likely to stay as in-patients for longer periods of time and thus become more severely disabled from re-entering society (Hardt and Feinhandler 1959).

The evidence from social psychiatric follow ups of patients with diagnoses of schizophrenia shows that the more opportunities they have for employment

the better their prognoses. Indeed socio-economic conditions are a better predictor of recovery than access to treatment; even optimal treatment (Ciompi
1984; Warner 1985; 2003). Also, the point about esteem or relative self worth
has been confirmed in studies looking at quality of life in different classes.
While people in all classes have negative experiences, the proportion of these
to positive experiences decreases with increasing class position. For instance,
Phillips (1968) found no class differences in the reporting of negative experiences. There were, however, significant differences in the presence of positive
experiences between high- and low-class respondents. The former were twice
as likely as the latter to report feeling excited, proud or interested by an event
during the last month than the latter. Phillips then concluded that lower-class
people have fewer positive experiences to buffer themselves against life's
stresses, which makes them more vulnerable to mental distress.

This is consistent with the findings of the longitudinal study of Myers (1974;
1975). It was found that, in all social classes, the greater the number of life
events, both positive and negative, then the greater the probability of psychiatric symptoms appearing. But non-lower-class people experienced a greater
proportion of positive events and this led to them being buffered from
symptom formation more often than lower-class people.

So, while it can be demonstrated unequivocally that social stress is correlated with social class, the evidence is still not clear about its *causal* role in
schizophrenia. The epidemiological evidence from social psychiatry seems to
point strongly at the role of social stress in recovery and relapse, but this is not
the same as deducing that social stressors actually cause schizophrenia. As we
will see later (Chapter 6), the clear traumatic stress of sexual abuse raises the
probability of most forms of psychiatric morbidity except for the diagnosis of
schizophrenia. This role of stress in relapse, rather than aetiology, may
account for the prevalence of schizophrenia being affected by social stress (but
not for the incidence of first episodes) and may explain why lower-class
patients recover less frequently.

In the case of depression and anxiety the underlying assumption has been
more clear cut, perhaps because minor morbidity is less strongly identifiable as
a biologically derived illness. Additionally, socio-economic inequality in
depression is heterogeneous and varies according to the way psychiatric disorder is measured, to the definition and measurement of SES, and to contextual features, such as region and time (Lorant *et al.* 2003). Stansfeld *et al.*
(2003) found that work is the main determinant of inequalities in depressive
symptoms in men, and work and material disadvantage are equally important
in explaining inequalities in depressive symptoms in women, while health
behaviours are more important for explaining inequalities in physical
functioning.

Wiggins *et al.* (2004) examined the link between common psychiatric symptoms and work. They found a complex relationship of social class to anxiety
and depression linked to changing employment status. They examined three
different ways of describing social position: (i) income; (ii) social advantage
and lifestyle; and (iii) social class. They found a relationship between mental
health and social position, when the latter was combined with employment
status. This relation itself varied according to a person's psychological health
in recent times. They concluded that the relation between social position and
minor psychiatric morbidity depended on whether or not a person was

employed, unemployed, or economically inactive. The relation was more evident in those with previously poorer psychological health. Among economically active men and women in good health, mental health varied little according to social class, status, or income. There was a traditional social gradient in psychiatric symptoms in those in work. However, in the unemployed group, a reverse gradient was found: the impact of unemployment on symptoms was greater for those who were previously in a more advantaged social class position.

Social class, social capital and neighbourhood

In most epidemiological studies there has been a tendency to treat the socio-economic status of individuals as a proxy for the social contexts in which they live (and *vice versa*). For example, we assume that poor people only live in poor areas and in poor areas there are only poor people. However, this can lead to the 'ecological fallacy' – the mistake of assuming that there are no individual class differences within specified localities. This fallacy may be particularly evident in large cities, such as London, containing many socially 'mixed' areas.

At the same time, there is some evidence that many cities and towns indeed have environmentally differentiated areas, even though the social boundary between them may be the difference between one street and the next (Macintyre, Ellaway and Cummins 2002). The distinct environmental features impact on all residents (independent of their class position or socio-economic status). In poor areas these features include a high combination of environmental stressors and the relative absence of opportunities for healthy behaviour. For example, if people are fearful of leaving their homes, then they will not go out walking or make social contacts regularly. Thus neighbourhood seems to have an independent effect on mental health. This suggests the need to distinguish between individually defined and neighbourhood-defined social position, as sources of mental distress. Example of this point are give in Box 3.1.

Given the sorts of findings summarized in Box 3.1, it is little surprising that the notion of 'social capital' has become an important consideration for both sociological investigators and for politicians seeking effective public mental health reforms. For example, a focus on social capital within communitarian reforms of Western capitalist societies has been central to the work of the American sociologist Amitai Etzioni (1995), who has influenced some aspects of social policy in Britain since 1997. Another influential figure has been Robert Putnam, an American political scientist, who has describes social capital as the: 'features of social life – networks, norms, and trust – that enable participants to act together more effectively to pursue shared objectives' (Putnam 2000) (see Chapter 2).

Social capital is a construct linking the embeddedness of individual social ties (social networks and social support) with the broader social structure. These ties might be bonds between family members or links with others in a locality or extended community – neighbours or those with a shared interest in an activity (Portes 1998). At an individual level 'cognitive social capital' describes the values, attitudes and beliefs that produce cooperative behaviour (Colletta and Cullen 2000). Other definitions emphasize structural or insti-

Box 3.1 **The neighbourhood as an influence on mental health**

- Residents of disadvantaged neighbourhoods report symptoms of depression independently of the effects of individual socio-economic characteristics (Ross 2000);
- Neighbourhood income is significantly related to the prevalence of major mental health problems and substance abuse (Goldsmith, Holzer and Mandershied 1998);
- Poorer neighbourhoods have been shown to provide fewer 'opportunity structures' for health-promoting activities than more affluent ones (Ellaway *et al.* 1997);
- The effects of place of residence on mental health are greatest among those who are economically inactive and hence more likely to spend the time at home. Those in more deprived neighbourhoods are less likely to be in full-time employment (Ellaway and Macintyre 2004);
- The 'ambient hazards' of chaotic localities have been associated with an increase in depression, anxiety and behavioural disorders (Aneschensel and Succoff 1996). People living in socially disorganized localities are more likely to experience psychological distress because of exposure to uncontrollable life events and psycho-social insults (Silver *et al.* 1999);
- People who report living in neighbourhoods with high levels of crime, vandalism, graffiti, danger noise and drugs are more mistrustful of those around them and the powerlessness which ensues amplifies the effect of neighbourhood disorder on mental health (Ross, Mirowsky and Pribesh 2001).

tutional level processes – for example 'collective efficacy', 'trust', participation in voluntary organizations and social integration for mutual benefit (Lochner *et al.* 1999).

Generating or regenerating social capital is assumed to be good for mental health. Focusing on repairing the breakdown of trust networks and relationships in an area is assumed to help reverse the processes of social inclusion. Thus the notion of partnership is commonly advocated – at a structural level between agencies and between social groups and social agencies. However, the obstacles to this communitarian vision of community healing are power discrepancies and barriers. Individuals within localities may not view community organizations or networks as representative of their interests or needs and therefore may be reluctant to engage in partnerships.

Equally, confidence in the benefits or outcomes of increased social capital is contested. The protective effects *vis-à-vis* mental health are not necessarily uniform across social groups. For example, Kawachi and Berkman (2001) suggest that gender differences in support derived from social network participation may partly account for the *higher* prevalence of psychological distress among women compared to men. Social connections may paradoxically increase levels of symptoms among women with low resources, especially if such connections entail role strain associated with obligations to provide social support to others.

Probably the most important and recurrent criticism of social capital, as a social reform strategy, is that it diverts attention from the need to reverse structural inequalities. Politicians can use it to claim the credit for social improvements, without any fiscal consequences for spending or political consequences for the ownership of the means of production. Indeed the linkage of social capital to economic efficiency and its health benefits tempt the politician with the prospect of actual *savings* for the State. This emphasis on process reform rather than structural reform has been a feature of New Labour policies in recent years. An indication that it reflects an adaptation of capitalism is that the political importance of social capital is endorsed by the World Bank (Colletta and Cullen 2000). Muntaner *et al.* (2001) suggest that social capital:

> . . . presents itself as an alternative to materialist structural inequalities (class, gender and race) and invokes a romanticised view of communities without social conflict . . . social capital is used in public health as an alternative to both state-centred economic re-distribution and party politics, and represents a potential privatisation of both economics and policies
>
> (p. 214)

Moreover the causal role of social capital in supporting well-being and preventing mental illness may not be as great as its advocates suggest. Ziersch *et al.* (2005) found that socio-economic factors were of relatively greater importance in determining mental health than social capital variables. Higher-income level and educational achievement were related to better mental health and mental health found to be higher within older age groups.

Similarly, Browning and Cagney (2003) found that affluence is a precursor to residential stability and its associated mental health benefits. Thus, a multi-dimensional view of 'capital' may be more useful in understanding the micro-social mechanisms which generate and maintain social inequalities. Cohen and Prusak (2001) note that the language of social *capital* may signify the reduction of human relationships to their financial value as a form of investment. Nonetheless, sociologists continue to use 'capital' in a fluid way, as a linguistic resource. For example, Bourdieu's work on *habitus* emphasizes the role played by various forms of capital (economic, social, cultural and symbolic) in perpetuating social inequalities (Williams 1995; Bourdieu 1997).

The relationship between poverty and mental health status

The discussion above seems to indicate that poverty should remain a strong causal focus in our understanding of mental health status. This focus allows us to explore the interaction between disempowerment and material deprivation. For example, if depressed groups are studied, black people are more severely depressed than their white counterparts with low socio-economic status (Biafora 1995). This could be accounted for by the double impact of oppression in this group (being poor and black).

Evidence of the link between poverty and mental health is evident in relation to other social groupings. Here are some empirical examples demonstrating this point. A study in Scotland found that financially deprived young people were twice as likely to commit suicide as their peers in more affluent localities (McLoone 1996). Brown and Moran (1997) found that single mothers had poorer mental health than those with partners. They were also twice as likely to suffer financial hardship even though they were also twice as likely to be in some form of full-time employment. These vulnerable mothers were trapped in conditions of poverty and isolation. Reading and Reynolds (2001) found that anxiety about debt was the best predictor of depressive symptoms in poor families.

An analytical advantage of focusing on poverty, rather than social class *per se*, is that it helps us to clarify a contradiction about mental health service utilization. Generally, in health care there is an 'inverse care law', that is, access to health care increases with increasing class status. However, the reverse appears to be the case in mental health care systems. Psychiatric services are dominated by patients from low social class backgrounds. Superficially this might suggest that those with the greatest need are being responded to. That is, given that poor people are more likely to be diagnosed as mentally ill, services are responding to their need. However, there is a problem with this logic. While most health care interventions are voluntary and ameliorative in intent in their response to the needs of sick people, in psychiatric services, involuntary detention and treatment are never far away. A proportion of patients are being forcibly detained and treated by the use of therapeutic law, some are notionally voluntary but de facto detainees, and others are genuinely voluntary but exist in a service context where the threat of coercion is ever present (Rogers 1993a).

In the light of these peculiar features about psychiatry, it might be more accurate to conceptualize mental health work as part of a wider state apparatus which controls the social problems associated with poverty (what has been increasingly called the 'underclass'). Once conceived in this way, it lowers our expectations that service contact should necessarily be about aiming for, or achieving, a gain in the mental health status of service recipients, given that the latent, and sometimes the explicit, function of psychiatry is that of successful coercive social control. The latter entails mental health services serving the interests of parties (such as relatives and strangers in the street) other than the patients they contain and treat.

Thus, poverty is an important focus for understanding the relationship between social class and mental health because it highlights the social control role of psychiatry in response to certain types of social crises and deviance. The social *consequences* of poverty become a dimension of understanding mental health in society. Poverty is also important in understanding the social *antecedents* of madness and psychological distress. These antecedents include interactions with other forms of oppression (such as racism, discussed above), the stress of poor living conditions and the impact of labour market disadvantage.

Relative deprivation has a greater impact on morbidity and GP consultation for stress-related conditions such as depression, anxiety and headache/

migraine. For all these conditions, higher levels of self-reported morbidity and a greater probability of consulting the doctor are associated with a cluster of social disadvantages – living in rented accommodation, unemployment, younger age and lower educational status. Relative deprivation is also associated with poorer mental health for this population of mothers of young children (Baker and Taylor 1997).

Labour market disadvantage and mental health

Reviews of the evidence on the impact of labour market disadvantage on mental health have found that unemployment has a predictable negative toll on both the unemployed individuals and their family members (Fryer 1995; Kasl *et al.* 1998). However, it is not a simple matter of unemployment being bad for a person's mental health and employment being good. Employment can bring with it stressors, as well as buffers, in relation to psychological well-being. Elsewhere (Rogers and Pilgrim 2003) we have explored this complexity, which can be summarized in the following points:

- Optimal mental health is correlated with secure, well-paid work, in which the worker has control over his or her tasks. While unemployed people have poorer mental health, those who are 'inadequately employed' (i.e. poorly paid, insecure and with unsatisfying tasks) have the poorest mental health (Burchell 1992; Graetz 1993; Dooley *et al.* 2000);
- This pattern of a hierarchy of mental health in relation to employment status (good work conditions being the best, poor work conditions being the worst and unemployment being in between) has been confirmed by longitudinal studies looking at changes of employment and their mental health impact (Kasl *et al.* 1998);
- Having a mental health problem is correlated with labour market disadvantage. For example, only one in four psychotic patients outside of their acute episodes are in employment and they are three times more likely to be unemployed than physically disabled people (Sayce 2000);
- The direction of causality between these findings is not always easy to trace, For example, depressed patients may lack the motivation and confidence to work (their primary disability renders them unfit for work). At the same time, there is strong evidence that psychiatric patients who are fit to work face predictable discrimination from employers (Sayce 2000).

Housing and mental health

The second broad set of antecedent factors relates not to employment status but to accommodation. However, it is important to note that while these are discussed separately for convenience here from employment factors, they are copresent and additive in the lives of many poor people. The following main points can be made about the link between housing and mental health:

- Poor accommodation produces stress reactions in inhabitants (Hunt 1990; Hyndman 1990);

- Some researchers have argued that mental health problems lead to homelessness rather than the poverty on the streets being a stressor which provokes mental ill health (Whitely 1955; Bassuk *et al.* 1984). Others argue that the reverse is the case (Hamid 1991);
- Arguments about the direction of causality at times have been driven by professional interests to retain psychiatric beds. Snow *et al.* (1986) undertook ethnographic fieldwork to assess the mental health status of homeless people and found, using standard diagnostic criteria, that only 15 per cent of a population of 991 were considered to be mentally ill. This empirical picture can be contrasted with the catastrophic discourse about deinstitutionalization in those who lobbied to retain large scale hospitalization of psychiatric patients which over-emphasized prevalence in homeless populations. For example, one British pressure group in the early 1990s in favour of retaining the mass segregation of patients (Concern) argued that 40–50 per cent of the homeless population was mentally ill and, moreover, that prison populations had grown in response to hospital closure (see Page and Powell 1991). The latter collection also contained articles emphasizing the need to retain the Victorian asylums and the highly dangerous nature of madness (Hollander 1991; Jacobs 1991);
- While homeless people are no more likely to be psychotic than other poor people, they are more likely to suffer from reactive depression (Gory *et al.* 1990) and they do have high rates of substance misuse (Toro 1998). Indeed substance misuse seems to be a good predictor of homeless status, whether or not an individual has a mental health problem. According to Teeson *et al.* (2000), in a cross-national review of the topic, 25–50 per cent of women and 50–75 per cent of men who are homeless also abuse substances;
- The small minority of homeless patients, who are both psychotic and abuse substances, represents a particularly vulnerable group. They are prone to both self neglect and violence (Soyka 2000);
- Psychiatric epidemiology suggests that homeless populations have different symptom profiles than other poor (housed) groups. Homeless people are more likely to abuse substances and fulfill criteria for anti-social personality disorder (North *et al.* 1997). Moreover, when homeless and housed psychotic patients are studied it is found that the former are more likely to have troubled social histories, including abuse and conduct disorders in childhood, criminal activity and substance misuse (Odell and Commander 2000).

Social class and mental health professionalism

In this section we address a set of factors which reinforce (rather than singularly create) class differences in mental health status. A number of studies have focused on the impact of the 'cultural gap' which can exist between clients and their treating mental health professionals (Horwitz 1983). The latter concept refers to more than class differences as it can implicate race and ethnicity as well as age, gender and sexuality. However, class is an important consideration when people with mental health problems engage with professional services. Poor patients are more likely to receive a diagnosis of schizophrenia than richer patients, who are more likely to receive a less stigmatizing neurotic label or be allotted one of affective disorder (depression, mania, or manic-depression). Poorer patients are more likely to receive biological treatments than psychological treatments. Poorer patients are less likely to be referred for psychotherapy, are rejected more often on assessment by specialists and drop out of treatment earlier (Pilgrim 1997). Poorer patients are more likely to be treated coercively than voluntarily.

Some of this picture could be accounted for by the simple issue of raised incidence of severe mental health problems in poor populations – i.e. the more severe mental illness profile of the latter warrants greater levels of coercion and biological treatments in mental health service responses. Sedgwick (1982) warned of the dangers inherent in social constructivist arguments in this regard. He commented that some critics of psychiatry wanted it both ways: on the one hand they argued that adverse material conditions cause severe mental illness (warranting more psychiatric services) and, on the other, they deconstructed, and thereby undermined, the legitimacy of diagnostic data demonstrating this causal relationship. They also complained of the social control role of psychiatric professionals.

However, as we noted in Chapter 1, constructivism and causationism can be reconciled. It is logically quite feasible that the material conditions of poverty raise the probability of mental distress in a population and that professional interests are at play and, within this, the role and 'world views' of psychiatric professionals. This might include the class and cognitive interests of mental health professionals operating, when they respond to low-class patients in contact with services and formulate this distress in bio-medical terms or in the thinly veiled value judgements of psychological interpretations. For example, clinicians tend to interpret psychometric test responses from lower socio-economic groups as reflecting greater psychopathology than similar responses from middle-class clients. Also, growing conditions of poverty significantly affects how people perform on tests of abstract thinking, intelligence and academic achievement (Franks 1993). Taken together, these processes point to both causal and constructed influences upon poor clients in service contact.

Poverty and other class-related phenomena remain neglected areas in the training of mental health professionals, with the latter not being exposed to the narratives of poverty, oppression and daily struggle which would sensitize them to the needs of their client group. Schnitzer (1996) suggests that mental health professionals typically question the responsibility, cognitive competence and moral sensitivity of poorer clients. This may reflect not just the secondary socialization (in their training) of mental health professionals but also their primary socialization (in their class of origin).

A number of commentators have pointed to the absence of notions of class and inequality in disciplinary knowledge which underpin mental health professionals' practice. For example, in mainstream psychiatry and psychology textbooks class, racial and gender inequalities receive little attention. Power inequalities are then marginalized and are seen as having little to do with psychiatric vulnerability or psychiatric management more generally (Horsfall 1997). Ussher (1994) points to the narrow focus of mainstream clinical psychology models, such as behavioural and cognitive behavioural therapy, which ignore class both at the level of theory and practice.

Lay views about mental health and social class

While there has been a social psychiatric epidemiology which maps the relationship between social variations and mental health, the views of people within different classes about the topic of mental health and social class has, until recently, been a relatively neglected area. As we have outlined above there is an extensive literature which maps and puts forward explanations for differences between groups in the population in terms of mental health status. Traditionally, there has been little interest in how people themselves construed their distress and oppression. However, more recently, there has been a growing interest in the understanding of lay knowledge. One of the arguments for this greater concentration is to augment gaps in professional knowledge about how ordinary people understand their health.

Blaxter (1990) has explored the views that people have about inequalities in health in general. In relation to mental health, lay people tend to adopt a relative, rather than absolute, view of mental health and social causation (Rogers and Pilgrim 1997). People in all social classes tend to view money problems as a central feature of mental well-being – though those from more middle-class backgrounds identify it as being more of a problem for working-class families. Similarly, work stress and stress related to common life events, such as bereavement and birth, were considered by working-class respondents to affect people similarly, albeit in different ways.

Perceptions of lay knowledge about help seeking are also important. The expectations of patients and prospective patients shape demand for, and use of, formal services. For example, in primary care settings lay people provide accounts of help seeking about mental health problems which are different from those offered by GPs (Pilgrim *et al.* 1997). Professionals emphasize diagnostic categories (like depression) based upon a symptom approach to presenting problems. By contrast, patients themselves understand their problems within a unique biographical context situated in time and place. These attributions within a life story include factors such as poverty, employment and unemployment, domestic violence and life events (like birth and death in the family).

Blaxter (1997) found that social inequality in health is not a topic which is very prominent in lay presentations, particularly among those who are most likely to be exposed to disadvantaging environments. Blaxter notes the way in which accounts of social identity have the potential to be self-devaluing, through the act of explicitly labelling and acknowledging inequality and poverty. Resistance to talk of class, in her respondents, was displaced by accounts of individual, private experience. Class was discussed though in more impersonal discussions of health as a wider social or political phenomenon.

Blaxter's work lends qualified support to the 'individualisation thesis': demonstrable objective inequalities in health are not reproduced subjectively by the actors they apply to, in the personal accounts given in qualitative research or in focus group discussions. Class identity and health are negotiated in lay talk as participants shift argumentatively back and forth between competing positions, and public and private realms, in the attempt to make sense of health and illness (Bolam, Murphy and Gleeson 2004).

Discussion

Some disease categories such as schizophrenia have been subjected to per-suasive critical deconstruction. For example, this diagnosis has been criticized for its lack of aetiological specificity, its lack of predictive validity and its lack of inter-rater reliability (Bentall, Jackson and Pilgrim 1988). It is a 'disjunctive' diagnosis. That is, two patients called 'schizophrenic' may have no symptoms in common (Bannister 1968). Some historians of the concept (Boyle 1991) have even demonstrated that the symptom profiles recorded in the late nine-teenth century, when Kraepelin and Bleuler constructed the disease entity, first called 'dementia praecox' and then 'schizophrenia', bear little relation-ship to the first rank symptoms which psychiatrists currently use in their diagnoses. In other words, the features of patients given the diagnosis of schizophrenia at its conceptual inception were not the same as those with the same label today.

These conceptual problems with schizophrenia are raised in this chapter because the diagnosis has been at the heart of the case for a class gradient in mental health. If the concept of schizophrenia is discredited by the critiques outlined, does this undermine our confidence in social causationist claims from over 60 years of social psychiatric research?

Also, we need to be aware when examining the relationship between social class and mental health, that the concept has itself become increasingly problematized within sociology. With the decline in the centrality of Marxism within social theory and its replacement by a mixture of other currents includ-ing feminism and post-structuralism, social class appears less frequently in the literature or is problematized by non-Marxists when discussing social stratifi-cation and societal disadvantage (Runciman 1990; Evans 1992; Goldthorpe and Marshall 1992; Westergaard 1992; Pahl 1993). Reflecting this trend, in the first edition of this book we provided only a section, not a whole chapter, on the topic. Parker *et al.* (1995: 46) in their social constructivist critique of psychopathology point out that:

> Although by its very nature a 'social' concept, implying a group, increas-ingly 'class' has been a term applied to individuals. Worse than this, classes are defined in the psychological literature, without any reference to the exploitation of labour, alienation or oppression ... Indeed class is heard of less and we now hear more of socio-economic status – an indi-vidualised variable. Pilgrim and Rogers' (1993) *A Sociology of Mental Health and Illness* [first edition] includes chapters on gender, race and ethnicity and age but only a section on class.

In response to this fair criticism we adapted our second edition of this book to include a chapter on social class, which is updated here. Parker *et al.* also raise an important point to consider about reducing class to an individualized vari-able, which can exclude a discussion of social processes. Moreover, sociological descriptions of social class divisions or groupings (poor/rich; employed/ unemployed and so on) do not automatically connote inequality.

Turner (1986) pointed out that terms such as 'inequality' or 'oppression' require that empirically described social divisions are then understood within an ideological framework of value-judgements. Conservative political values emphasize individual freedom rather than the minimization of social divisions. The notion of 'oppression' is more likely to be individualized within conservative ideology and not seen as a matter of social justice. (For this reason some conservative libertarians might champion the civil liberties of the mad who are constrained by the State.) The notion of 'exploitation' is obvious to the left-wing critic of capitalism but to its conservative supporters it is simply and laudably a matter of employers providing work for others. Earlier we also noted how conservative politicians have shown a preference for the term 'health variation' than 'health inequality'.

These tensions highlight a problem as well for radical social constructivists (like Parker *et al.* 1995). A critical realist paradigm would argue that there should be some irreducible materiality to poverty, which is not open to semantic manipulation or various contructions, a point made well by Pilger (1989). Pilger highlights the thrust of his argument about poverty by citing the humorist Jules Feiffer thus:

> I used to think that I was poor. Then they told me that I wasn't poor, I was needy. Then they told me it was self-defeating to think of myself as needy. I was deprived. Then they told me deprived was a bad image. I was under-privileged. Then they told me under-privileged was over used. I was disadvantaged. I still don't have a cent but I have a great vocabulary.
>
> (Feiffer, cited in Pilger 1989: 313)

This humorous point is used here seriously to indicate that arguments about the relationship between concepts (or 'constructions') and reality need to be understood in relation to both psychiatry and sociology. Psychiatry may well confuse the map with territory at times (with dubious diagnoses like 'schizophrenia' or 'depression'). At the same time, lay people as well as professionals can consistently spot when their contemporary rules of social convention are broken and when others are mad or miserable (see Chapter 2). Similarly, Turner may be correct to argue that social divisions do not automatically connote inequality, but empty pockets and empty bellies are material realities.

There is now a trend towards viewing social class as a complex mixture of discursive, material and psychological factors which interact to produce inequalities. This approach brings with it a stronger focus on the personal experience of relative deprivation for individual and collective identity and emphasizes how inequalities manifest themselves in everyday life. A focus on the social environment and its dynamics, by investigating indicators of income and material equality, social cohesion, self-efficacy and trust is likely to be the most fruitful way of progressing knowledge about health inequalities in mental health. Within this approach, it may be possible to link the nature and circumstances of service contact with wider factors affecting the types and experience of mental health inequalities.

Currently there is a split between one type of literature on inequalities in mental health status and another on the inequalities that service contact might perpetuate. However, as we have discussed earlier, there is evidence that service contact brings with it risks that can have a sustained negative impact on mental health. A better understanding of the relationship between service contact and its impact on quality of life and psychological distress would illuminate further our understanding of one aspect of the multi-factorial interaction noted earlier.

Apart from the displacement of Marxism as the central discursive focus of class within sociology, societal changes have brought with them difficulties in thinking simply about the concept and formulating and conducting empirical projects. For example, the traditional use of the Registrar General's classifications system has become less and less meaningful. Women can no longer be conceptualized as sharing their husband's class status – not just because this is now ideologically rejected in the wake of feminism but because marriage has declined in popularity (so it fails to capture the range of forms of interdependent cohabitation). Also women, not men, numerically now dominate the labour market.

Moreover, the old pyramid notion of class structure has been replaced by one which is nearer to a diamond, as traditional blue-collar factory production has been eroded but service industries have expanded. Consequently, white-collar work covers a variety of status and salary levels (from clerical low pay to rich executive earnings) and at the bottom of the diamond is a group of dispossessed people who are excluded permanently or semi-permanently from the labour market. This exclusion can be reproduced over several generations. The notion of oppression, which was previously associated mainly, or singularly, with low social class within Marxian sociology, is now linked to other social groups independent of their class position – women, black people, people with physical disabilities, people with learning difficulties, gay people, older people and, of particular relevance to this book, people with mental health problems.

Given the conceptual problems within both psychiatric epidemiology, discussed earlier, and the contested concept of class within sociology, we can make only very broad confident statements about social class and mental health. For example, it is safe to say that poverty contains causal influences which both create and exacerbate mental health problems. We cannot say definitively, however, that 'poverty causes schizophrenia'. We can say that being poorly employed or homeless increases the probability of mental health problem development, although we cannot, with certainty, say that *this* person has a mental health problem because they are poorly employed or homeless. We can say that the oppression and powerlessness, associated with low social class, disadvantage poor people during mental health service contact (they are more likely to have interventions imposed upon them and be treated with biological treatments than those in a higher class position), but we cannot say that these discriminatory service eventualities are only attributable to social class, because other variables, such as race or gender, might be alternative or coexisting determinants of professional action.

This chapter has explored a range of sociological aspects of mental health and social class. It is clear that whatever conceptual problems exist about understanding mental illness in the same way as physical illness, the social impact of low social class (especially its associated poverty) is similar for each. Basically, poorer people are significantly less healthy, both physically and mentally, than richer people. It is, however, more problematic to argue that there are social causes of specific diagnosed conditions (like 'schizophrenia'). This says more about the poor concept validity of diagnoses used by psychiatry than it does about the stress created for people by socio-economic inequality.

Questions

1 Does poverty cause schizophrenia?

2 Why are richer people mentally healthier than poorer people?

3 Discuss the relationship between housing and mental health problems.

4 Discuss lay views about mental health and social class.

5 Have changes in sociological interest in social class produced changes in sociological work on mental health and illness?

6 What are the strengths and weaknesses of the concept of 'social capital' in understanding mental health status?

For discussion

Think about people you know who have had mental health problems and discuss ways in which their social class background may have affected their lives.

Further reading

Blaxter, M. (1990) *Health and Lifestyles*. London: Routledge.

Rogers, A. and Pilgrim, D. (2003) *Mental Health and Inequality*. Basingstoke: Palgrave.

Warner, R. (1985) *Recovery from Schizophrenia*. London: Routledge.

Weich, S. and Lewis, G. (1998) Poverty, unemployment and common mental health disorders: population based cohort study. *British Medical Journal*, 317: 115–19

Wilkinson, R.G. (1996) *Unhealthy Societies: The Afflictions of Inequality*. London: Routledge.

Williams, S.J. (1998) 'Capitalising' on emotions? Rethinking the inequalities in health debate. *Sociology*, 32(1): 121–40.

Chapter **4**

Women and men

Chapter overview

Most of the discussion about mental health and gender has been about women. This chapter reflects this in both the sociological discourse and social-psychiatric research reported. However, in addition, the question of men and psychiatry is addressed. The chapter will cover the following topics:

- the over-representation of women in psychiatric diagnosis;
- does society cause excessive female mental illness?
- is female over-representation a measurement artefact?
- are women labelled as mentally ill more often than men?
- men, dangerousness and mental health services;
- gender and sexuality.

The over-representation of women in psychiatric diagnosis

Although most academic attention about the topic of this chapter has focused on women and mental health, the study of gender is a comparative exercise in which the relationship of men and women to psychiatry requires exploration. Overall, women receive a psychiatric diagnosis more often than men. However, diagnosis is gendered as is the site in which it tends to take place. For example, in tertiary services, such as medium and maximum-security hospitals, men, not women, are over represented. In secondary services (acute psychiatric units in local general hospitals) gender differences are not significant. The bulk of the diagnostic practices leading to overall female representation is accounted for by 'common mental disorders'. The latter are mainly diagnosed and responded to in primary care settings. The majority of those diagnosed are not referred to specialist mental health services.

Turning from overall numbers to type of diagnosis, a gendered pattern is evident:

1 Some diagnoses are not gendered, such as those of schizophrenia and bi-polar disorder (Mitchell *et al.* 2004), though in the former case it is diagnosed on average five years earlier in young men (Gelder *et al.* 2001);
2 Some diagnoses are inevitably limited to women, such as post-natal depression and post-partum psychosis. Some of these referring to the emotional concomitants of menstruation and the menopause are contentious;
3 Some diagnoses are overwhelmingly female, such as anorexia nervosa and bulimia nervosa (Van Hoecken *et al.* 1998);
4 Some diagnoses are overwhelmingly male, such as anti-social personality disorder (Tyrer 2000). The great majority of sex offenders (whether or not their conduct is classified as a psychiatric condition) are men;
5 Some diagnoses are more likely in men than women, such as substance misuse (Meltzer *et al.* 1994).
6 Some diagnoses are more likely in women than men, such as anxiety states, depression and post-traumatic stress disorder (Breslau *et al.* 1998; Fryers *et al.* 2004). Because women live longer than men higher female prevalence rates for both dementia and depression in old age also make a contribution to female over-representation.

Thus, female patients in points 2 and 3 and especially 6, account for the overall over-representation of women in psychiatric statistics. The above list summarizes the picture in North America and Europe. However, there are substantial international differences, which highlight the problem of taking psychiatric positivism at face value. For example, eating disorders are virtually unknown in developing countries (where the main challenge about food is not its refusal but its availability). In another example, in China (contra the western picture) women are diagnosed as suffering from mental illness more often than men but in a different way. The prevalence of depression and neurotic disorders is lower in Chinese than western women. However, the prevalence of the diagnosis of schizophrenia is significantly higher for women than men in China, which might be accounted for by the cultural tendency in that country for women to be disvalued and coercively controlled (Pearson 1995).

In a Western context community surveys in the last 30 years have consist-ently confirmed point 6 on the list above. For example, Walter Gove and his colleagues, focusing on higher female rates among married women than men, claim that women experience psychological distress more than men (Gove 1972; Gove and Tudor 1972). Blaxter (1990) also found that, throughout the life span, women report greater psycho-social malaise than men and the gap between the sexes increases in older people. Blaxter's self-reported factors included depression, worry, sleep disturbances and feelings of strain.

How, then, can this apparent excess of female over male 'mental illness' be explained? The reasons for the over-representation of women in mental health statistics are highly contested, with a number of competing explanations being evident in the literature. These explanations can be broadly categorized into three main perspectives:

• Social causation – does society cause excessive female mental illness?
• Artefact – is female over-representation a measurement artefact?
• Social labelling – are women labelled more often than men?

These three questions will now be explored.

Does society cause excessive female mental illness?

That mental illness is rooted in women's life experiences has been expounded by a number of commentators. Most of these explanations have focused on the link between the 'stress' of women's lives and mental disorder. Gove (1984) and his colleagues (Gove and Geerken 1977), who have written and researched extensively in the area of women's mental health, claim that the amount and particular type of stress experienced by women results in higher rates of female psychiatric morbidity. In particular, they look at two aspects of women's soci-etal role to explain why women experience more psychological distress than men. First, the lack of structure in women's roles (which tend to be more domestic than for men) makes them more vulnerable to mental distress because they have time to 'brood' over their problems. In contrast, men have relatively 'fixed' roles. According to Gove, this means that the necessity of responding to the immediate and highly structured demands of the workplace distracts men from their personal problems and this offers a degree of protection that is not available to women.

Citing community studies, Gove points to evidence that poorer mental health is found in situations where women are more likely to occupy nurtur-ant roles (e.g. divorced women who care for children have a higher incidence of mental distress than divorced men and women without children). It is hypothesized that the social demands and lack of privacy associated with this role may be a causal factor.

Evidence of social aetiology and depression among women comes from the research of Brown and Harris (1978), who identified different factors which together point to the social origins of depression. This picture of aetiology is sometimes referred to as a multi-factorial social model, where a wide selection of factors interacting with each other may be necessary preconditions for developing a psychiatric condition.

Brown and Harris draw attention to three groups of aetiological factors that need to be understood as interacting with one another to produce depression.

Vulnerability factors

Such factors might make women more susceptible to depression during a time of loss or in the face of another major negative life event. These biographical events include loss of mother before 11 years of age. Subsequent research linked this to the quality of care that followed this loss. Those with poor subsequent care were particularly vulnerable to depression (Brown *et al.* 1986). The absence of a confiding relationship with a partner also makes women more susceptible to depression, as does lack of employment (full- or part-time) outside of the home. The presence at home of three or more children is also a vulnerability factor. When the opposites of these factors were found to be present, for example high intimacy with a partner and the presence of a mother after the age of 11, they acted to 'protect' women against depression.

Provoking agents

These are factors operating in women's contemporary everyday lives, which may lead to depression, and include detrimental 'life events' such as loss through bereavement or marriage breakdown, or episodes of serious illness. Chronic difficulties as well as specific stressors are included here. The occurrence of these events determines *when* the depression will arise.

Symptom-formation factors

These factors determine the severity and form of depression. In Brown and Harris's (1978) research, depression was found to be more severe if there had been previous depressive episodes and the woman was aged over 50. These social factors were linked together in Brown and Harris's research with psychological variables (cognitive sets). Women whose personalities were characterized by low self-esteem were more likely to experience the onset of depression than those who had high self-esteem.

The work of Brown and Harris in the 1970s has been extended in the interim. More data has been collected and, recently, more theoretical issues have been raised by Brown and his colleagues. Brown *et al.* (1995) compared clinical and non-clinical populations in Islington, north London. Drawing upon the work of Gilbert (1992) and Unger (1984), they elaborate their position about depression and the experience of life events. They conclude that the probability of depression increases not necessarily with loss or threatened loss *per se* but with the coexistence of humiliation and/or entrapment.

Gilbert and Unger note that depression is commonly associated with feeling trapped and humiliated, such that there is an assault on the person's sense of self-worth and they have a blocked escape. The latter may then make the difference between a depressive and a non-depressive trajectory. For example, Brown *et al.* (1995) suggest that a woman being told that the paralyzed husband she is caring for will not recover might become depressed, but another, able to leave her violent or feckless partner, may feel liberated. Thus, being able to 'leave the field' may head off depression or reverse it in those already distressed.

The Islington study also highlighted more details about the risk factors associated with adverse childhood experiences. A third of the depressed women studied had experienced neglect or physical or sexual abuse in their childhoods. This subgroup had twice the chances of becoming depressed in one year, compared to those without such adverse antecedents (Bifulco *et al.*1992). These childhood events also increase the probability of anxiety symptoms. Brown (1996) suggests that this might account for the common coexistence of anxiety and depression in adult patients.

Rigorous research such as that of Brown and his colleagues can tell us a great deal about the possible direct and indirect influence of social factors in the cause of female mental illness. However, the extent to which we can accept the conclusions of research that suggests that women experience more mental disorder than men rests on the way in which both mental health and gender are measured. The epidemiological work of this type rests on medical constructs (Brown and Harris accepted 'depression' and other diagnoses measured by the Present State Examination). Likewise, work on prevention of mental health problems, in the wake of Brown and Harris's study, does not question psychiatric knowledge (e.g. Newton 1988). This is not the case with the next and subsequent positions.

Is female over-representation a measurement artefact?

The artefact explanation suggests that epidemiological measurement and its interpretation are faulty. From this point of view, some or all of the excess in psychiatric morbidity is not 'real', rather it is created by the design, assumptions and interpretations operating in social psychiatric research (using, for instance, the Present State Examination and the General Health Questionnaire).

As an example of a traditional causation study subjected to an artefact critique, we can take the work of Gove (1984) and his colleagues, which has been the centre of considerable debate. This research focused on female psychiatric morbidity and marital status and claimed to demonstrate that married women have greater levels of mental distress than married men.

Gove and his coworkers take marital status as an accurate indicator for identifying differences in mental health between men and women. However, there are variations in marital relationships and the ways in which particular features of the relationship, such as the degree of role differentiation and shared power, act as a risk or a protective factor. Marital status does not lead to a unitary role outcome for men and women. For example, the notion of nurturant role assumes the presence of children in the marital relationship, yet it is also the case that 25 per cent of children in the UK are now born outside of wedlock. Similarly, a childless woman in full-time employment may have little in common in terms of role with another married woman, without employment outside of the home, who is also a mother.

The evidence of a link between gender and mental illness based on marital status may also be challenged if other comparisons are made. For example, single status makes men, not women, more vulnerable to mental health problems. With regards to the explanatory links of different stressors associated with role, Gove does not explore why the same marital female roles seem to act as protective factors in physical illnesses. While married women have higher rates of hospitalization for psychiatric illnesses, married men have higher rates of admission for non-psychiatric illness than married women.

Finally, the definition of mental illness used by Gove to support his hypothesis that women suffer from problems more than men has been subjected to the criticism that he focuses exclusively on certain types of mental disorder, such as depression and phobias. He excludes other types such as organic conditions and personality disorders (Dohrenwend and Dohrenwend 1977). A review of community studies carried out during the 1980s showed that although rates for the most common types of disorder are generally higher for women than men, rates reported by one epidemiological study (Regier *et al.* 1988) showed an almost equal sex ratio by including drug dependency and personality disorders.

These critiques seem to point to the possibility that an apparent excess of female mental disorder may be an artefact of the construction of epidemiological research. However, subsequent research provides convincing evidence that undermines the artefact explanation and further supports the likelihood that women's greater risk of depression is a result of differences in roles and in their experience of life events. Nazroo *et al.* (1998) compared men's and women's experience of severe life events. Women were found to be at greater risk of depression than men when the event experienced involved children, housing and reproduction and where there was a clear distinction within households in roles between men and women. This suggests that women's increased risk of depression is a result of gendered role differences which are associated with differences in the type and experience of life events.

Similarly, in relation to marital violence, gender differences in rates of anxiety (which are higher among women) have been attributed to the nature and meaning of physical abuse experienced by women (Nazroo 1995). Female perpetrators of domestic violence are now nearly as common as males (Rogers and Pilgrim 2003) but on average the severity of violence is greater when women are victims. And the latter are more likely to present with post-traumatic symptoms following victimization. Research such as this, which focuses on the meaning and context of events provides us with a deeper understanding of the relationship between key variables identified by traditional social psychiatric epidemiology. Differences in the way in which men and women seek help from services may also account for their over-representation in mental health statistics – our next discussion.

Sex differences in help-seeking behaviour

There is not necessarily a direct relationship between experiencing symptoms and the decision to seek help. Symptoms are experienced more frequently than rates of medical consultation and admission to hospital suggest. Patterns and processes of help-seeking are influenced by people's experience of illness, the way in which services and professionals have responded to people in the past and the levels of social support and alternative health care resources available to them in the community (Rogers *et al.* 1998). In the case of psychological symptoms, it is likely that the 'clinical iceberg' is larger than is the case with physical illness, because of the stigma of mental illness, the perceived ineffectiveness of medical interventions and a greater tendency to deny symptoms.

Scambler *et al.* (1981) interviewed 74 working-class women and found that only one in 74 subjects who suffered 'nervous depression' or irritability consulted their GP, compared with one in 9 for sore throats. There is also some evidence to suggest that people with psychological symptoms delay seeking formal help for a long time. Rogers, Pilgrim and Lacey (1993) found that the time-lag between experiencing psychological symptoms and seeking professional help was more than one year for 20 per cent in their survey of 516 post-discharge psychiatric patients.

The relationship between experiencing symptoms is further complicated in psychological distress because of the high rates of formal referral by other people. In the study by Rogers and colleagues (1993), in nearly two-thirds of cases help was sought by others or in conjunction with others. Thus, a decision to seek formal help in the case of psychological distress is a complex process dependent on both the incipient patient's and others' notions of mental health problems and the translation of the experience of these problems (e.g. tiredness, hallucinations and so on) into a willingness to contact formal agencies.

Reported rates of symptoms in community studies may not be due to a greater incidence of mental disorder as measured by 'clinical symptoms', but a reflection of women's greater propensity to be disclosing about their symptoms. Self-reported morbidity is determined not only by the presence or absence of clinical symptoms but also by the perception and interpretation of symptoms by the person, together with their willingness to report illness in an interview situation. This entails a willingness to label/view problems in psychological terms and to seek help once a problem has been defined. Both these interlinked processes may be influenced by differences in attitudes, norms, values and expectations between men and women. Debating this issue in the 1970s, Dohrenwend and Dohrenwend (1977: 1338) commented that:

> Sex differences in the seeking of help correspond to attitudinal differences: women are more likely to admit distress . . . to define their problems in mental-health terms . . . and to have favourable attitudes towards psychiatric treatment.

Women, then, may be more likely to recognize and label mental illness than men or, put another way, men may be less likely to view their problems as psychiatric ones. There certainly appears to have been an assumption on the part of researchers that women are more likely to be able and willing to talk about their mental health than men. This may, in turn, account for the female focus of much of mental health research, which we will discuss later. An example of how researchers operated such an assumption is in the cited community survey of Brown and Harris (1978: 22), who are quite explicit that their choice of a female-only sample stemmed from a gender assumption:

It also seemed likely that women, who are more often at home during the day, would be more willing to agree to see us for several hours . . . most of the women we approached were willing to talk to us at length about their lives and appeared to enjoy doing so.

Women may also be more likely to act on their mental health symptoms than men by seeking professional help. Women are approximately twice as likely as men to refer themselves for psychiatric treatment. Men, on the other hand, have been found more frequently to seek help on the advice of others. Community studies suggest that, for those considered to be suffering from severe psychological distress (measured by the General Health Questionnaire) sex ratios for primary health care consultations are almost identical. However, in terms of overall rates of consultation with a GP, women appear to consult more than men (Williams *et al.* 1986; Rickwood and Braithwaite 1994).

It seems unlikely that this higher propensity to seek help is due to women having more spare time to visit the doctor than men. Women who combine maternal, domestic and employment roles have less time on their hands than employed men or housewives, and housewives work longer hours than employed men. However, Verbrugge and Wingard (1987) argued that women's roles, as part-time workers or housewives, may allow them greater flexibility (not time *per se*) to visit the doctor. Because of gendered assumptions about caring, women also make contact with GPs when taking their children to be seen for minor ailments. However, there is also some evidence to suggest that women with young children may put their children's health needs before their own, which inhibits them entering the sick role (Brown and Harris 1978; Rogers *et al.* 1999).

Additionally, it may be that higher rates of consultation are not due only, or mainly, to the active help-seeking actions of women. Women's own accounts of stress, anxiety and depression seem to suggest that women normalize the mental health problems they report (Walters 1993), which is not commensurate with problem recognition associated with help seeking from formal services. Moreover, a study of women's pathways to care in post-natal depression suggests that only one-third of women considered to be depressed by primary care professionals believed they were suffering from the condition. Over 80 per cent had not reported their symptoms to any health professional (Whitton *et al.* 1996). This suggests that contact with health services for other reasons, such as the seeking of health care for children, may allow for increased detection of problems which may contribute to seemingly higher consultation rates for female mental health problems.

Are women labelled as mentally ill more often than men?

A different explanation for female over-representation in mental health statistics is proposed by some feminist researchers, influenced both by labelling theory and constructivist frameworks. From this viewpoint, patriarchal authority, which seeks out and labels women as mad, is responsible for the over-representation. Women become vulnerable to being labelled mentally disordered when they fail to conform to stereotypical gender roles as mothers, housewives, and so on or if they are too submissive, too aggressive or hostile to men.

During the 1970s feminist writers began to argue that there is both a general cultural sexism, which renders women vulnerable to psychiatric labelling, and a specific sexism from professionals. For example Chesler (1972: 115) asserted that: 'Women, by definition (sic), are viewed as psychiatrically impaired – whether they accept or reject the female role – simply because they are women'.

More specifically, medical discourse is deemed to be patriarchal and misogynistic. Here, Chesler's analysis has much in common with those of other feminist writers on health and illness who have viewed male doctors as defining illness with reference to women's emotions (e.g. English and Ehrenreich 1976). The profession of psychiatry is, according to Chesler and others, numerically male dominated and permeated by patriarchal stereotypes of female inferiority. This situation has arisen as a result of a historical legacy. As medicine, including psychiatry, successfully professionalized during the eighteenth and nineteenth centuries, so women healers became marginalized and excluded from positions of power. This male domination influences the way in which psychiatric diagnoses are applied to women as well as the types of diagnosis and the rates at which they are applied.

There was evidence at the time of Chesler's writing that these patriarchal assumptions were not confined to psychiatry but operate in other parts of health services. Barrett and Roberts (1978) found that male GPs construed their middle-aged female patients to be overly neurotic and requiring minor tranquillizers more than male patients. The doctors also often thought that the distressed women who worked would be better off resigning and they expressed a greater sympathy for male counterparts. Goldberg and Huxley (1980) also found that GPs are not as likely to identify a psychological problem if the patient is a man. Milliren (1977) studied older patients and found that male GPs diagnosed women as suffering from anxiety symptoms more often than men. When the latter were diagnosed they were offered minor tranquillizers less often than women by the GPs.

Subsequently, Sheppard (1991) provided further evidence that GPs discriminate against women. Doctors were found to be more likely to refer women as candidates for compulsory admission than men. According to Sheppard, this reflects the sexist practices of GPs, because their decisions were not always confirmed. That is, many of the female referrals were not subsequently deemed suitable for compulsory admission by Approved Social Workers (social workers specially trained in mental health law). Social work is a predominantly female profession. This was considered by Sheppard to be evidence of women workers being able to counteract the sexist practices of the predominantly male group of GPs.

However, others found evidence of sexist stereotyping of female roles among social workers in relation to women with severe mental health problems (Davis *et al.* 1985). This suggests that having a predominantly female profession might not eliminate sexist practices. Similarly, Chesler's theoretical position rests on the premise that in the psychiatric profession women are massively outnumbered by men. Yet, statistics on the number of medical graduates embarking on psychiatry as a career suggests that psychiatry is rapidly becoming a less male-dominated system in terms of the ratio of male to female practitioners (Parkhouse 1991). This casts some doubt on the assumption that a numerically male-dominated psychiatric profession is solely responsible for sexist psychiatric practice.

It is likely that sexism in psychiatry has its roots in, and can be transmitted in, the type of knowledge, diagnostic categories and practices followed by the profession as well, which can still be called 'patriarchal' even when used by women doctors. Another dimension of feminist analysis has drawn attention to the assumptions inherent in the ideology of psychiatry. Disordered behaviour is defined according to what is considered normal or ordered mental health.

Research by Broverman *et al.* (1970) provided evidence of bias in the construction of notions of mental health and illness. This research showed that behaviour defined as 'male' was viewed by psychiatrists to be congruent with healthy behaviour, while behaviour defined as 'female' was not. Healthy women were in comparative terms considered to be more submissive, less independent and adventurous, more easily influenced, less aggressive, less competitive, more excitable in minor crises, seen as having their feelings more easily hurt, being more emotional, more narcissistic about their appearance and less objective than healthy men. Women were couched in primarily negative terms, even images of healthy women were perceived as less healthy than men. Fabrikant (1974) reported that male therapists rated 70 per cent of 'female' positive.

Those interested in gendered labelling emphasize that it is shaped by new technologies (not just psychiatric diagnosis *per se*). For example, the new SSRI anti-depressants have played a role in expanding existing categories of mental ill health among women. Metzl and Angel (2004) studied the impact of these new drugs on popular notions of women's depressive illness. What were previously seen as ordinary life events now had become categories, such as 'pre-menstrual dysphoric disorder'. The enlarged notion of gender-specific mental health problems was also found to be disseminated in the mass media.

Examples of negative stereotyping can be found even in biographical forms of psychiatric knowledge, such as psychoanalysis. Masson's (1985; 1988a) historical investigations of psychoanalysis reveal psychotherapists disbelieving reports from female patients of incestuous assaults on them, and compounding their distress through new abuse during treatment.

Gendered notions of mental health and illness seem to be prevalent among lay people as well as mental health professionals. Jones and Cochrane (1981) found from responses to a series of scales made up of terms depicting opposite personal characteristic (e.g. 'outgoing' versus 'withdrawn', 'sensitive' versus 'insensitive') that respondents clearly differentiated in the adjectives they chose to describe the differences between mentally ill men and women. In contrast, the terms used to describe normal women and mentally ill women were similar.

So far, a picture has been presented of how others have sought to define mental illness in a feminized way. As well as professionals and lay people constructing problems in this manner, there are also indications that patients conceptualize their problems in a sex-specific way. Rogers, Pilgrim and Lacey (1993) found that women were more likely to identify marital stress as the source of their difficulties. By contrast, men reported work stress to be of relevance three times more often than did women. This suggests that relationships in the domestic arena seem to take on a greater meaning for women than men. Women were also found to share their difficulties with others more readily than men. Women were more likely to choose their lay network of friends and neighbours as their first attempt to seek help.

There is some evidence to suggest that this willingness to disclose is reversed once contact has been made with professionals. A Dutch study (de Boer 1991) has claimed that problem formulation in therapeutic encounters is a product of the interaction of two different discourses – that of the therapist and that of the patient. Sex differences in 'problem formulation' were found in so far as men appeared to be more able to account for their problem in a therapeutic situation than women, who appeared to be more diffident. As a result, male influence on the definition and formulation of a problem at this stage may be greater than the influence of women.

A caution needs to be introduced about generalizing the willingness of women to disclose and seek voluntary primary care or outpatient contact compared to men. This picture seems to hold true for white patients in European and North American clinical settings. However, the literature on ethnic minority women suggests a tendency for them to under-utilize such voluntary service contact opportunities (Padgett *et al.* 1994). The latter US study found that black and Hispanic women had a lower probability of accessing out-patient services than white women from similar class backgrounds. Overall, if race and class differences are ignored, women use out-patient mental health services more than men (Rhodes and Goering 1994) but within the female picture are racialized subgroups which are treated differently. For example, when young black women do have service contact they are offered less psychological treatment than white women (Cuffe *et al.* 1995).

There has been a tendency to view the social causation and the labelling explanation as contradictory, i.e. the over-representation of women is caused by either women's social situation making them sick or the pathologizing of women by a male-dominated mental health service. However, to argue that the phenomena which have historically come to be constituted as mental illness have their roots in the difficulties of women's lives is not inconsistent with the view that the social nature and social consequences of defining a woman as mentally ill need to be emphasized.

The effects of labelling secondary deviance – women and minor tranquillizers

We introduced the notions of primary and secondary deviance in Chapter 2 when discussing labelling theory. Whatever the reasons why and how women enter the sick role in a psychiatric sense, a consequence is that they are subjected to more frequent medical and professional attention than men. They also tend to seek help and are diagnosed more frequently than men when suffering from problems that are dealt with by GPs. It is here that a controversy arose over the way in which women's problems are viewed and treated. In particular, attention has been directed towards the prescription of minor tranquillizers because of their dependency-inducing properties. Women consume psychotropic drugs in far greater quantities than men (Olfson and Pincus

1994). This is despite evidence which suggests that women express a strong antipathy to using drugs to solve their problems (Gabe and Lipshitsz Phillips 1982).

By 1980, the excess of the female rate of consumption was estimated as 2:1, with four-fifths of this consumption being attributed to minor tranquillizers and sedative hypnotics (both types of benzodiazepine) (Cooperstock 1978). Although, the dangers of benzodiazepines were well known by 1980, by the end of that decade the prescription rate was still over two-thirds of that a decade earlier, despite both litigation/campaigning from addicted users and cautions from professional bodies such as the Royal College of Psychiatrists (Medawar 1992).

The prescription of minor tranquillizers and antidepressants can be seen as a medicalized response to personal troubles. From this vantage point the benefits of a medical response are to remove personal responsibility from the individual for their problems. For example, the guilt and unhappiness associated with depression can be dealt with simplistically if it is framed as an illness, which can be relieved by mood-altering drugs, rather than the responsibility of the individual's actions and their social circumstances.

However, from a different perspective, the prescription and use of such drugs are viewed as a means of 'social control' because they transform social problems into medical ones. The social effects of treating personal problems by medical sedation were highlighted by Waldron (1977), who pointed out that the treatment of individual 'pathology' disguises its social causes and deflects attention from the need for political change to ameliorate the oppression of women.

Gabe and Thorogood (1986) found that women were most likely to find benzodiazepines to be a 'prop' in the absence of other means of support, such as paid work, adequate housing, leisure activities and so on. This was particularly so in the case of middle-aged women, who were less likely than other women to have access to resources with which to manage their everyday lives. Women tended to express ambivalent views about taking minor tranquillizers: on the one hand, they expressed the view that they gave them 'peace of mind', and on the other, they emphasized the dangers and dependency-inducing aspects of taking these drugs.

Paradoxically, perhaps, in publicizing the dangers of addiction, women who have been prescribed such drugs have been subject to what labelling theorists refer to as 'deviance amplification'. The media, in taking up the problem of minor tranquillizer dependency, has tended to reinforce images of women as helpless, dependent and passive victims of addictive drugs (Bury and Gabe 1990). Not only did their original behaviour or primary deviance expose women more frequently to an addictive prescribed drug but the consequent addiction then became associated with their gender.

Does this additional labelling of women imply that they are subjected to medical control more frequently than men? Their greater contact with services and the minor tranquillizer problem being labelled as a 'women's problem' might imply that this is the case. Certainly feminist scholarship has been instrumental in gaining a wider recognition of the ways in which women have been oppressed by being labelled as mentally ill. This in turn has led to the setting up of alternative services for women. According to Scambler (1998), these women's services retained a collective notion and awareness of the social by providing group support aimed at resocializing women to reject a subordinate position within domestic and social life.

However, as Scambler points out, being outside of State-provided services means that access to the voluntary women-only mental health services may be denied to those in most need. Moreover, Pilgrim (1997a) has argued that even feminist therapies retain the power discrepancies between therapists and patients inherent in all styles of psychotherapy and they retain many patriarchal elements intrinsic to the psychoanalytical legacy. (The main theoretical position underpinning women's services has tended to be psychoanalytical in orientation.)

As we noted in our introduction, it is not possible to make generalized claims about the overall predominance of mental disorder being an essentially male or female phenomenon. The nature and construction of mental health problems differ according to diagnostic category and cultural context. However, the discussion of male mental disorder is, compared with the feminist literature on women and mental health, rare. This corresponds to a more generalized tendency in the sociology of health and illness to focus on female rather than male health disadvantage (Cameron and Bernardes 1998).

An exception to this has been research conducted into male unemployment and mental health. There is evidence to suggest that the experience of unemployment is detrimental to men's mental health because of the dissonance this gives rise to between a masculine self-image and social expectations of men being in full-time paid employment (Hayes and Nutman 1981). Studies have also taken as their focus the variation in male mental health according to wider economic and employment opportunities (Warner 1985). However, if we put to one side these studies looking at unemployment, the sociological discourse about gender and mental health is female dominated. Let us look at two examples of the different considerations given by both psychiatrists and sociologists to men and women with regard first to dangerousness and then to sexuality.

Men, dangerousness and mental health services

Men's behaviour is more frequently recognized as being dangerous than women's. Indeed, men *are* violent more often than women in society, but consequently all men (including non-violent ones) may be subjected to stereotypical expectations. Just as women may be stereotyped as weak and ill, men may be stereotyped as being violent. Comparisons are sometimes made between the statistics which show women to be over-represented in mental health populations while men predominate in prison populations. This may be related to the type of social judgement which is made about 'rule breaking'.

The recognition both of mental disorder and of criminality involve judgements being made about a person's state of mind and their conduct. In conditions such as depression, the judgement being made is more about a person's anguished and irrational state of mind, judged by their social withdrawal and 'motor retardation'. By contrast, a criminal act is more about a person's self-interested motivation, judged by the manifest gain made from their offence.

However, both entail judgements about the relationship between mind and conduct – and weighing up the nature of this relationship decides whether the deviance ascribed is of a criminal or psychiatric type. As we noted in Chapter 2, these distinctions between rational or goal-directed, and irrational or incomprehensible, rule breaking are not always clear cut in the minds of either professionals or of lay people.

The connection between these considerations and gender is that men's conduct has been more associated with public antisocial acts, violent and sexual offences, drunken aggressive behaviour and so on, whereas women's behaviour has been associated more with private, self-damaging acts, where aggression is directed at the self rather than others. Depression, parasuicide, eating disorders and self-mutilation together summarize this tendency. Men are more likely to indulge in behaviour that is antisocial, and to be labelled as criminally deviant more than women. This is then reflected within psychiatry, in that men are more likely to have labels which refer to and incorporate the threat of their behaviour.

The notion of 'danger to others' is more frequently ascribed to male than female patients. The question of 'danger to self' is more complicated. Although women attempt suicide more frequently then men, the figures for actual suicide are consistently higher for men than women. However, a Finnish study of parasuicidal behaviour suggests that men make more gestures of suicide, as well as committing suicide more often (Ostamo and Lonnqvist 1992). Of course, suicidal and parasuicidal behaviours are ambiguous – they may be adjudged to be either self-injurious or antisocial or both. This may account for the prevalence being split between the two sexes and the contradictory findings about the ratio of such a split.

The affixing of diagnostic labels which imply 'dangerousness' and the focus on the behavioural consequences of a person's state of mind has corresponding implications. Female problems are more likely to be dealt with at the 'soft' end of psychiatry since, as we have already seen, they tend to be labelled with the type of problem that is usually dealt with in primary health care settings. Although such management is by no means always benign, as demonstrated by the negative effects of the reliance on minor tranquillizers discussed earlier, it more rarely requires compulsory admission. By contrast, men are more likely to be dealt with at the 'harsh' end of psychiatry as mentally disordered offenders in secure facilities.

Thus, once a label has been affixed, overall as a group, men are dealt with more harshly than women. This is especially the case at the interface between psychiatry and the criminal justice system. It is mainly men who are over-represented in the most stigmatized and policed part of the mental health system, the 'special hospitals'. Though many in these institutions are there for sex offences and other violent crime and their behaviour or threat to society might have warranted such a response, many have not been convicted of a criminal offence. The effect of such management can be seen not only in the negative media stereotypes portraying the inmates of such hospitals as 'animals', but also in recurrent government inquiries into the mistreatment of special hospital patients.

With regard to psychiatric referrals from the police, under section 136 of the Mental Health Act 1983 there is evidence to suggest that men are subject to arrest more frequently than women. Moreover, the police use handcuffs and detention cells more frequently for men than women (Rogers 1990).

Even where the differences in the rate at which a diagnostic label is attached are not great, the negative consequences of a label may be greater for men than women. This can be seen in the case of schizophrenia in Western countries, where, overall, there is little difference in incidence between men and women. There are, however, wide differences between the sexes in the incidence of the illness at different ages. It has been estimated that the occurrence is twice as great for men aged 15–24 than for women of the same age. For women the peak age is between 25 and 34 (Warner 1985: 231). This may reflect career- and work-related stress upon men at this stage in their lives.

Because men are diagnosed younger, when they are physically at their strongest, this may induce more coercive actions from professionals during a crisis. (We will return to the handling of aggression in black male patients in Chapter 5.) Additionally, a greater prevalence of schizophrenia in males has been reported for many developing countries. Just as the domestic role has disadvantages associated with it, as pointed out in the study by Brown and Harris, in other contexts it can be seen as a protective factor for women. One possible implication of this is that as the proportion of women in the labour force rises, so we can expect an increase in 'schizophrenia'.

The course of 'schizophrenia' is also, in some ways, more benign for women than men. Warner (1985: 142) reports that, historically, the proportion of patients discharged as recovered is consistently higher for women. Differences in prognosis have also been noted. In the World Health Organization (1979) international study of schizophrenia, proportionally fewer women were in the worst outcome group at follow up, and more were in the best outcome category. In industrialized countries women tend to have shorter episodes of schizophrenia.

If we look at other disease categories, then the male/female distinction drawn by feminist analysis above is only applicable to a Western social context. In other places, men do worse than women. For example, some cross-cultural studies of depression have shown a slightly higher proportion of men than women suffering from depression (Carstairs and Kapur 1976). While women take sick leave for minor psychiatric problems more often than men, the latter tend to be off work for longer periods (Hensing *et al.* 1996).

These studies suggest that it is the roles and context of people's situations that influence the type and rate of mental distress, rather than anything intrinsic or constant about being a man or woman. In some contexts, work outside the home can be a threat to mental health, just as the domestic environment can.

Gender and sexuality

Both gay men and lesbians present with more mental health problems than do heterosexuals and are more likely to abuse substances (King *et al.* 2003) Gay and bi-sexual men are four times more likely to commit suicide than their heterosexual equivalents (McAndrew and Warne 2004). This may reflect the stress created by homophobic reactions and the discrimination and violence that ensues in hate crimes (Huebner, Rebchook and Kegeles 2004). It may also reflect developmental challenges. Girls and boys growing up with an emerging realization about their homosexuality may struggle with a particular identity problem, over and above the general one when shifting from childhood to adulthood. In Britain the demonization of a gay identity in schools has sometimes been an explicit educational policy (Section 28). Thus the ascription of a form of devalued sense of self or 'otherness' to young gay people can operate at both lay and 'official' levels.

The psychiatric response to homosexuality in one sense has differed from responses to other types of 'problem' behaviour. During the mid twentieth century homosexuality was designated as problematic by psychiatrists. However, in the nineteenth century its assumed biological determination led not to active physical intervention (as was the case with madness) but with a fatalism which prompted little therapeutic interest (Bullough 1987). It was only when psychoanalytical and then behavioural therapeutic methods were introduced during the twentieth century that psychiatrists began to interfere with homosexuality and aspire to 'cure' the condition. At the end of the century, the gay liberation movement opposed and undermined this pathologization but did not eliminate it. The very optimism encouraged by these environmental/ psychological theories of mental disorder prompted professionals to be more interventionist with homosexuals. Moreover, both male and female homosexuality were problematized by psychiatry because they were problematized more widely in western society. As Al-Issa (1987: 155) noted: 'Deviation from gender role expectations is traditionally considered abnormal'.

Leaving aside psychiatry's response to homosexuality, have men and women been treated equitably? Certainly differences in society are discernible. Since the nineteenth century, male not female homosexuality has been designated as criminal. In Great Britain it is no longer criminal but it has a higher age of consent than heterosexuality (21 not 16 years). In the Isle of Man and Northern Ireland it remains illegal and it remains a court martial offence in the armed services.

Once more, as with dangerousness, differential legal and cultural assumptions about homosexuality seem to associate maleness and antisocial behaviour and lower such an expectation of women. This is also reflected in the therapeutic discourse on homosexuality. While most therapeutic schools have clinical reports, and even research on treatment outcomes, for both gay men and lesbians, male problems are alluded to more frequently or given a greater priority.

This prioritization of men as suitable cases for treatment was at its most exaggerated in the late 1960s and early 1970s, when behaviour therapists attempted to 'cure' male homosexuals using electric shock aversion therapy. More benign behavioural methods were used for lesbian patients requesting reorientation (such as desensitization and assertiveness training) but men were singled out for the aversion treatment. The latter not only failed to induce a shift of sexual orientation in gay men, it merely induced phobic anxiety and impotence in some of its recipients (Diamont 1987). However, even today, some psychiatrists still pursue a form of 'therapeutic optimism' about reorientating homosexual desire and identity (Spitzer 2003).

Another way in which male homosexuals suffer especially restrictive or punitive attention from the mental health system links to the point made earlier about secure environments. Because there are more men than women in secure psychiatric provision, this means that there are more gay men than lesbians living in closed systems. In such systems, homosexual behaviour is constrained by the lack of privacy permitted for sexual contact. Thus, advocates of women's rights in secure provision understandably complain of the plight of those lesbians who are incarcerated at the 'harsh' end of psychiatry (Stevenson 1992). However, it is logical to deduce that the infringement of homosexual rights must occur with a greater regularity for men than women, as the latter are under-represented in secure provision.

However, the more frequent constraints on male, rather than female, homosexual rights in secure provision need to be considered alongside the greater vulnerability of women, once they are in such environments. Those women who do find themselves in secure provision are more vulnerable than male patients to sexual harassment and assault, from both patients and staff. Such predatory attention from men is particularly relevant given the type of women appearing in conditions of maximum security. For instance, Potier (1992) reported that 34 out of the 40 female patients with a diagnosis of psychopathy at Ashworth Special Hospital had been sexually abused in childhood or adolescence.

Having addressed the question of dangerousness and sexuality, we can now see why men are treated more harshly than women by psychiatry more often, though the small ratio of women at the secure end of psychiatric services may suffer individually more than men. Thus the focus on the over- representation of women in psychiatric statistics and the relative absence of men from the sociological discourse may gloss over important questions of gender, which are about both women and men.

Discussion

The concentration on women and mental disorder is a relatively new phenomenon. Gove and Geerken (1977) found that of the 11 pre-Second World War studies reviewed, three showed higher rates of mental disorder for women, while eight showed higher rates for men. Following the Second World War, studies showed higher rates for women while none showed higher rates for men.

How might these changes be accounted for? They may be a result of changes in women's social situation and psychiatric practices. A further possibility is that feminist scholarship itself may be a factor in constructing women and mental health as an object of study. Put another way, the shift towards identifying higher rates of mental disorder in women may be the result of a change in discourse. As the discourse changes, so too do the objects of attention.

Identifying women as an object of study, in itself may accentuate the 'female character' of mental ill health, establishing it as an essentially women's problem. For example, the work of Brown and Harris is often cited in texts as evidence that depression is a female problem. From this it may be inferred that the same problems are not experienced by men. However, Brown and Harris did not set out to study men, who were excluded from the research design at the outset. Therefore, from this study we do not know anything about the nature of male depression. If research is directed at women, to the exclusion of men, it is likely to produce evidence that links depression to women's experiences and social roles. Also, in attempting to make women more visible, some feminist scholars may have made men relatively invisible.

Feminists make much of the social disadvantage under which women suffer. Indeed, socio-economic indicators do demonstrate unequivocally that, overall, women suffer greater material deprivation than men. Notwithstanding such evidence, it is clear that particular groups of men are also subject to social disadvantage. There may be substantial evidence that men make women mentally sick, by stressing and labelling them more often than vice versa. However, the existence of a large number of men who are mentally disordered and particularly disadvantaged means that an exclusive focus on women and mental health precludes a full picture of the relationship between gender and psychiatry.

Rather than focusing on men or women and psychiatry, comparative analyses of men and women along a range of dimensions, including treatment, behaviour and portrayal of images of abnormality, are needed. In addition to gender, other variables need to be taken into consideration in understanding the mental health of women and men. What is clear in understanding gender and mental disorder is the need to focus more on the context and meaning of the cause and experience of mental health problems.

As we have argued elsewhere, a close relationship with social psychiatry had created one form of sociological analysis, following Durkheim, of treating mental health problems as social facts. Useful as this may be at showing the social origins of mental health problems, an understanding of the relationship between agency and structure, when considering the gendered nature of mental health problems, is also required. A recognition of meaning and context is also relevant to responding to the differing needs of men and women using mental health services. We return to this issue in the chapter on treatment. As will be seen in the next two chapters, gender as a variable in mental health is overlain by age and race.

Gender and mental health have been considered extensively by sociologists. However, there has been an overwhelming focus on women. Paradoxically, this may have contributed to a discourse linking women and psychological vulnerability. It also disguises an underlying set of processes which make some men particularly vulnerable to coercive psychiatric treatment. Despite the continuing interest in gender and mental health, there is still not a clear sociological account of why women are over-represented in the way they are in psychiatric populations. This chapter has rehearsed some factors which can be seen as additive or competing in this regard.

Questions

1 Which factors might explain why women are over-represented in mental health statistics?

2 How are psychiatric diagnoses gendered?

3 Provide a socio-historical account of psychiatry's response to homosexuality.

4 What has *The Social Origins of Depression* (Brown and Harris 1978) taught us about gender and mental health?

5 Why do women take more psychiatric drugs than men?

6 Why have men been overlooked in sociological studies of mental health?

For discussion

Consider arguments for and against the notion that women are less mentally healthy than men.

Further reading

Barnes, M. and Maple, N. (1992) *Women and Mental Health: Challenging the Stereotypes*. Birmingham: Venture Press.

Bentley, K.J. (2005) Women, mental health and the psychiatric enterprise: A review. *Health and Social work* 30(1): 56–63.

Kaplan, M.S. and Marks, G. (1995) Appraisal of health risks: the roles of masculinity, femininity and sex. *Sociology of Health and Illness*, 17(2): 206–21.

Nazroo, J.Y., Edwards, A.C. and Brown, G.W. (1998) Gender differences in the prevalence of depression: artefact, alternative disorders, biology or roles? *Sociology of Health and Illness*, 20(3): 3112–30.

Chapter 5

Race and ethnicity

Chapter overview

This chapter will examine investigations into the relationship between mental ill health and race. We will focus on the psychiatric response to African-Caribbean, Asian and Irish people in Britain. Earlier epidemiological studies undertaken in the 1960s and 1970s tended to draw out fairly rough and ready differences about ethnic groups. A poverty of data, as much as theorizing, particularly the way in which ethnicity was classified in the British national census, produced forms of analysis based upon crude distinctions.

Since then, more informed epidemiological work has displaced some old assumptions and presents us now with a more complex picture. The burgeoning interest from within sociology and social psychiatry in research and scholarship about ethnicity and mental health also reflects changing norms about race and social exclusion.

The chapter will cover the following topics:

- theoretical presuppositions about race;
- race and health;
- the epidemiology of mental health, race and ethnicity;
- Asian women and the somatization thesis;
- Irish people and psychiatry.

Theoretical presuppositions about race

In the past, many social scientists rejected the use of the concept of race because of its association with a dubious anthropological tradition left over from the nineteenth century. The latter used the concept of race to make biological distinctions between groups, and assumed white supremacy. This can be seen in relation to eugenics, the 'science' of racial improvement, which was a backdrop to the development of both anthropology and psychiatry at the turn of the twentieth century.

In its most extreme form eugenics culminated in the mass extermination of 'racially inferior' groups in Nazi Germany, along with physically and mentally disabled people of any race (Meyer 1988). The sterilization of mental patients and the eventual killings were instigated by the German medical profession and endorsed by the Nazi Government. Thus, social policies influenced by eugenic principles have intertwined considerations of both race and mental illness. Medically supported initiatives about sexual segregation and steriliza- tion for all disabled groups were also found in the rest of Europe and North America. Nazi social policy extended this general trend. It took the exclusion of purported eugenic threat to its ultimate conclusion (hence the notion of the 'final solution').

Fernando (1988) pointed out that there has also been a long and strong medical tradition which has operated on the basis that the brains of black people are inferior to those of white people. So, the link between race and mental illness has historically been a close one and medical–scientific know- ledge has been far from neutral about the assumed relationship. It has played a significant role in the perpetuation of pejorative theories and oppressive practices about certain racial groups.

The notion of race within the social sciences has since then more typically been used to refer to 'race relations'. This involves the relationship between a dominant community and minority groups. In contrast, socio-cultural differ- ences between groups are usually referred to as 'ethnicity'. This term usually connotes a collective identity, so it embraces a subjective element for a person. The ways of life of different ethnic groups depend on a combination of their inherited culture and their relations with other cultures. (See Anthias (1992) for a discussion about the various ways sociologists have addressed the relationship between race and ethnicity.)

Some empirical studies find little support for notions of singular or primary identities, such as having a psychiatric diagnosis or being black. Instead they point to identities being multiple, complex and contingent (Sudbury 2001; Ahmad, Atkin and Jones 2002). For example, Nazroo and Karlsen (2003) used survey data of ethnic minorities to identify five main dimensions along which people defined their ethnicity. Two of these related to self descriptions. In addition people alluded to traditional identity, community participation and membership of a racialized group. Diversity exists about the balance of these multiple descriptions across and within ethnic minority populations in Britain.

Much of the debate about minority ethnic groups and health has centred on cultural difference as a way of explaining the differential experience of groups within the community (differences in language, values, norms and beliefs).

This type of analysis focuses on the individual, or their culture, and is concerned mainly with examining the role of prejudice and discrimination in determining differences in health behaviour and the use of services.

Within these debates, 'prejudice' implies a psychological concept in that it refers to a set of personal attitudes. Transcultural or cross-cultural psychiatry, for example, is concerned with how different ethnic groups are treated by mental health workers socialized in the ways of the 'dominant' culture (Rack 1982; Kleinman 1988; Tseng 2003). This position advocates initiatives aimed at challenging and changing prejudices through 'race awareness' training. This works on the premise of challenging the stereotypical and negative views about minority ethnic groups held by powerful individuals, like professionals.

Cross-cultural psychiatry began by focusing on the differing manifestations of mental disorders among diverse societies. More recently, it has broadened its focus as a means of incorporating social and cultural aspects of 'illness' into a clinical framework. This has meant that transcultural psychiatry focuses more than it did in the past on illness experience than on bio-medical notions of mental disorders viewed from the health practitioner's perspective. But what still tends to be missing from analyses based on prejudice is a consideration of the impact of inequality – how the latter is manifested in rates of psychiatric diagnosis, service contact and variable professional responses to black and other minority groups.

Race and health

Before we start our examination of race and mental ill health, a more general note will be made about race and health. An account which respects multi-factorial causality extends beyond a focus on racism alone. Smaje (1996) suggests that such a fuller account would need to take into consideration the following:

- *Genetics* Because of their eugenic associations social scientists may have a tendency to avoid genetic explanations. While most (75 per cent) of the genetic material of human beings is identical and most (85 per cent) of the genetic variation occurs between individuals not races, the latter do show some differences (about 7 per cent of variance). The upshot of this is that some racial groups are more genetically susceptible to certain disorders. For example, there are differential incidence rates of sickle cell disease and phenylketonuria in Africans and North Europeans;
- *Migration* This is a complex topic in itself. Migrants may encounter new health threats in their host country. Also the circumstances of migration may be traumatic both physically and psychologically (as in warfare). Alternatively, it may be linked to high expectations, achieved or dashed, when a migrant wants to move in order to make a new life. Economic motives for migration may lead to racialized patterns of living in the host country, when people of the same origin move to the same area to work in the same employment context. Low-paid work in poor areas of inner cities, for

example, may lead to health outcomes which affect not just the migrants but subsequent generations;

• *Material disadvantage*   While migrants may enhance their wealth by moving, they may at the same time be relatively deprived within their host country. Low pay, housing disadvantage and unemployment make migrants susceptible to the direct health impact of poverty;

• *Cultural factors*   Lifestyle, social networks and kinship differences from the host culture may lead to health losses and gains;

• *Racism*   The health impact of racism is twofold. First, the direct effect is that racially victimized people are prone to stress, injury and death. Second, the indirect effect is that racial discrimination in the housing and labour market produces lowered health outcomes.

The epidemiology of mental health, race and ethnicity

A number of studies have compared the prevalence of 'common mental disorders' (i.e. diagnoses of neurotic symptom presentation) between ethnic groups. Compared to their white counterparts African-Caribbean people have lower rates of diagnosed anxiety but higher rates of depression (Shaw *et al.* 1999; Sproston and Nazroo 2002). This general finding holds true for gender-specific constructs such as post-natal depression where the same pattern is discernable (Edge, Baker and Rogers 2004).

There are low prevalence levels of anxiety among Bangladeshi, Pakistani and Indian groups compared to their white British counterparts but there is a slightly different pattern for depression. Compared with the white British group, the rates of depression were similar in the Pakistanis and lower in the Indian and much lower in the Bangladeshi groups. Given that women have high prevalence rates of common mental disorders generally, the relative differences between white and South Asian groups are more marked for women than men.

These findings are consistent across a number of surveys. Psychiatric epidemiology has traditionally been tied closely in to service utilization. This is because the profession has been predicated on the relationship between diagnosis and the presumed need for service contact. Psychiatric epidemiology has been shaped by investigations of the need for services, rather than symptoms *per se* (Rogers and Pilgrim 2003). By contrast, *social* epidemiology links the genesis of mental health problems with broader social and economic influences which may differ. For example, job security for black rather than white men appears to be a more important factor in preventing 'depressive symptoms' (Zimmerman *et al.* 2004).

During the last 30 years some very general trends in racialized service contact have been identified. Cochrane (1977), analysed 1971 psychiatric admissions and found that rates for Irish, Polish and Scottish immigrants to England and Wales were higher than for native-born people. Rates for those born in the Indian sub-continent were lower, while the rate for Caribbean immigrants was virtually the same as for the English-born. This contrasts with the findings of two other studies carried out in the 1970s and 1980s. Dean *et al.* (1981), examining first admissions to hospital in south-east England for 1976, found one and a half times the expected numbers for Caribbean-born people than for

British-born people. Carpenter and Brockington (1980) recorded two and half times the rate of admission for Asian-born people and one and a half times the rate for African-Caribbean groups than for white British-born people.

Looking at the cumulative findings over a period of 30 years, there seems to have been more consistent evidence for the over-representation of African-Caribbean groups in admissions than Asian groups. Of all the studies conducted, only Cochrane's seems to indicate lower rates for African-Caribbeans (cf. Hemsi 1967; Rwegellera 1977; Carpenter and Brockington 1980; and Koffman *et al.* 1997).

Recently, Tolmac and Hodes (2004) found that black adolescents are still over-represented in mental health services, especially if they were born outside of the UK and had refugee status. However, some earlier studies had indicated that British-born blacks were more over-represented than migrants. This may reflect a change in forms of data collection shaped by changes in migration patterns, which now include particular stressors associated with refugee status. By contrast, 20 years ago the children of voluntary Caribbean migrants raised in Britain were studied.

For Asian groups the picture has been much more variable. Although Carpenter and Brockington found higher rates for Asians overall, Hitch (1981) found higher rates for Pakistani-born people and lower rates for people born in India than native-born. As well as providing a rather inconsistent picture, these studies suffer from a further methodological weakness. Although in the past they told us something about the rates of admissions among people entering Britain, they tell us little about admissions for different racial and ethnic groups within Britain as a whole.

In using place of birth as an indicator of racial and ethnic origin, black people born in Britain are not counted with people entering the country from Africa and the Caribbean. There have been attempts to deal with this shortcoming by recording ethnicity independently of place of birth. McGovern and Cope (1987) using this method found that more African-Caribbeans than expected, as measured against numbers in the general population, enter the in-patient system.

Hospital admission records are often incomplete and inaccurate. Consequently, they may be a poor indicator of the incidence and prevalence of mental disorder in the community. Hospital admission has traditionally been used as a measure of the incidence of mental illness among different racial and ethnic groups. However, this method may be misleading as admission is shaped in part by the supply side and demand-management policies. It is not only determined by community incidence. For example, a recent study conducted in the USA explored why there seemed to be higher admission levels in areas with higher concentrations of poverty and African American residents. It found that the admission trends were more likely to result from changes in hospital management and funding affecting access to hospital services than the socio-demographic make up of the local population (Almog *et al.* 2004).

Few studies have set out to measure the rates of mental illness among different ethnic groups in ordinary populations. One study carried out in Nottingham did not confine itself to hospital admissions (Harrison *et al.* 1988) but included all patients in contact with psychiatric services over a two-year period. The researchers estimated that the incidence rate of schizophrenia for African-Caribbean people was 12 to 13 times higher than that of the general population. In community studies of hallucinations, African-Caribbean people are found to experience them 2.5 times more often than white samples. However, only a quarter of the hallucinating black group fulfilled psychiatric criteria for a diagnosis of psychosis. Thus not only are there cultural differences in the reporting of hallucinations, these differences are not accounted for in most cases by a psychotic context (Johns *et al.* 2002).

In the psychiatric literature, two types of explanation predominate in attempting to explain the apparent over-representation of African-Caribbean people with schizophrenia and the under-representation of Asian groups. The first tends to look for reasons at the level of 'cultural difference'. For example, it has been suggested that the relatively low number of admissions for Asian groups is an accurate reflection of low rates of distress because of psychological robustness or fatalistic attitudes to suffering.

It has also been suggested that there may be a tendency to avoid contact with services in the Asian community because of the stigma attached to psychiatric conditions or because of the inappropriateness of existing services which results in low uptake. A particular controversy which surrounds the discussion of Asian mental health relates to the adequacy of western psychiatric research to respect diverse meanings of distress (see later discussion on somatization).

The second type of explanation in addition to this cultural consideration, suggests a vulnerability to distress related to an adverse environment i.e., social deprivation and unfavourable conditions, such as poverty, racial harassment and discrimination over housing. However, since few studies have systematically investigated the impact of external stressors on the mental health of black people, the consequences of racism in employment, housing and education have not been assessed adequately. Also, if the stressors of racism are the main explanation for poor mental health, and both African-Caribbean and Asian are affected by it, why is the former group over-represented in service contact but the latter is not? Compared to North America, there has been little substantial British public health research on health and race to answer this question (Karlsen and Nazroo 2004).

Black mental health groups themselves describe diverse forms of stress derived from racism, which affect their mental health. In one study, Afro-Caribbean users identified a variety of factors to explain their mental health problems. These included: problems of coping with adolescence and the education system, which builds up and then dashes expectations; growing up in a hostile environment with few positive images of black people; and parental and British white cultural input leading to confusion and conflict over identity (Frederick 1991). Another study has illuminated how Asian women tended to identify isolation and cultural differences as the root of their problems (Fenton and Sadiq 1991) while Asian men identified feelings of powerlessness as a result of unemployment or racism (Beliappa 1991).

It would seem that a simple social stress hypothesis, with poverty and racism predominating as causal variables, cannot be sufficient to account for the data available on psychiatric morbidity. After all, in poor inner city areas, Asian people as well as African-Caribbean people suffer recurrent racism. And yet, overall, the evidence seems to point to only the latter being over-represented in psychiatric records, not the former. This is not to argue that different racial and ethnic groups do not experience peculiar stressors, which lead to mental health problems emerging in particular individuals. But it would seem that such external stress is not a strong enough unitary explanation to account for the aggregate data on over-representation among African-Caribbeans (or the Irish, as we will see later).

Methodological cautions about findings

Community studies, as well as those that have examined admissions to hospital, have been criticized on methodological grounds, casting some doubt on the validity of their conclusions. Such criticisms include the unreliability and lack of conceptual validity of the diagnosis of schizophrenia, which means that data about ethnic groups is subject to a large margin of error (Sashidaran 1993). In the case of the Harrison study above, for example, critics have noted that:

> If one case was misclassified a 4 per cent change in incidence would be recorded. Likewise, if they [the researchers] had under-counted the number of people in the population deemed at risk by 200 the incidence recorded would be reduced by 40 per cent . . . (Francis *et al.* 1989: 161)

Fernando (1988) has also pointed out that because these studies tend to be suffused with cultural stereotypes, it is difficult to make accurate estimates about 'true rates' of mental illness among different groups. He cites the example of a study by Bebbington, Hurry and Tennant (1981), which attempted to explain the lower levels of minor psychiatric disorders, such as depression among Caribbean-born people, by their tendency to respond to adversity with 'cheery denial'.

Type of service contact

In addition to explanations which focus on 'cultural' differences, or vulnerability to mental distress according to ethnicity, another explanation for over-representation lies with the way in which others involved with psychiatric practice respond to black people. This issue will be considered in relation to initial service contact and subsequent treatment.

African-Caribbean people are much more likely than white people to make contact with psychiatry via the police, courts and prison. These African-Caribbean patients are also more likely to be young and male (Bean *et al.* 1991). Young black men are much more likely to come into contact with forensic psychiatry than white equivalents. During the 1980s migrant and British-born second generation black men were found to be referred 29 times more frequently than their white counterparts (McGovern and Cope 1987; Cope 1989). Also, the 'non-white' group had committed less serious offences prior to admission.

At each point of the processing of the criminal justice and mental health systems there appears to be a staged increase in discrimination. For example, Browne (1990) found that black defendants, deemed to be mentally vulnerable, were less likely than white defendants to be given bail and more likely to receive court orders involving compulsory psychiatric treatment. At the other end of the spectrum from coercive psychiatry, there is evidence to suggest that black people are under-represented in outpatient and self-referred services (Littlewood and Cross 1980) and are less likely than other groups to be referred by general practitioners (Hitch and Clegg 1980).

While psychiatric epidemiology has enumerated differences in sources of referral and rates of admission to hospital, it has provided fewer insights into *why* black people come into contact with specialist services in this way. Studies undertaken more than 20 years ago identified a number of inter-related factors. They focused on factors that were viewed as characteristics of black people themselves. It was suggested that the culture of black people made them more susceptible to being identified by lay people and the police. The crux of this argument was that black people express their distress in a culturally idiosyncratic way (Littlewood and Lipsedge 1982). It has been suggested, for example, that the manifestation of 'mental illness' predisposes African-Caribbean people towards police arrest because they present in a particularly disturbed or violent way (Rwegellera 1977; Hitch and Clegg 1980; Harrison *et al.* 1988).

There is a relative low level of registration with primary care services on the part of African-Caribbean people who are subsequently admitted to hospital (Koffman *et al.* 1997) and lower rates of treatment for depression compared to other ethnic groups when they are in contact with these services (Nazroo 1997). The place where behaviour takes place may also be significant. According to Bean (1986) if a greater part of young African-Caribbean social life takes place in public, then deviant conduct is more likely to be detected and dealt with by agents of the State, such as the police and psychiatrists, than is the case of white people, who have more of an indoor culture.

As was mentioned earlier, explanations which emphasize cultural difference have been criticized because they tend to make stereotypical generalizations about behaviour which may be erroneous. They also incline towards identifying the problem as being situated in the person's own culture, thereby viewing it as pathological. One of the logical conclusions of this approach is that to avoid detection as mentally ill, black people should adopt white ways of behaving (such as staying off the streets).

While a research focus on black culture runs the risk of contributing to a form of victim-blaming, a focus on the part played by other people in reacting to ethnic difference reframes the problem. It is not the conduct of black people in itself that is at issue but the way others react to it. Horwitz (1983) has noted that the tendency to label a person mentally ill increases with the cultural distance between the labeller and labelled. In other words, members of minority ethnic groups are more likely to be labelled mentally ill than dominant indigenous groups. This may lead to a predisposition on the part of white people in Britain to interpret black people's behaviour as signs of insanity and danger.

One study found that lay people were more responsible for initiating police action than police officers themselves. African-Caribbean people were also found to be less frequently referred by their relatives or neighbours and more frequently by strangers and passers-by than other ethnic groups (Rogers 1990). Thus, perhaps the conduct of black people is interpreted in a more negative light by the lay (white) public than is white conduct.

The way in which black people's behaviour is viewed, together with the high number of black police referrals, suggests a process of 'transmitted discrimination' (Reiner 1986). This entails the police acting as a conveyor belt or conduit for community prejudices about black people's behaviour constituting a threat to public law and order. This transmitted discrimination could then be compounded by other factors, such as a general conflictual relationship between young black men and the police and intensive policing strategies on inner city housing estates with large numbers of black residents. These factors contribute to raised levels of police detention of all forms of deviance, including mental disorder.

The relationships that black people and the police have with other agencies are also relevant. The policies and reactions of the local courts and psychiatric services have been found to be influential in how the police react when detaining someone they believe to be mentally disordered. A study conducted for the National Association for the Care and Resettlement of Offenders (NACRO) found that the large rate of psychiatric referrals may have been due to the sentencing attitudes of magistrates. Decision makers tended to err on the side of caution with black defendants considered to be mentally vulnerable (Browne 1990).

The pathways by which black people come to the attention of mental health services have led some commentators to view psychiatry as part of a larger social control apparatus which regulates and oversees the lives of black people (Mercer 1986; Francis 1989). That black people, and in particular young black men, are also over-represented in all parts of the criminal justice system suggests indeed that both the 'criminalization' and the 'medicalization' of black people are closely connected processes.

According to Francis (1989), higher rates of entering the psychiatric system via the criminal justice system indicate a coalescence of the criminalization and medicalization of black people. He argues for a much wider definition of what constitutes the psychiatric system to be adopted, which views it as an extended network of scientific expertise and professional practice. This would necessitate the position and management of black people being considered across a number of related state institutions, including schools, hospitals, social services, the courts and prisons. Francis suggests that this would highlight common practices and processes and bring together issues which have hitherto been analysed separately, such as the IQ testing of black children, which has led to high numbers being classified as 'educationally subnormal'.

In theory, admission to hospital and service use serve the function of responding to mental health need. A complementary theoretical position to that provided by Francis has been suggested by Smaje (1996) and Nazroo (1998) when explaining ethic inequalities in mental and physical health. Their analysis involves abandoning an emphasis on a-historical and decontextualized genetic and cultural factors, which has found favour in previous epidemiological work, and replacing them with a structural approach, which considers the fine-grain aspects of disadvantage faced by black people in society. The latter includes the experience of racism, ethnic identity and the relevance of 'group affiliation and culture while acknowledging the contingent and contextual nature of ethnicity' (p. 710).

Disproportionate coercion

During the 1980s, when only around 8 per cent of all admissions to hospital were compulsory, 20–30 per cent of African-Caribbean patients were detained involuntarily (Cope 1989). The rate was even higher for young Caribbean migrants. One study monitored detention rates over a four-year period and found this group to be compulsorily admitted at 17 times the rate for compulsory admissions made from the community and, under admissions via the criminal justice system, 25 times more frequently (Cope 1989). This pattern was confirmed by studies in the 1990s, which found that black people were over-represented in admissions to psychiatric hospitals (Bhui *et al.* 2003). They were more likely to be admitted compulsorily and to be placed in locked wards (Koffman *et al.* 1997) and were more likely to have been in conflict with the police (Commander *et al.* 1999).

Black people are generally treated in a more coercive way within the psychiatric system. Black patients are over-represented in locked wards, secure units and the Special Hospitals (Bolton 1984; Jones and Berry 1986; Mohan *et al.* 1997; Fernando, Ndegwa and Wilson 1998; Commander *et al.* 1999; Lelliott, Audlin and Duffet 2001). They are more likely to receive physical treatments than whites. Two studies have indicated the over-use of ECT for Asian and African-Caribbean patients (Littlewood and Cross 1980; Shaikh 1985).

The study by Littlewood and Cross also found that black patients were more likely to receive major tranquillizers and intramuscular medication, and were more likely to be seen by junior medical staff. Chen, Harrison and Standen (1991) confirmed these findings, noting that while no differences between black and white patients in medication levels were evident at admission, over time the black group received higher levels and were more likely to be prescribed depot medication. Littlewood and Lipsedge (1982), found excessive Caribbean detention to be independent of diagnosis, while Bolton (1984) found that black patients identified by staff as uncooperative, but not aggressive, were much more likely to be transferred to locked wards than white patients.

Likewise, Noble and Rodger (1989), who reported a longitudinal record of violent incidents in the Bethlem Royal and Maudsley hospitals in London, found that in their control group of non-violent patients, 50 per cent of African-Caribbean patients in the sample were detained formally or on a locked ward, whereas only 15 per cent of non-violent whites were managed in the same way. Black patients were also recorded to be violent more often than white patients, raising the question (for us but not the investigators) about a 'spiral' of expectations, similar to that found in authoritarian penal regimes. That is, staff treat black people more coercively than they do whites and so black people react to a discriminatory regime in a more aggressive way. This then prompts staff to behave coercively more often to incidents involving black patients, and the spiral continues.

Despite the widespread evidence of continuing over-representation of black people in compulsory admissions and in coercive interventions, these findings have not influenced policy or led to a strategy to ensure that services appropriately meet the need of the culturally diverse population in this country' (Bhui, Christie and Bhugra 1995; Morgan *et al.* 2004).

The shift towards taking into account users' views of services now has produced additional evidence that black patients experience their contact with services as being unsatisfactory and characterized by racism (Parkman *et al.* 1997; Secker and Hardy 2002). This trend is also apparent in the USA. There, Diala *et al.* (2000) found that African-American patients prior to service contact had more positive views than whites. After contact this was reversed. Studies which take wider accounts of the black community's perception of psychiatric services confirm that early service contact is avoided because it is associated with racism and mistreatment (Mclean, Campbell and Cornish 2003)

Black people's conduct and attributions of madness – some summary points

While it is clear from the evidence summarized earlier that black people are over-represented in in-patient settings and are disproportionately coerced, how is this trend explained? Three explanations can be gleaned from the literature on the subject, some of which has been touched on earlier: black people are mentally ill more often than whites; black people may be mentally ill more often but they are given the wrong diagnosis; psychiatric theory and practice is part of a wider racism. Let us now look at these three accounts in a little more detail.

- *The labelling may merely reflect actual incidence*   High rates of schizophrenia have been cited as an explanatory factor for the high rates of civil compulsory detention of psychotic black patients (Cope 1989). In other words, it is argued, black people become 'schizophrenic' more often than whites and therefore warrant more aggressive treatment in services. However, methodological uncertainties about the data on ethnic monitoring mentioned earlier, together with uncertainties over the diagnosis and aetiology of schizophrenia in general, and among black people in particular, cast doubt on this as an adequate explanation. The uncertainty over the aetiology of this disease category is indicated at the end of a study on the subject by Harrison *et al.* (1988) who identified a multiplicity of possibilities: potential biological differences in terms of genetic factors, neurochemistry, pre- and peri-natal trauma, virology, and immunology, as well as possible effects of living in decaying areas with high unemployment and poor housing.
  A desirable precondition of diagnostic validity is that a disease has a known cause. Schizophrenia has no known cause – it lacks 'aetiological specificity'. This adds to the other known difficulties of its diagnosis being both unreliable and not leading to any clear predictions about outcome (prognosis) (Bentall, Jackson and Pilgrim 1988; Boyle 1991). Thus the 'actual incidence' position about black people is extremely weak because the diagnostic category of schizophrenia is so problematic. These studies, which appeal to the evidence of over-representation being accounted for by the purported raised incidence of schizophrenia in black people, fail to engage with the problems of conceptual and empirical validity which attend the diagnosis. This represents a leap in faith rather than an example of scientific medicine.
- *Misdiagnosis* An alternative viewpoint is that admission rates for

'schizophrenia' and other psychoses do not necessarily reflect the incidence of these disorders in community populations. Instead, records may reflect biases in diagnostic practices. Fernando (1988) has suggested that it is the ethnocentric view of psychiatrists that has resulted in this misattribution of labels, such as 'schizophrenia', by imposing Western concepts with little regard for the cultures of non-western people. According to Littlewood and Lipsedge (1982), terms such as 'schizophrenia' and 'cannabis psychosis' are used when black people display disturbed behaviour. Evidence for the difficulties that psychiatrists have in affixing appropriate labels is derived from the observation that many more black, than white patients had their diagnosis changed over time.

The misdiagnosis hypothesis tends to leave unchallenged the fundamental assumption that high rates of psychopathology actually exist among black people. What is claimed instead is merely that the *wrong* label is being applied. For instance, from studying patients with 'religious delusions' Littlewood and Lipsedge suggest that patients with 'acute psychotic reactions' may be misdiagnosed as schizophrenic. This viewpoint does not challenge the validity of diagnostic categories themselves, nor the scientific status of psychiatric knowledge or practices. Transcultural psychiatry, of which the Littlewood and Lispsedge study is an example, has also been criticized on the grounds that it provides a simplistic notion of 'culture', which has been adopted by predominantly white psychiatrists about black client groups (Sashidharan 1986).

Fernando, Ndegwa and Wilson (1998) argue that the misdiagnosis hypothesis needs to be accepted only as a partial account of the data on African-Caribbean over-representation. In their view, in addition to the misdiagnosis hypothesis, other concurrent explanatory factors need to be taken into account, which include institutional racism and the conceptual inadequacy of psychiatric knowledge in its totality. Within such a wider critique of psychiatric theory and practice lies an account of why psychiatry is unjust and unscientific, to an extent, not just about black patients but also about its whole client group.

- *Racialized psychiatric constructs reflect and reinforce wider racism* Earlier we noted that police referrals to psychiatry reflected 'transmitted racism'. This starts with lay judgments about the meaning and perceived threat of black conduct by white onlookers. The police are called and refer on to psychiatrists. Both the police and psychiatrists are embedded in the same societal context as the public. A number of commentators have noted the tendency of psychiatric constructs to be shaped by this context. From this perspective, the notion of psychiatry as a scientific discipline, which remains unaffected by social forces, is rejected.

The way in which race and culture are inextricably bound up in the construction of disease categories is illustrated by a number of past and contemporary examples. For example, 'drapetomania' was defined by an American psychiatrist Cartwright in 1851, as a disease which made slaves run away: 'The cause in the most of cases, that induces the Negro to run away from service, is as much a disease of the mind as any other species of mental alienation, and much more curable, as a general rule' (quoted in Ranger 1989: 354).

Fernando (1988) points out the rise in racist categories is bound up with the institution of slavery and social control. Examples which have more relevance to contemporary psychiatry and the social control of black people are the constructs of 'cannabis psychosis' and 'schizophrenia'. Cannabis psychosis is a label which has been attached selectively to African-Caribbean people when British psychiatrists are perplexed by their behaviour (Ranger 1989). Psychosis is defined by the Royal College of Psychiatrists as a mental illness which 'cannot be understood as an exaggeration of ordinary expression'. As discussed in the chapter on gender, the notion of 'ordinary' here is based on dominant groups in society in terms of numbers, status and power. Thus, in Britain, 'ordinary' implies having a white skin.

Others have pointed to the racist assumptions underlying the theoretical tradition of Kraepelin, the German psychiatrist responsible for the development of the category and classification of schizophrenia (which he dubbed 'dementia praecox'). Kraepelinian theorizing, which dominates post- as well as pre-War western psychiatry, points to a 'tainted' gene pool as a causal factor in schizophrenia. This pool is associated with other forms of disruptive and dangerous conduct. These suggestions neatly fit racist stereotypes held about black people (Francis 1989).

Certainly it is well documented that German eugenic medicine, which underpinned the Nazi programme of racial hygiene and evinced the degeneracy theory of disability and dangerousness, also gives western psychiatry many of its presuppositions. Indeed, most standard psychiatric textbooks documenting the evidence for the heritability of schizophrenia (e.g. Gottesman and Shields 1972) report uncritically the seminal genetic research of Rudin and Kallman during the Nazi period in Germany (Marshall 1990; Pilgrim 2002a). Thus, assumptions about genetic inferiority and race are deeply ingrained in psychiatric theory.

The question of racist constructs relates to the wider question, about the capacity of western psychiatric knowledge to respond adequately to cross-cultural differences. Thus, even when psychiatric knowledge is not implicitly or explicitly racist, it is inevitably a product of its time and place. At present this means the dominance of ideas derived from nineteenth-century Europe, particularly the work of Kraepelin and Bleuler, which has been modified by later Anglo-American psychiatrists. This has culminated in the production of several versions of the American Psychiatric Association's Diagnostic and Statistical Manual in the US and the International Classification of Diseases in Britain. Both of these are predicated on earlier notions derived from Germanic psychiatry.

Even when less biologically and diagnostically orientated mental health workers have developed therapeutic rationales, such as Sigmund Freud in Europe, or Carl Rogers in the US, they are clearly western in their assumptions (for example about individualism and mind). Despite this, these psychotherapeutic systems are offered as being trans-historically and trans-culturally valid by their founders and followers (Pilgrim 1997a). In this sense they are not different to the bio-medical rationales offered by their competing colleagues in the mental health industry. Despite a much greater sensitivity to the racial biases of psychiatric constructs, they remain implicit in most epidemiological studies (Bhui and Bhugra 2001).

In summary, the picture drawn above about mode of referral, diagnosis, compulsory admission and psychiatric management indicates that black people (particularly young black men) are subjected more to the harsh end of mental health services than white people. However, there are exceptions to this pattern, which we will consider later when examining Irish people in Britain. First, we turn to another ethnic group in a British context.

Asian women and the somatization thesis

The focus within the psychiatric literature on the 'madness' of young African-Caribbean men masks an important, but until recently less explored, question related to the misery of Asian women. Studies of consultations in primary care show that South Asians consult with physical problems more frequently than compared to white/ British subjects (Goldberg *et al.* 1997). In particular, the rates and consultations for widespread musculo-skeletal pain are higher among South Asian groups than white groups (Allison *et al.* 2002).

The discourse from psychiatric researchers about this topic suggests that Asian women present their mental distress as bodily symptoms – the 'somatization thesis' (Currer 1986). This provides a case for an apparently legitimate form of medical management, i.e. doctors need to diagnose and treat an underlying mental illness (depression) despite the patient's somatic presentation. However, there are problems with this somatization thesis. Fenton and Sadiq-Sangster (1996: 69) point out that the presentation of bodily symptoms by Asian women is ambiguous for a number of reasons:

> It could mean several things: (a) a non-recognition of mental illness, so that ailments are always presented as somatic, (b) a non-recognition of the link between physical ailments and emotional states, (c) a presentation of ailments as somatic despite some recognition of mental distress, and (d) simply a non-presentation of mental symptoms to bio-medical doctors.

The assumption that physical distress is 'really' a mental illness may reflect a form of Western cultural imperialism on the part of the psychiatric profession. For example, according to Skultans (2003) psychiatric language in Latvia has been taken over recently by the diagnostic category of 'depression' and 'masked depression', which has replaced the more established language of somatic distress that was central to previous lay conceptualizations under Soviet psychiatry.

Skultans raises the argument that it might be assumed that a psychiatric rather than physical diagnosis raises the probability of a patient-centred approach to care. However, the language of depression does not in itself lead to a greater appreciation of, or engagement with, patients' subjective narratives. Indeed, conversely, doctors who begin by addressing their patients' physical discomfort and presentation keep an open mind about a range of narrative possibilities. By contrast, a point diagnosis of depression leads usually to the prescription of anti-depressants. The diagnosis and treatment then close down the need for further exploration.

Given this unexplored ambiguity, the psychiatric assumption of somatization in Asian women is a pre-emptive construction. The latter has a tendency to stereotype whole groups of people. Another example of this is in relation to the investigation itself of 'Asian' health. The attempt by medicine to seek a pattern of health in a variegated group of people from a large land mass (say the Indian subcontinent) containing several countries, religions and nationalities reflects a homogenization stereotype. Also, as Watters (1996) has pointed out, Asian people may encounter different styles and qualities of mental health services in various parts of Britain. Despite this, the psychiatric literature studying differences in hospitalization rates in Asian people assumes that these exist as a result of patient variables.

Watters (1996) criticizes researchers for a number of rash generalizations about Asian mental health. He includes the following examples: an uncritical acceptance of the somatization thesis; an assumption that Islam is a protective mental health factor but Hinduism is not; and the assumption that Indians have an easier migration experience than Pakistanis. Another example of pre-emptive stereotyping is the assumption that Asian culture fails to have a notion of psychological causation (Ineichen 1987).

A final point which the literature on Asian mental health highlights is the vulnerability of western medical knowledge. The somatization thesis implies that physical symptoms disguise a true mental illness. However, given the centrality of the heart in south Asian culture (Krause 1989; Fenton and Sadiq 1991), sadness is articulated readily as being in that area of the chest – the heart 'sinking' or 'falling' (*dil ghirda hai*). The sufferer is not 'disguising' depression but is simply experiencing their distress in that way. One analysis which seems to bridge the gap between cultural determinism and medical positivism can be found in a study of South Asian women's lay knowledge. Fenton and Sadiq-Sangster (1996), in a follow up to their earlier research, found that women describe and express mental distress in a culturally specific way but their descriptions did correspond with a number of the features associated with the western psychiatric category of depression.

A problem with western psychiatric positivism is that it assumes a neat division between mental and physical illness. It also assumes that the linguistic expression of emotions is transculturally stable (Pilgrim and Bentall 1999). However, cross-cultural comparisons reveal large variations in the use of words to describe subjective states. For example, some cultures have no word for 'anxiety'. The current western notion of 'depression' is a contemporary convention which may change in the future and was certainly different in the past. In the nineteenth century it was not used. Instead lethargy, weakness and low mood were labelled as 'neurasthenia' and extreme sadness dubbed 'melancholia' by psychiatrists. In China, the former term is still favoured over 'depression' by lay people and doctors (Kleinman 1988).

A recent study exploring widespread pain among ethnic minority groups suggested that for South Asian women in particular somatization or the notion of bodily pain was merely a starting point to providing a more wide-ranging narrative of pain and distress related to psychological distress and external social events (Rogers and Allison, 2004). Somatization may also reflect the way in which the family and the group is more important than individual autonomy in the expression and management of distress. In the study of widespread pain, the apparent lack of reference to *individual* coping strategies among the South Asian respondents was accompanied by an importance attributed to family members in dealing with pain and distress and an emphasis on a transfer of domestic and everyday duties to others.

In this context, mental health treatments which foster individualism (say through psychotherapy) may result in dissonance with family members, which might undermine, rather than engender, social support and the patient's sense of self-worth. As a result, as Kirmayer and Young (1998) point out, solutions that make sense from the perspective of Euro-American psychiatry may not be embraced by many Eastern cultures. For example, the Western assumption that disclosure and emotional catharsis lead to healing may not have a global application. This somatization thesis about Asian women may reveal more about the epistemological weakness and asocial approach of western psychiatry than the subjective weakness of its diagnostic targets.

Irish people and psychiatry

While most of the debates about psychiatry and race have centred on the diagnosis and treatment of black people, the smaller literature on Irish people in Britain points to factors other than skin colour in understanding over-representation in psychiatric records. (For a summary of this literature see Greenslade (1992) and Bracken *et al.* (1998).) If we take two broad measures of distress from official statistics (suicide and psychiatric admissions) we find that Irish people, despite their white skin, have in the past been over-represented.

Table 5.1 shows the picture for self-induced deaths from suicides and non-accidental poisoning according to official statistics reported by Cochrane (1977) in England and Wales, by country of origin. People from the West Indies have a low rate, whereas the rate for Irish people is high. The even higher figures reported for Germans and Poles probably reflects the large proportion of Nazi death camp survivors or their families. The Scots too have a higher self-induced mortality rate than those indigenous to England and Wales. It is important to note that Welsh data cannot be disaggregated as they

Table 5.1   Non-indigenous self-induced death in England and Wales

	Standardized mortality ratio	
Country of origin	*Men*	*Women*
All countries	100	100
Poland	221	207
Germany	177	239
Ireland (North and South)	154	149
Scotland	138	145
USA	98	198
India and Pakistan	100	122
West Indies	85	60

Modified from Cochrane (1997)

are collected together with English data sets by central government, although recently some internal Welsh studies are emerging.

Turning to psychiatric admissions, Irish immigrants have been more likely than Caribbean immigrants to enter hospital (Table 5.2). The diagnosis of schizophrenia is highest in Caribbean 'immigrants' (of all racial/ethnic groups). But Irish people going to the British mainland are significantly more likely to be labelled as schizophrenic than those born there. Previous studies suggested that the Irish are under-represented in records of schizophrenia in England (Clare 1974). The recorded incidence for schizophrenia is higher in Eire itself than in the rest of the British Isles.

The over-representation of Irish people in psychiatric populations has led some commentators to generate more questions than answers when proposing a multi-factorial research programme. This might require an understanding which would include Irish child-rearing practices, long-term effects of emigration, poverty, rates of obstetric complication, mental health service over-utilization, late male marriage age in rural communities and specific forms of personal alienation from the neighbouring ex-colonizer (Jones 1997).

The Irish on mainland Britain have the highest rate of diagnosis for most categories, including neurosis, personality disorder, depression, 'other' psychoses and alcohol abuse (Cochrane and Bal 1989). As a consequence of this overall over-representation, the Irish have the highest rate of admissions to in-patient facilities of all ethnic groups in Britain (Bracken *et al.* 1998). Unlike with the data on Afro-Caribbean people, the gender bias is less clear for the Irish, with a slight female, not male, preponderance. There is some evidence from a study of Irish-born Catholics living in the West of Scotland that the health gap (including mental health) is closing between Irish people and other white groups in the British Isles (Abbotts *et al.* 2001). However, the overall trend from studies in the past 20 years is that this gap undoubtedly exists. These figures indicate that race and ethnicity clearly are important, as far as mental ill health and psychiatric services are concerned. But given that the Irish are white, how can we make sense of their shared features with some black groups?

Two broad groups of interweaving features probably make the Irish vulnerable to mental health problems, one material and the other cultural, which overlap with the research agenda offered by Jones (1997). The material factors relate to the legacy of socio-economic disruption: poverty; famine; the military suppression of rebellion and insurrection; forced migration; and economic reliance on a neighbouring colonial power.

The cultural concomitants of these colonial and post-colonial material forces have involved a series of identity crises and confusions. As well as the

Table 5.2 Psychiatric admissions of immigrants (16+) per 100,000 in England

Origin by birth	Male	Female	All
Eire	1054	1102	1080
Northern Ireland	793	880	838
Caribbean	565	532	548
England	418	583	504

Modified from Cochrane and Bal (1989)

general history of the Celtic fringe of the British Isles being relevant – the suppression of language and religion by an occupying English colonial power, which for varying periods has been resisted – the internal ruling elites of Ireland have often been pro-English and have not always shared the same cultural identity of their subordinates in relation to language and religion (O'Mahony and Delanty 1998).

The latter authors also point out that the political hegemony of the Catholic Church has been linked to a conservative clerical nationalism, as well as an imposed civil culture which has: quashed intellectual dissent; been sexually repressive; subordinated women; and engendered a strict child-rearing style, both in the home and in an educational system under its monopoly control. Additionally, the clerical adjudication over sin by celibates has operated as a ubiquitous social control mechanism over the Irish laiety, creating mass self-doubt and guilt.

Some of the points made by O'Mahony and Delanty are also explored by Scheper-Hughes (1979) in her anthropological study of Irish mental health, although she traces ego-sapping child-rearing practices as much to the English colonial power as to the Church. The destructive cultural force of English colonialism and its possible mental health impact are also examined by Kenny (1985). Thus, Irish history is saturated, like other colonized countries, with an experience of exploitation, loss and separation from starvation and migration. But also there are peculiar religious and cultural forces which form a backdrop to Irish identity fragmentation. Together these may have been powerful historical sources of madness (and creativity) which cumulatively retain a contemporary resonance.

Discussion

There is an alternative way of viewing the debate on race and mental health, which goes beyond attempting to identify causal factors in the high incidence of mental illness among black and Irish people, or pinpointing prejudicial labelling practices. This focuses on the discourse of race and psychiatry.

As Foucault (1965) has argued, we live with an ingrained predisposition to view madness as essentially 'other'. The use of the Victorian asylums for warehousing the insane was a mechanism for bringing about a break in the dialogue between reason and unreason on the one hand, and society and the disturbed on the other. In our contemporary era, where large mental hospitals are now virtually extinct, the narrative of loss and difference is preserved in the status of becoming a patient. This is clearly expressed by Barham and Hayward (1991: 2), who note that people who receive a diagnosis of schizophrenia tend to be viewed as 'lost to the disorder'. They become a stranger to themselves and others. They become alien:

> Schizophrenia is more than an illness that one has; it is something a person is or may become. The person who has suffered a schizophrenic illness is someone in which a drastic rupture has been effected in the continuity of his or her biography ... some schools of thought, we

discover, do not accept there is an 'after' with schizophrenia, only a 'before'.

The current use of the English word 'alien' to describe an outsider or foreigner resonates with the early nineteenth century use of the term 'alienist' to describe an expert on madness. This notion of 'otherness', which characterizes the discourse on psychosis, fits well with a new type of racism. The latter is preoccupied with who should be included or excluded from the mainstream of society:

> The new racism is primarily concerned with mechanisms of inclusion and exclusion. It specifies who may legitimately belong to the national community and simultaneously advances reasons for the segregation or banishment of those whose 'origin, sentiment or citizenship' assigns them elsewhere.   (Gilroy 1987: 45)

Within this discourse, people from black and ethnic minorities are identified as an alien force responsible for national decline and social disorder. While the old racism, underpinned by eugenics, proposed sterilization and extermination, the new racism suggests banishment and exclusion. In the context of the British historical legacy of colonialism, the debate on race and madness may be seen as central to the inner workings of this 'new racism'. This chapter has reviewed the evidence on the mental ill health of groups of people, who are the legacy of British colonialism as ex-slaves, servants, imported service labour and, in the case of the Irish, have been implicated in a post-colonial armed struggle.

Academic and psychiatric literature alluding to race accentuates those mental illnesses which imply a threatening and hostile alien presence. Professional and academic texts then become part of a wider discourse about a threat to a traditional social order. This threat includes: terrorism; non-Christian faiths; alien diet; arcane cultural norms; violent street crime; illicit drug use and so on. These images may then reinforce, or even be used to justify, English racism and endorse processes of segregation, exclusion or banishment.

Mental health and anti-terrorist legislation may be conceptualized as being part of what Althusser (1971) called the 'repressive state apparatus', which allows for preventive detention without trial, and the segregation or exclusion of threatening or undesirable 'others'. Banishment and exclusion can be reinforced by powers under mental health law to repatriate mentally ill aliens. Entry to the country on psychiatric grounds can also be banned under immigration legislation (Rogers and Pilgrim 1989).

However, the legitimacy of repatriation has declined in a context where a growing proportion of black people are British-born. It has become logically untenable. British-born black people have no identifiable nation state to which they can be banished (whether it be to the Indian subcontinent or the Caribbean of their parents, suggested only now by neo-Nazi groups in Britain). Likewise, Europeanization has ensured that rights of residence will be protected for people from any part of the British Isles.

Coercive psychiatry, as part of the wider repressive state apparatus, offers itself as a post-colonial, Europeanized alternative to repatriation. Ideas about banishment to another country can be replaced by the mechanisms of exclusion and control afforded by the mental hospital, prison and physical treatments. Not only are black and Irish people more likely to be incarcerated in locked facilities, and restrained using physical treatments, they are concomitantly represented as the 'other' in the texts and practices of academics and mental health professionals.

Most of what is summarized in this chapter is part of a discourse in which threat predominates, not distress. For example, compared with the extensive psychiatric literature on compulsorily detained African-Caribbean men, there is relatively little to be found on the sadness and despair of Asian women living in the community (Beliappa 1991; Fenton and Sadiq 1991). Ironically, this picture of differential attention is reinforced by some critiques which concur with our points here about repressive control in a post-colonial context. For example, Fernando, Ndegwa and Wilson (1998) provide an elaborate and sophisticated critique of post-colonial psychiatry. However, while their book is entitled *Forensic Psychiatry, Race and Culture*, the great bulk of their analysis focuses singularly on black people. The Irish appear nowhere in the text, even though many of the authors' arguments would also apply powerfully to this ethnic group.

This chapter has summarized arguments and evidence about the mental health of African-Caribbean, Asian and Irish people in Britain. It has drawn attention to methodological problems of interpreting evidence about over-representation and discussed the errors of Anglo-American psychiatry using a diagnostic approach which is ill suited to people from black and ethnic minority populations. At the time of writing, the challenge of understanding the impact of post-colonial conditions upon formerly colonized groups of people, be they black or white, has become complicated by new migration patterns.

Asylum seekers and refugees are now coming to Britain often with experiences of recent trauma. Sociological accounts of this group of people are now invited to add to the literature on those once colonized by Britain. Whereas those of Irish, Caribbean and South Asian origin are now British (and so cannot be repatriated), white racism in Britain is being turned daily to this effect on others coming here in recent years. This is likely to produce different sorts of mental health profiles for these newcomers. In other words the mental health of migrants is determined both by their departed country of origin and by the conditions awaiting them in their 'host' country.

Questions

1 What factors need to be considered when understanding the relationship between race and health?

2 Discuss the evidence about the psychiatric treatment of African-Caribbean people in Britain.

3 What factors might account for the over-representation of Irish people in psychiatric admissions?

4 What problems are highlighted for psychiatric knowledge by the 'somatization thesis'?

5 Discuss ways in which psychiatric services could improve their response to Asian people.

6 Discuss the role of racism in the creation of mental health problems and the character of psychiatric services.

For discussion

Consider the ways in which your background has influenced your views about mental health in your own racial group and in that of others.

Further reading

Fernando, S. (1995) *Mental Health in a Multi-Ethnic Society*. London: Routledge.

Kleinman, A. (1988) *Rethinking Psychiatry*. New York: Free Press.

Morgan, C., Mallett, R., Hutchinson, G. et al (2005) Pathways to care and ethnicity: Source of referral and help-seeking. *British Journal of Psychiatry* Apr 186: 290–6.

Smaje, C. (1996) The ethnic patterning of health: new directions for theory and research. *Sociology of Health and Illness*, 18(2): 139–71.

Chapter **6**

Age and ageing

Chapter overview

In this chapter, the mental health implications of three phases of the life span will be examined under the following topic headings:

- emotions and primary socialization;
- childhood sexual abuse and mental health problems;
- social competence in adulthood;
- dementia and depression in older people.

Emotions and primary socialization

During childhood two factors become highly relevant to the question of mental health. The first is the emotional life of young people. The second is primary socialization – the ways in which newcomers learn how to become accepted and acceptable members of their parent society. Both of these factors are relevant for our purposes, because the field of mental health implicates distressed experiences and distressing conduct on the one hand and deviance from norms on the other.

As far as emotions are concerned, sociologists have drawn largely upon psychoanalysis. Freudianism has influenced a variety of social theories from structural functionalism to neo-Marxism (the 'Frankfurt School'). Psychoanalysis (see Chapter 1) offers a theory which connects the individual's inner life to their external social context. It provides an account of emotional life of individuals, while at the same time offering an explanation of how mental ill health is determined by society. (For a wider discussion of the sociological status of psychoanalysis see Jacoby (1975); Holland (1978); Hirst and Woolley (1982); Craib (1989).)

For Freud, civilization puts limits on the free expression and experience of emotions, particularly the instincts of sexual desire and murderous aggression. These limits lead to the need of the child to repress their antisocial feelings in exchange for family and societal acceptance. This battle between emotions and social conformity leads to the development of neurosis. However, Freudianism is a limited social theory. Freud's emphasis is on civilization (Freud 1930) leading to repression and neurosis. According to Freud, we are all neurotic (to some extent) for more or less the same reasons to do with balancing our instinctual needs with the constraints of reality made clear to us by our parents. Consequently, differences between social groups were not addressed systematically by his theory, although later analytically oriented writers explored women's issues (Mitchell 1974; Eichenbaum and Orbach 1982).

Freud offered an explanation for neurotic behaviour arising from anxiety. Later psychoanalysts also tried to address the question of depression (Bowlby) and psychosis (Winnicott and Laing) by looking at the impact of poor care and separation on the infant (from birth to two years). However, as an example of the divergent views within psychoanalysis, the influential work of Melanie Klein is distinctive because it focused on the pathogenic impact of the infant's inborn aggression (rather than poor care). By contrast, the work of Bowlby, Winnicott and Laing was heavily environmentally oriented – it emphasized parental privation and deprivation as the source of later mental health problems. Whereas Klein can be seen to blame the instincts for mental ill health, the 'environmentalists' can be seen to point the finger at parents, particularly the mother.

Thus, variegated psychoanalytical accounts certainly emphasize a general social backdrop ('civilization') to emotional development, but the nuclear family then becomes its main frame of sociological reference. Mainstream clinical psychoanalysis tends to play down or ignore variables other than the family, such as the particular stresses associated with class, race, gender, age and sexuality. It also ignores the potentially powerful role of extra-familial social institutions, such as the school, in shaping the child's identity and their emotional life. Those psychoanalysts who have strayed into these wider areas of theorizing have tended to leave or be expelled from their professional culture (Reich 1942; Laing 1967; Masson 1990).

Psychoanalysis also assumes family relationships which are 'triangulated', that is, based on a set of tensions, which engender anxiety, created by children relating to a mother and a father. We now know that in many modern complex societies children grow up in contexts other than this, e.g. those with single or homosexual parents. (For an analysis of the social administrative role of psychoanalysis see Miller and Rose (1988).)

Turning to primary socialization, there is a strong consensus across theoretical positions in both sociology and psychology that childhood is a special part of the life span. It is a time when most of the rules and mores associated with the society and particular class and culture which the child inhabits are learned. It is also a time when gender-specific conduct is acquired. The child learns what is expected of him or her both at their current age and in the future, through their exposure to adult models of conduct. They learn gradually to control their body and their emotions in order to perform competently and efficiently in the presence of others. They learn the importance of a shared view of reality with their fellows in gaining security and in meriting credibility. All these learned capacities are also bound up with an increasingly elaborate and defined sense of identity. Thus, socialization is about learning how to behave in a context-appropriate way in society and it is about a person gaining a confident sense of who they are.

The relevance of socialization for mental health is that children learn to behave confidently and appropriately, following rules and complying with norms. This competence can fail if the person lacks the intellectual capacity to grasp what to do (currently this is termed a 'learning difficulty' and used to be called 'mental handicap' or 'mental subnormality'). It can also fail if the person lacks confidence in their performance as a social actor (this might be a way of thinking about 'phobic anxiety') or if they are too sad to participate in everyday activities ('depression'). The competence can also be adjudged to have failed by others if the person fails to comply with everyday expectations of appropriate behaviour in context or they make idiosyncratic claims about reality. We will return to this later when discussing schizophrenia.

A final aspect of socialization relevant to understanding mental health is that children learn to control their emotions. The strong emotional expressions tolerated in childhood become less and less acceptable as the person matures into adulthood. Consequently, if an adult becomes more exuberant or sad than is deemed appropriate for the context by others, they may acquire the label of 'manic depressive'. (For a sociological summary of the tasks of socialization in childhood see Dreitzel (1973).)

In modern industrial societies, which are regulated by versions of rationality, adult conduct is marked by a capacity to comply with both moral propriety and rational rules. By young adulthood, those of us who act either immorally, incompetently or irrationally will be deemed by others to be either bad or sick. Sometimes, which of these it is – badness or sickness – may be ambiguous both for lay onlookers and experts. As was noted in Chapter 1, mental illness can be understood as a particular form of deviancy which is not characterized by malice aforethought or motivated by personal gain or gratification, as is the case in criminal behaviour.

Part of our expectation of normality is that people will be competent in their social role and that their actions will be readily intelligible to us. So, if a person is so fearful or sad that their competence breaks down we may account for this in terms of mental ill health. In everyday western terms they have had a 'nervous breakdown'. Likewise, if someone acts in a way which we cannot understand, we may account for this in terms of them suffering from mental illness. An example here would be a person talking to voices that no one else can hear. Either way, mental illness might be understood sociologically as failed or incomplete socialization.

Such a view is reinforced by the emphasis given by psychologists from different schools to the legacy of childhood on adult competence. Most psychologists assume that problems in childhood make the person susceptible to later mental health problems. Likewise, sociological models of depression in adulthood emphasize developmental vulnerability factors as well as current stressors (Brown and Harris 1978, discussed in Chapter 4). The social causationist model of depression from Brown and Harris involves a multi-factorial approach. As far as childhood is concerned, a strong case has been recently made for a uni-factorial causationist model, which links a variety of mental health problems to sexual abuse in childhood. Because of the strong evidence for this relationship, we will look at this in some detail.

Sociology, childhood and mental health

Social epidemiologists have been concerned with exploring the cumulative risk of poor mental health, starting with adversity in childhood. However, in general terms, the relationship between age and mental health has only occasionally been addressed directly by sociologists. By comparison, socially oriented psychoanalysts have explored the topic more thoroughly, as have developmental psychologists and child psychiatrists.

This picture may reflect the low status that children have had within mainstream sociology. As Mayall (1998) has pointed out, children have been 'regarded unproblematically, as socialization projects within the private domain'. It is only relatively recently that a sociology of childhood has begun to be established, which focuses on understanding children's social position as a minority group and as 'embodied' health care actors and explores inter-generational relationships.

To date, little of this type of sociological work has been undertaken in the area of mental health. There has been some interest in people's conception of health and illness through subjectively defined stages of the life course (Backett and Davison 1995) and in the impact of mental health risk at different points in childhood, adolescence and adulthood (Power *et al.* 2002). However, there has been little integration of the different dimensions of ageing within sociological thought (Arber and Ginn 1991). An exception is the work of Backett-Milburn, Cunningham-Burley and Davis (2003), who explored the social and cultural processes in different accounts of childhood, health and inequalities provided by children. They found that children display considerable emotional resilience and tend to play down the effects of relationship and material factors. At the same time children highlight how familial and personal challenges, such as bullying, divorce or learning difficulties constitute a set of commonly held childhood experiences which cut across differences of class and gender.

This type of study on childhood processes is important because of the emergence of roles and norms during primary socialization (both traditional topics of interest for sociology as well as social psychologists). For example, children, adolescents and adults who follow a certain sequencing of their social roles are assumed to be better adjusted than their counterparts who follow other life course patterns. In early adulthood this normative order is defined as first entering the paid labour force, getting married, and later having children. Both men and women seem to benefit from following the normative course of role transitions. However there are differences for different population groups. For example a recent US study suggests that African-Americans who work first, then have children, and later get married report better mental health than their peers who followed the normative order (Jackson 2004).

It is well recognized that the point at which young people become adults is historically and socially constructed. Changing views about when a person is a child and when they become an adult has been evident in recent mental health research. For example, it has been found that early pubertal timing is associated with increased mental health problems (Kaltiala-Heino *et al.* 2003) Additionally, the point at which children are considered to become adults has implications for identifying mental health trends. A study found that malaise symptoms in the age group 11–16 seemed to have a similar pattern to young adults suggesting that the boundary between childhood and youth might need to be set at an earlier age (West and Sweeting 2004).

Societal values also seem to define to an extent what is acceptable treatment and management of children and adolescents with mental health problems. For example, substantial media attention has been focused on the issue of psychiatric medication use and ECT for children. While the use of medication has increased dramatically over the past three decades, for both children and adults, the vulnerability and special social status attributed to childhood means that this group receives more emotive and controversial coverage. This change has led to concerns about the long-term impact of medication on the immature brain (Carlezon and Konradi 2004) and the ethical implications of parents consenting to treatment (Breeding and Bauman 2001).

Lay people express mixed views about the use of medication in childhood. In a study of the acceptable use of Prozac, specifically for children, a survey of US public opinion found that while just over half of the adults interviewed considered it appropriate to use Prozac for children or adolescents expressing suicidal intentions but there was growing opposition to the use of such medication for hyperactivity and other behavioral problems (McLeod *et al.* 2004).

Childhood sexual abuse and mental health problems

While the connection between sexual abuse and distress can be viewed as a uni-factorial relationship, this does not imply that there is a consistent outcome for all victims. Individuals do vary in their responses to similar abusive acts, and the severity of the abuse, its duration and the relation of the perpetrator to the victim have all been linked to variable outcomes (Finkelhor 1984). Another caution is that sexual victimization may be part of a wider picture of family disturbance which could be pathogenic. As Briere and Runtz (1987: 51) point out:

> Although symptomatology in adulthood may covary with early sexual abuse, in the absence of further data it is not clear whether the former is caused by the latter or whether both are actually a function of some third variable, such as dysfunctional family dynamics.

The risk of childhood sexual abuse seems to be enhanced by a number of factors, such as troubled inter-generational attachment relationships in families. These include problems in maternal adult functioning, a negative relationship between the grandmother and mother, and a disrupted pattern of care giving during the mother's childhood (Leifer *et al.* 2004).

Reviews of the literature on the immediate and long-term effects of sexual abuse on child victims come to the conclusion that there is strong evidence that they are significantly more prone to mental distress than non-abused children (Wyatt and Powell 1988; Cahill, Llewelyn and Pearson 1991). Moreover, the offspring of survivors of childhood sexual abuse are at greater risk of mental health problems than others (Roberts *et al.* 2004). Not only is this evidence compelling but it points to a wide range of effects which may account, in part at least, for the higher rate of reported mental health problems in women than men. Overall, girls are at greater risk than boys of sexual victimization. This is certainly true of intra-familial abuse (Rogers and Terry 1984) although there is some evidence that boys may be at greater risk from stranger-perpetrators (Abel *et al.* 1987).

The large gap between male and female victims in terms of rates of abuse and rates of distressing consequences may be accounted for in part by the greater readiness of female victims to disclose on both counts (Finkelhor 1979). Also, as we pointed out in Chapter 4, the discourse on females has been more wide-reaching than that on males, with the bulk of the research on prevalence of abuse and its effects being focused on women, not men (Becker 1988; Dimock 1988).

Sexual abuse makes child victims more likely than non-abused children to demonstrate the following:

1 aggression;
2 sexually inappropriate behaviour;
3 sexual aggression.

'Sexually inappropriate behaviour' refers to the tendency of victims to become sexually interested in peers and adults in a way which is unusual for their age group. 'Sexual aggression' refers to this process when it is associated with anger or violence. This trio of symptoms characterizing child victims of sexual abuse does not mean that they have only these problems. Other forms of distress reported include those suffered by non-abused psychiatric referrals (anxiety, depression, night terrors, language delay, hyperactivity, stealing, peer relationship difficulties, eating disorders and so on). However, the trio does seem to mark sexual abuse victims off from non-abused children with emotional problems.

A number of epidemiological studies now indicate that these immediate externalizing effects in childhood translate into adult problems of both 'acting out' and of experienced distress. Studies of long-term effects have been on both clinical and community populations. Here we will give an example from each. Briere and Runtz (1988) examined the records of 152 consecutive women requesting appointments at the counselling department of an urban Canadian community health centre. Table 6.1 summarizes their results.

The significant results in the far right column alert us to the symptom profile of the abused group. Notice the suicidal behaviour and the substance abuse, as well as the battered adult picture. This phenomenon of 'revictimization' is common in adult survivors of childhood abuse. There is some evidence that disproportionate numbers of victims are found working as prostitutes (Browne and Finkelhor 1986).

Other studies indicate that some victims also become perpetrators. Estimates of this vary. Longo (1982) reported that 47 per cent of male adolescent sexual offenders had been victims themselves. Becker (1988) reports a figure of 19 per cent in her adolescent sexual offenders' clinic.

The focus of the clinical discourse on sexual abuse is on male perpetrators and, with the exceptions just quoted, female victims. Recently, a minority interest in female perpetrators has emerged suggesting that they constitute between 1 per cent and 10 per cent of offenders. Women are much less likely to act alone than male abusers (though paedophile rings of men working

Table 6.1 Differences between sexually abused (AB) and non-abused (NAB) female attenders at a Canadian community health centre for crisis counselling (*n* = 152)

	% NAB	% AB	Sig. level
Current psychotropic medication	14.0	31.3	0.01
History of hospitalization	22.1	19.4	ns
History of attempted suicide	33.7	50.7	0.03
Battered as adult	17.6	48.9	0.0003
History of rape	8.3	17.7	ns
History of drug addiction	2.3	20.9	0.0005
History of alcoholism	10.5	26.9	0.02
Restless sleep	54.7	71.6	0.03
Nightmares	23.3	53.7	0.0001
Anxiety attacks	27.9	53.7	0.001
Trouble controlling temper	18.6	38.8	0.006
Desire to hurt self	18.6	31.3	0.07
Sexual problems	15.1	44.8	0.0001
Fear of men	15.1	47.8	0.0001
Fear of women	3.5	11.9	0.09
Derealization	10.5	32.8	0.0001
Out of body experiences	8.1	20.9	0.04
Chronic muscle tension	44.2	65.7	0.008

Modified from Briere and Runtz (1988)

together also exist). The infamous cases of Myra Hindley and Rose West illustrate this type of male-female collusion in a dramatic way because it culminated in several murders. Less dramatic cases, stopping short of death, receive less publicity.

Given that the data reflects a preponderance of female victims and only a small minority of female perpetrators, it alerts us to the problems of accounting for sexual abuse, simply in terms of adults repeating abusive relationships from childhood. The switching from victim to perpetrator is not inevitable, nor can it be invoked as a strong causal explanation of most abusive acts, as most victims of both sexes do not go on to become perpetrators.

Turning to an example of a community survey, Stein *et al.* (1988) interviewed 3132 adults in two Los Angeles areas – one predominantly white, the other Hispanic (Table 6.2).

The symptom profile of victims is confirmed again in this study. Drug and alcohol abuse is evident, as are anxiety and depression. Significant differences do not appear in the groups in relation to diagnoses of schizophrenia, mania and obsessive-compulsive problems. The final column shows the consistent pattern of victims being more likely overall to receive a psychiatric diagnosis than non-victims. Elements in this range of adult personal difficulties seem to be more amplified in victims of intra-familial abuse than for those abused by non-relatives. Not only do they suffer the psychological impact of assault common to all victims, they also struggle with a particular sense of betrayal and stigma.

Finally in this section it is worth noting the likely underestimate of childhood sexual abuse as a social problem. The actual rate of childhood sexual abuse is difficult to ascertain because of a reluctance to disclose a traumatic and stigmatised event. A recent study indicates the pervasiveness of a reluctance to disclose with (78 per cent) of women interviewed about their experiences indicating that they had not told anyone about the sexual abuse when it happened. The most common reason for this was fear of not being believed (Lundqvist, Hansson and Svedin 2004).

The stigma of the abused victim and the shame and criminality of the perpetrator make accurate empirical estimates of child sexual abuse particularly difficult but logically suggest underestimation. Baker and Duncan (1985) suggest child sexual abuse rates of 0.25 per cent for relative and 10 per cent (12 per cent female and 8 per cent male) for non-relative abuse in Britain. If these are

Table 6.2 Lifetime prevalence of psychiatric problems in those sexually abused (AB) and those not (NA) in childhood ($n = 3132$)

	Men		Women	
	% NA	% AB	% NA	% AB
Alcohol abuse	23.2	35.7	4.1	20.8*
Drug abuse	7.8	44.9*	3.1	13.7*
Severe depression	3.9	13.8	5.5	21.9*
Phobic anxiety	7.0	6.5	12.5	34.2*
Any psychiatric diagnosis	34.0	71.2*	24.0	58.6*

* Significance level of 0.05. Figures summarized from Stein *et al.* (1988)

accurate estimates, around 4.5 million British adults are victims of earlier sexual abuse. In the US, Russell (1983) reports much higher rates in her community survey of women – 38 per cent reporting one experience of sexual abuse before 18 with 4.5 per cent of the sample reporting abuse by their biological fathers or stepfathers.

Prevalence rates of abuse victims of around 30 per cent are quoted by studies of psychiatric outpatient records (Gelinas 1983). This range of estimates poses a problem of interpretation. If Russell's estimates are correct, then it would appear that while the rates in the community of reported sexual abuse are high, this is not translating into a proportionate number of victims becoming psychiatric patients. What is implied instead, as with the Brown and Harris study of female depression in the community, is that there is a 'clinical iceberg' (see Chapter 1), with only some of the abuse victims presenting for professional help. By contrast, if the Baker and Duncan data is more accurate, then it would appear that sexual abuse during childhood is being reflected more closely in prevalence rates of psychiatric disorder.

Social competence in adulthood

One of the most controversial questions in current debates about mental health is the nature of schizophrenia (Bentall 1990; Boyle 1991). This diagnosis is the most common one given to those deemed to be suffering from a 'major mental illness'. It is also the one which is given most commonly in young adulthood. Orthodox psychiatric descriptions depict the schizophrenic as a person who is socially withdrawn and who suffers disturbances of cognition (thought disorder and delusions), perceptions (hallucinations) and emotions ('flat' or 'inappropriate' affect).

Psychiatrists are divided or uncertain about the cause or causes of such symptoms. Some argue that 'schizophrenia' is a genetically programmed 'time bomb' which explodes in adolescence, disturbing the functioning of the brain and the person. Others follow the view of Winnicott (1958) that it is an environmental disease, resulting from poor maternal care in the first year of life, leaving the person psychologically weak and without a secure sense of self. Adolescence marks a time when the person's sense of identity and capacity for independence is under scrutiny and strain, making them vulnerable to psychotic breakdown. Others have attempted to render schizophrenic behaviour intelligible within the confused and confusing communication pattern of the patient's family (Laing and Esterson 1964).

Because of weak aetiological agreement, schizophrenia is particularly vulnerable to labelling and constructivist critiques (Bentall, Jackson and Pilgrim 1988; Boyle 1991). If the diagnosis is stigmatizing to its recipients, and of little use value to researchers, then such critiques become predictable. Boyle, for instance, notes that one of the conceptual weaknesses of the diagnosis is that it rests solely on symptoms, not signs. Consequently, it can never be validated in any way other than a circular fashion. Put simply, a person is deemed to be schizophrenic because of their oddity and they are deemed to be odd because they are suffering from schizophrenia. Boyle draws an analogy with diabetes.

There, the subjective experience of fatigue can be checked against signs of hyperglycaemia in a blood test. Schizophrenia rests on value judgements about the person's unintelligible behaviour but has no equivalent of a blood test. This does not imply that diagnoses of physical illness cannot be deconstructed, nor does it imply that value judgements are absent in physical diagnoses. However, it does point to the particular construct validity problems of a diagnosis of schizophrenia and other 'functional' psychiatric disorders.

The questions begged for sociologists about schizophrenia are thus mainly about how it is negotiated or ascribed. This tack has been taken most systematically by Coulter (1973). He argues that focusing on debates about aetiology obscures the ways in which madness emerges, first through social negotiation in the lay area and then in professional confirmation (a diagnosis). Coulter focuses on everyday expectations of normality and competence. For instance, in relation to hallucinations he argues that to maintain our credibility in a social group there has to be a consensus about what our senses detect around us. In most contexts, if a person sees or hears something which others do not, then their credibility, and therefore their social group membership, is jeopardized. However, it is possible in certain contexts that such idiosyncratic capacities might strengthen rather than weaken their credibility and group status. The Christian mystic and some African medicine men are expected to have extraordinary visions. Indeed, their social credibility may rest on having these abnormal experiences.

In some cultures where hallucinations are valued positively, the bodily circumstances which increase the probability of their occurrence (fasting, fatigue, drug taking and so on) are often contrived deliberately. Al-Issa (1977) notes that, in western society, hallucinations offend rationality. Most of us suppress idiosyncratic perceptions because we learn that they are valued negatively. The 'schizophrenic' in contrast makes the mistake of, or is driven to, acting upon their idiosyncratic experiences. Community surveys indeed point to estimates of between 10 per cent and 50 per cent of the 'normal' population who hallucinate (Bentall and Slade 1985).

Thus, atypical idiosyncratic perceptions are not intrinsically pathological (although most western psychiatrists may insist that this is the case). Whether hallucinations are deemed to indicate a gift or a defect depends on the roles people occupy in particular cultures. Likewise, weird speech patterns are highly valued in those Christian sects which respect the ability to 'speak in tongues' (or 'glossolalia') (Szasz 1992; Bentall and Pilgrim 1993). Outside of these sects, in everyday western life, they may be taken to be an offence to rational discourse and so encourage attributions of mad talk from their fellows. Later these may be reframed as evidence of schizophrenic thought disorder by a psychiatrist.

Some recent sociological accounts of madness have gone beyond Coulter's point about the attribution of unintelligibility and explored the meaning of patient narratives as a pathway to understanding how people live with a psychiatric diagnosis. Once a young person receives a diagnosis of 'schizophrenia' then they reflect on their pre-existing sense of self. These reflections on identity are not always negative (Dinos, Lyons and Finlay 2005). This ambiguity can be contrasted with the tendency of significant others to see the patient as being 'lost' to the illness (Barham and Hayward 1991).

All of these ambiguities generated by contextualized approaches to narratives or the meaning of specific unusual experiences ('symptoms' in Western medical terms) can be contrasted with a traditional view from medical naturalism or positivism. Generally, psychiatrists have tended to conceive of thought disorder as a stable set of cognitive idiosyncrasies or failures: woolly thinking, vagueness, bizarre content, neologisms (invented new words), poverty of thought, fixed and rigid or repetitive expressions. Similarly they have simply assumed that hearing voices is inherently pathological. However, these medical attributions are extracted from the contexts in which judgements are made about social competence.

Coulter emphasizes that, in fact, people may be judged sane by their fellows and yet often manifest such cognitive failures. Following Coulter, what matters are the circumstances in which in one social setting such speech oddities are judged or are valued to indicate madness (by lay people) and confirmed subsequently as schizophrenic illness by psychiatrists. When we discussed labelling theory earlier in Chapter 2 this was described in terms of 'contingencies'.

For Coulter, there are no abstract defining qualities of schizophrenic thought, but there are social settings in which the thoughts of some people are judged to be meaningless or illegitimate. These settings, and the decisions associated with them, involve family members and neighbours at home, or strangers in public places, who appeal for the attendance of psychiatric professionals to deal with a discomforting situation. In other words, madness, like the sanity with which it is contrasted, is socially negotiated. Consequently, the best that sociologists can do is to describe the particular contexts in particular cultures in which ascriptions of madness are made. To do this, knowledge of norms and competence are vital for the investigator. The latter is really studying a moral order and the way in which social actors attempt to maintain its stability by correcting or removing offending group members.

While most cultures across time and place have some notion of oddity or madness, because norms of sanity vary, this notion is not constant. Nor is there a transcultural or trans-historical consensus on what causes oddity or how to respond to it when it emerges (Sedgwick 1982; Horwitz 1983). Each culture may have a notion of what it means to lose one's reason but these notions vary across time and place and so undermine the claims of modern western psychiatry that 'schizophrenia' and its symptoms are a stable set of factors to be studied.

When we considered labelling theory earlier, the work of Scheff was noted. For Scheff (1966) mental disorder is 'residual deviance', i.e. left over after criminality and other bad conduct are considered, but not attributed, by observers. 'Schizophrenia' for Scheff was then the 'residue of the residue' – a catchall ascription of madness, when other forms of mental disorder had been considered and rejected.

The diagnosis of schizophrenia predominates in young adulthood because that is when role expectations based on rational rule following and goal orientation are highlighted. It is the age when the rationality of work and parenting are demanded of, and by, those involved. The schizophrenic defies or violates these expectations.

Dementia and depression in older people

It is commonly assumed that in old age biological determinants take on a greater significance in accounting for deterioration in social competence, in conditions described collectively as the 'senile dementias'. Over half a million people in the UK suffer from the best known of these (Alzheimer's Disease), a figure projected to rise to a prevalence of 750,000 over the next 15 to 20 years (Alzheimer's Disease Report 1992).

However, the salience of dementia in mental health services and its purported biological causes in older people may be exaggerated. As well as people with dementia needing social support to maximize their quality of life and avoid physical jeopardy, there are many more older people with cognitive problems who have no proven neurological condition. Kitwood (1988) points out that Alzheimer's dementia can only be properly diagnosed post-mortem. Moreover, some people who are clearly confused and suffering impaired memory show no post-mortem neurological signs, whereas others who are not demented may show neurological deterioration. The loss of personhood which accompanies the progression of dementia has also been linked to the notion of 'social death'. Those who are close to the sufferer come to believe and sometimes act as if, the person is already dead (Sweeting and Gilhooly 1997).

Another point to note about dementia is that while it is mainly a problem of old age, it can occur, albeit more rarely, in middle age (pre-senile dementia). An example of an even younger population being affected is the small but increasing incidence in CJD among teenagers and those in their 20s, which appears to be causally related to eating products of cattle infected with BSE during the 1980s.

There is a secondary mental health impact of dementia which affects informal carers (Morris, Morris and Britton 1988). Stress reactions are common in this group of carers, although some other studies highlight positive as well as negative psychological features of the caring role (Orbell, Hopkins and Gillies 1993). In Chapter 11 we examine the problematic status of the concept of 'carer'. However, here we will note that, in those with advanced dementia, direct physical care is demanded in a way which is usually not implied in younger patients with diagnoses such as schizophrenia.

While dementia may have become a dominant modern culture image of becoming elderly, depression is actually more prevalent. While the prevalence of dementia is about 5 per cent in the over 65s, rising to just below 20 per cent for those over 80, depression is much more common in the younger age band of older people. In Britain, community surveys indicate prevalence rates for depression of between 5 per cent in Edinburgh (Maule, Milne and Williamson 1984) and 26 per cent in Newcastle (Kay, Beamish and Roth 1964) for people over 65. Other studies more typically quote rates of 11 per cent to 15 per cent (Copeland *et al.* 1987).

About 2 per cent of the UK population of over 65s is in residential care. In this particular population, the prevalence of depression rises dramatically. A London survey of 12 old-people's homes revealed that around 40 per cent of the residents were depressed (Mann, Graham and Ashby 1984). Surveys in Sydney, Australia (Snowden and Donnelly 1986) found one-third of the residents depressed and a similar survey finding was reported from Milan, Italy (Spagnoli *et al.* 1986). Mild depression is more common in older women than men and it is also more prevalent in those suffering from physical illnesses (Brayne and Ames 1988).

The extent of the association of depression and physical ill health is shown by a study of 100 patients referred over a 30-month period to a psychogeriatric service with depression (Dover and McWilliam 1992). The authors found that only 3 per cent of the men and 20 per cent of the women patients were physically well. The rest had a variety of serious complaints including cancer, cardiovascular disease, arthritis, deafness and respiratory problems. Sixty-five per cent of the sample had 'multiple illness'. Moreover, many of the drug treatments for some of these physical disorders are known to cause or amplify depressed mood, suggesting an iatrogenic component in this group of depressed physically ill patients. The association of depression with physical illness in old age is highlighted by a recent review of several studies of medical (i.e. not psychiatric) in-patients which concludes that only one in five recover from their lowered mood state before death (Cole and Bellavance 1997). Suicide rates also increase in the older age group, and this is mainly accounted for by the high rates of male deaths.

What are the social implications of the data from psychiatric epidemiology of depression in older people? Starting with the very high rates of depression in residential homes, there are three explanations for these prevalence rates, which are not mutually exclusive:

1 It could be that *those selected to enter these homes* have been adjudged by relatives or professionals already to be in poor mental health, or vulnerable because of their lonely and under-supported home conditions (hence their referral to the homes).
2 The *under-stimulating environment* of these homes may induce apathy and morbid introspection (in the jargon of psychiatry 'dysphoria'). This has led some psychiatrists of old age to speculate that the homes may contain a number of people who are not 'clinically depressed' but who, instead, suffer from environmentally induced dysphoria, which may dissipate with a more stimulating care regime (Pitt 1988). Such a construction on the data of course assumes that there are clear demarcations to be made between clinical descriptions of 'true' depression and other experiences, such as apathy, anomie, listlessness, sad brooding and so on. Some other psychogeriatricians have pointed out that, in fact, it is not easy in the bulk of cases of sad old people to pigeonhole them as being 'ill' or 'not ill' (Murphy 1988).
3 Being moved to a residential facility is disruptive, entails a loss of previous surroundings and may mark a loss of personal control or autonomy. This *imposed disruption and loss* may have a depressing toll on the old person.

Turning to the community data on depression in old age, there are other explanations that could be offered for depression in old people, who are not in residential care.

1 The probability of *physical illness increases with age* and this in turn makes older people vulnerable to depression (Post 1969). However, Blaxter (1990), studying the self-reported physical and mental well-being of people across

the life-span, found that overall psycho-social well-being improves relatively in old age. This could be partially accounted for by the lower expectations of life quality in old age leading to an under-reporting of distress.
Another factor is the dramatic improvement in the self-reported psycho-
social well-being of richer people living in more comfortable surroundings
(see below).

   An implication of the association of physical illness and depression is that
good and effective physical care of depressed, poorer older people may have
an ameliorative impact. Murphy (1988) suggests that the provision of aids
for associated disability and other practical help to lessen the dependency of
older physically ill people on their relatives may raise morale in the family
system and thereby help lift depression.

2 Relationships that have accumulated during the life-span are lost. Spouses,
friends and siblings die off around a surviving older person, making that
person prone to *the aggregating effect of grief*. Depression in old age may be
understandable in whole or part as cumulative grief.

3 Another social vulnerability factor is that of *material adversity*. In a community study of life events preceding depression in old age, Murphy (1982)
found that poorer people who had experienced housing and financial
difficulties were more prone to depression (of both mild and severe propor-
tions) than better-off older people. Blaxter (1990) found that the psycho-
social well-being of older people varied significantly with social class. Social
classes 1 and 2 improved with age overall but those in social classes 4 and 5
deteriorated. (For a discussion of class and other variables affecting social
support see Wenger (1989).)

4 Another consideration is the *role of supportive and confiding relationships*.
Lowenthal (1965) found, like Brown and Harris (1978) in their study of
younger women, that the presence of a stable confiding relationship was a
protective factor against depression in old age. She also found that those
most vulnerable are old people who try to form relationships and fail, rather
than people who have coped throughout life alone. Murphy (1982) found in
her community survey that 30 per cent of those reporting the lack of a
confiding relationship were depressed. Given that 70 per cent of this group
were not depressed, a multi-factorial model of vulnerability and protective
factors seems to be indicated (as with Brown and Harris (1978)).

5 A final depressogenic factor to consider is that of *abuse in old age*. Eastman
(1984) suggested that estimates of abused older people in the US vary from
600,000 to over a million. As with the abuse of children, prevalence and
incidence are difficult to investigate accurately, given that abusers will typically deny the act. When the abuse occurs at the hands of paid carers, their
job is at stake, as well as their reputation. Estimates of elder abuse rates in
Scandinavia vary from 8 per cent to 17 per cent of older victims across
Denmark, Sweden and Finland. In one of the Swedish samples 12 per cent of
relatives admitted violence (Hydle 1993).

   Some authors extend the notion of elder abuse to medical neglect and
iatrogenic disease in hospitalized older people (Gorbien, Bishop and Beers
1992). They include here: poor skin care; poor infection control; failure to
make accurate physical diagnoses; leaving frail elders to risk falls; and
inadequate dietary provision (as a cost-cutting method). The immediate and
long-term negative psychological effects of abuse are difficult to ascertain. It

is self-evident that sexual or emotional abuse or physical violence against, or neglect of, old people will not enhance their mental health.

A complicating factor is that confused older people who suffer from dementia are prone to violence themselves at times which may trigger reactive aggression in some of their care givers. In one study (Paveza *et al.* 1992) it was found that in the year following a diagnosis of Alzheimer's Disease, 15.8 per cent of patients and 5.4 per cent of their carers were violent. Usually, age as a perpetrator risk factor for violence is linked to youth, but dementia raises the probability of violent acts in (one group) of older people.

Service provision for older people is skewed towards providing for dementia. However, recently there has been some effort to provide for older people experiencing depression from within primary care. Treatment regimes for depression seem to mirror those being provided for other groups experiencing depression, which focus mainly on the use of anti-depressants (Baldwin *et al.* 2003). More normalized activities might seem to offer amelioration. For example, gardens have been identified as a 'therapeutic landscape'. Gardening activities have been found to offer comfort and opportunity emotional and spiritual renewal. Communal gardening activity on allotments has been found to contribute to psychological well-being through the provision of a mutually supportive environment which enhances emotional well-being through combating social isolation, contributing to the development of social networks and enhancing the quality of life and emotional well-being of older people (Milligan, Gatrell and Bingley 2004).

Discussion

The sociological consideration of the life-span and mental health is clearly uneven. At the start of life, socialization is considered to be important and there is certainly no shortage of interest in this arena of social determinism. Indeed, the consensus is very strong within social science that upbringing, acculturation and rule learning are all necessary considerations about societal functioning and the relationship between the individual and the collective. Admittedly, some have complained that this theorizing has been exaggerated (Wrong 1961) but, generally, primary socialization is given a privileged position in a variety of sociological (and psychological) theories. We noted at the start, though, that the sociological connection between primary socialization and mental health has been relatively under-scrutinized.

Psychoanalysis, a form of socialization theory itself derived from the psychological treatment of people with mental health problems, seems to have had a pervasive influence on different types of sociology. As far as childhood is concerned, sociological interest thus far has been theory-dominated. Despite this wide-ranging theoretical discourse about socialization, few sociologists have done empirical work on childhood and its problems (although there is the work of Russell and Finkelhor in the area of child sexual abuse and James and Prout (1990) who have studied 'normal' children).

The evidence of child sexual abuse we reviewed has, ironically, posed particular problems for clinical psychoanalysis. This theoretical framework, which has appealed so strongly to so many sociologists, has found itself accused of a central cultural role in suppressing evidence of the sexual abuse of children. This is because of Freud's reversal of his theory in 1896. Prior to then, Freud tended to believe women patients' recollections of incest from childhood. After that time, Freud succumbed to the more comforting notion that these represented subjective fantasies on the part of patients. This then became the accepted 'wisdom' when dealing with patient-reported abuse by Freud's clinical followers (Masson 1985).

When we turn to the core of psychiatry interventions in young adulthood and beyond sociology became enmeshed with a social movement in the 1960s to challenge or discredit clinical theory and practice (see Chapters 2 and 7). Scheff's labelling theory and Goffman's critique of the asylum from within symbolic interactionism were associated with 'anti-psychiatry'. The retreat from this association with political activism and 'counter-culture' was then reflected in the sociology of mental health. The latter became more theoretical with the emergence of post-structuralist appraisals of psychiatric discourse. This was, in part, a reaction against the humanism and civil libertarianism which had been associated with anti-psychiatry. These post-1960s sociological approaches can be contrasted again historically with the earlier epidemiological tradition of the social causationists. The latter have not disappeared from the map of the sociology of mental health, given the community survey approaches of, for instance, Brown and Harris and Murphy in the 1970s and 1980s.

The main sociological deductions about mental health problems in older people have, mostly, to be made from clinical researchers (social psychiatrists like Murphy). Consequently, harder data is considered from epidemiological surveys at the expense of sociological theorizing. While sociologists have theorized childhood extensively, but done little empirical work, they have done little in either realm as far as old people and their mental health problems are concerned. What theory does exist about later life has come from depth psychologists and has been poorly tested empirically (e.g. Erik Erikson's life-stage theory) or is from a position that emphatically privileges the individual over society (e.g. that of Carl Jung).

This relative absence of sociological work on the mental health of older people may reflect a lesser-valued group of people who are consequently as readily ignored by sociologists as they are by other people of employable age. This leaves older people being studied in the main by clinicians or by those who have taken a particular interest in social policy rather than social theory (e.g. Walker 1980; Townsend 1981; Wenger 1989). 'Gerontology' as a hybrid academic discipline overlaps with, but is not a sub-discipline of, sociology. While sociologists have contributed substantially to gerontology (Fennell, Phillipson and Evers 1988; Jefferys 1989) the specific issue of mental health remains largely absent from their ambit of interest.

Thus, there are three main questions for sociologists given the above summary. First, should they now immerse themselves more in empirical research about childhood and mental health? Given that so many articles of faith have been linked to the theoretical assumptions of this period, for instance that the events of the formative years are predictive of adult personal functioning, sociologists could test their theoretical assumptions against longitudinal investigations. Second, will psychiatric professionals and their diagnostic and treatment activities be the continued focus of interest for the examination of adult mental health or will sociologists seek out new topics and dimensions of inquiry? Third, will sociologists be able to apply their liking for theorizing to the grey topic of older people, or will the latter continue to be scrutinized mainly by clinicians and social policy researchers?

This chapter has taken three periods in the life-span (childhood, young adulthood and old age) and examined their implications for mental health. The importance of socialization has been emphasized and disputes about its meaning and relevance discussed. Adulthood brings with it expectations of role-rule consistency which mentally ill people challenge in their functioning. The social factors discussed in old age draw our attention to the importance of depression, not just dementia. They also highlight that ageism is present in sociological interest in mental health.

Questions

1 Why has the concept of primary socialization been so important in social science?

2 What is the relevance of primary socialization for adult mental health?

3 Discuss the impact of childhood sexual abuse on adult mental health.

4 What does the diagnosis of schizophrenia tell us about social norms?

5 What social factors influence the mental health of older people?

6 The sociology of mental health and illness is ageist – discuss.

For discussion

Think about your own family and others you know and consider the link between age and mental health within their relationships.

Further reading

Bifulco, A. and Moran, A. (1998) *Wednesday's Child: Research into Women's Experience of Neglect and Abuse in Childhood and Adult Depression.* London: Routledge.

Bright, R. (1997) *Wholeness in Later Life.* London: Jessica Kingsley Publishers.

Coulter, J. (1973) *Approaches to Insanity.* New York: Wiley.

Gearing, B., Johnson, M. and Heller, T. (eds) (1988) *Mental Health Problems in Old Age*. London: Wiley.

Kitwood, T. and Bredin, K. (1992) Towards a theory of dementia care: person-hood and well-being. *Ageing and Society*, 10: 177–96.

Chapter 7

The mental health professions

Chapter overview

The questionable legitimacy of categories of mental illness (discussed in Chapter 1) extends to the roles, identities and functions of mental health workers. The explicit control function of mental health professionals, alongside their role as paid carers, has meant that they have often been scrutinized in a more critical light than many other groups of health professionals. This chapter will cover:

- theoretical frameworks in the sociology of the professions;
- mental health professionals and other social actors;
- sociology and the mental health professions;
- the impact of legislative arrangements and service redesign.

Theoretical frameworks in the sociology of the professions

When sociologists first began to investigate professionals they provided a set of rather flattering descriptions. This was because, by and large, they were prepared to accept definitions provided by professionals themselves. These tended to emphasize that practitioners have unique skills, which are put altruistically at the service of the public. This early credulous view has now changed substantially in the light of many critical accounts of the professions. For example, Illich (1977a) talks of medicine being a 'threat to health' and of welfare professionals being 'disabling' (Illich 1977b). Others reviewing the rise of the new middle class have accused welfare professionals of manipulating both the rich and poor in society for their own interests, as both providers and users of services (Gould 1981). Gouldner (1979) goes as far as speculating that professionals are coming to dominate not just public services but industrial, and even military, life.

Despite these criticisms (ironically by and large from professional academics), for many ordinary people the word 'professional' still tends to imply both special skills and ethical propriety. It implies competence, efficiency, altruism and integrity. Hence, the converse of this is the everyday notion of what it means to be 'unprofessional' – to behave incompetently, inefficiently or unethically. As for contemporary sociologists, they largely agree on some basic characteristics of professionals:

1 Professionals have grown in importance over the past 200 years and expanded massively in number during the past century;
2 Professionals are concerned with providing services to people rather than producing inanimate goods;
3 Whether salaried or self-employed, professionals have a higher social status than manual workers;
4 This status tends to increase as a function of length of training required to practise;
5 Generally, professionals claim a specialist knowledge about the service they provide and expect to define and control that knowledge;
6 Credentials give professionals a particular credibility in the eyes of public and government alike.

However, beyond this rough consensus, there is much debate about how professions might be understood sociologically. Here we will look at some of the main frameworks used within sociology to understand professions.

The neo-Durkheimian framework

Overviewers of the field of the sociology of the professions (Saks 1983; Abel 1988) emphasize a certain progression of events. At first, as has been mentioned, sociologists tended to simply categorize the professions and describe their work uncritically. Claims of special knowledge and altruism were taken at face value. This early sociological depiction of positive qualities was dubbed the 'trait' approach to the professions. A parallel and equally uncritical approach to the professions was provided by the structural functionalist accounts, which saw the professions as a static or stable social stratum which offered a socially cohesive role (Parsons 1939; Goode 1957). Durkheim saw professions as providing a disinterested integrative social function. They were one of the social forces which counterbalanced the tendency of ego-tistical individuals to fragment society. For the Durkheimian tradition, pro-fessions are a source of community for one another and stability for the wider society they serve. They regulate their own practitioners, ensuring good practice by establishing codes of conduct and punishing errant colleagues. They regulate their clients in their interest and in the interest of their host society.

The neo-Weberian framework

Those in the Weberian tradition (Freidson 1970; Abel 1988) emphasize that the professions develop strategies to: advance their own social status; persuade clients and potential clients about the need for the service they offer; and corner the market in that service and exclude competitors. Two notions in particular emerge from this picture for those following Weber.

Social closure

Collective social advancement rests upon social closure. By cornering the mar-ket, professionals offer a service which is closed off from others. A monopoly is gained to work in a specialized way with a particular group of clients (e.g. medical practitioners treating sick people) so that other occupational groups seeking a similar role are excluded. This closing off also means that only those inside the boundaries of the profession can scrutinize its practices – others are denied access and are kept in a state of ignorance. In order for professionals to maintain their social status they must convince those on the outside of their boundaries that they are offering a unique service and so they develop various rhetorical devices to persuade the world at large of their special qualities. To do this they must justify a peculiar knowledge base that has a technical or scien-tific rationality on the one hand, but that, on the other, is not so easy to understand that anybody can use it. Medicine as a whole can be seen to pro-vide such accounts to the world. However, this persuasion is precarious. The growth of alternative medicine (Saks 1992) is testimony to this, as are the doubts about the coherence and credibility of psychiatric knowledge which we examined in Chapter 1.

Professional dominance

The second main feature of this Weberian picture is that of professional dom-inance. Professionals exercise power over others in three senses:

1 *They have power over their clients*. The latter, convinced of the need for the service they are offered or seek, are dependent on professionals. An imbal-

ance of specialized knowledge keeps the client in a state of ignorance, insecurity and vulnerability. This power imbalance is reinforced if the professional operates on their own territory rather than that of their client, for instance by treating people in hospital rather than their own home.

2 *Professionals exercise power over their new recruits.* Thus, a dominance hierarchy is common in professions, with senior practitioners and trainers exercising control and discipline over their juniors. Power enjoyed in the upper ranks of a profession can only be secured by submission and deference in earlier junior days, as trainees are dependent on their superiors for career progression.

3 *Professionals seek to establish a dominant relationship over other occupational groups working with the same clients.* Professionals may seek to exclude existing equal competitors or they may seek to usurp the role of existing superiors. In medicine, in addition to excluding competitors (e.g. orthopaedic specialists who have kept chiropractors and osteopaths out of official health service practice) they also subordinate them (obstetricians directing the work of midwives) or limit their therapeutic powers to one part of the body (e.g. dentistry and optometry).

Thus, power relationships are of central importance to neo-Weberians. These are about gaining and retaining power over clients, new entrants and other occupational groups working with those clients. One way of thinking about the neo-Weberian focus is in terms of horizontal relationships between professionals and those they work with, as colleagues or clients, in order to sustain or extend the material advantages, status and comforts of middle-class life in society.

The neo-Marxian framework

When we look to the Marxian tradition, power relationships are also important, but now the focus is on vertical structural relationships. The question to be answered by neo-Marxians is: 'where do professionals fit into a social structure which is characterized by two main groups: those who work to produce wealth (surplus value) in society (the working class or proletariat) and those who own the means of production and exploit these workers and expropriate surplus value as profits (capitalists, the ruling class or the bourgeoisie)?' Marx gave scant attention to the third group of interest to us: those functionaries or 'white collar' workers who were neither exploitative capitalists who owned the means of production nor workers who produced goods and profits for their bosses in exchange for wages. Consequently, those sociologists upholding a Marxian tradition of analysis have had a number of conceptual difficulties with the professions.

Three positions have been taken up by neo-Marxians about the professions. The latter are deemed either to be part of the ruling class or part of the proletariat, or to constitute a separate and new social class holding contradictory qualities. The first type of claim is made by Navarro (1979) who argues that, for instance, the medical profession actually constitutes a part of the ruling class in capitalist society.

By contrast, Oppenheimer (1975) claims that the 'knowledge-based' professions have had control over their work eroded by the state bureaucracies which employ them (they have been subjected to 'bureaucratic subordination'). As a result, their control over their specialized skills has diminished ('deskilling') and consequently they have become part of the working class ('proletarianization'). Oppenheimer understands the collectivist strategies of professions as being no different from traditional trade union defences of working-class terms and conditions of employment. This contrasts with the neo-Weberians, who point to such collective action as being about upward social mobility. Thus, the neo-Weberians are clearly much more critical of the professions than Oppenheimer, who treats them with the sympathy implied by their status as an exploited group of workers who are vulnerable to wage erosion and unemployment.

Clearly, Navarro and Oppenheimer cannot both be totally correct if they claim to operate within the same sociological tradition started by Marx. Their apparent opposition is rescued by a third group of neo-Marxians who argue that they are both partially correct. This group, exemplified by the work of Carchedi (1975), Johnson (1977) and Gough (1979), emphasizes the contradictory position of professionals in capitalist society. They are not capitalists but they serve the interests of the latter. They are not full members of the proletariat (as they do not produce goods and surplus value) but they are employees and so they share similar vulnerabilities and interests of the working class. For instance, mental health workers would be seen in this contradictory position as being both agents of social control acting on behalf of the capitalist state and employees of that state and so vulnerable to the same problems of any other group of workers.

Eclecticism and post-structuralism

The above picture of competing views is complicated further by many analysts of the professions drawing liberally on more than one tradition. For instance, Parry and Parry (1977), when discussing the rise of militant trade unionism within the junior ranks of the British medical profession in the 1970s, utilize Weber's notion of closure and Oppenheimer's proletarianization thesis. They go as far as arguing that Weber actually anticipated Oppenheimer's insights and thus they see no dispute between the Marxian and Weberian types of analysis about modern professions.

As we will see later in relation to the mental health professions, it is now common for sociologists to approach their work eclectically – they draw on more than one theoretical tradition. For some this has become an explicit prescription for analysis. For instance, Turner (1987: 140), when discussing health professions, comments that 'a satisfactory explanation of professionalization as an occupational strategy will come eventually to depend upon both Weberian and Marxian perspectives'.

One important shift in social theory, post-structuralism, now goes beyond eclecticism. One of its main intellectual leaders, Foucault considers that social analysis entails examining a:

> . . . heterogenous ensemble consisting of discourses, institutions, architectural forms, regulatory decisions, laws, administrative measures,

scientific statements, philosophical, moral and philanthropic propositions – in short the said and the unsaid.

In particular, Foucault and his followers are concerned to map out discourses associated with particular social periods and places. This notion of discourse includes both forms of knowledge and the practices associated with that knowledge. For this reason, the notion of 'discursive practices' might connote more accurately the focus of the post-structuralists when discussing the professions.

The Foucauldians provide a different way of looking at applied knowledge in professional work. They have no notion of a clear or stable power discrepancy between professionals and clients or between dominant professions and subordinate ones. Power is dispersed, it cannot be simply and easily located in any elite group. While it is certainly bound up with dominant discursive features of a particular time and place, these may change and they may be resisted. For Foucault and his followers, ways in which the person (the body and mind of the individual) is now described or constructed (measured, analysed and codified) are central features of contemporary society. Medicine and professions close to it have had a central role in this regard with their interests in diagnosis, testing, assessment and observation and the treatment, management and surveillance of sick and healthy bodies in society. However, in the post-structuralist account there is a failure to endorse the notion of self-conscious collective activity of professionals, to advance their own interests or to act on behalf of the capitalist state.

As we will see later, the mental health professions have been of particular interest to post-structuralists. This is probably because of the 'psy complex' having a chronic surveillance role in relation to mental patients and because it has been associated with two types of discourse. The first of these emphasized segregation and acting on the body (physical treatments) and the second emphasized the construction of the self via a set of psychological accounts (counselling and psychotherapy). The attack on the body and the construction of the self represent two key ways of understanding the activities of mental health professionals.

The above four general sociological frameworks have been the most influential in understanding the professions. As we will see below, in relation to mental health work, other sociological approaches have also been influential. These include symbolic interactionism, the sociology of knowledge, the sociology of deviance and feminist sociology. Before we discuss these let us look at the relationships which mental health workers have with other key social actors.

Mental health professionals and other social actors

A number of professional groups contribute to mental health work. The most obvious collection – psychiatrists, clinical psychologists, social workers, psychiatric nurses, occupational therapists, art therapists, counsellors and psychotherapists – is employed with the explicit assumption that mental health work is their main role. For this reason, they, or their practice and knowledge, are sometimes referred to as 'the psy complex' by post-structuralists (Ingleby 1983). One way of approaching the sociology of the mental health professions is in terms of seeking out examples within the above sociological frameworks which apply to mental health specialists. However, it would be misleading to give the impression that this core group in the mental health industry provides the only professional input in terms of contact with people entering the patient role or in terms of the negotiation of what constitutes a mental health problem. A variety of other personnel are also implicated, including general practitioners, the clergy, the police and social services care or case managers.

DeSwaan (1990) makes the point that members of the public are encouraged through personal contact with professionals and their clients, and through the media, to frame their personal difficulties in professional terms. He calls this process 'proto-professionalization'. For DeSwaan, what start as personal troubles or discomforts about a person's relationship with others can be framed as problems amenable to specialist help, even before contact with professionals occurs.

While DeSwaan focuses on the voluntary presentation to professions by those seeing themselves as suffering these difficulties, as we noted in Chapter 6, Coulter (1973) points out that members of the public also look to professions to rescue them from discomfort or threat caused by others whom they deem to have a mental health problem. Thus, the public are centrally involved in inserting mental health problems into the domain of professional activity in two senses. Sometimes they label themselves in advance as having a problem amenable to specialist help. At other times they look to professionals to help them cope with the distress, threat or anxiety which results from the conduct of others.

Thus, consideration of non-specialist professionals and lay people is important to understand how specialists obtain and retain their mandate of authority about mental health. We can think in terms of four groups of social actors who interact with one another to define the field of mental health problems:

1 The State (represented by politicians, civil servants and managers);
2 Mental health specialists;
3 Professionals who are implicated in mental health work some of the time (GPs, the police, the clergy) but who do not claim a specialist role;
4 That section of the general population that is already convinced of the need to frame their own distress or other people's troublesome conduct in professional terms – lay people who have been 'proto-professionalized'.

The increasing recognition of the coalescence of lay and professional perspectives and involvement in mental health, evident in the work of DeSwaan and Rose, highlights a parallel process of the changing knowledge base and territory of mental health professional work. There has been a blurring of boundaries between mental and physical health work and models of health and illness. Disciplines across medicine and nursing have embraced the notion of 'holism'. Portmanteau models such as the 'biopsychosocial' model are gaining increasing popularity, particularly as a paradigm which challenges the reductionist and bio-medical emphases of traditional health professionals (Dowrick *et al.* 1996; Pilgrim, 2002a).

'Emotional labour' has also become a focus of mental health specialist and generalist health workers alike as well as forming a focus of the analysis of work of non-professionals undertaking 'people work' (e.g. air hostesses) (Hochschild 1983). The terrain of professional health work, particularly mental health work, has also changed. More work now takes place in the more 'open systems' of primary and community care. Institutionalized ways of responding and relating to patients inside organizations have given way to community- focused work. The need to obtain entry to patients' houses in order to carry out work has reduced the gap between professionals and patients – in so far as access becomes the object of negotiation between two parties, whereas in institutionalized settings it has frequently been taken for granted.

'Fringe work' which refers to a series of activities that professionals are not expected to do or 'supposed' to engage with (de la Cuesta 1993) assume a higher profile when professionals work increasingly in the community. The growing recognition of the mental health component of a wider range of health problems amongst different population groups and presented in primary care is evident in the rise in numbers of primary care counsellors employed to deal specifically with referrals from GPs and other primary care professionals.

Sociology and the mental health professions

Let us now return to the models described earlier within the sociology of the professions. The neo-Durkheimian approach is rarely visible in the contemporary sociological discourse about professional life, although it can still be found in the writings of mental health professionals when they are generating a 'public relations' view of their own work. Examples of this can be found in relation to psychiatry (Clare 1976) and clinical psychology (Marzillier and Hall 1987).

Below, we start by acknowledging that many studies have drawn upon more than one theoretical framework. We then look at some purer sociological frameworks before addressing the influence of theoretical models from the study of deviancy, professional knowledge and patriarchy. The latter are important in addition to the work of the sociology of the professions because they come at the question of professional practice from a starting point other than the specialists themselves.

In regard to the other groups we have just noted (non-specialists and lay people), deviancy theorists are interested in the negotiation of deviant roles, like that of becoming a psychiatric patient. While professionals are central to this, they are not the only group of social actors implicated. Likewise, sociological investigations of the transmission of knowledge start with an interest in knowledge but then look to how professionals are a vehicle for its reproduction, possession and modification. Feminists start from a wider interest in the male domination of women in society and then look to particular sites of this domination, like professional practice.

Eclecticism and post-structuralism

Many of the attempts to understand mental health professionals have drawn upon more than one theoretical base. For instance, the extensive work of Andrew Scull on the development of psychiatry during and since the nineteenth century draws heavily upon Marxist ideas. Scull explains the rise and maintenance of psychiatry in terms of its functional value for economic order and efficiency under capitalism. The segregation of the mad and the delegation by the State of powers to doctors to keep madness under control are central to Scull's thesis. His emphasis is on the role of psychiatrists as agents of social control employed by the State to contain the threat of one section of a poor underclass – the mad.

However, when explaining the finer dynamics of how doctors purged lay administrators from the asylums and sought upward social mobility for themselves, he uses a Weberian notion of 'closure', as in this example:

> Modern professions are not simply the dominant or most important providers of a particular service; instead they effectively monopolize a service market . . . During the nineteenth century, mad-doctors manoeuvred to secure such a position for themselves and acceptance of their particular view of the nature of madness, seeking to transform their existing foothold in the market place into a cognitive and practical monopoly of the field, and to acquire for those practising this line of work the status prerogatives 'owed' to professionals – most notably autonomous control by practitioners themselves over the condition and conduct of their work.
>
> (Scull 1979: 129)

Similarly, a work which builds heavily on the work of Scull is Baruch and Treacher's (1978) analysis of the functioning of psychiatry in Britain, which emphasizes the professional dominance of psychiatrists. In the Marxian tradition, they highlight the economic factors which both precipitate mental distress and are consequent upon a person entering the role of psychiatric patient. However, they also draw liberally for the latter purposes on the work of Parsons, albeit with critical reservations. They also refer positively to the post-Marxian social critic Illich, as well as to Scull, in their 'medicalization' thesis about the transformation of madness into mental illness by doctors. Indeed, while Baruch and Treacher, like Scull, could be labelled as 'Marxist functionalists', they begin their book with a long quote from Illich's *Medical Nemesis*. (The ideological position of Illich is contested. His anti-professionalism has given comfort to critics of both right and left and his alternatives to current forms of social organization contain a mixture of libertarian and authoritarian elements.)

The medicalization of madness thesis and the emphasis on psychiatrists as agents of social control is by no means limited to neo-Marxians. Right-wing libertarian critics from within psychiatry have constructed social histories of their profession with these emphases as well. The best example of this is the work of Szasz (1971), who argues that psychiatrists are for the modern State what witch-finders were for the Church in mediaeval times. The work of Szasz also echoes some of the analysis of Foucault, which is described later.

In another analysis of twentieth-century psychiatry, Ramon (1985) looks at services and the professions of psychiatry, psychiatric nursing and psychology. She dubs these for her purposes as the 'psy complex', echoing a post-structuralist term but at the same time firmly endorsing the political economy approach to welfare professionals given by the Marxist Gough (1979) we noted earlier (Ramon 1985: 21).

Turning to the analysis of a different profession – clinical psychology – eclecticism is evident again. Pilgrim and Treacher (1992) describe the historical development of the profession and its recent functioning. The profession in Britain has gone through four phases: psychometrics (1950s), behaviour therapy (1960s), therapeutic eclecticism (1970s) and managerialism (1980s). When theorizing the meaning of their description, Pilgrim and Treacher endorse the partial advantages of post-structuralist, neo-Weberian and neo-Marxian models for their data analysis. Psychologists have been mainly concerned with voluntary relationships (see discussion of post-structuralism later). They have tried to usurp the role of a dominant profession (psychiatry) to some extent and they have sought, via a campaign of registration, to attain a State-endorsed monopoly over psychological practice. Psychologists have demonstrably served the social administrative requirements of the capitalist State by seeking to regulate the behaviour of children and people with mental health problems and learning difficulties.

In addition, Pilgrim and Treacher draw attention to questions of gender and race in understanding some of the features of the profession being white and male dominated (see later). These examples of eclecticism reflect that the earlier advice of Turner (1987) about the need to integrate Weberian and Marxian frameworks has been anticipated by a number of sociologists.

Foucault's (1961; 1965) early writings on mental health began quite close to the Marxian emphasis on social control. However, he diverged from Scull's analysis on two counts even at this stage. First, he puts the beginnings of segregation at an earlier point, the 'great confinement' of the mid-seventeenth to mid-eighteenth century. Scull argues that most of the mad were still roaming free in society at the beginning of the nineteenth century and it was not until the mid-nineteenth century that the State asylum system was well established to segregate madness. Second, Foucault emphasized the moral, not the economic, order. While Scull argued that psychiatry functioned to aid and abet economic efficiency, Foucault argued that psychiatry existed primarily to deal with those who offended bourgeois morality and rationality. For Foucault, segregative psychiatry was not concerned with either medical cure or economic efficiency *per se* but with moral regulation.

Miller (1986) notes that Foucault's work is essentially a 'prehistory' of psychiatry. It is then extended by Castel (1983) into the period when the profession became more firmly established in the nineteenth century. The moral regulation theme continues about the role of the alienist or psychiatrist. Madness now had to be dealt with within the rules of the emerging bourgeois 'contractual' society. During this period the psychiatric profession did not go unchallenged but it retained its central role in relation to the asylum.

The third phase of interest to post-structuralists has been the changes in psychiatry during the twentieth century (Castel, Castel and Lovell 1979; Armstrong 1980; Miller and Rose 1988). Here, four interweaving themes can be identified:

- psychiatry as a professional enterprise is no longer restricted only to the asylum;
- its practices are no longer only associated with coercive social control;
- large bands of the population have been induced into an individualized state of psychological mindedness about their existence, via the media and education; and
- following from the last two points, voluntary relationships involving lengthy conversations about the self are now sought out by the public and deployed by professionals (versions of counselling and psychotherapy) (Rose 1990).

The move beyond the asylum can be linked roughly to changes in practices during the First World War when the problem of shellshock required a new response to mental distress (Stone 1985). Psychotherapy began in earnest at this point: out-patient clinics were set up after the war and centres of excellence, like the Tavistock Clinic, which celebrated the legitimacy of psychoanalysis, were established. Psychoanalysis had been attacked or ignored by psychiatrists before 1914. After the war, the Tavistock Clinic became associated with a wider cultural emphasis on the individual and the family, for instance, by promoting explanations of delinquency and mental distress, which were purported to arise from poor mothering.

Of central importance in this account is the rejection of the coercive social control emphasis of Scull and the 'anti-psychiatrists'. For instance, Miller and Rose argue that the psy complex has increasingly emphasized voluntary relationship, which is sought out and appreciated by clients: 'We argue that it is more fruitful to consider the ways that regulatory systems have sought to promote subjectivity than to document ways in which they have crushed it' (Miller and Rose 1988: 174). DeSwaan's notion of 'proto-professionalization', mentioned earlier, also operates with a similar assumption about a cultural consensus between professionals and lay people that their everyday troubles can be solved by conversations (counselling and psychotherapy) which focus on, celebrate and construct, the 'self'.

However, the post-structuralist account still emphasizes the role of professionals in 'regulating' the everyday lives of their clients (Donzelot 1979). Abbott and Wallace (1990: 6) note that the caring professions:

> not only aim to change and control behaviour, but also help to structure the context of social and cultural life in a more general sense . . . [T]hey create both the object of intervention – the neglectful mother, the wayward teenager, the bad patient – and at the same time make these the targets of their intervention. Intervention is designed to normalize, to make subjects conform to the defined norms.

Thus, differences of opinion between sociologists about the regulatory role of professionals seem to hinge on differences of emphasis. The post-structuralists (and Parsons (1951) in his discussion of the sick role) emphasize a process of consensual decision making, some of it implicit or unconscious, wherein the client either comes to agree with, or already accepts, professional definitions of the nature of their problem. Social regulation occurs by agreement and with actual (or perceived) benefits to the client. By contrast, the Marxian tradition emphasizes the enforced imposition of a view on the client by professionals acting as agents of the state. The first of these suggests that the power to regulate emotional life and norms of conduct is diffuse or dispersed. Power cannot be located 'inside' any one particular group of social actors. Rather, it is understood as a relationship or discourse shared by several parties. The second account clearly locates power in the hands of professionals who dominate their clients at the behest of their state employers. Maybe both types of account are credible. Patients do seek out help in voluntary relationships. In addition, sometimes, professionals impose themselves on patients – they lock them up and give them treatments they do not consent to freely.

Because post-structuralist writers about mental health have tended to focus on twentieth-century developments, their emphasis has tended to be on the disciplinary, rather than repressive, power of psychiatric experts. This has led to a skewed post-structuralist interest, with Foucault's early concern with repressive power being replaced by an emphasis on psychological interventions which are 'anxiously sought and gratefully received' (Pilgrim and Rogers 1994). This shift emphasizes the role of the secularized confessional in modern society in Foucault's later writings:

> The confession has spread its effects far and wide. It plays a part in justice, medicine, education, family relationships, in love relations, in the most ordinary affairs of everyday life and in the most solemn rites: one confesses one's crimes, one's sins, one's thoughts and desires, one's illnesses and troubles; one goes about telling with the greatest precision whatever is most difficult to tell.
>
> (Foucault 1981: 59)

This role of the confessional is discussed in more detail in relation to mental health work by Rose (1990). He suggests a number of points in this regard:

1 Psychotherapeutic assumptions can be found to operate now in general medicine, education, advertising, and journalism and business management. They are not limited to the work of mental health experts.
2 A countervailing discourse has also emerged from some social critics about a 'modern obsession with the self' and a 'tyranny of intimacy in which narcissism is mobilised in social relations'.
3 Modern psychotherapeutic rituals mimic and displace the older emphasis on religious or spiritual pilgrimages. The growth of Protestantism with its emphasis on individual guilt and responsibility marked a bridge between mediaeval religion and the modern culture of the self and individualism. Alongside this emerged the 'civilizing process' (Elias 1978) in which self not State control became important; the growth in importance of etiquette and manners. Thus, a repressive State form of control was increasingly superseded by self-control.
4 New versions of the confession like counselling and the psychological therapies became means by which identities were inscribed upon their subjects. Mental health work produces 'the subjectification of work', 'the psychologization of the mundane', 'a therapeutics of finitude' and a 'neuroticization of social intercourse'. What Rose points to in these phrases is the way in which

work, common life transitions, disappointment, death and our intimate relationships are now framed within mental health discourses.

5 Following Foucault, Rose offers a triple aspect on psychological treatments. First there are moral codes in the language and ethical principles of therapy. These imply some notion of 'the good life' and are thus implicitly or explicitly normative. Second, there are ethical scenarios which are the sites or contexts in which the moral codes operate – social work practice, the courts, the private consulting room and so on. Third there are techniques of the self, which are developed to codify the exploration, definition and confrontation of the self in therapy (Foucault 1988). These techniques are not a unitary body of knowledge but a wide range of models which produce narratives of the self – heterogeneity of approach characterizes the psychological treatments.

6 These features of mental health work are not guided by the hidden hand of capital (cf. the neo-Marxian view of the professions) nor by the conscious collective self-interest pursued by professionals according to the neo-Weberians (see later). Instead, the main orientation of modern mental health work is one of reconciling or aligning the needs of individuals with the social, political or organizational goals which form the social context of therapists and their clients.

Having outlined the post-structuralist perspective of mental health work, we now turn to the application of an older sociological approach.

The neo-Weberian approach

This has already been mentioned in relation to clinical psychologists seeking a monopoly on psychological practice and on their boundary dispute with psychiatry (Pilgrim and Treacher 1992). It was also an important aspect of the study of a psychiatric unit by Baruch and Treacher (1978), in terms of the strategies which consultant psychiatrists used to maintain their dominant position in the mental health team working with in-patients.

In another study of psychiatrists, their relationship with the police has been analysed in terms of professional dominance. The transactions that occurred between the two occupational groups when people deemed to be mentally disordered in public were taken for psychiatric assessment by police officers (under section 136 of the Mental Health Act 1983) were studied. The same study also found that psychiatrists operated a number of strategies to exert control over how the patient was dealt with. The technical knowledge of the profession was a focus for psychiatrists' dominance over police officers. Even though police officers identified mental disorder with the same technical efficiency as psychiatrists, the latter insisted on depicting the police as lacking in the credentials to understand or manage the client group. The police were not in fact interested in encroaching on the territory of psychiatric practice. Nonetheless, psychiatrists acted to ward off a form of encroachment on their professional power that they perceived to be coming from police officers.

Sociologists who try to understand specific groups of professions usually find it necessary to appreciate how practitioners perceive their own role and that of others. The next wider sociological tradition to be discussed highlights this.

Symbolic interactionism

This approach can be found in Goffman's (1961) classic study of asylum life and of how the patient role is imposed on admitted psychiatric patients. What matters in this 'microsociology' are the meanings which are negotiated by various social actors involved in a drama or ritual. Goffman talks of 'degradation rituals', when the patient's identity is removed as they enter the psychiatric patient role (see later). This type of approach was extended by Braginsky, Braginsky and Ring (1973) (discussed further in Chapter 7).

The symbolic interactionists can also be found in studies of how psychiatrists and other mental health workers see and justify their role. Goldie (1977) interviewed psychiatrists in order to understand the meanings they attached to their knowledge base and their perceived superior status compared with non-medical staff. He also observed and took accounts from other members of mental health care teams about how they understood their particular expertise and powers. From this data he built up a picture of how psychiatrists maintain their mandate of authority in the field of mental health and how subordinate professions both challenge and maintain that mandate.

More recently, another study has examined the different mental models held by different members of mental health teams within this negotiated order (Colombo *et al.* 2003). While a pragmatic imperative exists to make a service work and to complete daily tasks, it is clear that these contain strains and compromises about implicit models which permeate the intentions and actions of staff. For example, psychiatrists still overwhelmingly operate a diagnostic treatment approach to mental illness. They work alongside others who do not share this view but prefer an alternative model (psychotherapeutic or social).

In another study of a psychiatric team using participant observation and interviews, Emerson and Pollner (1975) investigated the ways in which professionals classified their work with different types of patients. In particular, the investigators were interested in looking at how less acceptable work, such as the compulsory detention of patients in emergency duties, was conceived by workers. They found that this 'dirty work' or 'shit work' was accounted for by workers who preferred the morally superior role of being benign therapists. The dirty work conception derives from earlier work by Hughes (1971), who sees it as an aspect of all professional activity entailing a practitioner being obliged to 'play a role of which he thinks he ought to be a little ashamed of morally'. For Emerson and Pollner, the dirty work of acute psychiatry is that of social control – involuntary admission to hospital. In order to distance themselves from this explicit and morally dubious role, practitioners will point out that it is not really typical of their duties, that it is forced on them by circumstances or that they use the opportunity to help the patient as best they can.

The symbolic interactionist approach has been given new relevance, given that mental health service reformers are seeking to take account of the role of lay people in quality improvement programmes (Milne *et al.* 2004). (We return to the importance of 'users and carers' in the final chapter.)

The influence of the sociology of deviance

It is not surprising that some investigations of mental health work have started with the social negotiation of psychiatric patienthood, rather than looking at a particular profession. Coulter (1973) studied how social crises in the domestic arena became reframed as psychiatric illnesses. A similar approach can be found in the work of Scott (1973), who tried to map out the powers available to professionals, prospective patients and significant others to establish or maintain the deviant role of mental patient. Scott talked of the 'treatment barrier' to describe the loss of agency occurring once the identified patient was labelled as ill. This process of placing illness inside an individual obscures the roles and responsibilities of all the parties in the transaction and is consequently an impediment to change.

Goffman's work has already been mentioned but it is important to note that his study of hospital life supplied us with important concepts related to the negotiation of deviance: 'the betrayal funnel' and the 'degradation ritual'. The former refers to the conspiratorial relationship which necessarily develops between relatives of identified patients who have been forcibly admitted to hospital and the receiving professionals. Goffman called this conspiracy 'the circuit of agents that participate fatefully in the passage from civilian to patient status'. The 'degradation ritual' refers to the removal by professionals of a person's everyday identity and a stripping away of their usual sense of self. They are labelled with a diagnosis and normal signals of their individuality (such as their own clothes) are removed.

This emphasis on the involvement of professionals in negotiating a deviant role can be found in Bean's (1980) study of psychiatrists, social workers and GPs who compulsorily detain patients. In this study, Bean was testing the validity of claims arising from Lemert's (1974) work on group interaction, an extension of labelling theory about the treatment of one set of rule breakers (criminals) and checking how this model applied to another group of rule breakers (those diagnosed as being mentally ill). The principles of this model of deviancy are concerned with rules, their enforcement by parties (i.e. professionals) with designated powers, and how rule enforcement may or may not lead to an outcome which is intended. Bean's interest in testing the limits of this theory in the field of mental health work involved his observing the conduct and statements of professionals (the 'rule enforcers') in their work when admitting patients to hospital compulsorily.

The influence of the sociology of knowledge

Some sociologists have tried to understand the workings of particular professions in terms of the knowledge base they employ. Within the neo-Weberian tradition this sociology of knowledge approach is evident in the work of Freidson (1970) when examining the general character of modern professional life. In relation to mental health workers, Sheppard (1990) has compared psychiatric nurses with social workers within such a framework. He takes the lead from Atkinson (1983), who advocates the need to examine 'the relationship between education, practice and the organization of occupational groups'. The rationale here is that a close look at that relationship will reveal how the assumptions about the knowledge will shape professional practice and illuminate how practitioners defend the legitimacy of their particular role. Following from this, empirical studies of professionals should attend to the meanings that practitioners attach to their work (in line with symbolic interactionism discussed above).

Sheppard (1990) suggests that social workers and community psychiatric nurses (CPNs) might in some respects overlap in the type of work they do with clients, but a closer look at the knowledge base of each profession also points to differences. Social workers are influenced, albeit inconsistently, by social science. CPNs, in contrast, are preoccupied more by a focus on mental illness – how to account for it and how to respond to it. This means that practitioners accept psychiatric (i.e. medical) models of explanation and treatment or they react against them (i.e. take on board 'anti-psychiatry' arguments). Their background is not within social science but is tied instead to a medical body of knowledge. Also, because of their role in relation to mental health law (social workers approved for this purpose are required to detain patients compulsorily), social workers may be more concerned with legal definitions of work rather than the nature of distress and its treatment.

The influence of feminist sociology

Feminist sociology has emphasized the subordinated role of women in three senses when discussing the caring professions (Gamarnikow 1978; Hearn 1982; Crompton 1987; Abbott and Wallace 1990; Witz 1990): (1) women are more likely to be subordinated as clients; (2) women on average occupy lower-status positions within professions; (3) those occupational groups which are numerically dominated by women (like nursing) are more likely to be subordinate to male-dominated professions (like medicine). However, because of the history of male asylum attendants being used to physically control lunatics in the nineteenth century, psychiatric nursing has been more male dominated (and working class) than general nursing (Carpenter 1980).

Pilgrim and Treacher (1992) found that female clinical psychologists are less likely to occupy managerial and professional leadership positions than men. Moreover, they found that conservative male elements in the profession also lamented the greater proportion of women to men on the explicit grounds that this implies an inferior status and induces a decline in salary levels (Humphrey and Haward 1981; Crawford 1989). Feminism has also stimulated new forms of therapeutic practice which are tailored to women's needs (Eichenbaum and Orbach 1982).

The impact of legislative arrangements and service redesign

We deal in a general sense with legislation in Chapter 10 but there are some specific implications of legal arrangement which are relevant to discussing the role of mental health professionals. In the current British context there are two main implications.

First, at the time of writing, the government is proposing radical changes to the 1983 Mental Health Act in order to reconfigure powers of coercive control outside of hospital settings. (This is expressed misleadingly as an intention to improve mental health – the suggestions are called the 'Draft Mental Health Bill' (Department of Health 2004).) These proposals have provoked an unprecedented alliance of opposition, which includes all of the mental health profession, including psychiatry. The Royal College of Psychiatrists has expressed its concern about the risk-management implications of these proposals and is critical of the way in which it would undermine the professional ethos of a care profession. Similarly, strong objections have come from clinical psychologists who emphasize the importance of voluntarism and trust in negotiating personal change in those with mental health problems.

Earlier, the notion of 'dirty work' was noted. Although there have been a range of specific objections raised by the mental health professions, at their centre is a concern that their work will become more and unacceptably 'dirty' at the behest of the State. There is a fear that working relationships with patients will become more, not less, difficult and that expectations imposed on professionals about the management of risky behaviour will be unreasonable.

A second legal change in the offing, of relevance to the mental health professions, is in relation to shifts from self-regulation to more State control of professional standards. As Price (2002) notes, there is an important logical and political difference between the State regulating specific practices and it regulating professional groupings that award titles and maintain a professional register. At present in Britain the tradition has been of the latter but now changes are occurring which signal some shift to the former. For example, clinical psychologists, to date, have operated a voluntary scheme about their continued professional development (ongoing post-qualification learning). Henceforth, they will be obliged to record and demonstrate this in order to retain their legal right to practice. The more the activities of a profession are specified (rather than its practitioners' credentials being simply formally held on a register) the more its legitimacy can be undermined. For example, a critical account of credentialism in clinical psychology offered by Hayes (1998: 36) notes the following about individual professions or 'guilds'. It has many neo-Weberian resonances noted earlier:

> Up until recently guild forces have resisted practice guidelines foreseeing interference and restriction. Guilds have preferred to emphasize the certification of people over procedures, in part because this approach has been shown over the centuries to provide an extremely effective method of enhancing economic success and professional power of particular groups. The problem with certifying people is that is an extremely ineffective way of ensuring quality. It is not by accident that although the first meaning of license in the dictionary is 'lawful permission', the second is 'excessive liberty'. People with license do sometimes take license. When one's judgment is officially sanctioned, it is but a small step to disconnect judgment from careful and defensible reasoning and base it instead on mere personal preference.

At the start of this chapter, we noted that critical accounts of professions displaced credulous ones in sociology but that lay people still retain a positive concept of professionalism. However, this lay view is now being undermined by major scandals about respectable professions. Examples of this in Britain include the detection of the mass murderer GP, Harold Shipman, the removal of body parts of dead babies at Alder Hey Hospital without parental consent and the recurring pattern of sexual misconduct among mental health professionals (Allsop 2002; Pilgrim 2002b). This sort of very publicly debated evidence about the professional abuse of power has increased the confidence of politicians in introducing specific rather than general forms of legal regulation.

Another point to note is in relation to quasi-legal constraints on professional autonomy. These refer to formal government policies and structures, which hedge around 'clinical freedom'. For example, since 1997 the government has introduced clinical governance arrangements in the NHS which are designed to ensure service improvements. The implementation of this policy has necessitated the bureaucratic subordination of professional power to managerial power. Another example is the setting up of the National Institute for Clinical Excellence (NICE) and the Commission for Health Improvement to provide guidance on good practice and to monitor service standards.

The debates about specific versus general State regulation are occurring at a time when the government is also redesigning health and social care services. This is having substantial consequences for occupational roles under current and envisaged service changes. In the field of mental health, psychology graduates have been introduced to support low capacity in primary mental health care. The increasing integration of health and social care has generated new models of mental health support workers. New forms of service, such as crisis resolution, assertive outreach, early-intervention (for psychosis) services and treatment centres for those with a diagnosis of personality disorder are merging. They are generating roles which are new or they are creating new forms of role blurring between the existing mental health professions.

Discussion

This chapter will end by drawing attention to the twin problems of uncertainty when discussing the mental health professions. The first problem is about the professions themselves. What are they up to? Are they concerned with ameliorating distress or with controlling deviant behaviour (or both)? To what degree are they effective in either of these roles? This question is addressed when we discuss treatment in Chapter 8. In whose interests do they work – themselves, their clients, the general public, the State, patriarchy? What role does power play in their operations? Are they impartial benign practitioners or partisan oppressive enforcers of social conformity, deriving their role from wider inequalities of power (based on race, class and gender)? Do they crush individuality or celebrate and construct it? Any critical student of the mental health professions or critical practitioner within their ranks is drawn to these types of questions in one form or another.

The second problem relates to the lack of consensus on the part of sociologists when attempting to provide answers to these questions. Answers are provided but sometimes they concur with the work of others and sometimes they do not. The mental health professions represent a contested area of sociological inquiry, which is rendered less contentious by eclecticism but remains contested nonetheless. Post-structuralism is only an acceptable resolution for those accepting the epistemological current of post-modernism. Although many are part of that current, not all sociologists are post-modernists.

Both sides to this uncertainty characterize the discourse about mental health work at present. Two questions in particular will continue to tantalize social scientists for the foreseeable future. First, how do mental health professions with such a weak, controversial, contradictory and poorly credible body of knowledge (see Chapters 1 and 8) continue to maintain a mandate to regulate the lives of those they deem to be mentally unfit? Second, with the apparent mixture of coercive and non-coercive power operating in mental health work, how might the tensions and contradictions of the professions be understood?

The post-structuralists seem to come nearest to providing answers to these questions but they leave a number of loose ends. They notoriously ignore gender relationships (Rose 1990). They also understate the continuing role of coercive social control enjoyed by professionals and suffered by service users. Also, traditional epidemiological research seems to suggest that predictable inequalities in mental health derive from real differences between social groups, which are independent of a professional discourse or set of interventions. Arguably, professionals diagnose and respond to these differences, they do not simply create them in cahoots with other social actors. How then do we resolve questions about whether apparent differences in mental health between social groups are real outcomes of social inequality or constructed by-products of psychiatric discourse?

The work of mental health professionals is important to sociologists not only because of the character of their operations, strategies or practices. Professionals might also be deemed to account for the very existence of 'the mentally ill' in modern society on the one hand, or they might represent a set of occupations which respond to real socially determined forms of personal distress and social deviance defined by lay people on the other.

This chapter has explored a variety of sociological approaches to mental health work. The diversity reflects wider unresolved disputes within the field of the sociology of the professions. In turn, these disputes are connected to divisions within social theory, with post-structuralism representing the most recent participant in debates about how health professionals are to be understood in society. As we note in the latter part of the chapter, sociological currents outside work on the professions have also been influential in some investigations of mental health work. The sociological perspective taken determines the reader's sympathy for, or criticism of, mental health workers.

Questions

1 Compare and contrast two perspectives from the sociology of the professions and apply them to mental health work.

2 'Mental health professionals and their patients are trapped in the same discourse' – discuss.

3 Are mental health workers agents of the State?

4 Whose interests are served by the work of psychiatric professionals?

5 What advantages are offered by sociological eclecticism when understanding the mental health professions?

6 Discuss the role of non-specialists in mental health work.

For discussion

Would you trust a mental health professional to help you if you were distressed? Consider this question by rehearsing what would encourage you to seek help and what would make you cautious.

Further reading

Allsop, J. and Saks, M. (eds) (2002) *Regulating the Health Professions*. London: SAGE.

DeSwaan, A. (1990) *The Management of Normality*. London: Routledge.

Pilgrim, D. and Rogers, A. (1994) Something old, something new . . . sociology and the organisation of psychiatry. *Sociology*, 28(2): 521–38.

Rose, N. (1990) *Governing the Soul*. London: Routledge.

Samson, C. (1995) The fracturing of medical dominance in British psychiatry. *Sociology of Health and Illness*, 17(2): 245–68.

Chapter **8**

The treatment of people with mental health problems

Chapter overview

This chapter will examine the ways in which the treatment of people with mental health problems might be understood sociologically. In particular the two connotations of 'treatment' will be explored – one related to technical aspects of therapy, the other to do with the way in which people are treated as part of a moral order. The chapter will cover the following topics:

- therapeutics;
- a brief social history of psychiatric treatment;
- criticisms of psychiatric treatment;
- the moral sense of 'treatment';
- the social distribution of treatment;
- the impact of evidence-based practice on treatment;
- tackling social exclusion as a focus of treatment;
- governmentality and therapy.

Therapeutics

The term 'treatment', when used to refer to therapeutic procedures, assumes a view of people being ill and reflects a commonly shared 'therapeutic discourse'. 'Talking treatments' or 'drug treatments' or 'electro-convulsive treatment' (ECT) (in the USA this is called 'electroshock treatment') are common descriptions, whether they are from advocates or critics. We will look at these procedures but also examine a broader notion of 'treatment'. How are people with mental health problems treated in the broader moral and political sense? This section will summarize the social history of psychiatric treatment before going on to examine recent criticisms of that legacy.

A brief social history of psychiatric treatment

Sedgwick (1982) notes that two broad responses to emotional problems can be traced to antiquity. On the one hand, attempts have been made to tamper with the bodies of people with emotional afflictions, for example douching them in water or drilling holes in their skulls to allow evil spirits to escape. On the other hand, in ancient times good counsel was also purported to be of help. Thus, there are certain stable transhistorical themes, one somatic (today's biological psychiatry) and the other conversational (today's psychological therapies or talking treatments).

In the twentieth century, Western psychiatry developed an eclectic mixture of these interventions. Those entering the role of psychiatric patient will be prescribed physical interventions (drugs or ECT) or some version of psychological treatment, or a combination of the two, with the former typically predominating. In the late nineteenth century this was not the case. Psychiatrists at that time had a narrow interest in lunatics in their asylums. These were assumed to have disordered brains and were therefore treated accordingly. Physical treatments were very limited and crude. By the 1930s, psychotic in-patients were being treated only with paraldehyde, chloral hydrate, laxatives and cold baths (Bean 1980).

There was little or no interest in psychological treatments or in non-psychotic disorders until the First World War created a crisis of legitimacy for the dominant bio-determinist model of psychiatry. This was built on the assumption that lunacy, alongside other forms of deviance like criminality and idiocy, was a result of a 'tainted' gene pool. This hereditarian emphasis was formalized with the emergence of the pseudo-scientific discipline of eugenics. Eugenicists were convinced that racial improvement necessitated the resistance to external contamination by an alien racial stock and to the internal contamination by the tainted genes of the lower classes. The latter threat was amplified by their purported greater fertility.

With the First World War, 'England's finest blood' began to break down with 'shellshock'. Later this psychological disability was called 'battle neurosis' and then 'post-traumatic stress disorder'. The officers and gentlemen and their lower-class volunteer subordinates could not be construed as being genetically inferior. Consequently, the tainted gene model of psychiatry virtually constituted a form of treason. To add to the problem for the hereditarian position, officers were breaking down at a higher rate than lower ranks. This crisis of legitimacy for the hereditarian model created a space for other approaches to mental disorder, especially psychoanalysis and its derivatives. Versions of psychotherapy were the stock-in-trade of the 'shellshock doctors' of the time and in the treatment centres like the Tavistock Clinic, set up after the war, to treat compensation cases of the new disorder. A fuller version of this shift from biological to psychological approaches in treatment can be found in Stone (1985).

Thus, by the end of the war, psychiatry began to become more eclectic, although a pattern was already discernible of neurosis being treated psychologically and madness being treated with physical means. The latter began to predominate again in the inter-war years, boosted in confidence by the appearance of insulin coma therapy in 1934, prefrontal leucotomy in 1935, and ECT in 1938.

Mainstream psychiatry after the Second World War marginalized the aetiological role of psychological factors and talking treatments. The main textbooks of that period, which were to dominate post-war psychiatric training, reasserted the Victorian bio-determinism of the profession's founders (Mayer-Gross, Slater and Roth 1954). Once major tranquillizers were introduced in the mid-1950s, psychiatrists could begin to make the claim, which is often repeated today, that these drugs opened the doors of the hospitals and paved the way for community care. This claim, though common, is unfounded. In-patient numbers were already dropping before the introduction of major tranquillizers and the reasons for deinstitutionalization are multiple (see Chapter 9).

While it is generally conceded by most commentators on twentieth century psychiatry that it developed eclecticism (Ramon 1985), the bias towards physical treatments remained strong. Despite the incorporation of social and psychological aetiological factors into modern psychiatry, it has tended to reject the centrality of their relevance compared with purported biological causes (Royal College of Psychiatrists 1973). Alternatively, they have been given equal consideration but they still legitimize the disease model and the authoritative power of medicine in the diagnosis and treatment of people with personal and social problems.

By the 1970s, this revision of the medical model by Clare (1976) was described as a 'portmanteau model' by Baruch and Treacher (1978) to indicate that the disease formulation now takes more on board without being undermined. However, by the 1990s after a declarations of the 'decade of the brain' such a portmanteau or 'biopsychosocial model' was on the retreat from biological psychiatry within the profession as a whole (Guze 1989; Clare 1999; Pilgrim 2002a).

The limited eclecticism of psychiatry is illuminated by trends in the content of mainstream psychiatric journals during the twentieth century. While there was a broadening in the scope of psychiatric interest to include mental disorders, such as neurosis and substance misuse and personality disorder, there was an enduring interest in biological treatments of mental illness with relatively little coverage of the alternatives, such as psychoanalysis or social psychiatry. Thus there seems to be a lack of evidence to support the notions that explanatory paradigms used by psychiatry changed much over the course of a century (Moncrieff and Crawford 2001).

As well as psychiatry now offering a mixed therapeutic approach, biased towards drugs and ECT, other mental health professionals vary in the types of treatment they offer. Psychiatric nurses might provide client-centred counselling following the humanistic psychologist Carl Rogers or psychoanalytically oriented 'psychodynamic' psychotherapy, either individually or in groups. Some nurses are trained as specialists in cognitive-behavioural therapy. A similar eclectic mix can be found in the approach of clinical psychologists to treatment (Cheshire and Pilgrim 2004).

Criticisms of psychiatric treatment

Throughout medicine, therapeutic preferences are evident. Certain treatments may predominate, but they coexist with lesser-used alternatives. They also wax and wane in popularity with clinicians. In recent times they have also been subjected to wider social and cultural influences. The media and 'public opinion' have been influential in changing the regulatory frameworks and provision of drugs. Mental health work is no different in this sense. However, it has been controversial for particular reasons, which go beyond the pattern of fads and fashions typical of wider curative medicine:

1 Following Sedgwick's observation above, there is still a broad and unresolved tension between somatic and conversational modes of treatment. The overwhelming dominance of the first of these, especially in response to madness, has led to disaffection among service users;
2 All therapeutic approaches have been attacked for their iatrogenic effects. Iatrogenic effects are those caused by the treatment itself. The term 'side effects' is a common version of this notion when talking about drug therapy. It is more accurate to speak of 'unwanted effects' or 'adverse effects', rather than 'side effects';
3 Each approach has been attacked for its ineffectiveness in ameliorating distress.

These criticisms will now be elaborated.

Why have physical treatments tended to predominate?

From a user's perspective, the fact that psychiatric treatments are biased more towards drugs and ECT is indeed a problem. Not only do patients (understandably) expect their subjective sense of well-being to improve as a result of psychiatric treatment, they have higher expectations of the helpfulness of psychological and combined treatments than physical interventions alone (Noble, Douglas and Newman 2001). Despite these expectations, in most mental health services physical treatments predominate or are simply the only form offered or imposed. When asked in an open-ended way, people with a diagnosis of severe mental illness tend to describe service responses which are overwhelmingly limited to medication (Rogers, Pilgrim and Lacey 1993; Kilian *et al.* 2003). The strong bias towards drugs reflects bio-medical professional preferences at the expense of user choice.

Six mutually reinforcing contributory factors can be put forward to suggest why such a bio-medical bias exists.

1 The *medicalization of psychological abnormality* in the nineteenth century entailed a biological emphasis. Scull (1979: 165) quotes the following from the *Journal of Mental Science* in 1858: 'Madness is purely a disease of the brain. The physician is the guardian of the lunatic and must ever remain so'. For doctors to ensure their jurisdiction over madness they had to assert or prove that it arises from some sort of physical pathology. Accordingly, the use of physical treatments is consistent with a bio-deterministic aetiological theory. If such a position is not persuasive, then arguably mental illness is actually a sort of social, educational or existential, not physical, problem. As an indication of this, psychoanalysis, the prototype of the modern talking treatments, became divided in its early years about whether analysts needed to be physicians.

2 During the 1960s, when large mental hospitals came under attack from a variety of sources, an opportunity was created for psychiatrists to shift their site of operation into *mainstream medicine*. Their preferred service delivery model was that of the District General Hospital psychiatric unit. Baruch and Treacher (1978) point out that this allowed psychiatrists to make a bid to rejoin mainstream medicine and thereby compensate for the low status traditionally enjoyed by their medical specialty. Whether this has actually led to an improvement of their status within medicine is uncertain. However, aligning itself with general medicine was made more credible by the content of its interventions being like other medical procedures (i.e. physical treatments; see Chapter 8). In the USA Kleinman (1988) also noted that medication use, and the professional image of psychiatry as a poor relation trying to improve its medical reputation, were intertwined.

3 Physical treatments are legitimized and encouraged by the *profit motive*. Drugs are a well-known source of profits for their producers. In addition to the profits accruing from the sale of psychotropic medication, these companies also sell drugs to offset the side effects of major tranquillizers (e.g. induced Parkinson's disease). Drug companies promote their products through expensive advertising campaigns and sponsored events.

4 Although millions in each international currency are spent yearly on psychotropic drugs, they are still arguably *cheaper to deliver* than labour-intensive talking treatments. For instance, minor tranquillizers (discussed in Chapter 4) are a cheap and quick way of disposing of emotional problems in the surgery. Likewise, a reliance on major tranquillizers to dampen down the agitation of psychotic patients, older people and those with learning difficulties has been a cheap alternative to crisis intervention, intensive family support and psychological programmes.

5 If psychiatry exists, among other things, to control disruptive and unintelligible conduct, then physical treatments are highly suited to this purpose because they can be *imposed in the absence of cooperation*. Medication, psychosurgery and ECT can, in certain circumstances, be imposed on people against their will, whereas it is very difficult to conduct talking treatments with resistant subjects. Indeed, most psychotherapists argue that consent is a necessary precondition for any form of their treatment and that this condition of free choice is clearly compromised by a client being captive (Pilgrim

1988). However, group therapy has been used inside secure psychiatric facilities. Indeed, the therapeutic community approach to treatment is arguably well suited for social control as it uses group pressure and conformity to realign deviant conduct.

6 Although discoveries about the behavioural impact of psychotropic drugs have often been a result of accident rather than design, once the effects are demonstrated and they are patented and marketed by drug companies, they provide a *spurious illusion that biodeterminism has been proven* (bringing us back to point 1 above). The drive for pharmaceutical companies to produce both innovative and 'me too' compounds for profit has entailed their stimulation of biological psychiatric research both directly via research funding and indirectly. In the latter regard, Healy (1997) noted that even the patient who is drug 'treatment' resistant becomes a curious conundrum for neurospsychiatric researchers to solve using expensive medical technology to scan (live) and slice (dead) brains. The very use of that expensive technology then confirms the legitimacy of biological reductionism within psychiatry.

Minor tranquillizers

The benzodiazepines ('minor tranquillizers') have been discredited for their addictive qualities. They are only effective in symptom control for around ten days, with 58–77 per cent of recipients reporting sedation effects of the drugs (drowsiness, lethargy and memory disturbances). Thirty per cent of those taking these drugs for more than a few weeks will develop withdrawal symptoms, including panic attacks, insomnia, tremor, palpitations, sweating and muscle tension (Tyrer 1987). In a small percentage (under 5 per cent) more severe problems, including epileptic seizures and paranoid reactions, might occur. During the 1980s, the scale of iatrogenic addiction prompted a popular protest movement coordinated by MIND and the TV programme *That's Life*, which led to litigation against the drug companies supplying minor tranquillizers (Lacey 1991). When they are used in older patients, minor tranquillizers can also lead to mental confusion and falls, necessitating emergency medical treatment.

Sociologists have illuminated the role and impact of wider social influences, institutions and processes on the use and acceptability of minor tranquillizers. Bury and Gabe (1990) demonstrated the role of the media in legitimizing the social problem status of minor tranquillizers. The same authors presented an analysis of events surrounding the suspension of the licence, by the British Licensing Authority in 1991, for the widely used sleeping tablet Halcion (triazolam) (Gabe and Bury 1996). They identify four elements within these events: the claims-making activities of medical experts; legal challenges; the role of the media; and the response of the State. Together these have made a contribution to minor tranquillizers becoming a public and governmental issue rather than a purely clinical matter.

In relation to the same controversy about Halcion, micro-sociological factors within organizations like the Licensing Authority, have been offered as an alternative to the account by Gabe and Bury (Abraham and Sheppard 1998). These micro-factors include professional interests and the internal organizational arrangements and processes within institutions for reviewing and presenting data. Abraham and Sheppard suggest that these are more important than broader extra-organizational social influences in determining whether or not a drug remains widely available or is withdrawn from use (cf. Gabe and Bury 1996). It may well be that both accounts are applicable – it seems likely that social processes at both micro and macro levels are likely to sway the extent to which drugs are viewed as acceptable by authorizing bodies, the medical profession, the public and the State.

While there has been a significant reduction in the use of benzodiazepine drugs in recent years, a question has arisen about what should replace them as a strategy for managing anxiety-based mental health problems. Moreover, despite criticisms of the drugs they are still prescribed. They remain a quick and cheap response to complex psycho-social presenting problems in primary care settings (Groenewegen *et al.* 1999; Johnell *et al.* 2004; Pelfrene *et al.* 2004).

Major tranquillizers

The phenothiazine major tranquillizers, also called 'neuroleptics' and 'anti-psychotics', create the iatrogenic problems of Parkinsonism (trembling), akathisia (inner restlesness) and tardive dyskinesia. The latter is a group of disabling and disfiguring movement disorders, including pronounced facial tics, tongue flicking and jerking limbs. Estimates of its prevalence in those prescribed major tranquillizers vary from 0.5 per cent to 50 per cent with a mean of 20 per cent (Brown and Funk 1986). The probability of the iatrogenic effect occurring increases the longer the drug is prescribed, the larger the dose and the more other drugs are given in a 'cocktail' (technically called 'poly-pharmacy') (Hemmenki 1977; Warner 1985). When larger doses are given ('megadosing') fatalities are also risked, warranting the invention of a new diagnosis for iatrogenic death from phenothiazines – the 'neuroleptic malignant syndrome' (Kellam 1987).

Given the serious dangers associated with neuroleptics, the degree of complacency about their use on the part of professionals has attracted particular sociological interest. Brown and Funk (1986) traced how the evidence about tardive dyskinesia was available to psychiatrists in the late 1960s. And yet, throughout the 1970s and 1980s major tranquillizer prescription rates were undiminished (they actually increased in frequency and in dose levels). Active and passive forms of professional resistance to the recognition of tardive dyskinesia as an iatrogenic epidemic were evident in this period. Some clinicians acknowledged its existence but challenged data on its claimed prevalence or argued that the therapeutic benefits outweighed the iatrogenic risks. Others simply failed to change their prescribing habits without comment.

Brown and Funk claim that two theories (professional dominance and labelling) have some merit in accounting for this professional resistance to change. Both acknowledge the importance of the powerless social position of patients. The labelling theory account suggests that the powerless position and low social status of psychiatric patients renders them both unimportant and invisible. Consequently, their treating psychiatrists do not take their complaints about 'side effects', or their concerns about the debilitating effects of the drugs, seriously. Instead, doctors tend to be concerned only with the effectiveness of the drugs in symptom reduction (assessed by them, not the patients themselves).

The professional dominance theory focuses on the relationship between the status of psychiatry as a medical specialty and the role of physical treatment (see earlier). Brown and Funk endorse a similar picture, with psychiatry tying itself to physical medicine and its attendant biological trappings. Given this preoccupation with collective professional status, unfortunate consequences of biological treatment (like tardive dyskinesia) are ignored, denied or rationalized by clinicians. According to this theory, the needs of patients are ignored in favour of the political needs of their treating psychiatrists. A study of psychiatrists and recipient views of major tranquillizers (Finn *et al.* 1990) showed that both groups concur on the risks and 'bothersomeness' of side effects. However, 'psychiatrists saw side-effects as significantly less bothersome than symptoms when considering costs to society' (Finn *et al.* 1990: 843).

It is, perhaps, not surprising that patients who experience the side effects are often reluctant to comply with the regimen. In its depot form this type of medication results in an even more disempowered perception of the treatment process (Kilian *et al.* 2003) What is, perhaps, more surprising is that given the range and severity of side effects, non-adherence rates for major tranquillizers are the same as for other types of non-psychiatric medication. The problems associated with traditional major tranquillizers (the phenothiazine group of drugs) seem to apply less to a new generation of drugs, dubbed the 'new anti-psychotics'. These are more efficient at symptom reduction and are less liable to create movement disorders in patients. However, there is the risk of life-threatening blood disorders with some versions of the new anti-psychotics.

The sociological significance of the prescribing and compliance with anti-psychotics extends beyond the issue of the adverse effects and practices of the profession of psychiatry. Psychiatric patients' 'non compliance' with medication has emerged as a significant social problem. Images of deinstitutionalization, often promoted via the media, have become synonymous with the occurrence of socially unacceptable behaviour by ex-psychiatric patients living in the community. Within this oft-publicized scenario, medication has been depicted as a valid means of managing and controlling people who are viewed as a potential threat to the social order. Compliance with these drugs has come to be seen as an indicator of the success or failure of 'care in the community'. In this sense, the need for patient compliance derives not only from public pressures about managing psychiatric patients appropriately but also it is a central tenet in the management of mental health problems more generally.

The closure of mental hospitals was predicated on the assumed effectiveness of major tranquillizers. The introduction during the late 1960s of depot medication can be seen as an early attempt to devise a strategy for the more efficient control of patients' behaviour in the community. (It involves patients being injected with long-acting drugs in their home or at a clinic.) Depot medication was uniquely marketed as a means of ensuring the receipt of medication which was not contingent on patients' consent to treatment on a daily basis or their daily self-administration of pills.

The effectiveness of neuroleptics has been assumed by professionals, politicians and relatives' groups who emphasize the importance of treatment compliance for discharged patients. This has extended to legal proposals to enforce medication compliance in community-based patients in Britain – a policy already implemented in some parts of the USA (Dennis and Monahan 1996). However, the effectiveness and acceptability of major tranquillizers have been strongly challenged. For example, Cohen (1997) notes that:

- only one in three medicated patients fails to relapse;
- chronic use of the drugs leads to a reduction in social functioning;
- to date, few researchers have attended to user views of being medicated.

The reviewer concludes that '. . . the overall usefulness [of neuroleptics] in the treatment of schizophrenia . . . is far from established' (p. 195). In relation to their iatrogenic effects Cohen concludes that the 'neuroleptics' near-sacred reputation as 'antipsychotics' is equalled only by their record as one of the most behaviourally toxic classes of psychotropic drugs' (p. 201).

Extending the point about assumed utility of the drugs, major tranquillizers have been viewed as the principal means of preventing 'the revolving-door patient' phenomena. They are a central plank of 'out reach' care, case management, the care programme approach, supervised discharge and the management of those with 'a severe and enduring mental illness'. However, the centrality of medication to mental health policy has been problematic. The iatrogenic effects of medication have also become a focus of critical scrutiny and this has received greater publicity than at the time when Brown and Funk were discussing the topic in the 1980s.

The negative effects of major tranquillizers have been the focus of criticism from campaigning and mental health user organizations. Policy makers are now faced with balancing the need to maintain medication adherence, with the risks of iatrogenesis (Rogers and Pilgrim 1996). This dilemma has become increasingly difficult for policy makers to manage in a cultural context of high sensitivity to risk, the emergence of a consumerist philosophy within the health service, and the growing acceptance of the legitimacy of lay perceptions and assessment of medicine within modern health care systems.

The receipt of major tranquillizers occurs in a context of the wider meaning and symbolic significance that 'schizophrenia' has for patients in their everyday lives and of a policy context which stresses the need to survey and control the behaviour of people living in the community. For this reason, self-regulatory action in this group of patients has been found to be less evident, and the threat and application of external social control is greater than in relation to other groups of patients taking medication for chronic conditions (Rogers *et al.* 1998).

People taking antipsychotic medication do not see – as mental health professionals do – side effects and symptoms as separate issues. Instead, they describe drugs as 'good' or 'terrible', an indication of the total impact of their treatment and the impact that it has on well-being. The latter is defined by service users as normality of function, feelings and their appearance to the outside world (Carrick *et al.* 2004).

Antidepressants

Antidepressants have been associated with a number of disabling effects, including tiredness, dry mouth, loss of libido and impotence, blurred vision, constipation, weight gain and palpitations. The tricyclic version of this type of drug was implicated in around 10 per cent of deaths from self-poisoning in Britain in the early 1980s.

Tricyclics have now been superseded by the selective serotonin re-uptake inhibitors (SSRIs), which are less toxic. In older people a decline in suicide has been directly attributable to prescribing this type of anti-depressant (Gunnell *et al.* 2003) However, as these drugs have gradually superceded the tricyclics, new issues have emerged which suggest that the newer antidepressant drugs carry serious risks that may outweigh any benefits. This is particularly the case when prescribing these drugs in the treatment of depression in childhood and adolescence and warnings have been issued regarding the increased risk of suicide-related behaviour (Whittington *et al.* 2004).

The prescription of antidepressants for a range of psycho-social problems and their associated distress (reduced diagnostically and monolithically to 'clinical depression' (Pilgrim and Bentall 1999; Dowrick 2004)) is shaped by a number of factors. These include patient and professional characteristics, the interaction between them, the type of treatment setting and form of health-care system. Sleath and Shih (2003) found in the USA that insurance status is influential in determining which type of antidepressant is prescribed. Patients belonging to a health management organization that had capitated visits were four times more likely to receive older rather than newer antidepressants.

As with the newer 'anti-psychotics' discussed above, the regular use of newer antidepressants has met with accusations of another false dawn, as new iatrogenic problems are identified and initial hopes of curative power are queried. For example, reviews of studies of antidepressants versus psychological therapies in randomized controlled trials suggest that both are clinically effective in the short term, separately and combined, but no treatment is good at preventing long-term relapse in those who have had a depressive episode in their lives (Fisher and Greenberg 1997).

Initially it was claimed that the SSRIs were not dependency forming. This has now proved to be a false claim. Moreover, and more dramatically, they have been linked to claims of raised risk of both homicidal and suicidal behaviour (Healy 1997). SSRIs have also played a role in extending the medicalization of a range of ordinary experiences of distress. For example, Metzl and Angell (2004) examined an increasing range of female experiences, which have been medicalized by their treatment with the newer antidepressants. These include 'pre-menopausal dysphoric disorder (PMDD)', 'post-partum depression' and 'peri-menopausal depression'. Moreover, categories of depressive illness have expanded to incorporate what were previously considered normal life events such as motherhood, menstruation and childbirth.

These points about antidepressants indicate that medications have complex life cycles, with diverse actors, social systems, and institutions influencing who they are prescribed to and how they are used. Cohen *et al.* (2001) point to the way in which a medication life cycle evolves and mutates with social and technological change. The drug companies, the medical profession and patients themselves contribute to these changes in prescribed drug use.

Psychological therapies

As far as the psychological therapies are concerned, it is not self-evident that they are benign, simply because they are physically non-invasive and generally preferred by service users. Two types of iatrogenic problems arise in psychotherapy. The first is the so called 'deterioration effect' – where symptoms get worse during the normal course of therapy (Bergin 1971). The second set of problems is to do with the personal abuse suffered at the hands of unethical practitioners who exploit the power discrepancy existing, under conditions of privacy, to gain emotional or sexual gratification from their clients (Jehu 1995; Pilgrim and Guinan 1999).

By the mid-1990s over half of the malpractice suits taken out by people with mental health problems about their treatment at the hands of psychiatrists and clinical psychologists in the USA involved the distress created by sexual abuse by therapists (Schoener and Lupker 1996). Such has been the crisis of confidence thrown up by evidence of these iatrogenic effects of psychotherapy that some previously committed therapists have recommended the abandonment of therapy in favour of some type of self-help or have issued strong warnings to patients about the risks, as well as of the potential benefits, of psychotherapy (Masson 1988b; Smail 1996; Pilgrim 1997a).

Nonetheless, users of in-patient services still ask for talking treatments, complaining that these are on offer less frequently from psychiatric services than physical treatments. Exclusion from such treatment seems to reflect a tendency to treat neurotic patients more readily in this way. There is mixed empirical evidence on this issue. On the one hand, psychotic patients seem to be more prone to deterioration effects than less disturbed patients (Bergin and Lambert 1978). On the other hand, there are claims of significant positive effects of psychotherapy with psychotic patients (allowing the latter also to avoid the problems associated with major tranquillizers) (Karon and VandenBos 1981).

Just as medication use and the professionalization of psychiatry are interconnected (see earlier) professional questions also surround the differential use of psychological treatments. During the early professionalization of clinical psychology, its bid for therapeutic legitimacy centred on the behavioural treatment of neurosis. Psychologists tended to leave the treatment of madness to biological psychiatrists (Eysenck 1975). However, in the past 20 years psychologists have taken an increasing interest in the treatment of psychosis (Bentall 2003). As a consequence, the costs and benefits of physical and psychological treatments now need to be considered for all groups of patients as the unstable division of labour between psychiatrists and clinical psychologists has shifted.

Despite the user disaffection about bio-medical treatments in psychiatry and an expressed preference for talking treatments, given the risks of the latter, this does not imply that they are more cost-effective than drugs and ECT. Indeed, it could be argued that in some ways drug regimes are more open to public accountability than are the talking treatments (Pilgrim 1997b). For example, provided that clinicians cooperate with them, drug protocols can make prescribing practices amenable to audit (by managers or even service users). By contrast, the effective elements of talking treatments largely relate to 'nonspecific' effects of the therapist or therapist–client interaction. Good outcomes in psychotherapy are not linked to particular models but to these benign, supportive or inspirational practitioner variables, or the synergies for change created by some client–practitioner interactions but not others (Lambert and Bergin 1983). It is much more difficult to audit such inter-subjective factors than it is to set down guidelines about good drug-prescribing practice. Also drug-prescriptions are public and impersonal, whereas psychotherapy is private and personal. The latter features seem to be linked to user preferences (to have their idiosyncratic experiences taken seriously). However, these are the very reasons why talking treatments are liable to create deterioration effects because incompetent or abusive practitioners are shielded from public view.

Talking treatments, as their name indicates, rely on talk as a resource for personal change. In doing so, they professionalize ordinary human processes: the production and coproduction of human narratives. Psychological therapies professionalize narrative work and then generate expert meta-narratives. The latter then inform the preferred model of the practitioners through illustrative and justificatory case studies. Psychotherapeutic expertise implicitly or explicitly privileges these preferred meta-narratives, with competition existing between professionals about which one is superior.

Thus, this professionalization of narratives could be criticized for undermining the legitimacy and effectiveness of ordinary relationships, which when working well contain elements of clarification, reflection and social support. Indeed, the 'non specific' effects indicated earlier from psychotherapy outcome research suggest that the main elements of change are common to any helpful conversation between human beings such as rapport, empathy, trust and support (Barker and Pistrang 2002; McQueen and Henwood 2002).

Forms of lay and professional talk are on a continuum with shared characteristics. The professionalization of talk may obscure this continuum when privileging therapeutic narratives. One way of viewing psychological therapies is that they provide the opportunity for helpful conversations which, for contingent reasons, are missing from a client's personal and social context (Pilgrim 1997a).

Why is there a problem of legitimacy about the effectiveness of psychiatric treatment?

In addition to criticisms about the role of psychotropic drugs in sedating disruptive individuals, drug treatments have been criticized for being ineffective at symptom control. Mention has already been made of the short-term value of minor tranquillizers. Public knowledge about debates of the effectiveness of major tranquillizers is less evident. The psychiatric literature indeed suggests that they are effective at reducing the probability of relapse (Hirsch 1986). However, the extent of this impact is quite modest according to one oft-quoted study. Crow *et al.* (1986) reported that 58 per cent of patients receiving the drugs were deemed to relapse within two years, compared to 78 per cent of a control group receiving a placebo. Indeed, there was only a 12 per cent difference between the two groups according to the original data. (The latter were corrected statistically but without explanation prior to publication.)

We have already mentioned that there is mixed evidence about the effectiveness of psychotherapy. Behavioural critics of verbal psychotherapy have maintained that spontaneous remission from symptoms accounts for positive change in two-thirds of neurotic patients (Eysenck 1952; Rachman 1971). These doubts, plus those mentioned earlier from internal critics about deterioration effects, have certainly rendered psychotherapy problematic. Indeed, the overall estimate of psychotherapy is that it is only of marginal (though positive) utility because the gains it achieves are offset by deterioration effects and spontaneous remission (Bergin and Lambert 1978).

As for behavioural psychotherapy, this has been subjected to two types of criticism. The first relates to the limited value of behavioural work for the gamut of mental health problems referred to psychiatric services (Yates 1970). The second criticism is that it slavishly adheres to, rather than challenges, cultural norms. An example of this was the role taken up by behaviour therapists in seeking to convert homosexual men into heterosexuals by using electroshock aversion therapy (see Chapter 4).

Thus, the legitimacy of psychiatric treatments is undermined by different but inter-related dissatisfactions. First, there is the problem of effectiveness per se – no form of treatment claims startling improvement rates (let alone 'cure') (Pilgrim 1997b). Second, given this poor showing in symptom reduction, the iatrogenic effects of treatment become particularly salient. 'Side effects' might be tolerated if significant therapeutic benefits were also experienced by patients but with high iatrogenic effect rates and low symptom reduction rates, treatments become highly problematic (Breggin 1993). Third, the use of treatments to ensure conformity (e.g. aversion therapy) and quell disruptiveness (e.g. major tranquillizers) has highlighted, and stimulated opposition to, the normative and coercive role of psychiatric interventions (see Chapter 10). Fourth, currently there is a variable gap between the evidence for effective interventions in clinical trials and these treatments being used effectively in actual services (see later discussion on evidence- based practice).

The moral sense of 'treatment'

In everyday parlance 'treatment' has moral as well as medical connotations. Certain medical specialties have been exposed to particular critical attention as far as this non-medical notion of treatment is concerned. One of these is gynaecology and the other is psychiatry. This might imply that certain aspects of the person need to be treated with particular sensitivity by medicine.

The final essay in Goffman's critique of the mental hospital, *Asylums* (1961), is subtitled 'Some notes on the vicissitudes of the tinkering trades'. He analyses the mental hospital and the medical model of treatment as if it were a service industry directed towards the repair of damaged parts of society (psychiatric patients). If we accept Goffman's metaphor of psychiatry as a repair industry then we can examine how its 'customers' are treated.

To begin, the scope of psychiatry needs to be restated. At one end of a spectrum of psychiatric service provision is a picture of enforced detention and imposed treatments. In Britain we have the maximum security Special Hospitals, Regional Secure Units and in-patients detained under 'mental health law' in open hospitals or psychiatric units. At the other end of the spectrum are out-patients who attend voluntarily to see a therapist of their choosing in a variety of state-provided and private therapeutic facilities. In between are patients who hover around a centre-ground of services, which contains a mixture of both voluntary and coercive practices. Depending on their conduct, they may drift or be propelled suddenly towards one or other end of the spectrum.

What separates the two ends of the spectrum is essentially the question of free choice. If the mental health industry does indeed provide a service to its patients then we would expect it to manifest certain characteristics. Service industries provide options and opportunities for customers in pursuit of a product of their preference. Rotten products which customers found noxious or aversive would quickly disappear from the range of offers made by the industry. A person experiencing some form of self-defined psychological problem or distress would have the resources (financial and cognitive) and the options to freely choose a form of amelioration. How does the mental health industry fare over this issue of free choice? We will explore this question by addressing two more which are begged. Who is psychiatry's client? And what is the extent of informed consent given to patients?

Who is psychiatry's client?

One of the ambiguities surrounding psychiatric work is whether or not the identified patient is the actual client of the service. Clearly, some party other than the patient is being served under those sections of the Mental Health Act which empower professionals to remove a person's liberty and/or impose treatment interventions against the patient's will. Coulter's work (described in Chapter 6) on decision making about madness in the lay area traces such a process. Professionals are summoned in order to resolve a distressing drama to those around the patient. Similarly, when members of the public contact the police about a person acting bizarrely in the street it is clear that the client of the police-psychiatrist 'disposal' is not the patient, although quite who psychiatry is serving in this instance is ambiguous. Is it the distressed and perplexed member of public making the first police contact, is it the police themselves, or is it both?

Clearly, if a person is detained without trial, and they are interfered with without consent, then it is difficult to conceptualize them as 'customers' or 'clients' of psychiatry. Instead, the terminology favoured by the psychiatric service users' movement would seem to be more appropriate, of 'recipients' or 'survivors' (see Chapter 11). On the other hand, if a person chooses freely to make contact with a mental health worker, to seek help with a personal difficulty, in this instance they would seem to have a genuine 'client' status. However, even with this voluntary contact there is still a sense in which the client does not enjoy the same rights and privileges as other types of customers accessing a service industry.

The question of informed choice

This can be examined with reference to five criteria set out by Bean (1986). Bean suggests that to understand whether or not genuinely informed consent takes place in psychiatric services, we must ask the following questions:

1 Are the patients aware of themselves – are they competent at making judgements on their own behalf?
2 Do those who are assumed to be aware of themselves (relatives and professionals) use that awareness to act morally?
3 Do professionals supply comprehensive and comprehensible information to
   patients?
4 Are patients subjected to pressure or coercion when they are in receipt of
   psychiatric treatment?
5 Is consent to specifiable actions offered by professionals to patients?

Answers to these questions, suggested below, point towards psychiatric practice being problematic on all five counts:

Insight

Professionals may override the need to seek consent from patients about
treatment if they believe that the patient is lacking in insight into their condition. However, three problems with the notion of insight can be noted:

1 Insight tends to be defined in a *circular way*. That is, insight means that a
   patient agrees with their psychiatrist. Sanity and madness are socially agreed
   notions and where agreement breaks down in a psychiatric encounter
   between doctor and patient, then the more powerful party has their view
   upheld. Consequently, the patient may lose their right to refuse treatment.
2 Even if we take it to be non-problematic, on the first count, then mental
   illness is conceded by professionals often to be *episodic in nature*. Given this,
   how do psychiatrists know for sure when a person is aware and when they
   are not aware?
3 Given that professionals concede that psychotic patients who lack insight
   may be competent in certain regards (for instance the paranoid patient who
   can wash, dress and make money on the stock market) how can psychiatrists
   specify what insight actually means in terms of *cognitive and social competence*? Clearly, a patient may be aware of some things when they reflect on
   themselves but not of others; this is probably true of everybody. None of us
   can be aware of everything relevant to our existence all of the time. None of
   us can know our own minds for certain. (Indeed, if we are exposed to the tenet
   of psychoanalysis we are all encouraged to believe that the bulk of our
   mind is unconscious.) And yet, despite our ubiquitous failure to be fully
   self-aware, we get by most of the time in most of our lives.

Beck-Sander (1998) deconstructed psychiatric literature referring to insight
and found it to have weak construct validity. She found that the concept was
used by professionals to indicate four separate patient features:

1 *Treatment compliance* – when this is a defining feature of insight, then it is
   assumed that to resist treatment is necessarily irrational. This is a dubious
   assumption given the iatrogenic effects of psychiatric treatments discussed
   earlier. Indeed, if all patients were fully informed of these effects, treatment
   compliance would probably decrease generally.

2 *Psychological mindedness* – this can be found in the psychiatric literature as another proxy indicator of insight. It refers to insight as a reified defence operating inside patients which purportedly protects them from the pain of their illness. Thus, those with more insight are deemed to be more distressed, whereas those lacking insight are cut off from the pain of the purported disease process they are experiencing.

3 *Prognosis is also used at times by psychiatrists as a circular indicator of insight* – those with more insight are deemed to have shorter periods of relapse into psychosis and the inverse is deemed to be true for those with less insight. This professional reasoning is *post hoc* and tautological. Moreover, given that prognosis is determined by a number of external, as well as patient characteristics, such as socio-economic opportunity and societal discrimination, then how can we ever know whether insight is a defining single feature when prognosis is good or bad for a particular patient?

4 *Pathophysiology* – this is offered at times by some psychiatrists as a correlate of insight. That is, purported neuropsychological dysfunction in psychosis is offered as an explanation for why psychotic patients lack insight into their condition. This is, of course, a possibility, much as cerebral bleeding accounts for the brain damage which affects the short-term memory and orientation in time and space of some dementing patients. The problem with this argument is that, by definition, the functional psychoses are not organic conditions, at least they are not demonstrably so at present. They are defined by symptoms alone because biological markers (true signs) are absent, despite substantial bio-medical and neuropsychological research into the psychoses.

Thus, the whole question of competence or self-awareness is problematic. Despite this, professionals have powers to treat patients without their consent and they do so using the notion of 'lack of insight', as if it were non-problematic. Moreover, this purported lack of competence on the part of psychiatric patients is the very rationale for why negotiation about consent is either deemed to be unnecessary or futile. Despite this, there is no evidence that psychiatric patients are actually less able than medical patients to understand what is told to them. Soskis (1978) found that, in fact, psychiatric patients knew more about the side effects of drugs they were receiving than did medical patients. (Showing that if they are told they understand.) However, the psychiatric patients were less likely than the medical patients to be told why they were receiving the medication. This indicates that psychiatrists are less willing than physicians to discuss diagnosis and rationale for treatment with their patients.

The morality of others

The discussion above showed that, collectively, psychiatrists have not acted morally in relation to the needs and vulnerabilities of patients. Major tranquillizers are one of the main groups of treatments imposed on resistant recipients. Practitioners have also acted immorally in the case of the abuse of patients by psychotherapists. Thus, psychiatric therapists are prone to fail Bean's second criterion.

Comprehensive and comprehensible information

This question is the one most commonly addressed by disaffected users of services. Whether the disaffection is caused by drugs, ECT or psychotherapy, the recurrent complaint is that patients are not supplied with enough information about the advantages and disadvantages of the treatment offered or imposed. The minor tranquillizer campaign led to litigation against the drug companies and the prescribing doctors, which focused on both iatrogenic effects and the withholding of information at the time of prescription about these effects. The same has been true of litigation about major tranquillizers in the US (Brown and Funk 1986). Rogers, Pilgrim and Lacey (1993) found that 60 per cent of a sample who had received major tranquillizers reported not being informed of their purpose, and that 70 per cent of this group were unhappy about the amount of information they had been given. Similar findings have been reported in studies in the USA (Soskis 1978; Lidz *et al.* 1984). These complaints would indicate that psychiatry is found to be lacking according to Bean's third criterion.

Coercion

Despite legal safeguards under mental health legislation detained patients may be injected forcibly with drugs or given ECT or psychosurgery against their will. They can also be forced into isolation ('seclusion') without consent. The question begged is whether informal patients are genuinely in the patient role voluntarily. Rogers, Pilgrim and Lacey (1993) compared those in their sample who felt their voluntary admission had been genuine with those who felt it to be not genuine. In the first group, 21 per cent reported some degree of coercion, whereas in the second group 80 per cent felt coerced into going into hospital. Similar evidence of coercion during 'voluntary' admission to psychiatric facilities has been found in the US (Klatte *et al.* 1969). Bean's fourth criterion is failed by psychiatry.

Specifiable actions

Bean points out that real informed consent cannot be consent to anything and everything. Instead, it must be consent to a specific action or circumscribed set of actions. If it were consent to anything then this would give arbitrary powers to professionals. Indeed, in secure psychiatric provision, in particular, it is commonplace for patients to be subject to the regime of what Goffman called a 'total institution': all activities and interventions are determined by the regime of the hospital. When this is the case, patients have little or no moment-to-moment powers of decision making. In effect, they abandon their right to agree or disagree to specifiable actions on admission or it is taken away from them.

Even in less coercive surroundings, if professionals do not give a full account, in advance, of what is to happen when a treatment is carried out, then they are not giving patients the right to agree to specifiable actions. For example, biological psychiatrists may be paternalistic about withholding information on major tranquillizers (in case it may worry the patient). Psycho-analysts may evade questions about their technique as part of their technique (to provide a blank screen for the patient's projections). Thus, for different reasons, both physical and psychological therapists may evade specifying their intended actions in relation to the patient they treat.

Having now discussed both the problems of identifying psychiatry's client and informed consent, let us return to Goffman's criteria of a good repair service industry. In essence he argues that such a service would have the following features (with our queries about the gap between principle and practice in brackets):

1 The workshop of the industry would be benign and would prevent a deterioration in the condition that required repair; (Mental health services are clearly not always benign. Coercion is ever present and treatments can be damaging.)
2 Transporting the part in need of repair to the workshop would not introduce new forms of damage; (Entering services is stigmatizing and can be distressing.)
3 The damaged part is not linked inextricably to its possessor. That is, the owner can be separated from their damaged part for a defined period of time until it is repaired; (The damaged part and its possessor are one and the same. Mental illness is about a flawed or deviant self. This is why a psychiatric diagnosis has such profound implications, as a patient's credibility as a social actor or citizen is questioned, possibly for life.)
4 Those providing the service and those using it enter into the repair contract voluntarily and with mutual respect. (Mental health law exists to enforce the relationship between service providers and service recipients.)

The social distribution of treatment

One of the paradoxes of psychiatric treatment is that it inverts the 'inverse care law'. The latter, which generally holds true for people with physical health problems, refers to the phenomenon of those in the greatest need, as a result of their socially created illness, having the poorest access to the health care system. Not only are richer people healthier than poorer people, they also access better treatment from both publicly funded and private health care systems. The opposite is true of mental health care systems at least as far as in-patient care in Britain is concerned.

In the light of the stigma attached to mental health services and the role of psychiatry, some of the time in the coercive control of socially disruptive behaviour, then it is little surprising that some social groups are more vulnerable to service receipt than others:

1 black and ethnic minority populations receive greater in-patient attention and physical treatments than white populations in Britain and the USA;
2 in-patients are usually poor. They are often unemployed and unemployable;

3 women are in receipt of more psychiatric treatment than men, although a caution here is that more men are treated coercively than women.

When we examine the research on receipt of voluntary out-patient attendance in mental health services, then a different picture emerges:

1 the utilization of long-term psychotherapy is inversely related to age (over 65), race (black) and years of schooling (Olsen and Pincus 1994);
2 in the USA black and Hispanic women utilize out-patient facilities less than white women (Padgett *et al.* 1994);
3 black war veterans in the USA receive less intensive treatment for post-traumatic stress problems than white veterans;
4 black people drop out of out-patient family therapy earlier on average than whites (Kazdin, Stolar and Marciano 1995). This finding needs to be seen in the context of the failure to incorporate cross-cultural counselling into mainstream services.

The impact of evidence-based practice on treatment

In the past ten years there has been the emergence of research knowledge and evidence as means of controlling and improving the development and quality of health care services. The extent of its formal academic impact in the field of mental health is shown by the appearance in 1997 of a dedicated journal, *Evidence-Based Mental Health*.

The rising popularity of 'evidence-based practice' (EBP) is linked to the imperatives of health policy makers to control service costs. It has also been overlain by a discourse on concern to assess the health benefits and risk of technology and treatments (Faulkner 1997). These concerns can be seen as rhetorical devices, which include the purported strengths of multi-disciplinarity and benefits to users of cost-effective treatments. It is common now for all parties to accept in principle, evidence as a basis for clinically effective and cost-effective interventions. The randomized control trial (RCT) remains the 'gold standard' of EBP, while evidence-based or lay knowledge and qualitative methods are afforded a lesser place. In the area of mental health there are particular problems in applying the experimental conditions of the RCT to services:

> In RCTs, treatment fidelity is ensured, contaminating variables such as dropouts are eliminated and specific symptom reduction outcomes are investigated. In contrast in actual services, treatment fidelity cannot be assumed, people drop in and out of service contact and their presenting problems are often complex and not limited to specific symptoms ...
>
> (Pilgrim 1997b: 569)

However, there have been specific aspects of treatments which have been evaluated along standardized criteria and guidelines in actual services. There is evidence too that the rhetorical devices of quality and evidence can be harnessed to empower mental health users to challenge mainstream psychiatric practices. Notwithstanding the relatively weak position of mental health quality standards compared to physical ones the trend towards EBM is increasing in the mental health arena. While this is very much a nascent and marginal trend, the insertion of criteria of quality into mental health services is likely to influence what comes to be acceptable knowledge about mental health service development. Two examples are given here of how a user perspective on treatment effectiveness can challenge professional definitions of evidence-based practice.

Disputed evidence about ECT

The use of ECT, controversial since its inception, illustrates the challenge of addressing patients' perspectives in the evaluation of health care technology. Despite widespread professional acceptance of ECT, service-user groups have often opposed its use. This illustrates how differing conceptions of evidence can affect the evaluation of technology. It also provides an example of the value of a more complex definition of the significant outcomes of treatment and the way in which they can shape health policy (Heitman 1996). Professional definitions of good outcomes and those offered by treatment recipients may not always coincide. While some users' groups focus on ECT as an irredeemable barbarity perpetrated by professionals, some individual patients endorse it as a life saver, while others harbour life-long resentment about its use in their care (Rogers *et al.* 1993).

Official professional accounts of ECT (Royal College of Psychiatrists 1995) have given no hint of this mixed consumer perspective on the treatment and insist that it is safe and effective, even for children. With such discrepant views about outcomes between psychiatrists and their patients about ECT, services became a contested site for competing interest groups both in terms of their viewpoints and the evidence invoked to support them.

A recent literature review-based study designed to ascertain patients' views of the benefits of ECT (Rose *et al.* 2003) suggested that at least one-third of patients reported persistent memory loss. This 'meta analysis' of patient perspectives suggested that the current conventional wisdom from the Royal College of Psychiatrists that over 80 per cent of patients are satisfied with ECT and that memory loss is not clinically important is misleading.

Users' views as evidence in service research

Some work on users' experience of mental health services, with its roots in symbolic interactionism, has considered the experience of users to be worthwhile in its own right. This has been incorporated, to some extent, into a health outcomes approach to policy development, as has been pointed out by Godfrey and Wistow (1997: 326):

> The Department of Health has placed great importance on evidence-based purchasing rooted in the assessment and measurement of health outcome

... We draw upon users' conceptions of acute mental health service to examine users' conceptions of outcomes ...

In a narrow policy approach, the accounts of users get transformed from narratives situated in their biographical context to a set of potential outcomes with which to measure the success, or otherwise, of a service. The knowledge base – qualitative methods transformed and presented as something 'new' – is a form of 'methodolatory' increasingly common in health service research which loses sight of social theory (Pilgrim and May 1998). A more holistic approach to outcomes would address a users' perspective which considers the entire course and experience of mental illness, i.e. the meanings of users and significant others of 'becoming' and 'being ill'.

The utility of a more holistic approach to outcome work was confirmed by Felton *et al.* (1995). Their study examined whether employing mental health consumers as peer specialists in an intensive case-management programme can enhance outcomes for clients with serious mental illness. They found that clients served by mental health teams with peer specialists demonstrated greater gains in several areas of quality of life and an overall reduction in the number of major life problems experienced. They also reported more frequent contact with their case managers and the largest gains of all three groups in the areas of self-image and outlook and social support. Other research advocates the use of user perspectives in informing future clinical governance strategies, for example the clinical practice guidelines should consider how to harness what users are already doing to manage risk because they cannot always rely on staff to do this for them, particularly in volatile environments such as acute psychiatric wards. A set of identified contextual risks which users manage were found to include avoiding risky situations/individuals, seeking protection from staff, and pushing to get discharged.

Tackling social exclusion as a focus of treatment

Historically, the types of psychiatric treatment discussed earlier have predominated in the mental health field. However, a departure from a mental illness paradigm is evident in recent calls for the more active promotion of positive mental health. This trend in the mental health field reflects a shift evident more generally in health promotion and fits broadly within the contemporary and dominant approach to health promotion, which includes three areas: consumption, lifestyle and risk. Burrows, Bunton and Nettleton (1995: 2) describe the new paradigm thus:

What is distinctive about health promotion is the attention that it gives to the facilitation of healthy lives: the idea that it is no good just telling people that they should change their lifestyles without altering their social, economic and ecological environments. People must be able to live healthy lives. Health promotion aims to work not only at the level of the individual but at the level of socio-economic structures to encourage the creation and implementation of healthy public policies such as those concerned with transport, environment, agriculture and so on.

The shift in the area of mental health can be seen in the expansive and holistic definition of health adopted by the World Health Organization in the 1980s: 'By the year 2000, people should have the basic opportunity to develop and use their health potential to live socially and economically fulfilling lives' (WHO 1986). Recently, the active promotion of mental health has been evident in the government's approach to public health and health promotion. At the level of health policy too the recent Green Paper 'Our Healthier Nation' advocates a multi-sectoral approach to mental health problems and advocates action to be taken at government, locality, and individual levels (Department of Health 1998).

Two features evident in this trend are the move in the epidemiology of mental illness away from a traditional psychiatric paradigm and the acknowledgement given to lay perceptions of positive mental health. With regard to the latter, sociologists have been party to this reorientation by engaging in a research agenda examining lay epidemiology (described in Chapter 2). This orientation has also placed a higher value on strategies for maintaining mental health.

Those who have researched in this area have identified both proactive and reactive lay action, self-reliance, cognitive strategies (taking up a particular psychological stance to everyday events) and stress-reducing activities, such as sport, as common mental health strategies (Rogers and Pilgrim 1996). The focus of the amelioration or management of mental health problems has also shifted. Lay management strategies of dealing with mental health problems have been given a higher priority than previously in formal health promotion strategies, including those with professionals (Trent and Reed 1997).

A further commensurate shift among some working in the mental health field is in efforts to actively manage or 'treat' social exclusion and marginalization. The latter are viewed as causing or exacerbating mental health problems in areas of poverty and deprivation, over-crowding and unemployment.

To an extent this has also been adopted as a central part of official mental health policy; for example this is evident in this statement of the National Institute for Mental Health (http://www.nimhe.org.uk/priorities/socialinclusion.asp):

> NIMHE starts from a commitment to supporting the efforts of mental health service users and local organisations in delivering access to the mainstream opportunities that are so important to hope, ambition and recovery . . .

Those with enduring mental health problems have emphasized the importance of enhancing, sustaining, and taking control of their mental health. In line with this, the potential of health professionals' interventions is seen as 'empowering' people with long term mental health problems by attending to the form of professional interaction with patients (e.g. quality of communication continuity of care they provide) and where this takes place (Kai and Crosland 2001).

In their current guise the health goals of people with serious mental illness are viewed as being most likely to improve when personal power is advanced through treatment partnerships and community opportunities. Corrigan (2002) has suggested that strategies that may enhance treatment partnerships include:

- an emphasis on hope and recovery rather than on poor prognosis;
- treatment plans that are collaborative rather than unilateral decision making that is perceived as (or is) coercive;
- treatment services provided in the person's community rather than places which are physically and personally distant.

Communities that substitute stigmatizing attitudes and discriminatory behaviors with reasonable accommodation and a 'realistic' view of mental health problems are seen as key requirements facilitating the work and independent living opportunities.

Family support services in one London Borough is an example of one such mental health intervention that focuses on finding effective ways of working with vulnerable families affected by experiences of racism, bullying, mental health difficulties, domestic violence or child abuse through the active participation of those being targeted (Gray 2002).

Governmentality and self-help

Some sociologists have argued that we now live in a therapeutic society in which therapeutic ideas are not confined to clinical and hospital settings but permeate most areas of everyday life. 'Governmentality' in contemporary societies is achieved by the self-regulation of our conduct and feelings and the internalization of psychological knowledge. The point is made by Rose (1990: 10):

> Through self-inspection, self-problematization, self-monitoring, and con-fession, we evaluate ourselves according to the criteria provided for use by others. Through self-reformation, therapy, techniques of body alteration, and the calculated reshaping of speech and emotion, we adjust ourselves by means of the techniques propounded by the experts of the soul.

This analysis has increasing salience for understanding cultural trends and the popularity of psychological ideas and therapies and the promotion within official policy making of therapeutical interventions designed to promote individual responsibility and control through population-based training programmes (such as the Expert Patient Programme in Britain or Chronic Disease Management Programme in the USA). These *public* health policies are designed to encourage *individuals* to take control and responsibility for their illness and their lives. They emphasize self-assessment, self-monitoring of risk and self-efficacy in managing health and illness in everyday life.

Giddens (1991) talks of the notion of 'lay re-skilling' where technical knowledge is reacquired or reappropriated by lay people and routinely applied in the course of their day-to-day activities. 'Lay re-skilling' can be framed as a trend towards the demedicalization of society with a return to notions of 'natural' rather than technical forms of healing – non compliance with medical treatment and the growth of complementary therapies are examples of this. Alternatively it can be seen as lay reappropriation whereby individuals use medical technology for their own ends and this is thus seen as a means of liberation rather than oppression. In line with this, self-help, self-care and self-treatment are all growing trends in mental health, as in physical health, especially in response to 'chronic disease' or 'long-term conditions'.

Self-care has been a salient but embedded activity of some new social movements connected to a wider societal view about the need for change (see Chapter 11). A good example of this in the field of mental health is the Hearing Voices Network. This mainly consists of people, mainly with a diagnosis of schizophrenia, who explore the different meanings which might be attached to a person having auditory hallucinations within their biographical context:

> People who hear voices and their families and friends can gain greater benefits from de-stigmatising the experience, leading to a greater tolerance and understanding. This can be achieved through promoting more positive explanations which give people a more positive framework for developing their own ways of coping and raising awareness about the experience in society as a whole.
>
> (www.hearing-voices.org.uk)

However, the trend towards self management that has begun to emerge over the last few years, alluded to earlier, is unconnected with this social/political campaigning ethos. Instead, policy innovations such as the Expert Patient Programme have focused on professionally devised packages designed to save professional time in cash-strapped services.

Richards (2004) has contrasted the core elements considered by professionals and users to be important about self-help. Professionals focus on: pressures on professional time for one to one treatment; technique-based interventions; evidence-based practice; health technology delivery methods (books, computers); common mental health problems (e.g. anxiety and depression); early treatment; and cost effectiveness. By contrast, service users focus on: self-determination; empowerment; lifestyle; social networks; recovery; serious mental health problems; personal development as a reaction to negative experiences of mental health services; and chronic disease management. Thus self-help, self-management and self-surveillance have ambiguous features. They are both an extension of professional power/knowledge and an opportunity to resist it by those with mental health problems.

Discussion

This chapter has looked at how patients are treated by the psychiatric service. The sociological discourse about this topic has tended, itself, to be divided between the poles of the spectrum of service delivery mentioned earlier. On the one hand, it has been concerned with critically exposing treatment as mystified coercive social control. On the other hand, it has become pre-occupied with those psychological interventions which are 'anxiously sought and gratefully received'. Sociology is a mirror to the divided territory of psychiatry and, arguably, it contributes to that division.

Psychiatric treatment remains in a precarious state of legitimacy. This uncertainty is then amplified by the doubts about the effectiveness of both physical and psychological therapeutic approaches and the complaints that have accumulated about the iatrogenic effects of these treatments. The con-tradictory picture of psychiatry, mixing as it does both coercion and voluntar-ism, and an eclectic range of treatments from leucotomy to psychoanalysis, also increases the gap between expectation and reality. If patients entering the psychiatric system expect lengthy explorations of their biography and actually get a cursory interview, followed by a prescription for antidepressants, then the chances of disappointment are great. Likewise, if people look to psychiatry as a source of comfort during times of personal confusion and distress and actually encounter an impersonal controlling regime, with professionals who serve third parties rather than the patients they are supposedly treating, then disaffection is, again, likely.

The uncertainty surrounding the legitimacy of psychiatric treatment is also amplified by the structural inequalities in access to the range of its interven-tions. In other words, as we have explored elsewhere in the book, not all social groups are represented evenly throughout the spectrum of psychiatry. Some receive much harsher treatment than others. Black people are less likely to receive psychotherapy and more likely to receive medication and ECT. They are also more likely to be treated coercively than white people, with the excep-tion of the Irish in Britain. Richer clients can afford to pick and choose between therapists in private practice, whereas poorer clients have to take what is given by state-employed professionals in their particular locality. Those diagnosed as being psychotic are less likely to receive psychological treatments than those who are diagnosed as being neurotic. Men are over-represented at the 'harsh' end of services.

If entering the psychiatric system *ipso facto* entailed being treated well, then those groups which are over-represented (like black people) would view them-selves as being in receipt of preferential treatment. The fact that over-representation is instead a source of concern and anger to these groups, reflects the suspicion with which psychiatry is viewed (as being an oppressive part of the extended state apparatus of control). Sociological investigations of how psychiatric patients are treated (in both senses of the word) may need to take on board this complexity and these contradictions. Up until now, two main 'camps' of sociology might be seen to have been warring about how to describe and understand psychiatric treatment. The humanistic bias of symbolic inter-actionism, exemplified in the work of Goffman, contributed to the notion of 'anti-psychiatry' and focused on the degradation of the individual and their loss of citizenship. The anti-humanistic bias of the post-structuralists con-ceives only of discourses which patients and therapists contribute to (or are trapped in). According to this view, individuals are produced, rather than destroyed, by psychiatry.

The psychological technologies, like the psychotherapies, are indeed now deeply implicated in modern secular society, contributing to the regulation of a moral order and promoting the contemporary importance of the 'self'. Arguably, the same is true of an approach which emphasizes the promotion of positive mental health. The problem for the post-structuralist position is that the old humanistic, anti-psychiatric arguments about the coercive power of the State are still highly pertinent to those groups which continue to be its particular target. It is not surprising that such groups remain hostile to psychiatry, rather than receiving it gratefully when contributing to 'productive power'. Sociology cannot ignore either the productive technologies of the self or the destructive potential of coercive psychiatry. Both have to be considered together.

In this chapter we have covered a wide range of considerations about psychiatric treatment. This has included reviewing the literature on specific forms of treatment and the social forces which shape its production and maintenance. Sociologists have contributed to a critical discourse about treatment along with the 'anti-psychiatrists' and disaffected service users. At other times, sociologists have suggested that psychiatry is part of a wider set of processes of governmentality. Overall, sociological scrutiny (exemplified in the work of Goffman) has tended to expose the logical contradictions of treatment. At the same time, the influence of Foucault has focused more on productive power rather than the coercive role of psychiatry in society.

For the foreseeable future, sociologists are likely to retain an interest in both of these aspects of professional mental health work. However, the notion of social exclusion and the need to reverse the effects of the role of being a psychiatric patient through social and economic opportunities suggests a broadening focus to the traditional notion of treatment. This may mean that mental health workers and psychiatrists in particular will be placed in the increasingly ironic position of ameliorating the distress caused by the labelling, treatment and management created by their own professional actions.

Questions

1 Does psychiatry produce or crush subjectivity?

2 How can non-compliance with psychiatric treatment be understood?

3 Why does the 'inverse care law' not apply in psychiatric services?

4 What problems are associated with the concept of insight?

5 To what extent does Goffman's work on large mental hospital life still apply today?

6 Discuss the rationale for evidence-based mental health care and barriers to its success.

For discussion

Consider whether you would be prepared to volunteer for psychiatric treatment if you became psychologically distressed. What would be the pros and cons to consider in this decision?

Further reading

Breggin, P. (1993) *Toxic Psychiatry*. London: HarperCollins.

Fisher, S. and Greenberg, R.P. (1997) *From Placebo to Panacea: Putting Psychiatric Drugs to the Test*. London: Wiley.

Gabe, J. and Bury, M. (1996) Halcion nights: a sociological account. *Sociology*, 30(3): 447–70.

Pilgrim, D. (1997) *Psychotherapy and Society*. London: SAGE.

Romme, M. and Escher, S. (1993) *Accepting Voices*. London: Mind.

Trent, D.R. and Reed, C.A. (1997) *Promotion of Mental Health*. London: Ashgate.

Chapter 9

The organization of mental health work

Chapter overview

This chapter will explore the changing organizational form of mental health work under four main headings.

- the sociology of the hospital;
- the rise of the asylum;
- the crisis of the asylum;
- responses to the crisis;
- community care and reinstitutionalization;
- public health, primary care and the new technology revolution.

The sociology of the hospital

Despite attempts by policy makers to move the focus of health care towards primary and community care, in modern western societies, the hospital has remained at the centre of health care systems. When analysing the organization, sociologists have tended to use as a working model the general hospital which deals with acute physical illness. The way in which the modern general hospital has been depicted provides a benchmark with which the mental hospital can be compared.

The modern hospital, with its high-technology equipment, elaborate procedures and specialized skills has frequently been viewed as an outcome of 'scientific developments' and medical progress over the last century (Tuckett 1976). This assumption has led a number of sociologists to comment that the modern hospital is an example of Max Weber's notion of a 'bureaucratic organization'. Sociologists of organizations have identified characteristics of the 'typical' modern hospital that have been influenced by Weber's ideal type.

Hospitals are complex organizations, which process inputs (patients) in a way which materially changes them (in this case cures them). Perrow (1965) identified three factors which determine the way in which organizations function:

1 the *cultural system*, which sets the legitimate or formal goals;
2 *technology*, which is the means for achieving these goals (in the hospital this includes the types of therapeutic techniques in use);
3 the *structure* of the organization in which techniques are embedded and person-power organized as a means of achieving the set goals.

Hospitals, like other complex organizations, such as factories and schools, operate on the basis of an inter-dependence between technology and structure. Cost-effectiveness and the efficiency of providing and operating sophisticated technology may determine the type of hospital service. For instance, specialist radiography equipment may have been responsible for the demise of small cottage hospitals and the relocation of services and staff to centrally based larger general hospitals.

Hospitals are characterized by a highly specialized division of health labour (what Durkheim termed 'organic solidarity'). This can be seen in hospital wards organized around the plethora of sub-specialties of medicine (e.g. ENT wards, radiology, orthopaedics, rheumatology, cardiac units, gynaecology and obstetrics and so on) and the strict demarcations between the roles and tasks of different health occupations.

The third characteristic of the modern hospital is its complex authority structure and command system. A system characterized by increased specialization, and the need to service patients round the clock every day of the year, necessitates a complex administrative structure. In Britain, the NHS has witnessed a struggle between bureaucratic and clinical authority in running hospitals. Weber's notion of the former refers to a system of officers in a hierarchical relationship and rationally organized by means of a system of rules and regulations. In contrast, clinical authority has tended to operate on the basis of the dominant professions, which usually means the autonomy of individual consultant medical practitioners.

The problems encountered by administrative reorganizations of the NHS, which were aimed at achieving a more coherent and rational means of organizing and delivering health care, may well be due to a clash between these dual lines of authority. For example, in surgical services, clinical authority at a local level, with consultants deciding to do a large number of operations, may well subvert the long-term planning and budgetary arrangements set by non-clinical managers. One of the aims of the introduction of managerialism to the NHS during the 1980s was to overcome this dual authority. This was done by amalgamating the two strands, making clinical directors responsible for the management and delivery of health care. The introduction of clinical governance into the NHS in 1999 strengthened this shift towards bringing the medical profession under managerial control.

Given this description of the general hospital, how did the the psychiatric hospital built in Victorian times look? The structure and organization of the large mental hospital did not fit the ideal type of the general hospital. Its architectural design and daily functions were organizationally incongruent in terms of therapy, structure and location. For example, while the general hospital is geographically located for easy access, many of the large Victorian asylums were deliberately built away from centres of populations. The lack of fit between institutional forms inspired by thinking in the nineteenth and twentieth centuries norms regarding health care delivery led to a crisis within these organizations. This crisis formed the focus of a critique of the institution, which emanated from a number of sources.

The rise of the asylum

The segregation of lunatics into large institutions took place over the final three centuries of the second millennium in Europe and North America. Psychiatric historians do not agree on the precise timing of this shift or on the exact explanation for its occurrence (Foucault 1965; Rothman 1971; Grob 1973; Scull 1979). Tracing the creation of large institutions can help us understand their demise but this involves the examination of competing historical claims.

A conventional and conservative account suggests that the asylum is viewed as part and parcel of medical progress and an increasingly humane way of dealing with 'mentally ill' people. For instance, Jones (1960) stresses the humanitarianism behind the reform movement leading to the Lunatics Act 1845. This Act compelled county authorities to establish asylums and enforced their regulation via a centralized Lunacy Commission and a system of medical records. Much of Jones's account centres around the official reports of Metropolitan Commissioners between 1828 and 1845 and the role of government-appointed bodies (such as Parliamentary Select Committees), which drew public attention to the poor state of workhouses and private madhouses.

The establishment of early institutions modelled on the moral treatment regime of the York Retreat is described as arising from 'the consciousness felt by a small group of citizens of an overwhelming social evil in their midst' (Jones 1960: 40). In fact, moral treatment failed to transfer from the early charity hospitals like the Retreat to the State-run asylums, although its image dominated the rhetoric of asylum reformers (Donnelly 1983). Jones (1960: 149) sees the implementation of the 1845 Act in a humanitarian light: 'Ashley and his colleagues had roused the conscience of mid-Victorian society, and had set a new standard of public morality by which the care of the helpless and degraded classes of the community was to be seen as a social responsibility'.

Critical historians reject this more conventional account of events. The incarceration of mad people in asylums is seen as inextricably linked to the wider-scale containment of social deviancy: the poor in workhouses and criminals in prisons. The accounts of alternative histories vary. Scull (1979), a Marxist, suggests that mass confinement (of which the asylum system constituted an integral part) was a product of urbanization, industrialization, and professional forces during the first half of the nineteenth century. The development of capitalism, with its demand for wage labour, meant that the existing means of poor relief was ill-equipped to deal with social deviance produced by the new market economy. Thus, the old outdoor system of relief in operation since the Elizabethan Poor Law was replaced by mass incarceration in institutions.

From the beginning of the nineteenth century a gradual process of segregation took place. Poor, able-bodied people (that is, those fit to work) were sent to workhouses, which were orientated towards instilling 'proper work habits'. These people were separated from those that could not work, which included those deemed insane and in need of incarceration in asylums. At the same time, ideas about madness were changing. It became recognized as a loss of self-control and not, as previously, a loss of humanity. These changing values were influenced by the exposure of the brutal treatment of those in madhouses. This encouraged the abandonment of mechanical restraints and it endorsed regimes such as the York Retreat.

These new social values permitted a greater willingness to accept a medical view of madness, the ascendance of which Scull attributes to the entrepreneurial leanings of medical practitioners, who were at the same time making efforts to professionalize and expand. Lucrative pickings were to be had by the profession trying to capture the madhouses previously run by laymen. Rather than having to attract patients to them, the asylum provided them with a ready-made and captive clientele.

Unlike Jones or Scull, Foucault (1965) does not concern himself with the specifics of the history of institutions. He views the *Hôpital Générale* at the end of the seventeenth century (where at one time 1 per cent of Paris's population who were 'incapable' of productive work were incarcerated) as symbolizing a new concept of madness. The spirit of capitalism, which Foucault traces from the enlightenment onwards, promotes rationality, surveillance and discipline. Reason becomes separated from unreason. This separation out of unreason, whereby madness comes to be seen as the lack of the faculty of 'logos', is symbolized in the replacement of lepers by lunatics. The latter became the new 'race apart'; and their confinement followed.

Critical histories therefore challenge self-congratulatory versions of history, which tend to mask the interests of powerful sections of society, such as the psychiatric profession and the central capitalist State. However, Rothman

(1983) suggests that there are problems with critical, as well as conservative, histories because in both accounts 'conception triumphs over data'. According to Rothman, a focus on ideology, whether it is humanitarianism (Jones), capitalism (Scull) or surveillance (Foucault), can divert the historian's attention from the complex empirical reality of specific individual cases. For example, Scull's emphasis on the economic, Rothman claims, is overstated. The early American system of asylums appeared in the absence of a market economy. Ideas about madness, he suggests, can be influenced by idiosyncratic factors other than those associated with a capitalist mode of production (for example, ideals related to localized political activity and religious doctrine).

Sociologists in the 1960s were party to critical arguments about the dehumanizing effects of the asylum when the direction of mental health policy was clearly focused around whether or not to proceed with mass hospital closure. With the passage of time, when hospital closure and resettlement has become the norm, more recent sociologically informed commentary suggests that the history of the asylum is a contradictory one, particularly when seen in the context of the rise in new forms of surveillance, ways of dealing with psychiatric patients, and in a society which is arguably no more tolerant of psychiatric patients than previous generations.

Gittens's (1998) socio-historical analysis of a large psychiatric hospital in Essex based on the biographical narratives of staff and patients who lived or worked in the hospital suggests contradictions and paradoxes about the way the asylums were. In relation to women patients it is clear for example that the hospital, based as it was on men-only or women-only wards constituted a 'women-only space' and true asylum in a social context in which there was little such space in external community life. Moreover, the hardships and restriction of asylum life need to be balanced against the external social, economic and political conditions during the heyday of the asylum, such as extreme poverty, unemployment and wars which affected people's abilities to cope with difficult material and personal situations. The ambiguous history of the asylum is captured in the conclusion to Gittens's book reporting her study:

> There has been a tendency to see the old asylums as isolated, inward-looking institutions that may have benefited staff, but rarely patients, while 'community care' gives patients greater opportunities in the wider world. In closer scrutiny what I have found in this study, as in history – and life – generally, is a great deal of contradiction. In some ways, conditions have improved for those suffering mental illness, in other ways they have not. Some people have benefited enormously from changes over the past few decades, others have not.
>
> (Gittens, 1998: p. 220)

These different histories and interpretations point to the way in which accounts of psychiatric organizations are themselves socially constructed and influenced by the particular point in time in which they are written. We turn now to the processes underlying the dismantling of the asylum system. Again, competing explanations influenced by different perspectives and reading of events provides a complex and contested picture of the causes of hospital rundown and closure.

The asylum system was problematic from its inception. The ideals of 'moral treatment' were abandoned almost immediately. The system rapidly became overwhelmed by the numbers admitted with chronic conditions. Political pressures were encountered to keep costs down. Although the dominance of the institution began to wane from the 1930s onwards, with a gradual reduction in the number of asylum residents, it was not until the late 1950s and early 1960s that it was faced with a sustained analysis and critique. These criticisms will now be examined.

Ronald Laing, David Cooper, Franco Basaglia and Thomas Szasz were psychiatrists who challenged traditional professional theory and practice. (Collectively they were dubbed 'anti-psychiatrists', although only Cooper conceded the label.) They were concerned to develop services to patients based on voluntary psychological approaches and consequently they attacked current coercive, biological and institutional psychiatry. Goffman (1961), in his seminal work *Asylums*, considered the mental hospital to be a 'total institution'. This he defined as a place of residence with a large number of people isolated from wider society, for lengthy periods of time, which runs according to an enclosed and formalized administrative regime. Goffman described four types of total institutions:

1 those which care for the incapable and 'harmless' (such as nursing homes and hospices);
2 those which provide for those who are perceived as an unwanted threat to the community (for example, sanatoriums for people who suffer from TB);
3 those which cater for the dangerous people where the welfare of the inmate is not paramount (for example prisons and prisoner of war camps);
4 those that are designed for people who voluntarily decide to retreat from the world, for instance for religious purposes (monasteries and convents).

The old asylums were examples of the second type of total institution. Secure psychiatric provision (medium-security units and high-security hospitals like Ashworth and Broadmoor) are remaining examples. Model (or Weber's 'ideal type' of) total institutions possess a number of characteristics. All aspects of life are conducted in the same place. Activities always take place in the presence of others and are strictly timetabled and geared towards fulfilling the official aims of the institution rather than the needs of individuals. A strict demarcation exists between 'inmates' and staff.

The crisis of the asylum

On entering the mental hospital (the 'in-patient' phase of the patient's 'moral career') individuals underwent what Goffman called the 'mortification of self'. 'Self' is not used to refer to a personal attribute. Instead it is conceptualized as being constructed by the pattern of social control which exists in an institution. The mortification of self occurred as a result of two stages. On entering the hospital a person was deprived of their previous identity through regimentation. This entailed stripping a person of their previous affirmation of self, movement was restricted, clothes worn on entry replaced with pyjamas or hospital-owned clothing, and personal belongings such as money and jewellery taken away. Goffman referred to this manner of entering the hospital as a 'degradation ceremony'. Once on the ward, inmates were invited to disown their former selves through a devaluing of past lives in 'confessionals' with staff and in-ward groups. Daily life on the ward was subjected to close and constant scrutiny, making privacy an impossibility.

Although Goffman's work was undertaken in an American context, similar analyses were being made of British mental hospitals. This British work was carried out by researchers who accepted psychiatric knowledge as being legitimate. Although their work was critical of custodial care, they need to be distinguished from the 'anti-psychiatrists' (whom Wing (1978) went on to attack). Moreover, their work is more empirical in its methodology than Goffman's study, whose work can be dismissed or queried as being theoretically elegant but weak on substantive evidence, beyond his own participant observations.

By contrast Wing (1962) drew attention to the social withdrawal and passivity of hospitalized patients, which could be correlated with length of stay and was independent of clinical condition (i.e. psychotic symptoms). Wing and Freudenberg (1961) demonstrated how such signs of institutionally induced apathy could be quite rapidly reversed if chronic patients were placed in a stimulating work environment. Brown (1959) and Brown and Wing (1962) demonstrated the severe effects of institutionalization and showed that sustained efforts by clinicians to reverse these effects could be demonstrated by comparing hospitals with custodial and more therapeutic policies. Nonetheless, the same pattern of withdrawal and apathy being correlated with length of stay was evident in all three hospitals. Brown and Wing cautioned that although enthusiastic medical leadership in the better hospitals could improve the functioning of chronic patients, these could be reversed by others later. Moreover, they commented: 'it is unlikely that the functions of an energetic reformer can be built in to the social structure of an institution' (p. 169).

Scott (1973) highlighted the passivity and symptom-inducing effects of the mental hospital and its attendant illness model, which he viewed as forming a 'treatment barrier' between professional and client. Russell Barton's *Institutional Neurosis* (1959) is traceable to his observations of Nazi concentration camp inmates. Inmates surrounded by corpses and excreta refused to move from the huts they were living in. Their bizarre attachment was compounded by stereotypical pacing. Barton noted the similar stereotypical behaviour in the closed and unstimulating environment of 'backward' life in large mental hospitals after his return to civilian medicine in England.

This Anglo-American critique of the mental hospital from the 1960s was augmented by later work. Braginsky, Braginsky and Ring (1973) found that acute patients wanted to leave hospital but that chronic patients took no interest in their clinical condition. Instead they found ways of remaining invisible to staff, while maximizing the comforts they could find in the hospital. These patients actively wanted to stay in hospital in preference to the uncertainties of poverty on the outside.

At the very time that the service-users' movement was emerging (see Chapter 11) and the large hospitals were on the brink of eventual collapse, Martin (1985) reviewed the failures of caring in British mental institutions between 1965 and 1983. During that period, ten inquiries of national significance took place into incidents and bad conditions within British mental illness and handicap hospitals. The problems forming the basis of complaints (which were often exposed by 'whistle-blowing' staff) ranged from inhumane, brutal and threatening behaviour by staff to lack of care through negligence and indifference.

Since the publication of Martin's work, mistreatment in large institutions continues to be exposed, for instance in Broadmoor and Ashworth Special Hospitals during the early 1990s. Thus his analysis is pertinent wherever the character of the total institution is retained. Recent accounts from Eastern Europe, where patients are sometimes kept in cages inside hospital wards indicate the contemporary relevance of critiques of hospital care from Goffman to Martin.

Two questions were posed by Martin: how do trained carers come to behave contrary to professional standards? And how have hospitals been arranged in such a way that abuse and neglect have not been prevented? Martin found that some other organizational goal (such as staff convenience or public safety) had implicitly usurped the goal of caring ('the subordination of care'). He also identified six types of isolation, which largely answered the second question. These were:

1 *Geographical isolation.* Most large institutions were situated out of main town centres, and even where they were not they were cut off from local communities;
2 *Immediate isolation* referred to the fact that wards within hospitals were often isolated from one another and operated as little 'fiefdoms'. Martin found that it was only a small minority of wards within each hospital investigated which formed the basis of complaints;
3 *Personal isolation* referred to situations in which individuals were left in charge of large numbers of difficult-to-manage patients. Untrained and isolated staff were often left to cope with unbearable conditions;
4 *Consultant isolation.* The worst wards were found to be those rarely visited by the responsible consultant, with everyday management being left to junior medical staff. Thus, professional abdication of responsibility and lack of leadership was an important factor;
5 *Intellectual isolation* referred to a lack of professional stimulus, staff development, and access to training opportunities;
6 *Privacy* was a prerequisite for abuse; patients who were regularly visited by relatives were not usually the focus of complaints.

The structural nature of this isolation led a number of social scientists to have a pessimistic stance towards the possibility of reforming the internal workings of large institutions. As we noted earlier, even those accepting the legitimacy of psychiatric theory and practice, such as Brown and Wing, questioned the reformability of psychiatric hospitals (even before the series of inquiries burgeoned after the mid-1960s). Whether or not all attempts at reform are futile is a moot point. However, what can be pointed out is that hospital scandals have continued where large hospitals exist – they are predictable sites of abuse and 'the corruption of care'.

Responses to the crisis

An early attempt to humanize the large impersonal isolated institutions was to introduce a more personal democratic approach to care. Therapeutic communities (TCs) – small units or wards designed to make the social environment the main therapeutic tool – were pioneered in Britain during the Second World War by psychotherapeutically orientated psychiatrists. The number of soldier patients suffering from the stress of warfare meant that the individual model of therapy became untenable because of scarce staff resources. These army psychiatrists were encouraged to experiment with a variety of group methods to increase staff cost-effectiveness. The twofold objectives looked for in therapeutic communities were identified by Main (1946) as the need to resocialize patients who had become dependent as a result of traditional hospital practices; and the use of the hospital environment as a therapeutic agent through establishing social participation. The latter was considered to be particularly valuable in treating people with neurotic conditions.

Later in civilian life, the TC approach was adapted more often to treat people with a diagnosis of personality disorder (Warren and Dolan 2001). The modification of the institution to form a TC has been reviewed sociologically by Manning (1989). These reviews focus on examples, such as the Henderson Hospital in Surrey, where the *whole institution* was involved. In other places a TC approach implemented piecemeal in a larger custodial setting tended to peter out. For example the rapid turnover of acute psychiatric units with their 'revolving door' patients and bio-medical treatment regime have tolerated the TC model poorly.

Inherent to the TC ideal was the belief that the social structure of the ward, group atmosphere, and ward morale were important elements in the therapeutic endeavour of psychiatry. Central to these objectives was the need for rapid change in the organization of the hospital in order to make it more flexible and egalitarian. Attempts were made to break down the traditionally rigid and hierarchical role divisions between staff and patients, and decisions on the running of the TC were to be decided through group discussion. The latter measure was designed to promote communication between staff and patients.

TCs developed rapidly during the 1960s but soon after they became marginalized. Thus, their success in changing mainstream psychiatric theory and practice has been modest. The main weaknesses seem to stem from their organizational form. Perrow (1965) has pointed to the shortcomings of TCs as viable organizations. In particular he points to the failure to change fundamentally the social structure of the organization, which he traces to the failure of the TCs' 'technology' (or the means used for reaching the set goals).

The wider organization (the mental hospital), of which TCs formed only a small part, continued to operate custodial practices and the bureaucratic and professional structures remained relatively impervious to change. This limitation was clearly recognized in Italy, where TCs were seen as only a preliminary step towards the total dismantling of the asylum system, which came to be viewed as unreformable. In describing the psychiatric reforms in one Italian locality, Franco Basaglia states that they were:

> More akin to the political struggles which broke out in other areas of social life in the 1960s, breaking up established institutions and exposing their shortcomings, than to avant-garde psychiatric experiments like the therapeutic community in England or *la psychiatrie institutionelle* in France.
>
> (Basaglia, in Ingleby 1981: 185)

The 'technology' for reaching the set goals of therapeutic communities was not enough to change a custodial culture and existing structures. In other words, the group work and social environment were not effective in changing sets of superordinate institutional relationships. Only one of Perrow's three conditions of organizational functioning were present and so the effectiveness and viability of TCs were undermined by the total institution. Certainly, the success of the TC, as an ideology or therapy, was limited in persuading British psychiatry to move away from a medical model, as indicated in an interview with Maxwell Jones, a pioneer of TCs, in 1984: 'For orthodox psychiatry it [the therapeutic community ideal] has provided a name to be wheeled out whenever it wants to defend Britain's reputation as the country which pioneered social psychiatry and to be conveniently forgotten otherwise' (*The Guardian* August 1984).

A radical alternative to trying to humanize the institution was the run-down and ultimate closure of large mental hospitals. In the later part of the twentieth century many countries followed a policy of hospital run-down and closure, often referred to as 'deinstitutionalization'. The latter is also used inter-changeably in some policy texts with the terms, 'decarceration' or 'desegregation'. In 1954 there were 154,000 residents in British mental hospitals. By 1982 this had fallen to 100,000. In other countries the degree of deinstitutionalization has been even greater. For example, in Italy between 1968 and 1978 the asylum population fell from 100,000 to 50,000.

The various clinical and research critiques of institutional life may not have been influential in changing policy. Scull comments that the work of social scientists on the disabling and custodial function of the asylum was not accompanied by evidence of greater public tolerance towards emotional deviance. In some cases, as in the work of John Martin discussed earlier, social scientists were probably more *witnesses* to the crisis of the institution than *participants* in crisis resolution or policy reform.

The reasons thought to be responsible for deinstitutionalization are multiple and contested, and implicate a complex set of inter-relationships between the medical profession, public morality, the State and political economy. A number of different accounts have been offered for deinstitutionalization policies, which we will consider in turn.

The 'pharmacological revolution'

The 'pharmacological revolution' is a frequently cited explanation for hospital run down. Simply put, it suggests that advances in medical treatment of mental illness permitted patients to be discharged from institutions *en masse*. According to this view of change, the introduction of major tranquillizers in particular enabled the alleviation of symptoms in psychotic patients, allowing large numbers of asylum residents to move into the community. Its explanatory power is still expressed in recent respectable psychiatric textbooks. For example:

> The introduction of chlorpromazine in 1952 made it easier to manage disturbed behaviour, and therefore easier to open wards that had been locked, to engage patients in social activities, and to discharge some of them into the community
>
> (Gelder *et al.* 2001: 769)

This account of deinstitutionalization generates both theoretical and empirical difficulties. For example, it cannot explain why community care policies were applied to a range of care groups such as people with learning disabilities and older people, who are not psychotic. They are not, therefore, the supposed target of 'anti-psychotic' medication. However, in later years at times the true role of these drugs as *tranquillizers* to suppress difficult behaviour showed through in their (mis)use with non-psychiatric patients, such as agitated older people and difficult-to-manage people with learning disabilities.

More importantly, a number of studies demonstrate that an increased pattern of discharges occurred *prior* to the widespread use of major tranquillizers. Nor did the introduction of psychotropic drugs appear to accelerate the rate of discharges. The pattern of the fall remained consistent with that preceding their widespread use. In a few countries in-patient numbers actually rose after the introduction of chlorpromazine, see Table 9.1.

The notion that medical intervention was principally responsible for 'decarceration' may have been deduced from a reading of the official statistics produced on mental hospital inmates of the time. However, Scull (1977: 83) points out that a reading of these sources of data may have led to erroneous interpretations being made, since they mask '. . . earlier changes at the local level and obscure the degree to which the fall in overall numbers, when it did come, represents a continuation rather than a departure from pre-existing trends'.

Thus, according to Scull, while psychotropic medication has helped manage deviance post-deinstitutionalization (through the control rather than permanent alleviation of symptoms), it was not responsible for the genesis of this policy. The retention of the unfounded claim of a 'pharmacological revolution' in recent texts, such as Gelder and colleagues', points up professional interest work in the preferred depiction of mental health policy history.

Other analyses of data sources indicate that organizational factors and social policy initiatives are responsible for changes in the location of psychiatric practice. Table 9.1 shows the growth in the number of psychiatric beds in a number of European countries post-Second World War, which ran counter to run-down in the UK and the US. While the type of increased bed use varied from one country to another (in some it was short-term beds, in others new specialist facilities) the point is that in-patient care increased during a time when the major tranquillizers were widely and increasingly utilized.

Table 9.1 Post-war growth of psychiatric beds in Europe

Country	Year	No. psychiatric beds
Belgium	1951	19,841
	1970	26,553
Austria	1950	9,868
	1975	14,314
Italy	1954	88,241
	1961	113,040
Spain	1949	25,571
	1974	42,493
Federal German Republic	1953	86,640
	1975	112,791

Source: Adapted from World Health Organization Statistics Annuals

Economic determinism

This is an alternative explanation for 'decarceration', by Scull (1977). He uses the term to describe the '. . . State sponsored policy of closing down asylums', which he relates to changes in social control mechanisms. Scull contends that with the emergence of the welfare state, segregative control mechanisms became too costly and difficult to justify. The cost inflation of mental hospitals prior to, and after, the Second World War was brought about by the elimination of unpaid patient labour and increased cost of employees as a result of the unionization of labour. The latter had the effect of contributing to the doubling of unit costs (because of the cost of a shorter working day and holiday entitlement).

The maintenance of ex-patients on welfare payments and the 'neglecting' of community care becomes a more viable State policy. The reality of community habitation for ex-inmates, according to Scull, has been an unmitigated disaster for the majority. The inhumanity of the asylum has simply been replaced by the negligence of the community: 'the alternative to the institution has been to be herded into newly emerging "deviant ghettoes", sewers of human misery and which is conventionally defined as social pathology within which (largely hidden from outside inspection or even notice) society's refuse may be repressively tolerated' (p. 153).

A problem with Scull's account is that it is more applicable to the 1980s, when fiscal savings were undoubtedly the driver for changes in social policy in relation to a range of patients with long-term conditions. The fiscal crisis of the State thesis fits less readily, though, with the immediate post-war period when he claims deinstitutionalization started. However, although the time frame is wrong, there is certainly evidence that the driver of fiscal savings eventually found its time, at least as a partial explanation for hospital run-down.

Changes in the organization of medicine: a shift to acute problems and primary care

The history of the large hospitals was bound up with the warehousing of chronic madness. However, during the twentieth century the ambit of psychiatry changed in a number of ways. By the end of that century mental health services also dealt with a range of other problems, such as neurosis, personality disorder and substance misuse. The shift had been occurring since the First World War when male neurosis (in the form of shellshock) entered centre stage. Also, a professional norm developed within psychiatry about the need to treat acute psychosis (with two-thirds of patients being deemed to recover permanently or have their symptoms eliminated until another acute episode).

The rhetoric of the 'pharmacological revolution' described earlier boosted this change in professional attention. Specious curative descriptions began to emerge in medicine such as 'anti-psychotic' and 'anti-depressant' medication. There was a focus on acute, not chronic, problems and the development of acute psychiatric units in District General Hospitals, with a limited number of beds (Baruch and Treacher 1978). This move aligned psychiatry with other medical specialties. In other words the desegregation was primarily of *psychiatrists*, to boost their medical respectability. (We will return to this point in Chapter 10.)

At the same time, it was becoming evident that conditions such as 'depression' (the 'common cold of psychiatry at once familiar and mysterious' (Seligman 1975)) and 'anxiety' could be contained in primary care. The great majority of patients with these 'common mental disorders' either did not seek help or were treated only by GPs, an arrangement still applicable today (Goldberg and Huxley 1980). Thus the remaining picture is that the bulk of people deemed to have mental health problems never access specialist services.

This change in the character of the medical framing of emotional deviance has been emphasized by some social constructivist analysts such as Prior (1991), who avoids both economic and technological determinism. Rather than attempting to identify causal mechanisms, his aim is to describe the object, ideology and organizational arrangements which constitute contemporary psychiatry. Prior argues that the target of psychiatric practice changes over time. Each new object is accompanied by a different type of clinical practice and organizational setting. For example, the nineteenth-century view of madness took as its focus the brain and forms of degeneracy, which demanded exclusion and control in the asylum. In contrast, the concepts of 'psyche' and 'the unconscious' in Freudian theory centred around the concept of 'mind'. The rising popularity of psychoanalytically informed ideas also started to cloud the distinction between normal and pathological behaviour which, according to Ramon (1985), helped destigmatize mental illness.

These new ideas required a socio-medical organization conducive to intimate therapeutic encounters between individual client and therapist. Prior argues that the lack of fit between modern psychiatric theories of the mind and madness necessitated the organizational change described as 'deinstitutionalization'. Prior perceives the 'therapeutics of mental illness at the end of the asylum age' as being widely dispersed. There is dual responsibility for mental health between medical and social services. The latter focus on aspects of

patients' lives, such as 'social networks', employment and family relationships, the former are subdivided between nursing and medical input. Medical
input takes as its focus the physical characteristics of the patient, diagnosis and
physical therapies such as ECT and psychotropic drugs. The object of focus, for
nursing in particular, centres around improving patient behaviour. However,
such a focus on behaviour is not compatible with a hospital milieu since, by
definition, it necessitates the patient's contact with society, both to test the
patient's behavioural competence and extend their behavioural repertoire.
The attendant therapeutic endeavours, which centre around such things as the
'normalization' of behaviour and the building of social networks, thus require
a community environment rendering the hospital 'functionless'.

Prior's analysis avoids the assumptions inherent in the economic interest
argument of Scull and the pharmacological revolution position of official
accounts. However, a set of empirical questions which are important in assessing the merits of the different theoretical positions that have emerged around
deinstitutionalization remain unanswered. For example, although there has
been an expansion of psychodynamically informed therapies and a greater
focus on the social relationships of patients, it is a moot point whether a bio-
medical hospital-centred psychiatric practice has actually been replaced with
extra-hospital activities.

Community care and reinstitutionalization

With a number of years passing now since the decarceration of chronic
patients, there is evidence that relocation has positive outcomes for individuals in some service settings. In Italy for example, where there has been a
careful tracking of post-institutional careers, a recent study has shown the way
in which a population characterized by a long history of illness and severe
disability underwent a radical change in care setting and living arrangements
with favourable outcomes (Barbato *et al.* 2004). In particular, this has been
indicated by the absence of adverse events or clinical deterioration and by
some improvement in social behavior. The results confirm that most patients
with long-term mental health problems can successfully leave psychiatric
hospitals and live in community residences.

There remains substantial confusion surrounding the meaning of the term
'community care', which reflects a lack of clarity over the ultimate goals of
such a policy. In practice, community care currently refers to mentally disordered people receiving 'care' in non-asylum settings. For example, the District General Hospital psychiatric units in Britain noted above are considered
to be part of community care (a back-up facility when those in community
settings develop acute difficulties).

While no country has created a mental health care system that can function
without 'acute' psychiatric wards for the admission of people with mental
health problems, some countries, such as Italy, show that it is possible to
minimize their use. However, this remains the exception rather than the rule.
Generally, the acute psychiatric ward environment does not generate mental
health gain. A census of standards on these wards at the end of the 1990s
indicated that most were 'non therapeutic' (Sainsbury 1998). MIND, Britain's
largest mental health charity currently has a 'Ward Watch' policy to track

conditions on these wards. Indeed, there is an emerging picture similar to the one about the old Victorian asylums: it may be that acute hospital units are inherently unable to provide a therapeutic culture (Quirk and Lelliott 2001). The reasons for this are multiple and similar, but not identical, to why their large predecessors failed as care environments (though they succeeded as sites of permanent or semi-permanent segregation – a form of apartheid determined by mental state):

- Because acute units retain a bio-medical emphasis they maintain the spurious illusion, pointed out in Goffman's final essay in *Asylums*, that they can act as a breakdown services, like a repair garage. (A problem is brought in, fixed and then sent out mended.) In fact, the technological emphasis on medication does not provide this repair service because despite their curative titles, psychiatric medications only control symptoms in some people some of the time. They do not cure the conditions diagnosed by psychiatrists. Even if they did, psychiatric drugs logically should work independently of setting – after all most community-based patients are already medicated. When admission is effected to enforce poor compliance with medication, then once more the aversive aspects of coercion are experienced by patients.
- Acute units are charged with a coercive control role. The majority of patients are detained compulsorily or are aware of compulsion being invoked. This culture of compulsion is a poor starting point for active collaboration in change from patients.
- The increased risk associated with 'co-morbidity', especially psychotic patients who abuse substances, means that the limited bed capacity in acute units has been increasingly reserved for patients who are mainly there because of their assessed risk *to others*. In other words, acute units implicitly serve the interests of third parties and so are not able to be 'patient centred'.
- The presence of raised levels of risky behaviour in small mixed ward environments has led to physical and sexual assaults (on both patients and staff). On-site substance misuse has brought with it an illicit cultural network of non-patients bringing alcohol and illegal drugs into the ward environment. The control of substance misuse on site has necessarily become an organizational priority for the staff. With this comes a distrustful surveillance role in relation to patients; an anti-therapeutic process.
- Staff tend to withdraw into their own space (the nursing office) and potential therapeutic staff–patient contact diminishes. The patient experience of this milieu is one of oscillating anxiety and boredom. These emotional states are not conducive to personal change or mental health gain.
- Like the old asylums the acute units are isolated from their community context. Here Baruch and Treacher (1978: 223) describe this in their early case study:

  . . . staff members were effectively 'institutionalized' – they rarely made domiciliary visits to their patients and they were not involved in the communities from which their patients came, so they could never develop an understanding of the patients' way of life or devise methods for using community resources to help the patients.

Since these early comments from Baruch and Treacher, other studies have confirmed the problems for staff of creating a therapeutic mileu in acute units. Medication still predominates and psychological interventions remain scarce (Lelliot and Quirk 2004). Staff morale remains low and patient dissatisfaction high (Norton 2004). (Indeed consultation exercises about mental health care tend to elicit user responses which focus narrowly on complaints about in-patient regimes.)

If these 'non-therapeutic' acute units are the back stop for non-hospital services, what are the latter? Community care is constituted by a variety of activities and services. The main initiatives evident over the past 20 years include psychiatric services in primary health care settings, the expanded use of community psychiatric nurses, the development of community mental health centres, the provision of domiciliary services, the development of residential and day care facilities, an increased emphasis of voluntary services and informal care by relatives and friends, and the relocation of mental health responsibilities from the secondary care sector to primary care.

There has been a rapid development of certain community resources. For example, between 1977 and 1987 Community Mental Health Centres in Britain expanded from one to 54 (Sayce 1989). Psychiatric services delivered via primary care are another area of expansion. However, it would be misleading to exaggerate the extent of reprovision from hospital-based services to the community. Mental health provision in Britain is still largely hospital-based. In the US, where a longer period has elapsed since the Community Mental Health Act 1963 than since the British NHS and Community Care Act of 1990, the old, large State asylums have simply been replaced by a network of smaller, private in-patient facilities. Even in the USA, Community Mental Health Centres were forced under fiscal pressure to shift to a custodial role (Samson 1992).

Samson insists that the US has never had proper community care but that instead a variety of economic and professional pressures have ensured a policy of reinstitutionalization. Consequently, he argues that those who attack the 'failure' of community care policies are actually attacking a straw man, given that what has actually happened is deinstitutionalization followed by reinstitutionalization. Similarly in Britain, the theory of community living has often been replaced by the practice of deinstitutionalization. The political objective of community care was first mentioned in the Mental Treatment Act 1930 and, by the 1970s, there was a bipartisan political goal of transferring people out of institutions. Yet, it was only in 1985 that the first British mental hospital actually closed.

By the late 1980s, 85 per cent of resources spent on mental health by the State were still bound up with hospitals (Sayce 1989). Data supplied by the Department of Health in 1992 showed both numerical losses and gains to hospital-based psychiatry. Although the number of psychiatric beds decreased from 193,000 in 1959 to 108,000 in 1985, by 1985 there had been a rise in the number of small psychiatric hospital facilities from 303 to 492. And even though hospital resident numbers dropped by 24 per cent between 1980 and 1990, psychiatric facilities still contained 36 per cent of all hospital beds by the latter year. In 1990 there were more than 50,000 psychiatric in-patients in England alone, at any one time. Moreover, despite a steady decline in the number of people occupying hospital beds since the 1960s, short-stay admissions rose dramatically, creating 'revolving-door' hospital care, rather than fully fledged care in the community.

By 2000 there were just over 100,000 admissions to English psychiatric units. However, an indication of the rapid throughput was that only 3.2 per cent stayed for longer than 90 days. Less than 1 per cent stayed for more than one year (Thompson *et al.* 2004). At the same time, these quick turnover units nearly always operate at 100 per cent bed occupancy. They are unable to provide either the stable place of residence offered by the old asylums or the continuity span required for a therapeutic community approach to be effective.

Despite the growth in the popularity of CMHCs as ideals at a local level (Sayce found that even in localities where there were no centres, policy makers thought they should have one), they have remained on the margins of community care. They are often established in the face of opposition from conservative forces within the psychiatric profession (Goldie, Pilgrim and Rogers 1989) and are not included in official government plans for replacing asylum beds, as they were, for example, in Italy. As new services they have been subjected to greater scrutiny and evaluations than hospital-based services.

New day places to replace hospital beds were not only slow in coming (between 1975 and 1985 only 9000 new places were made available (Audit Commission 1986)), they were overwhelmingly placed on hospital sites. Similarly, although there was a decrease in the number of in-patients, as out-patients they still attended hospital premises for their appointments. Domiciliary services – the visiting of people in their own homes by mental health professionals – today constitutes only a tiny proportion of this total.

A more recent health economic review of spending on mental health services (Sainsbury Centre for Mental Health 2003) still indicates a strong inertia about resources being bound up with hospital-based activity aimed at coercive control. Government spending was increased after 2000, in order to expand mental health services but the report concludes that this intention is unlikely to be successful. Although mental health is designated as a priority in health policy, proportionally the growth in expenditure on it, compared to other forms of State spending, has been slower. As a result, in proportional terms, the share allocated by the local State to mental health services is now actually falling. Also there has been slow progress in the timetable to implement the National Service Framework for Mental Health (Department of Health 1999). The Sainsbury Report estimates that in order to meet the deadlines, current expenditure allocated by central government for mental health services would need to be doubled.

Another factor indicating that mental health services continue to have a 'Cinderella' status relates to the range of peculiar costs or budgetary pressures experienced by them. These include debt repayment, staff shortages (which lead to expensive short-term agency payments) and the increasing prescribing costs, associated with the introduction of new and expensive psychotropic medications.

A look at the breakdown of spending on mental health services reveals socio-political priorities. For example, table 9.2 illustrates this point. The table indicates that there is a socio-political emphasis on social control (the combined items on acute facilities, secure provision and mentally disordered offenders). These items account for nearly 40 per cent of government spending on mental health services. This can be compared with the amount spent on

Table 9.2 Service expenditure 2002/03

	Per cent
Community mental health terms	17.2
Access and crisis services	6.6
Clinical services including acute in-patient care	24.6
Secure and high dependency provision	12.3
Continuing care	12.2
Services for mentally disordered offenders	1.1
Other community and hospital professional teams/specialists	1.6
Psychological therapy services	4.6
Home support services	2.1
Day services	5.3
Support services	1.5
Services for carers	0.3
Accommodation	10.3
Mental health promotion	0.1
Direct payments	0.1
Total direct costs	100.0

From Sainsbury Centre for Mental Health (2003)

Money for Mental Health London: Sainsbury Centre for Mental Health.

mental health promotion – a mere 0.1 per cent. Psychological therapy services only receive 4.6 per cent of spending (suggesting a bio-medical inertia in the mental health care system). Other non-hospital based services, which are meant to signal a service reconfiguration towards community-based interventions are lagging behind the political rhetoric of the chapter on mental health in the NHS Plan (Department of Health 2000). Between them the items on new assertive outreach, crisis resolution, early intervention and services for carers, account for less than 7 per cent of spending.

A final consideration about the problem of reinstitutionalization and the inertia of hospital-oriented State funding is the interaction of political interests which have impeded shifts to ordinary living and fuller citizenship for people with mental health problems. The old asylums were a total solution for the social problems associated with mental abnormality. In particular, they provided three main functions:

• semi-permanent or permanent accommodation;
• treatment;
• social control.

All of these functions occurred concurrently in one institution. Whatever disadvantages the old asylum system had for their inmates (by creating a form of disabling apartheid) as well as advantages (see comments from Gittins earlier), the socio-political benefit for others was that a group of non-conformist, troublesome, worrisome and economically inefficient people were segregated. Mental abnormality was swept away or 'warehoused' out of the sight and mind of the majority of free citizens. The consequences of demolishing these warehouses are thus obvious. The three functions would still be required by society for both economic efficiency and the maintenance of a moral order but now they would have to be reconfigured or reconstructed.

This political challenge has tempted cautious politicians to hold on to revised forms of institutional care and encouraged them with new forms of legal measures to ensure the coercive control of community-based patients (see Chapter 10). In addition, this new context of acute units provided the psychiatric profession with an opportunity to retain its traditional preferred link between power and beds. Moreover, the shift to DGH in-patient units was also an opportunity to increase the professional standing of a low-status medical specialty. Families troubled by patients in their midst would also look to new forms of safe residential disposal. Thus, a confluence of interests emerged in the final quarter of the twentieth century to retain a hospital focus to mental health work, despite the run-down of the asylum system. However, this has placed unrealistic expectations upon DGH units.

The interest groups just described have become immediately aggrieved about the inefficiency of the units compared to the old asylums, as the shift in scale means that the new units cannot replicate all the functions of the old hospitals. This led to diverse demands in response. Some of these centred on requests for more beds (from psychiatrists and patient- relative pressure groups) or calls for a halt to the run down of the old asylums. Others demanded greater community support to reduce the need for admission (user groups).

It can be seen then that the prioritizing of control, professional preferences to treat in in-patient settings and the continued need for people with mental health problems to be accommodated together place pressure upon smaller scale hospital facilities. This pressure created such political anxiety in the mid-1990s that in Britain ministers opted to slow asylum run-down and keep high investment levels in beds (Department of Health 1997). In response, critics argued that the three functions noted above should be dealt with as separate policy questions: accommodation implies social housing not hospitalization; treatment needs to be cost effective and its appropriate siting clarified; and risk management should be dealt with rationally, not prejudicially (Pilgrim and Rogers 1997).

The macro policy context together with the micro behaviour of professionals making and dealing with mental health referrals determine the pace and success of community care. A comparison of community-based care for those patients with a diagnosis of schizophrenia in Verona and South Manchester indicated that the organization of services in the former resulted in shorter hospital stays as a result of better integration between hospital and community services (Gater *et al.* 1995).

Public health, primary care and the new technology revolution

With the fragmentation of old structures like the asylums there has been greater attention paid to considering the cause and solution of mental health problems within a public health context. Previously, psychiatric epidemiology and the treatment of mental disorders were separated conceptually. With the rise of a 'new' public health, which integrates lay with traditional epidemiology, and the emergence of a strong primary health care agenda, epidemiology and treatment are coming closer together as the hospital disappears as the symbolic focus of treatment. Attention shifts instead to inequalities in mental health (discussed in Chapter 3), prevention and the notion of 'positive mental health'. Alongside this within mental health policy, problem management stretches beyond the structural and organizational arrangements of traditional health services.

The policy response to mental health problems here implicates local and central players, community resources, the environment and individual action. Thus, the focus has moved to incorporate aspects of employment, social, community and voluntary organizations in the prevention and management of mental health problems. Within this scheme where service contact is needed, primary care is privileged over specialist mental health services. That is, the optimal service response is cast in settings which are as close as possible to the place where the genesis of mental health problems originate and are expressed.

A final and further change is related to the way in which new technologies and information systems have changed the organization of psychiatry. The widespread availability of technology, together with the community location of the overwhelming majority of patients, has changed the face of how mental health services are organized and delivered. This change, in turn, is likely to dramatically alter the power relationships between providers and recipients of mental health services.

The proliferation of the use of new forms of mental health services is likely to be reinforced by the cultural shift towards the acceptance of evidence-based health care discussed in Chapter 8. For example, telephone counselling for patients with 'minor depression' from a primary care base has been found to be both efficient and effective (Lynch, Tamburrino and Nagel 1997) as has undertaking a psychiatric assessment and diagnosis over the telephone (Kobak 1997). Remote treatment of depression by telepsychiatry has been shown to be as effective as face-to-face therapy (Ruskin *et al.* 2004).

The ambiguous legitimacy that mental health care professionals hold in the eyes of users is reinforced by research which evaluates the outcomes of services organized along different lines. A randomized controlled trial compared face-to-face meetings with professionals and another group who used an electronic self-help computer programme in the form of a 'voice bulletin board'. Clients were found to be eight times more likely to participate in the computerized programme and were more satisfied than the group receiving face-to-face contact (Alemi *et al.* 1996).

'Telepsychiatry' has become increasingly popular and in traditional terms has been viewed as effective as, and more efficient than face-to-face encounters. Remote treatment of depression delivered by means of telepsychiatry and in-person treatment of depression were found to have comparable outcomes and equivalent levels of patient adherence, patient satisfaction and health care costs (Ruskin *et al.* 2004).

Professionals' use of computer packages and the fashion for 'stepped' and collaborative care takes mental health care out of any one organizational context and introduces new problems in terms of the surveillance and 'follow up' of patients. An aspect of this challenge, which has become the focus of professional and academic interest is the notion of 'continuity of care'. A combination of assertive community treatment, case management, community mental health teams and crisis intervention have been found to reduce the likelihood of patients dropping out of contact with services (Crawford *et al.* 2004).

The internet and computer-based programmes, by simplifying communication and being readily accessible directly to people, have the potential to 'cut out' professionals altogether from the care process. This also overcomes the problems caused by geographical location and variable personal quality (mechanical responses can be standardized). It is likely that the use of the Internet directly empowers users of mental health services by allowing them to feel in control of their treatment and everyday life more generally. (The issue of users as providers of care is returned to in Chapter 11.) Equally, if not more, important is the rapid increase in mutual non-professional support. The social isolation and 'poverty' of social networks have been a recurrent theme in the literature on people with long-term health problems.

One of the most important consequences of the technologies is the rapid increase it allows in mutual non-professional support. The anonymous helper in an electronic conference or the support group on the Internet provide the basis of a radical shift in mental health support. It has emerged as an unpredicted and major force in the global organization of mental health care.

Discussion

The old mental asylum system can be thought of as representing part of the modernist project, although other forms of total institution, like the monastery, stretch back to feudal times. But while the monastery was guided by theological considerations, the asylum was peculiarly modern because rationality was its guiding organizational principle. Reason, not faith, now permeated the total institution. The pursuit of rational scientific knowledge about lunacy became the aim of modern psychiatry, even when such an aim was rhetorical rather than real. Accordingly, the elimination of mental disease was seen as a possibility, through its systematic organization and treatment in purpose-built institutions designed to segregate embodied irrationality from everyday life. There was no longer what Foucault called a 'dialogue between reason and unreason', rather the latter was trapped and codified by the former.

This Victorian project is now largely over (save relics of the psychiatric total institution like the high security hospitals). The crisis of the asylum emerged not only because of considerations of cost but also because of changes in the discourse about mental abnormality and its treatment, in both the lay and professional areas. In Chapter 7 we summarized the expansion of the ambit of psychiatry after the First World War, and Prior (1991) argues for a more recent flux in psychiatric theory and practice. The asylum could not adapt to these changes and so its therapeutic legitimacy edged more and more towards crisis – but what of the asylum's replacements?

We have discussed two British responses: community mental health centres;

and District General Hospital Units. This divided response suggests that both a continuity with Victorian modernism and a post-modern break has taken place, as far as the organization of mental health work is concerned. The CMHC is consistent with a definition here by Clegg (1990: 53) of post-modern organizations, which are:

> forms of emerging organization that bear little or no relation to modernist variations on the theme of bureaucracy. These organizations are 'de-differentiated' . . . flexible, niche marketed and have a multi-skilled workforce held together by information technology, networks and subcontracting.

The emergence of the CMHC seems to confirm the notion that mental health care delivery is moving into a different era. In this organizational context, role-blurring removes the strict division of labour typical of the hospital. The key worker system and multidisciplinary working brings with it genericism and an increased individual responsibility for practitioners. Outreach work with clients decentralizes or diffuses the locus of power away from the professionals' organizational base. Even that base has lost its architectural salience compared with the hospital: the more successfully 'normalized' it is the more it looks like an ordinary house. The knowledge base used by the professionals is eclectic (incorporating biological, psychological and social notions). Moreover, no two CMHCs are exactly the same.

This picture of diversity and eclecticism in the CMHC no longer squares with Perrow's model of the hospital outlined at the start of the chapter. However, what does square with such a model is the DGH psychiatric unit. This seems to represent a continuity with the modernist project of Victorian psychiatry. Its power is clearly focused and centralized. There is the retention of a division of labour within the clinical team, and between clinicians and managers. Consultants continue to lead a pyramid of clinical power – they head up multi-disciplinary teams, even if their authority is less evident than in the past. Their power has been subordinated to some extent now to the rules of general management (a bureaucratic process) and the modern hospital has been subjected to some extent to the non-bureaucratic principle of marketization. So, while the contemporary DGH units represent a strong continuity with the nineteenth-century asylum, the psychiatric profession is enduring peculiar new stresses.

Another difference between the old and new is literally visible. The architectural form of the DGHU is actually more clear-cut than the old Victorian hospital, especially when it occurs in the post-war, high-rise, concrete block. In the Victorian asylum the expansive grounds might have been mistaken for a public park, whereas the modern hospital block containing cramped wards with low ceilings, and no internal or external exercise space, has become a caricature of an impersonal, modern, urban building.

As Samson (1992) notes about the US experience, new hospitals for old marks reinstitutionalization (or it could be dubbed 'trans-hospitalization') not community care. Consequently, if the Victorian asylums were found lacking as therapeutic institutions, then it is likely that this will also be the case for the DGH psychiatric units. With a much smaller physical capacity for beds than the old asylums, these new units are increasingly becoming a focus for the expert coercive regulation of high-risk patients. Locked wards have returned ('Special Care Units') and risk assessment and risk management have become the anxious daily preoccupation of staff. Substance misuse on site has added to this role and brought an illicit drug culture into psychiatric settings (to add to the official pre-existing one of prescribed medication routines). Despite their recent title of acute 'mental health services', these units, more than the Victorian hospitals, have now inherited the displaced function to restrain and segregate, albeit for shorter periods, those deemed to be a risk to themselves or others. They are not about mental health but are very much about mental pathology.

A further fragment of the post-modern condition of psychiatry lies with the rise of new technologies in managing mental disorder, where organizational arrangements are largely irrelevant. Directly accessible information to users, via the Internet and to professionals via telemedicine, signals the beginning of a new form of organization and delivery of mental health services.

This chapter has focused on the rise and fall of the asylum and the ambiguities which attend our current post-asylum world. A variety of factors have contributed to the demise of the old large mental hospitals, some of which have been economic and others ideological in influence. What the current social policy controversies surrounding care in the community highlight is that the old hospitals contained the three inter-weaving functions of care, control and accommodation. Any new arrangement about the organization of mental health work will also involve these functions. Controversies have tended to emerge for the very reason that critics (serving a variety of interests) have complained that government has still not delivered the correct blend of care, control and accommodation.

Questions

1 Why were the large mental hospitals closed down?

2 Why were the large mental hospitals not closed sooner?

3 Do new arrangements about mental health care reflect our post-modern condition?

4 'The pharmacological revolution is a myth' – discuss.

5 'Scull's fiscal crisis of the State thesis was 20 years out of time' – discuss.

6 How might new technology shape community mental health work?

For discussion

If you, or a friend or relative, had a long-term mental health problem how would you like services to be organized in response? When discussing this question, think about the points raised in the chapter about care, control and accommodation.

Further reading

Audit Commission (1994) *Finding A Place: A Review of Mental Health Services for Adults.* London: HMSO.

Baruch, G. and Treacher, A. (1978) *Psychiatry Observed.* London: Routledge.

Martin, J.P. (1985) *Hospitals in Trouble.* Oxford: Blackwell.

Richards, D.A., Lovell, K. and McEvoy, P. (2003) Access and effectiveness in psychological therapies: self-help as a routine health technology. *Health and Social Care in the Community*, 11(2): 175–82.

Chapter **10**

Psychiatry and legal control

Chapter overview

This chapter will examine the role of mental health legislation, which is a central feature in the relationship between the State and mental health service activity. It will cover the following topics:

- legal versus medical control of madness;
- mentally disordered offenders;
- socio-legal aspects of compulsion;
- the globalization of compulsion;
- professional interests and legislation;
- dangerousness.

Legal versus medical control of madness

During the early nineteenth century, in Britain as well as other emerging capitalist economies in Europe and North America, the systematic control of madness began. The system involved the State setting out laws and prompting, or prescribing, public spending on asylums. The building of county and borough asylums was encouraged by the County Asylums Act of 1808. These suggestions were made mandatory by the Lunacy Act of 1845, which led to a rapid enlargement of the State asylum system. This system came to displace a very varied picture of control. Prior to 1845, lunatics were dispersed in a range of places – small private madhouses, bridewells, poor houses and workhouses. This dispersal was unregulated and cases were not systematically recorded (Donelly 1983).

The Lunacy Act 1890 prescribed that admissions to hospitals and treatment would be governed by statute. It also ensured that the control and supervision of inmates would be overseen by government bodies. At first during the twentieth century, such safeguards and powers increasingly involved the legal profession. But later, diagnosis and admission were seen primarily as the concern of the medical profession. This is the viewpoint underlying both the Mental Health Act 1959 and, in a softened form, the current British legislation, the Mental Health Act 1983.

Historically, legalism has been used to counter what have been viewed as the deficits of medical management. Similarly, the assertion of a medical view of mental disorder has been resorted to at times when legalism was considered to have failed. The tension between legalism and medical control permeates the implementation of mental health legislation. This is true of both civil compulsory admissions of non-offender patients and mentally disordered offenders.

It is not only the psychiatric profession that has resisted the intrusion of law into its work. The use of the law in the mental health area has also been criticized by some social scientists. For example, Jones (1960), a prominent social policy analyst, argued that there are severe limits to what the law can achieve in mental health services. Jones considered that good practice is likely to be fostered through adequate resource allocation and the development of professional norms and values. She believed that the latter would enhance the appropriate attitudes, skills and treatments needed for the compassionate management of mentally disordered people and inter-professional cooperation. A strict legal framework might inhibit this process. Thus, the use of the law in her view should only be as a last resort.

From a different standpoint, Rose (1986) has argued that legalism is just another form of control that does not ultimately benefit the patient. Instead, he argues that not only does legalism not constrain psychiatric discretion but it also disguises the wider political context of the delivery of mental health services and thereby depoliticizes the debate over how psychiatry is organized and operates: 'legality is merely one mode of regulation and body of professional expertise amongst others, neither conceptually more rigorous, nor necessarily more effective in bringing power to account' (p. 209). Rose's criticism centres on the tendency of legal measures to individualize problems.

Legalism has had a chequered history with regard to fostering positive values about mental abnormality. The Lunacy Act 1890, for example, led to wide-scale stigma around madness and 'certification', because it allowed only for the forced admission of people to mental asylums via the courts. The Mental Treatment Act 1930 attempted to rectify this by introducing the possibility of voluntary admission to hospital, which, it is argued, fostered a more sympathetic attitude to emotional deviance.

Bean (1980) found that, under the Mental Health Act 1959, which represented a swing back from a legal to a medical control, there was an absence of adequate checks and control mechanisms. Over-zealous psychiatrists sometimes placed patients in a vulnerable position by permitting them to be deprived of their liberty for considerable periods of time. Bean related this to the nature of therapeutic law with its open-ended clauses and standards, which leads to a tendency towards *ad hoc* rule enforcement and the playing down of the importance of general rules. In other words, where there is a clash between the views of medicine and legal requirements, medical demands tend to be privileged.

Over the last two decades there has been a global trend towards balancing the medical dominance of therapeutic law with a greater legal presence with a view to giving greater weight to the individual rights of patients. A recent ethnographic study carried out in Sweden examining such arrangements seems to suggest that nothing much changes when the legal role is formally extended. Psychiatric norms and values still dominate patient–professional inter-action and the outcome of assessments. Even in a legally dominated context those with mental health problems are treated as patients rather than adverse parties and there is an inbuilt bias to the proceedings – it is assumed from the beginning that they are mentally ill. There is a tendency for their credibility to be viewed as suspect and expressions of 'sane' behaviour are seen as a temporary effort at self-composure. Where mental health is concerned, an informal atmosphere is often adopted which is atypical of other legal proceedings. This further militates against a view of the patient as a valid legal party (Sjostrom 1997).

Mentally disordered offenders

Forensic psychiatry is concerned with the management of those who are 'doubly deviant' – those who are considered to have committed a criminal act and who are deemed to be mentally abnormal. Forensic psychiatry is charged with the management of lawbreakers and others who come before the courts. Thus, its area of jurisdiction is principally in relation to referrals from the criminal justice system and those patients who are detained in hospitals subject to restriction orders.

The view of control discussed at the start of this chapter locates power in the hand of State organizations and agencies and their professional employees (psychiatrists and lawyers). Foucault provides an alternative view of the emergent relationship between psychiatry and the law. Psychiatry's involvement with penal law in the eighteenth and nineteenth centuries came about with the shift from a criminology that focused on the offence and penalty, to one concerned with the crime, the criminal and means of repression. The shift from crime to the criminal meant that the focus changed from what must be punished and how, to who must be punished:

> It is not enough for the accused to say in reply to that question 'I am the author of the crimes before you, period. Judge since you must, condemn if you will'. Much more is expected of him. Beyond admission, there must be confession, self examination, explanation of oneself, revelations of what one is.
>
> (Foucault 1978: 2)

For Foucault, psychiatry took its place in the legal machinery through the concept of 'homicidal mania' (a killing that took place in a domestic setting in the absence of any apparent motive) in the latter half of the eighteenth century. From this moment, crime and insanity became the same thing. He illustrates this type of crime/insanity with reference to notorious cases: a mother who kills her child; a man who breaks into a house, kills an elderly woman and departs without stealing and fails to hide himself; a son who kills his mother with whom he has always got on well. Psychiatry justified its involvement in order to make the unintelligibility of this type of crime intelligible. By claiming that insanity manifested itself in crime and vice versa, forensic psychiatry adopted a different focus of interest from the rest of the profession.

Foucault links forensic psychiatry to a type of public hygiene where the focus is on the 'societal body' and social danger rather than the 'individual soul'. Homicidal mania represents insanity in its most harmful form – minimum warning, maximum consequences – which only a specialist eye can detect. According to Foucault, forensic psychiatry's claim to monomania did not include a desire to take over criminality and was not a form of psychiatric imperialism. Rather, it was a means of justifying its function, namely the control of danger emanating from the human condition.

The problematic status of personality disorder

Although the overwhelming concern of the State and psychiatry during the nineteenth century was lunacy, 'moral insanity' was also described:

> The moral principles of the mind are strongly perverted or depraved; the power of self government is lost or greatly impaired and the individual is found to be incapable not of talking or reasoning upon any subject proposed to him, but of conducting himself with decency and propriety in the business of life.
>
> (Prichard 1835, quoted in Ramon 1986: 215)

The concern of the State to utilize medical facilities to control bad behaviour (in the absence of formal evidence of psychosis) continued in the twentieth century. The current legal definition of psychopathy appears under the Mental Health Act 1983 as: 'a persistent disorder or disability of mind (whether or not including significant impairment of intelligence) which results in abnormally aggressive or seriously irresponsible conduct on the part of the person concerned'.

A problem with this legal definition is that it maps poorly onto preferred professional ones. For example, the use of the term 'psychopathy' in law approximates to those of 'anti-social personality disorder' and 'dissocial personality disorder' codified by the American Psychiatric Association (1994) and the World Health Organization (1992) respectively. However, to complicate matters, there is a strong clinical tradition of using the word 'psychopath' to describe people who show overlapping symptoms of three types of personality disorders (anti-social, histrionic and narcissistic) (Cleckley 1941; Hare 1991). Some but not all of those with this clinical profile become criminals.

While early psychiatry was concerned with 'moral insanity', during the twentieth century it began to codify many other types of personality disorder. By 1994 the American Psychiatric Association described ten types, in addition to that of anti-social personality disorder (the approximate conceptual legacy of 'moral insanity'). One of these, 'borderline personality disorder', is used commonly to describe female prisoners who are emotionally unstable.

Personality disorder has been controversial for a number of reasons:

- As its etiology is not known, it is described tautologically by its symptoms and its symptoms are accounted for by the existence of the disorder; (For example, a man is deemed to be psychopathic because he rapes children. His raping of children is then explained by his psychopathy.)
- In the light of the above, it is impossible to disentangle attributions of personal abnormality from social deviance (Blackburn 1988; Parker *et al.* 1995);
- The types of personality disorder described are not coherent and separate but overlap in clinical presentations, undermining the validity of specific diagnoses (Pilgrim 2001);
- Mental health professionals are divided about the treatability of personality disorder. By definition, personality refers in the professional discourse to stable and unchanging personal attributes. If a personality is deemed as abnormal then it cannot (or would not be expected to) change. Despite this there is some empirical evidence that people with a label of psychopathy offered psychological interventions reoffend less often than those untreated (McGuire 1995; Skeem, Monahan and Mulvey 2002). Thus psychopathy itself may not be treatable but the overall probability of specific offending behaviours may be reduced in *groups* of patients with the diagnosis. This then leads to a further challenge; risk prediction in *particular cases* is difficult to estimate.

The logical and empirical vulnerability of any diagnosis of personality disorder created by these doubts and criticisms has not deflected either the State or some parts of the psychiatric profession from using personality disorder as a legitimate notion and rationale for social control. Such a continuing political and professional imperative has been divisive though. Mainstream psychiatry showed evidence of wanting to reject psychopaths as patients worthy of their attention but personality disorder is part of the bread and butter work of forensic psychiatry. In the Mental Health Act 1983 a treatability clause had to be inserted to prevent open-ended professional decision making. It stated that if a patient is suffering from psychopathic disorder, treatment must be likely to 'alleviate or prevent a deterioration' of the person's condition.

Why is psychiatry divided in this way about psychopathy? The answer may lie in the lack of responsiveness to treatment of this group of patients. However, this could well apply to other psychiatric diagnoses. For example, the limited success of treating 'schizophrenics' with major tranquillizers has not led to mainstream psychiatry wishing to diminish its contact with this group. A more plausible explanation is connected to changes in segregative control.

Ramon (1986) traces the change in the psychiatric stance towards psychopathy to developments in psychological approaches just after the Second World War. Then, soldier patients showing evidence of psychopathic disorder began to be treated in therapeutic communities. The move away from segregative control in mainstream psychiatry meant that the method to control antisocial behaviour became less feasible. Forensic psychiatry in contrast still had the segregative means to effectively manage such deviance.

Indeed, it seems to be that the precondition of the psychiatric detention of this group is governed by the demands of security and public threat, rather than mental state. As patients who have committed offences, they are likely to be detained for a period at least commensurate with the gravity of their offences (Norris 1984; Peay 1989). This is true also for those who have committed minor offences. An American study, using a large random sample of misdemeanor defendants, found that those with a psychiatric history were 'criminally sanctioned more severely than defendants without psychiatric records, and defendants with relatively extensive psychiatric records were even more severely sanctioned' (Hochstedler-Steury 1991: 358).

The importance of the psychopath to forensic psychiatry (in both numerical and therapeutic terms) illustrates the two systems which it tries to bridge. By definition, the mentally disordered offender qualifies for entry into both the criminal justice and mental health systems. This raises particular dilemmas and questions which arise out of a merging of two types of deviance, criminality and mental disorder. Explicitly stated, should individuals be dealt with in the system designed to deal with the criminal aspects of their behaviour (i.e. in prison) or should they be treated for their mental disorder in hospital? This can be framed in terms of the psychiatrization versus criminalization of deviance.

The arguments for psychiatrization are made on the grounds that hospitalization of mentally disordered offenders is less stigmatizing and hospital treatment benefits patients more than do prisons. Prisons are unable to provide the environment or range of treatments that a health care regime can (Abramson 1972). A policy initiative stemming from this reasoning is the diversion of mentally disordered offenders from custody projects, which are also informed by the prevailing ethos of community care. Others (Monahan 1973; Fennell 1991) see psychiatrization as resting on dubious grounds. They point out that mental hospitals are not stigma free. Arguably, in Britain the association of the high-security hospitals like Ashworth and Broadmoor with notorious serial killers and gangsters means that they are far more stigmatizing than prisons.

There are also doubts over whether medical treatment regimens are superior. As discussed earlier, those labelled as psychopathic make up a significant proportion of those in high-security hospitals, yet there is little evidence to suggest there is an effective treatment for antisocial behaviour. There is evidence that the 'recidivism' rate is lower for those coming out of hospital, i.e. discharged forensic patients are less likely to reoffend than mentally disordered offenders discharged from prison (Fennell 1991). But this may be attributed to the conservative discharge policies of hospitals, which are driven as much by 'security' considerations, as it is to changes in the mental state of patients. 'Psychopaths' in high-security hospitals receive longer periods of detention, on average, than their counterparts in mainstream prison provision, as judged by equivalent index offences (Peay 1989).

There are two main arguments underlying a criminalization position. The first relates to a moral and philosophical argument that both those who are designated mentally ill and those who are not should be treated as humanely as possible. That is, poor and 'brutalizing' conditions should not exist in either the prison or mental health systems (Monahan 1973). Reforming the prison system has also been argued for on pragmatic grounds. Fennell (1991) suggests that there will always be situations which do not permit the rapid transfer of mentally disordered offenders out of the prison system. Prisoners may not meet the legal criteria for transfer or transfer cannot be arranged quickly enough. Additionally, transfer may not always be the fairest option for prisoners. Sentences are often suspended for prisoners who spend time in hospital and recommenced if a person is transferred back to prison. (That is, there is no remission for the period that they have been treated as patients, and so their detention is extended beyond their sentence.) Moreover, increased diversion into psychiatric facilities is unrealistic, given the burden on existing facilities and the failure to rapidly develop more regional secure facilities. Fennell argues for a proper legal framework for psychiatric treatment in prisons to be established as a means of improving the standard of care that is currently provided. One policy option which tries to bridge the gap between these two positions was proposed by the Tumin Report (Woolfe and Tumin 1990). This suggested that adequately staffed psychiatric intensive care wards in the NHS be provided inside prisons.

The debates about the comparative merits of criminalization and psychiatrization are mainly in relation to different ways of controlling and containing offender patients. Alongside these arguments about which institutional structures (penal or health care) should take precedence is evidence of a coalescence of systemic processes. There has been a shift in *both* mental health and criminal justice facilities towards an actuarial policy (Armstrong, 2002). The latter refers to the emphasis on risk calculation as the main procedural guide to professional action in both systems.

While the penal system traditionally aimed to rehabilitate offenders, and the psychiatric system aimed to treat patients, in recent years both aspirations have been displaced by an emphasis on risk minimization. Treatment and rehabilitation in different ways are orientated towards the reform of the deviant individual. Treatment ideologies, prior to the emergence of actuarilism, had, to some extent, influenced rehabilitation interventions for some prisoners. For example, prisons have contained therapeutic communities as part of their rehabilitative strategy. By contrast, actuarial management is more about using *diagnostic* methods to efficiently contain the social threat of groups of deviant people, wherever they are contained. Both actuarial and treatment approaches are examples of how mental health assessments and interventions have permeated the criminal justice system.

The persistence of a problematic concept: the case of 'dangerous and severe personality disorder'

In recent years, the British State has exerted its right to impose an administrative concept of personality disorder in order to cut through or over-ride professional ambivalence (Department of Health/Home Office 1999). This has involved the construction of and use of a new category of 'dangerous and severe personality disorder' (DSPD) and new legislation has been devised to provide legal backing for the pre-emptive detention of people who have had this label applied to them. The impasse over which sector (prison or health service) has responsibility for the management and containment of people with personality disorder has in part been resolved by this State intervention, which includes the development and funding of new services.

The solution to the tensions posed by the precarious validity of personality disorder noted above would not have been resolved without the intervention of the State, which refused to rely upon 'medical science' alone. Manning (2002) has shown, through the use of actor network theory (Law 1992) and the analysis of policy networks, the mechanisms behind the effective intervention of the State in this arena. It managed to secure a practical policy outcome, despite the controversies surrounding the description and treatability of personality disorder rehearsed above. The State funded and promoted professional networks and research designed to achieve the outcome it desired. It even named and promoted this sponsored network, as the 'Virtual Institute of Severe Personality Disorder' (VISPED).

Key players within forensic psychiatry, and others in the academic medical and criminological centres of excellence, were recruited into the policy development. Money was made available to generate both research capability and capacity. Younger people were attracted into the field through PhD, post-doctoral and other research fellowships. 'Pilot' services were funded and evaluated. The characterization of the new service as a 'pilot', when it actually looked like the final version, acknowledged the difficulties of a thin evidence base. At the same time, it warded off criticism from professionals and engaged them in a policy development, which could build upon what had been started by government initiative.

The research capacity and activity has been put in place to furnish the technical capability of DSPD diagnosis, assessment and treatment, in the classic manner of the sociology of 'translation' whereby the network has enrolled, co-opted and disarmed the key elements, technical and human, and stabilized the development and production of new knowledge. If the research falters in this quest, then the government may not be able to hold the network together against the sceptics, and the 'translation' may unravel.

Socio-legal aspects of compulsion

A key difference in the societal response to people with mental health problems and those with physical health problems is the commonplace use of compulsion. The historical theme, of most societies physically constraining madness, was simply formalized when the legislative arrangements of the nineteenth century we alluded to earlier came into being.

Szasz (1963) has argued that as long as there is legislation authorizing compulsory detention there can be no genuine voluntary admission. The latter status is vulnerable to threats of invoking the former. Bean has used the term *'coactus voluit'* ('at his will although coerced') (1986: 5) to describe voluntary admission. In his research into compulsory admissions to hospital Bean found that assessing psychiatrists sometimes gave patients a 'Hobson's choice'. Patients were informed in a non-negotiable way of their impending admission or told that if they did not come into hospital voluntarily they would be compelled to do so (Bean 1980). A substantial minority of patients, who are admitted to hospital as voluntary patients, regard themselves to be there under coercion (Rogers 1993a).

This illusory status of voluntary patients has become less relevant practically in recent years in Britain, in the wake of large hospital closures. A consequence has been that the smaller number of in-patient beds have been reserved overwhelmingly for involuntary cases. In the early 1980s, notionally, only a minority of patients was involuntary and the bulk was voluntary. This balance is now inverted. A second illusion can now be dispelled because of the smaller in-patient infrastructure. While the professional campaign of psychiatrists to move from the old asylums to new District General Hospital Units was based on a rhetorical alignment with mainstream curative general medicine (Baruch and Treacher 1978), by the turn of the twenty-first century, these units had been reduced to holding units for risky patients. Many of the latter had multiple social problems and used drugs or alcohol.

By the 1990s, the prospect of these units being treatment centres, in line with the medical rhetoric and aspirations of the 1970s had disappeared. They had become 'non-therapeutic', with patients feeling unsafe and often describing a deterioration in their mental health as a result of hospital admission (Sainsbury Centre for Mental Health 1999; MIND 2004). Acute psychiatric units have now effectively become small madhouses. The recent challenge for the State has no longer been about the lawful control of those admitted to and controlled in hospital (this is taken care of by existing legislation in 1983). The main social administrative challenge is now in relation to the bulk of patients living in the community, who 30 years ago would have lived and died in the asylum system. When such patients episodically developed acute psychotic symptoms they were already in hospital (to be controlled). Now they are not. Consequently, the socio-legal challenge is to set out new provisions to control these patients when required.

In the United States 'involuntary outpatient civil commitment' (IOC) is now widely accepted as a principle in mental health services. Although the use of such powers are still relatively rare, over the last 20 years most States have passed legislation that permits involuntary outpatient intervention on the basis of a need for treatment. Some patients have been placed on IOC indefinitely and the penalty for non-compliance has varied from no action to automatic readmission, depending on the State involved (Maloy 1992).

In the last 15 years 'Community Treatment Orders' (CTOs) have been advocated at different times in British mental health policy debates which would entail the forced medication by injection with psychotropic drugs of people in their own homes. Advocates for the introduction of legislation permitting this forced treatment argued that a small number of patients were prone to 'relapse' and could not be relied on to take medication. This gave rise to a number of philosophical, ethical and practical difficulties. Who would administer the medication? Although psychiatrists would prescribe it, community psychiatric nurses were reluctant to take on the responsibility for administering drugs, which they viewed as potentially damaging to their relationship with patients. There were also problems related to who would receive compulsory treatment, given the limited effectiveness of major tranquillizers in treating certain patient groups and the strong opposition to the idea on the part of patient advocacy groups.

Although formal attempts by psychiatrists in Britain to negotiate powers of compulsory community treatment failed in the late 1980s, the issue was revisited by politicians in the mid-1990s, when a series of embarrassing incidents occurred in public involving psychiatric patients. As a result, new legislation was introduced to ensure active follow up in the community with powers to recall non-compliant patients to hospital (the Supervised Discharge Act 1995 modified the 1983 Act). This legal adaptation of the 1983 Act was reinforced by a raft of procedures including a register of 'at risk' patients and the Care Programme Approach. These administrative mechanisms were a governmental attempt to systematize risk management in the community. The impact of the British legislation still awaits the outcomes of formal evaluation research.

Huxley (1990), for example, describes case management as a system in which care is provided through individually planned combinations of different sources of support. In contrast, research which places the issue of coercion centre stage simultaneously places the issue of ethics high on the agenda. The term 'aggressive outreach' (used in the US) as opposed to the British notions of 'Care Programme Approach', 'care management' or 'assertive outreach' suggest tenacity and surveillance on the part of mental health professionals, which goes beyond paternalistic benevolence. In both types of research positive outcomes include measures of the extent of contact that people with mental health problems have with their worker and a reduction in hospital admission rates.

However, the issue of control is more explicit when some terms are used compared to others. In 1998 the British government began a process of reviewing the 1983 Mental Health Act. At that time it made clear its intention to implement new powers of compulsory conveyancing to hospital to ensure treatment compliance. The new British Draft Mental Health Bill (Department of Health 2004) is the most recent attempt of government to find lawful ways of controlling community-based patients.

The emergence of in-patient units as crucibles of coercive control (when they originally aspired to be treatment units to generate mental health gain or recovery from acute episodes) poses a major problem now for professional rhetoric about 'mental health care'. Where legal rules govern admission, discharge and daily decision making and action in between, in what sense can professions like psychiatry and mental health nursing maintain an ethical stance of caring for patients? Pols (2001) studied this clash of functions and ideologies in the work of mental health nurses in the interactions with in-patients. She found that legal measures to define 'doing good' (the patients' 'right to treatment') and those which were inherited from a non-legal paradigm of professional ethics interfered with one another.

The forced integration of professional paternalism with its preferred voluntary approach and one in which professional action is shaped and expected by legal requirement is also highlighted in the Draft Mental Health Bill (Department of Health 2004). In order to make the Draft accessible to ordinary people, the government produced an 'easy read version' which contained the following the statement:

> It is better if people with a mental disorder can live the life they want with the right help and support but sometimes they have to have treatment which they do not agree to.
>
> (Department of Health 2004: 4)

By making such legal rules accessible to all, ordinary people are arguably becoming party to their own oppression. This is part of the rationale in the Bill to shift towards lawful measures of community control but it continues an older theme in the discourse of professional mental health work. That is, it is presumed that care or treatment, whether given with or without the permission or cooperation of the patient, is still the same care or treatment. The (dubious) professional and political assumption here is that the content of care is independent of legal rules. Pols (2001) points out that this is a rhetorical avoidance of actual outcomes in services, where compliance with legal rules inevitably affects patient–staff relationships. It is not merely a matter of patients having treatment 'which they do not agree to'. It is also that any such failure to agree triggers an interaction with staff, which alters the very nature of any treatment received or imposed upon patients.

This point opens up two different interpretations of the link between compulsion and treatment. On one side is the State, most psychiatrists and some sociologists (e.g. Gove 1975) who assume that the impairments of mental disorder include a failure on the part of the patient to request what is needed, due to a lack of insight. In this view, compulsion ensures that those without insight into their real needs are given access to interventions which are good for them. The law is being used as a vehicle to ensure patients have the treatment they need (one version of 'doing good' in Pols analysis above). On the other side are those who assume that compulsion is largely driven not by patient needs (actual or assumed, expressed or not expressed) but by the needs of others to maintain social order. This position has been taken in the main by dissident psychiatrists (e.g. Szasz 1963) and by sociologists studying the social control of residual deviance (e.g. Scheff 1966).

The globalization of compulsion

Variability exists in relation to the extent to which a national or State culture is authoritarian or liberal and this affects the extent to which compulsion is used in its mental health services (Brakel, Parry and Weiner 1985; Ramon 1988; Cohen 1989; Dingwall, Tanaka and Minamikata 1991). As well as these international variations, there have been signs in the last 50 years of global convergence occurring in relation to mental health law. These include a change from the use of terminology such as 'insane' and 'lunatic', to 'mental illness', reflecting a worldwide trend towards medicalization. Latterly this may also signal globalization. For example, in the last decade there has been a gradual convergence of therapeutic law with many countries adopting similar definitions of mental disorder and legal processes. Evidence of this is in the consensus statement issued by the World Health Organization (2001) offering 10 recommendations:

- provide treatment in primary care;
- make psychotropic drugs available;
- give care in the community;
- educate the public about mental health and mental health problems;
- involve communities, families and consumers;
- establish national policies, programmes and legislation;
- develop human resources (for an adequate mental health service workforce);
- link with other sectors;
- monitor community mental health;
- support more research into biological and psycho-social causes of and treatment for mental health problems.

The list as a whole reflects the interest groups influencing WHO policy and the trends or aspirations for good practice in countries across the globe. For the purpose of this chapter the third recommendation is important (as the community, not hospitals, will increasingly become a site of compulsion) and so is the sixth which in full is:

> Mental health policy, programmes and legislation are necessary steps for significant and sustained action. These should be based on current knowledge and human rights considerations. Most countries need to increase their budgets for mental health programmes from existing low levels. Some countries that have recently developed or revised their policy and legislation have made progress in implementing their mental health care programmes. Mental health reforms should be part of the larger health system reforms. Health insurance schemes should not discriminate against persons with mental disorders, in order to give wider access to treatment and to reduce burdens of care.
>
> (2001: 3)

The WHO suggests then that mental health legislation is a desirable global outcome. It also assumes that such legislation (which defines the conditions of compulsion and safeguards against its misuse by the State and professionals) is a sign of progress. Thus the WHO is not signalling the need to abandon legal powers of compulsion, only the need to standardize these powers, in the light of 'current knowledge and human rights considerations'. In developed countries, which have had such legislation for many years, the critique of legalism is now well rehearsed (e.g. Campbell and Heginbotham 1991) but it is not reflected in the WHO's wish list. In the last five years, government proposals to revise the 1983 Mental Health Act to reflect a post-institutional world have intensified this critique from user groups and some professional groups. For example, for a while the British Psychological Society advanced the case that dedicated mental health law should be abandoned completely and replaced by one on dangerousness (complimented by one on disability rights).

Professional interests and legislation

In England and Wales, the 1959 Mental Health Act established the medical profession as the key party involved in making applications for compulsory admissions. This was based on the view that mental illnesses require medical treatment. This principle remained unchanged in subsequent mental health legislation in 1983 but is slowly being modified.

Under the prospective proposals other professions are to have a greater role which brings into the frame previously excluded professional groups such as clinical psychologists. Part of this move has taken place under the guise of promoting generic and inter-disciplinary working. However, it is clear that workforce shortages at least in the UK might be partially responsible. Also, when the psychiatric profession is ambivalent about the management of some patients (as it is in relation to those with a diagnosis of personality disorder), the State can call upon practitioners in other professions to act as agents of social control. The British government has recommended recently that the Responsible Medical Officer role (inhabited to date by psychiatrists) should be abandoned now in favour of the wider 'Clinical Supervisor' role. The latter would include appropriately trained psychiatrists, psychologists and social workers.

Social workers have traditionally performed a subsidiary and facilitative role (although this may change under future legislative arrangements). They are the personnel charged with bringing the patient to the attention of the psychiatrist and are thus subordinate to medicine. Bean (1986) views the social worker's role in compulsory detention as due to a historical accident. Certainly, as a predominantly female occupation, social work did not have access to the structures and territory that the male medical profession had when capturing jurisdiction over the control and management of mental disorder (Witz 1990). This is evident in the position that social workers have been ascribed in mental health legislation.

Intra-professional, as well as inter-professional power and status are also implicated. 'Approved Social Workers' (ASWs) are expected to have 'expertise' in mental health, which their peers do not. They are charged with interviewing patients in 'a suitable manner' and seeking alternatives to admission wherever possible. These roles and responsibilities set ASWs apart from generic social workers. However, unlike the professional politics of nursing in relation to the 1983 Act described later, social workers did not seek or aspire to this enhanced status. It was imposed from outside. There were concerns over the competence and commitment of social workers to carry out their expected responsibilities from those informing and drawing up the new legislation. The reluctant imposition of external professionalization on social workers led to disputes between the social workers' trade union NALGO and their employing authorities. Extra payments were demanded for what were viewed as new responsibilities, and these demands were accompanied by a boycott of ASW training programmes. Social workers did not see their interests in competing with the knowledge and skills of other mental health professionals by increasing their own expertise in mental health, preferring instead to adopt an industrialization strategy (Oppenheimer 1975).

Psychiatric nursing, along with other branches of the profession, has, for the last 20 years, been engaged in strategies to move from being a semi-profession to a fully autonomous profession. This can be seen in attempts to develop a unique body of knowledge (e.g. nursing theory) and engaging in research. Recognition by the State of the responsibilities and authorization of certain duties is also a prerequisite for the professionalization of an occupation. The 1983 Act gave psychiatric nurses 'holding powers' to detain voluntary patients who wish to leave hospital (section 5 (4)). During the six-hour period that registered nurses are authorized to prevent a person from leaving, a medical practitioner must consider whether a 'full' holding power should be used. According to Bean (1986) this new power was not really necessary. Existing medical powers and common law provide for the physical restraint of patients.

The power granted to nurses thus represented a capitulation to demands for greater recognition of their role, in the context of one of the nursing unions resisting the acceptance of a patient from a special hospital: 'Threats of industrial action, even from members of one union, can seriously disrupt and place patients in a vulnerable position. The holding power under the 1983 Act was an obvious attempt to placate trade union demands' (Bean 1986: 51). Thus, nurses used trade union tactics to gain increased State recognition of their professional status and role. This presents something of a contradiction within the professional ideology of psychiatric nursing. On the one hand, claims to an original body of knowledge rests on nursing's unique skills of 'caring' (as opposed to the curative claims of medicine); on the other, increased professional power was sought via their coercive role in relation to psychiatric patients. The supervisory role of new legally backed community control has also fallen to mental health nurses outside of a hospital context. This has provided nurses with greater voice and weight in mental health matters nationally but has had unforeseen negative consequences for nurse–patient relationships (Wells 1998).

Dangerousness

This section will first deal with violence to others and then suicide.

Violence and mental disorder

While public prejudice, backed up at times by the views of politicians simply assumes that mental disorder predicts violence to others, the considered empirical position about this relationship has varied over time. Broadly three phases can be identified:

1 *The negative relationship phase.* Studies of the relationship between mental disorder and violence between 1925 and 1965 suggested that people with mental health problems were actually less violent than the general population (Rabkin 1979).

2 *The small positive relationship phase.* After 1965 this position went into reverse. Link *et al.* (1992) found that after 1965 the median ratio was one of 3:1, with patients being more violent than non-patients. A number of factors could account for this reversal. First, episodic violent acts were historically contained in mental hospitals, when nearly all patients where chronically warehoused, with the range of potential victims being highly restricted in closed settings. This changed as more and more patients were treated in the community. Second, the community settings for patients were often risky environments–poor and socially disorganized with high rates of crime. Third, these environments also contained access to substances which could be abused less readily in hospital settings. Reviewing this small positive relationship, Monahan (1992: 510) noted that:

> None of the data give any support to the sensationalized caricature of the mentally disordered served up by the media ... Compared with the magnitude of risk associated with the combination of male gender, young age, and lower socio-economic status for example, the risk of violence presented by mental disorder is modest. Compared with the magnitude of risk associated with alcoholism and other drug abuse, the risk associated with major mental disorders such as schizophrenia and affective disorder is modest indeed. Clearly, mental health status makes at best a trivial contribution to the overall level of violence in society.

3 *The disaggregated data phase.* During the 1990s a further analysis of the small relationship revealed a complicated inter-relationship between clinical factors, personality factors and contextual factors (Blumenthal and Lavender 2000; Pilgrim and Rogers 2003). An increasing number of studies began to address specific aspects of the relationship between mental state and violence. The following summarizes these findings:

- Ambiguous findings have been evident about the link between psychosis alone and violence in community settings. Swanson *et al.* (1990) found that psychotic patients who did not abuse substances were three times more dangerous than their non-patient equivalents over a period of a year. By contrast Steadman *et al.* (1998) found that psychotic patients who did not abuse substances were no more likely to be violent than their neighbours. Given that violent acts are quite rare it is also worth noting that even in the Swanson *et al.* study, their findings only pointed up 7 per cent of violent compared to 93 per cent non-violent patients. This is why the summary of the small aggregate relationship by Monahan above refers to a 'trivial contribution'.
- Substance abuse predicts violence. People, whatever their mental state, who abuse alcohol and some other substances (such as crack cocaine) are significantly prone to violence and other risky behaviour, such as dangerous driving. Some drugs do not predict violence though, most notably the opiates (though they do predict other forms of criminality to feed the

habit). Substance abuse also is the best predictor of violence in psychotic patients (Steadman *et al.* 1998).

- The diagnosis of mental disorder which best predicts violence is that of a type of personality disorder (anti-social/dissocial/psychopathic). This is hardly surprising. As we noted earlier this diagnosis is typically defined tautologically by persistent violent habits. Broad diagnoses alone of mental disorder (such as personality disorder in general) or mental illnesses such as 'schizophrenia' are very poor predictors of violence.
- Ambiguous findings exist about the role of individual symptom and treatment variables. For example, compliance with medication reduces the risk of violence (Swartz *et al.* 1998). Command hallucinations with hostile content predict violent acts (Junginger 1995). Taylor (1985) also found that this was the case for hostile delusions. However, other studies have not demonstrated a relationship between hallucinations or delusions and violence (Teplin *et al.* 1994; Appelbaum *et al.* 1999; 2000). Violent ruminations seem to predict violence in those who abuse substances (Grisso *et al.* 2000). Indeed the consistent theme in the recent literature is that psychopathic disorder and substance misuse are strong predictors of violence but psychosis per se is not.
- Independent of clinical and personality variables, some times and places shape dangerousness more than others. When patients are discharged into richer areas they are less dangerous than in poorer areas (Silver *et al.* 1999). The latter areas of 'concentrated poverty' contain what Hiday (1995) calls 'violence inducing social forces'. In these poor community contexts, patients are more prone to be both the victim and perpetrator of crimes.

Having summarized the phases of empirical investigation about the overall or aggregate link between mental state and violence a prospective question is begged: can violence be predicted in individual cases? A number of criticisms can be raised in relation to the possibility:

1 *The empirical attack.* This is a body of research evidence which suggests that accurate prediction is impossible: 'It now seems beyond dispute that mental health professionals have no expertise in predicting future dangerous behaviour either to self or others. In fact predictions of dangerous behaviour are wrong about 90 per cent of the time' (Ennis and Emery 1978: 28).

2 *The political attack.* From a libertarian position, Szasz (1963: 46) has argued that prediction violates patients' civil rights:

> Drunken drivers are dangerous both to themselves and to others. They injure and kill many more people than, for example persons with paranoid delusions of persecution. Yet, people labelled 'paranoid' are readily committable, while drunken drivers are not . . . Some types of dangerous behaviour are even rewarded. Racecar drivers, trapeze artists, and astronauts receive admiration and applause . . . Thus, it is not dangerousness in general that is at issue here, but rather the manner in which one is dangerous.

The libertarian critique from Szasz has been echoed by other critics (e.g. Sayce 2000) who have argued that singling out mentally disordered individuals for particular scrutiny in relation to dangerousness is discriminatory. This point can be highlighted by the use of a table (Table 10.1) which identifies the contingent judgments and outcomes applying to a variety of social groups.

3 *Professional dissent.* The third source of attack emanates from some mental health professionals. Because predicting dangerousness is tied to social control, some professionals worry that it is incompatible with a caring and therapeutic role. They resent and resist becoming society's police officers for informal rule rather than law infringement. Risk minimization pushes professionals into conservative decision making to avoid false negatives (predicting the absence of risk when a patient then goes on to be dangerous). This type of decision making encourages professionals to take a distrusting attitude towards patients in general. The discussion earlier about the way in which legal rules and obligations interfere with professional ethos of care is relevant to this point.

These various examples demonstrate that psychiatric patients are only one of many groups that we might consider when thinking about degrees of dangerousness and socio-legal sanction. The question is whether or not psychiatric patients are offered the same rights as others in the table. For instance, currently in Britain people of known dangerousness (like those in cells 4 and 6) are morally condemned but not legally restrained. By contrast, many psychiatric patients who are no proven threat to others are compulsorily detained under the Mental Health Act.

Table 10.1 Mental health and dangerousness

	Sick				Well			
	Law breaker		Law abiding		Law breaker		Law abiding	
	Detained	Free	Detained	Free	Detained	Free	Detained	Free
Dangerous	1	2	3	4	5	6	7	8
Non-dangerous	9	10	11	12	13	14	15	16

Cell 1: Mentally disordered offenders.
Cell 2: Mentally disordered offenders prior to detection.
Cell 3: Civil compulsory admissions to psychiatric hospitals.
Cell 4: People who are HIV+ who indulge in unprotected sexual intercourse.
Cell 5: Convicted prisoners.
Cell 6: Drunken/speeding car drivers.
Cell 7: Prisoners of war.
Cell 8: Members of the SAS.
Cell 9: Petty criminal prisoners who are psychologically disturbed.
Cell 10: Petty criminals on probation.
Cell 11: Old people forcibly hospitalized under the 1948 National Assistance Act because they live in insanitary conditions.
Cell 12: People in the community who are depressed.
Cell 13: Prisoners guilty of 'white collar' crimes like fraud.
Cell 14: Unapprehended shop lifters.
Cell 15: Victims of child abuse who are taken into care.
Cell 16: The assumed societal norm.

Suicide and mental disorder

The social control of psychiatric patients, both in hospital and community settings, is not limited to the question of violence to others. Mental health services are also concerned with reducing the incidence of self-harm and self-neglect. Rates of suicide among psychiatric patients are high for a number of reasons. Their labour market disadvantage places them in a demoralized and devalued position. Their primary disability may include profound feelings of anomie, aimlessness, worthlessness, low mood and low self-esteem, as well as angry feelings which can be trapped and turned inwards. The secondary disability created by psychiatric treatment may be both demoralizing (when coping with drug side effects and stigma) and an opportunity to act suicidally (the option to self-poison with prescribed psychiatric drugs).

The differential way in which psychiatric patients are treated when violent or potentially violent is also true of self-harm. In Britain suicide is not illegal. Despite this, suicidal patients, when identified, are treated in a peculiar way – coercion is applied. The question of suicide in psychiatric populations is thus more contradictory in a legal sense than that of violence to others. The latter in any population, general or psychiatric, is judged to be both immoral and illegal. By contrast, suicide is not illegal and its moral status is contested. Another example of the differential rule application to psychiatric patients in relation to suicide is more subtle and implicit.

When psychiatric patients are suicidal, it is assumed that their intentions are governed singularly by their mental abnormality. However, suicides in non-psychiatric populations are evaluated in a range of ways, which might include a notion of a temporary imbalance of mind, but other motives can be ascribed as well. These include a notion of rational intelligibility, when for various reasons, it is obvious why a person has little or nothing to live for (e.g. severe pain or physical disability or traumatic loss of significant others). Similarly, for reasons noted earlier, psychiatric patients might, for very good reasons, feel devalued and disabled. And yet, suicidal intent or action on their part tend only to be interpreted as irrational. Thus, while the *post hoc* attribution of mental abnormality may be applied to any person committing suicide, there is a greater tendency for this to occur with people who are already psychiatric patients.

Psychiatric diagnosis is a weak predictor of suicide. For example, those with a diagnosis of depression have a 15 per cent lifetime risk of suicide and for those with a diagnosis of schizophrenia it is 10 per cent (Morgan 1994). This means that the overwhelming majority of those with a psychiatric diagnosis do not commit suicide, although more do so than in the general population. When specific personal and social factors are taken into account, rather than diagnosis, then predictive validity increases. These factors include: drug and alcohol abuse; single or separated status; male gender; low social class; unemployment; poverty; previous parasuicide; age (variable according to diagnosis); and recent violence (received or given) (Platt 1984; Jenkins *et al.* 1994).

When suicide is reframed as a social, rather than individual, phenomenon then a range of public policy factors can be identified in relation to primary prevention. For example, in the US suicide rates are lower in States with tight gun control than those with lax control. An Australian study revealed that

85 per cent of gunshot deaths were linked to distress rather than criminal action (Dudley, Cantor and Demoore 1996). Suicide has increased with motor car use over the past 20 years (via carbon monoxide self-poisoning) but it decreased when North Sea (non-toxic) gas was introduced in Britain in the 1970s. Given that self-poisoning is a common means of suicide, then lax prescribing of psychiatric drugs by the medical profession increases suicide rates, as does the widespread availability of some over-the-counter drugs like paracetamol.

Impact on patients of their risky image

The legal and empirical debate about dangerousness and mental illness and how to assess risk does include considerations of moral and ethical issues. However, notwithstanding the importance of the latter, sociologically there is a much wider agenda than assessing the points at which it may be considered legitimate or illegitimate to use coercive control. The conflation of violence with mental illness and its expression in language, its importance as a cultural construct, and its impact on the everyday lives of people with psychiatric diagnoses are also worthy of our attention. There is evidence, for example, that psychiatric patients internalize the stigma of dangerousness in a way which comes to impact negatively on their self-image. This has been illustrated in a recent study of the meaning and management of neuroleptic medication in its recipients (Rogers *et al.* 1998). This is illustrated by this patient who was interviewed in the study who had no personal history of violent acts or intentions. He reports his reaction to having been told that he had a diagnosis of 'schizophrenia':

> . . . the word frightened me to death because books I've read and programmes on telly like, when I heard the word like 'schizophrenic', the word 'schizophrenic' at that time meant to me, I'm not bloody safe. I'm not safe. I'm a dangerous person and that sort of thing, and I'm likely to, be talking nice and calm to someone and the next minute I'm going to be getting a knife or something like that to them you know and I said no, I'm not accepting this . . . that word does frighten people, if you were to tell somebody that I was a schizophrenic oh my God you know the first thing they'd say you know is 'I think you'd better keep away from him'.

In this chapter we have been mainly concerned with the way in which psychiatric patients have been contained and confined within psychiatric facilities or in the community by the provisions of therapeutic law. The shift towards community settings has nonetheless brought to the fore the issue of the rights of psychiatric patients to be involved in the mainstream of society and to participate in the planning and delivery of the mental health services they receive. British legislation, most notably the NHS and Community Care Act 1990, has encouraged the direct participation of service users in the planning and management of care services. However, legislation which encourages and promotes the notion of consumerism in mental and community services does not, in itself, ensure change.

The meaning and purpose of user involvement and how service users can best be represented and power shared cannot be legislated for but requires more fundamental changes to take place outside a strict legal framework (Bowl 1996). However, with the rise of the users' movement there has been growing attention placed on the need for a set of positive rights linked to the notion of citizenship. This perspective has stressed the need for equal opportunities about, and rights of access to, employment and housing for all psychiatric patients (Rooke-Matthews and Lindow 1997).

Psychiatric patients are singled out and treated in a separate way by legislation. First, involuntary patients admitted to hospital under civil sections of mental health legislation have no one to act as their advocate to retain their freedom at the time of admission. They have only the right to argue for their freedom after their detention. Second, they can be singled out in terms of their potential rather than their actual behaviour. Thus, therapeutic law is used for purposes of preventive detention. While criminals have a prescribed period of detention, mental patients do not, in the sense that legal powers allow their periods of detention to be renewed. Criminals lose their liberty as a consequence of a proven transgression of the law. Mental patients can lose their liberty even if there has been no such transgression – to offend public or family rules of decorum is all that is required. And even when a patient has committed an offence, they are not prescribed a defined period of detention if they are sent to a secure psychiatric facility.

Thus, Szasz is correct to point out that psychiatric patients are treated in a particularly discriminatory way in modern society. Moreover, some people who are not labelled as mentally disordered are manifestly dangerous (like those in cells 4 and 6 of Table 10.1) yet they suffer none of the infringements of liberty imposed on non-offending psychiatric patients. This discrimination against psychiatric patients is not implicit or covert, as is the case in so much of sexual and racial discrimination, but is explicit and legally legitimized.

Although British mental health legislation seemingly exists to protect the rights of patients, it actually helps facilitate this discrimination, rather than alleviating it, since it frequently fails to adequately protect or enhance patients' civil liberties or their quality of life. Instead, the law legitimizes 'the institutionalization of society's unfounded prejudice and fear regarding madness'. The latter phrase is used by Campbell and Heginbotham (1991) when arguing that there is little justification for maintaining a separate legislative framework for those considered to be mentally disordered.

Discussion

The inter-dependent relationship between the legal and psychiatric systems has been explored in this chapter. Having reviewed the interplay between legal and medical control, it seems that their conceptual separation, and assumed antagonism, does not always translate neatly into practice. Currently, the two feed off one another or form complementary contributions to the constraint of mental abnormality. In Britain, for instance, both lawyers and doctors sit on Mental Health Review Tribunals. The Mental Health Act Commission, which arose out of legislation (the 1983 Act), contains both doctors and lawyers.

Moreover, although the Commission is a manifestation of legalism, it enshrines the collegial loyalties enjoyed by doctors. For instance, it appoints and pays second-opinion doctors to review the appropriateness of the treatment of detained patients at the hands of other doctors. Disagreements with the 'treating psychiatrist' are uncommon.

Thus, arguably, in the field of mental health, lawyers and psychiatrists are bedfellows, not adversaries. The Draft Mental Health Bill, being debated as we write, replays this theme but extends the professional involvement beyond psychiatry to include psychology and social work. If brought into law it will change the precise structures at the interface of mental health services and the legal system, particularly in relation to the Mental Health Act Commission and the role of Tribunals. However, their replacement structures will still involve the inter-mingling of lawyers and mental health professionals and the rules governing them will reflect the current resolution between legal and health professional views.

A wider approach to understanding mental health care and coercion from within the social sciences and health services research is likely to add to analysis provided from within the existing legal framework. A greater focus on social and contextual aspects of violence and mental health suggests a response at a different level (for example, a public health agenda about mental health). Additionally, the adoption of a patient-centred approach to the framing of questions of care and control in coercion research is likely to balance the dominance of disciplinary approaches from within psychiatry and the law. The social construction of violence and mental illness at a socio-political level, the wider role played by services and professionals and the risks faced by patients living in the community should arguably be at the centre, rather than at the periphery, of research and analysis on coercion.

Legalism has played an important role in the field of mental health. It has set certain limits on medical power and discretion. It has also codified two separate social processes which are at odds with one another: the rights of patients to exercise choice; and the rights of professionals to impose their actions against the wishes of patients. Psychiatric patients have also had special legal provision when they commit criminal offences. The legal rules applied to them have been different to those of other offenders, highlighting the special (arguably discriminatory) way in which people with mental health problems are treated. This special treatment also applies to self-injurious behaviour. Although suicide itself is not illegal, suicidal intent detected in people with mental health problems can trigger peculiar forms of lawful control.

Questions

1 Should dangerous psychiatric patients be treated differently to other dangerous people?

2 Discuss the evidence about mental health status and dangerousness.

3 What contradictions exist in mental health law?

4 In which respects did mental health law in Britain change during the twentieth century?

5 Can consumerism operate while we have coercive mental health law?

6 Should mental health legislation be abandoned?

For discussion

Consider the different ways in which psychiatric patients might be denied informed consent and examine legal options to improve their lot in this regard.

Further reading

Aldridge, D. (1997) *Suicide: The Tragedy of Hopelessness*. London: Jessica Kingsley.

Bean, P. (1986) *Mental Disorder and Legal Control*. Cambridge: Cambridge University Press.

Monahan, J. and Steadman, H.J. (eds) (1994) *Violence and Mental Disorder*. Chicago: Chicago University Press.

Redley, M. (2003) Towards a new perspective on deliberate self harm in an area of multiple deprivation. *Sociology of Health and Illness*, 25(4): 348–73.

Sjostrom, S. (1997) *Party or Patient?: Discursive Practices Relating to Coercion in Psychiatric and Legal Settings*. Borea: Spinettstraket.

Chapter 11

Users of mental health services

Chapter overview

This chapter will explore the different ways in which those who use mental health services can be understood sociologically. These are not merely different perspectives. They reflect the changing role of psychiatric patients in mental health services and in wider social life. A shift over a 30-year period, from patient to provider highlights this point. The wider social and cultural influence of users, within and beyond health service provision, is also explored, particularly in relation to the formation of the mental health users' movement.

The following topics will be discussed:

- the diffuse concept of service use;
- the relatives or 'significant others' of psychiatric patients;
- users as patients;
- users as consumers;
- users as survivors;
- users as service providers.

The diffuse concept of service use

In the British context, the term 'user' of mental health services has generally been accepted in recent years. The term is eschewed in the USA because of its narrow connotation of drug misuse. There, user groups tend to prefer the term 'patient', 'ex-patient' or 'survivor' (the last of these is also common in Britain).

There is a deeper problem, not related to terminology, about the concept of 'service use'. Psychiatric services provide, among other things, one form of social control in society. As a consequence, social groups other than designated patients benefit from the existence of mental health services. Moreover, some of these groups have regular service contact. The legal framework in Britain recognizes this.

Mental health legislation has traditionally been split into two broad parts – one about civil sections and the other about mentally disordered offenders. This separation implies, and at times spells out, that mental health services will serve a range of statutory and civil groups in wider society: the criminal justice system, social services, the immigration service, primary health care and relatives of people entering the psychiatric patient role. Even strangers in public places are served indirectly because the police can detain people reported to them who are thought to be mentally disordered.

These legal administrative arrangements indicate that many groups other than identified patients effectively constitute users of mental health services. Some of these relationships have been discussed in earlier chapters. Here we will focus on the relatives of psychiatric patients before considering patients themselves in the next section.

Relatives or 'significant others'

Whether or not psychiatric patients enter the role voluntarily or involuntarily, it is not unusual for their relatives (or 'significant others') to be interested parties about service contact. Not only might they be involved in formal decision making about hospital admission, they might have previously been involved in engendering, coping with, and eventually informally labelling the incipient patient's mental abnormality, prior to formal psychiatric diagnosis. Also, once professional interventions are triggered, relatives may have service contact as visitors. Sometimes they act as advocates for patients (demanding improved services). Sometimes they might express concern that services are not being coercive enough in ensuring treatment compliance or in prematurely discharging patients.

Within some treatment rationales relatives are framed by professionals as implicit or adjunct service clients in order to engender change in the patient or minimize the chances of relapse in their condition. Because of wide-ranging powers of professional discretion within services, this imputed role is variegated and relatives may not always be informed of the assumptions operating about them in a particular service setting. A number of examples of this point can be given.

- *Family role in etiology.* In the controversial model of 'schizophrenia' being intelligible within mystifying and dysfunctional family communication patterns, some professionals sought to engage with relatives to render the patient's behaviour and experience intelligible or to trace causal antecedents (Lidz, Laing and his colleagues, Bowen and Jackson). A critical review of this strand of therapeutic work is provided by Howells and Guirguis (1985);

• *Family role in relapse.* A less controversial model relates to relapse. Here, professionals do not necessarily question either the validity of psychiatric diagnosis or the role of genetic factors in causality. Instead they argue that relatives who are intrusive and emotionally labile (high on 'expressed emotion') place stress upon mentally ill people which increases the probability of relapse in those diagnosed as depressed or schizophrenic. Within this model, relatives may be contacted in a process of 'psycho-education' in order to reduce levels of 'expressed emotion' during their contact with the identified patient. This work is summarized by Jenkins and Karno (1992). It has been critiqued by Johnstone (1993);

• *Relatives as risk assessors.* A paradoxical effect of the above two therapeutic approaches is that they may have changed professional norms about the credibility and involvement of family members. However, involving families by asking their views about risk in their relative-patient increases the accuracy of risk assessment and efficiency of risk management (Klassen and O'Connor 1987);

• *Relatives as perpetrators and victims of abuse.* Leaving aside the particular controversy noted above about family etiology in 'schizophrenia', the families of people with a psychiatric diagnosis, may be sites of victimization. In Chapter 6 we discussed the raised levels of diagnosis in survivors of childhood sexual abuse. The 'schizophrenia' literature may be contested about causal antecedents, but the long-term post-traumatic effects of childhood abuse are clear. In the other direction, some relatives may at times become the victims of violence at the hands of children who are psychiatric patients (Estroff and Zimmer 1994).

Over and above these variable professional assumptions operating about the antecedent and current role of relatives for psychiatric patients, family members have also become an important self-organizing lobby. In Britain, groups such as SANE (Schizophrenia A National Emergency) and Rethink (previously the National Schizophrenia Fellowship) have significant input from relatives. In the USA, the National Alliance for the Mentally Ill is dominated by relatives' interests (Manthorpe 1994). These groups focus on lobbying politicians and professional organizations nationally and locally. Sometimes they also set up direct support services in localities. The lobbying power of relative-dominated groups has been evident in recent years in Britain. In the past it has been commonplace for these groups to seek and gain publicity about mental health issues like community care and violence.

In Britain the amalgam phrase of 'users and carers' has been common in the discourse of mental health service management and government policy (Department of Health, 1999; 2002). Up to now we have deliberately avoided the notion of 'carer' in this section for a number of reasons.

• Relatives may or may not subjectively care for their patient relative; the

notion of 'care-as-emotion' cannot be taken for granted in a family relationship. They may dislike the identified patient or they have even made a
contribution to the development of their mental health problem;
• Relatives may or may not offer practical care – shelter, tangible support and
domestic tending;
• Patients themselves may, when not in hospital, be the carer of their
non-mentally ill relatives (e.g. their children and elderly parents);
• Sometimes those offering a caring role to someone who is mentally distressed are not family members;
• Relatives of patients may want to preserve their identity as a partner, wife or
husband and may not feel comfortable with the ascribed role of 'carer'
(Forbat 2002; Forbat and Henderson 2003).

For these reasons, caution needs to be exercised, purely on logical grounds,
about conflating the term 'carer' and 'relative' or assuming that the role of
carer is accepted by those it is applied to. Despite this complexity, there is a
literature, which has used the term 'carer' simplistically to mean family relatives acting in the interests of patients. For example, there is the review book of
Family Caregiving in Mental Illness (Lefley 1996). The extensive literature it
contains depicts relatives singularly as victims of care burden created by
(genetically caused) mental illness.

Another conceptual problem with this 'burden'-focused literature is the
tendency to see mental illness as creating similar political demands for relatives and patients alike. As a consequence, the self-advocacy movements (NB
plural) of patients and their relatives have not properly been separated for
academic analysis and are assumed to arise for similar reasons and to have the
same interests (see for example, Watkins and Callicutt 1997).

Elsewhere (Rogers and Pilgrim 1996) we have argued that social scientists
should avoid stereotypical assumptions about the role of family members.
Sociologically we deciphered two dominant currents of professional discourse – one which tends to blame relatives for their etiological role and the
other which tends to sympathize with the martyrdom created by 'care burden'. It may be that relatives can be both victims of circumstance when, for
example, struggling to cope with a disruptive and distressing son or daughter,
and a causal source of distress when, for example, they abused an incipient
patient in childhood. A whole range of other contingent styles of relating can
exist between prospective and current patients and their relatives.

The stress of living with people who have severe mental health problems
can itself lead to distress in relatives. For this reason, it is not unusual for
relatives to seek professional help for their own emotional difficulties and
thus become patients themselves (Perring, Twigg and Atkin 1990). It is little
surprising that relatives, when asked, will express the need for services to
support them as well as the primary identified patient (Goldberg *et al.* 1993).
Within the mental health field, this image of the 'carer' is changing. The
activities of health services management and research have meant that 'carers'
are increasingly conceived of as a separate interest group from both
professionals and users groups. They are distinctive in the way in which they
conceptualize mental disorder.

A survey of different stakeholders illuminated the value placed on different
aspects of care in primary care mental health (Campbell *et al.* 2003). Overall,

GPs rated a low number of practice level indicators as valid (41 per cent) (e.g. access, information treatment effectiveness) while carers rated the highest number valid (over 90 per cent). The reasons for the differences in what was seen to count as high-quality mental health care is likely to be an expression of different interests. GPs are likely to want to restrict the demand placed on their services to manage mental health. The high number of items mentioned by carers is likely to be an expression of the extent to which needs associated with mental health, from their perspective are not being met. Similarly another recent study exploring the commitment to various models of mental disorder (psychotherapeutic, medical, social, cognitive behavioural and so on) indicated that, compared to users and other practitioners, 'informal carers' were non-committal. A slight preference was shown for the medical and family models (39.2 per cent and 24.2 per cent, respectively) (Colombo *et al.* 2003).

Having discussed the wider notion of service use and looked at patients' relatives, we will now discuss the specific question of what services might describe as the 'identified patients' – people who formally enter the sick role voluntarily or against their will. We will examine the different ways in which the psychiatric patient's voice has been portrayed or conceptualized. We concentrate on four views of mental health service users, which reflect different discourses and interests:

- users as patients;
- users as consumers;
- users as survivors;
- users as providers.

Users as patients

The main way in which users of psychiatric services have been portrayed is as objects of the clinical gaze of mental health professionals. This is clearly seen in the academic literature which forms the basis of most psychiatric and psychological knowledge. Clinical research in the area of mental health has tended either to exclude the views of patients or to portray them as the passive objects of study. Their individual characteristics and feelings are mostly variables to be 'controlled out' in order to ensure valid results. For example, up until fairly recently the Medical Research Council has prioritized the funding of 'schizophrenia' research, with an emphasis on promoting genetic and biological studies. Evaluation of services to patients and user evaluation of services and treatment was given little mention. Explicitly or implicitly, 'mental patients' are portrayed in a way which emphasizes their pathology. A review of the literature provides a number of interesting examples of this claim. Here we mention four forms in which patients are denied a valid viewpoint.

The disregarding by researchers of those users' views that do not coincide with the views of mental health professionals

In an early attempt at providing a genuine user perspective, Mills (1962) found some interesting results. The study, which mainly used the accounts of patients and their relatives, found that users of services preferred contact with non-professionals to contact with social and health services personnel. When the latter were 'from a different social class [they] were often received with hostility'. The greatest forms of support were regarded as coming from people such as the local publican, the secretary of the local darts club and home helps, who were seen to provide 'down to earth common sense'. However, a reviewer of this work appeared to dismiss this errant view of services on the grounds that it could not be cross-validated.

> It is hard to believe that there were no sympathetic and sensible social workers in the area . . . The material is taken very largely from patients and their relatives and no attempt at validation appears to have been made. Since some of the patients were suffering from paranoia, and others from depression, it would have been a basic precaution to check the objective value of statements with the medical records or the responsible psychiatrist.
>
> (Jones 1962: 343)

This criticism insists that patients' views are to be treated with inevitable suspicion and that a professional view inevitably carries a greater claim to validity or truth.

The notion that psychiatric patients are continually irrational and so incapable of giving a valid view

Discussions around informed consent, which are relevant to the administration of treatments and participation in research programmes, also tend to invalidate the views of users. 'Schizophrenics' are a particular group thought inherently incapable of giving genuine informed consent. This is not infrequently linked to the high rate of 'non-compliance' to prescribed medication:

> Since the majority of clients with schizophrenia deny their illness, special difficulties are encountered in the criteria for understanding the nature of the psychiatric condition ... Denial is a major psychopathological mechanism which can impair appreciation. . . .
>
> (Davidhazar and Wehlage 1984: 385)

Why those labelled as schizophrenic should 'deny' their 'illness' is left unexplored. There is an assumption that this is due to a lack of 'insight'. That is, patients fail to agree with the opinion of their treating psychiatrist, which in itself is viewed as a symptom of mental illness. In the example given, the diagnostic label of schizophrenia is taken as a neutral one that can only be of benefit to patients.

Assumptions about the inability of patients to hold valid opinions are held by therapists of all kinds. This is summarized in a literature review of consumer satisfaction with mental health treatment by Lebow (1982: 254), who notes that therapists often suggest that the consumer cannot adequately judge the treatments they are given:

> Distortion is seen as inherent in consumer evaluation because of the client's intensity of involvement in treatment and impaired mental status, and the client is viewed as lacking the requisite experience to assess treatment adequately. Consumer satisfaction is regarded as principally determined by transference projections, cognitive dissonance, unconscious processes, *folie a deux*, client character, and a naivety about treatment, rather than an informed decision process reflecting the adequacy of treatment.

Patients and relatives are assumed to share the same perspective, and where they do not, the views of the former are disregarded by researchers

Another tendency in clinical work that superficially gives credence to the consumer voice is the conflation of the patient's view with that of their relatives. This is evident in a study which set out to examine the impact of the Mental Health Act 1959 (Hoenig and Hamilton 1969). The authors of the study conclude that: 'On the whole, [therefore] the general picture given here is of a large degree of satisfaction on the part of patients and their relatives . . .' (p. 130). However, if one scrutinizes their results in detail, there are some important contradictions. While 84 per cent of the relatives' group was favourably disposed to the admission of the patient, only 47 per cent of the patients were content to be admitted, with 43 per cent being reluctant. Yet, the implication of these findings, which seem to suggest, on close reading, that the interests of these two groups may at times be divergent, was not noted by the researchers. Moreover, disquieting results were glossed over and excused by referring to patient pathology. For instance, complaints made by patients about services were dismissed thus: 'Their complaints referred to rough handling by nursing staff. It must be remembered that they were rather sick patients, and it was also not within our brief to verify individual complaints . . .' (p. 126).

Framing patient views in terms which suit professionals

Often, lay conceptions of mental health problems are researched in such a way that there is little room for people to express their own views about the subject in hand. One example, from a psychologist's perspective (Furnham 1984) involved a research design aimed at examining lay people's conceptions of 'neuroticism'. Leaving aside the problem of representativeness (the experimental group was 'a fairly homogeneous young, well-educated sample'), such questionnaires leave little room for self-expression, since all the items are predetermined as standardized items by the researcher, with no open-ended questions.

Even where credence is given to the freely expressed views of patients, there is a tendency on the part of some researchers, who are also mental health practitioners, to adopt a 'victim-blaming' approach. This approach tends to leave practitioners' own role and that of their service unquestioned. One example of this is a study which found that clients attending a psychiatric day unit found it stigmatizing (Teasdale 1987). Patients preferred to 'hide' the reasons for attendance, because a label of 'mental illness' was experienced to be unhelpful. The analysis focused on the need for clients to be helped, 'to arrive at unambiguous personal interpretations and management of the stigmatising reaction of the local community' (p. 345). It is suggested that this might be achieved 'if they [the patients] are supported in their attempts to understand and manage the resulting stigma, then the social and thera-peutic effectiveness of the service should increase'. The professional's signal role in alleviating stigma was outlined as the 'need to encourage clients to be open about their fears and to help them demystify the idea of psychiatric care'.

Users as consumers

An alternative way of conceptualizing psychiatric patients is not as the objects of clinical interventions but as consumers of services. The term 'consumerism' implies the existence of choice between products, and an active insistence on value for money. Consumerism in one form or another has informed health policy making in Britain since the beginning of the 1980s. It is often linked to the introduction of general management principles in the NHS, which tended, when it was first introduced, to modify the clinical view of services. The administration of the health services by consensus decision making among different clinical groups was replaced by the concentration of responsibility for services and management in the general manager. Part of this trend towards general management has involved what Offe (1984) has referred to as the 'commodification' of welfare services. This has introduced the logic of the wider economic system into the health service. An example of this is the ten-dering out of health service catering and laundry services. Another example can be seen in the previous Conservative government's attempt to introduce an internal market for services by creating 'purchasers' and 'providers' of services under the NHS and Community Care Act 1990.

One of the effects of this philosophy has been a growing acknowledgement of the importance of consumer satisfaction. Starting with the second Griffith's Report (DHSS 1988), the importance of the health service being accountable to the patient has been emphasized. The importance of consumer choice has also been stressed in recent government consultative documents on primary care. Thus, there is now a clear acceptance within health policy circles that more credence and authority should be given to a user perspective. Attention given to psychiatric views and levels of satisfaction with services has, until recently, tended to lag behind other client groups using health service facilities. This is likely to have been a result of the assumption that the accounts of psychiatric patients lack credibility. However this has changed, due in not small part to the impact of users' voices in the mental health arena. Three examples are illustrative:

- the involvement of service users is now viewed as essential for high quality services in the National Service Framework for Mental Health (Department of Health/Home Office 1999);
- in 2003 there was the formation of the 'Commission for Patient and Public Involvement in Health' and all NHS Trusts now have a duty to carry out a range of activities related to service user involvement, under section 11 of the Health and Social Care Act 2001;
- the National Institute of Mental Health for England has incorporated the agenda of users as 'experts by experience' and invited the input of user/ survivor experience in a discussion forum. It was launched for people who use services to discuss the future of mental health services and other important issues in a safe, non-judgmental environment. (See www.nimhe.org.uk/ usersurvivor/index.asp)

There are a number of difficulties associated with viewing patients as consumers. Although general management has encouraged in the NHS a market-influenced system permitting consumer choice, the extent to which the health service has actually achieved this has been restricted by the 'clinical autonomy' exercised by the medical profession in treating patients. Britten (1991) showed that consultants who adhered to a bio-medical rather than psycho-social model of illness were less likely to agree with a proposed policy of patient access to their own records. Professionals sometimes claim that patients do not wish to know that they are ill.

There are also doubts about whether users of health services are currently in a position to make informed choices. Customers of health care do not have the same access to clinical knowledge as health care professionals, who have many years of training and experience on which to base their choices. Informed consent, in which the benefits and negative effects of treatment are made available to patients, has only recently been acknowledged as an area which needs attention. As we noted in Chapter 8, patients do not have access to information about their treatment whereas professionals do. In particular, there is the bias set up by professionals selectively withholding information which might alarm or demoralize the patient.

There are also objections to the notion of consumer being used specifically in relation to psychiatric patients. 'Consumer' tends to denote a positive choice from a range of alternatives. As one user representative put it:

Consumer tends to be rejected because of its connotations with Tory consumerism but also because consumer implies you are getting something of value. The majority of people in the users' movement do not feel that they have consumed anything of value and many say quite clearly that the real consumers of mental health services are relatives, the police and the state.
(Cited in Rogers and Pilgrim 1991: 136)

Since this research, the British government has changed but the connotation of patients as consumers has been retained by the Labour administration's health policy since 1997. Clearly, then, being a 'consumer' of health services is

	Market forces		Professional power
	−	+	
Psychiatric patient		Private patient	+
Acute medical/surgical NHS patient		Complementary medicine user	−

Figure 11.1 Typology of health consumers.

a complex affair. In order to understand the health care consumer's position, and in particular that of the psychiatric patient, we also require an analysis in terms of their relationship to market forces on the one hand, and professional power on the other. Figure 11.1 provides a way of conceptualizing these variables, putting psychiatric patients in a context of other medical service users. It can be seen that there are some areas of health care to which the term 'consumer' seems more applicable than others.

Complementary medicine (bottom right) provides a service predominantly in the private sector where market forces operate most freely. (There is little provision for alternative medicine within the NHS.) This allows for free competition between individual practitioners who compete for patients. Prices charged for therapies take place in a competitive environment. The necessity for social control on the part of professionals is also minimized. The typical person who chooses alternative medicine is middle class, articulate, and consults for non-life-threatening illness, under a voluntary contract which involves regular but limited service contact. Here the term 'consumer' seems to be highly appropriate.

The private patient using conventional medicine (top right) can choose health care according to the range of private hospitals available. However, professional control is greater than in the case of the complementary medicine user. General practitioners control access to specialist medical services, so the patient is not totally free of professional constraints. Moreover, in terms of professional power, in the private sector the internal constraints (such as complaints procedures and health authority policies) which govern clinical practice in the NHS are absent. Here the term 'consumer' is plausible, but the power of professionals to impede or dictate consumer choice renders it problematic.

Professional power is still influential in relation to NHS acute patients. However, this is arguably not as strong as in the private sector given the constraints placed on professional dominance through policy making and fiscal arrangements determined by the State. For example, as well as the gatekeeping function of GPs, the NHS acute medical patients' free choice is constrained by the rationing of health services made available by health authority funds (see Figure 11.1, bottom left). If demand outstrips supply (clinical resources of manpower and technology), access to public health care is usually rationed according to the notion of a waiting list. In other instances, such as kidney dialysis, other selection criteria may also apply. In the case of fertility treatment for example, sexual orientation, marital status, socio-economic status, and number of existing children are factors which may be taken into consideration in permitting the uptake of services. Thus, the term 'consumer' becomes more dubious in this group of service recipients, given limited resources and mechanisms to filter out 'unworthy' cases.

Users of psychiatric services (top left) experience professional power even more acutely, while being denied the freedom to choose their therapist or service (compare this with the consumer of alternative medicine). Psychiatric patients can be forced into the sick role by means of compulsory admission. Even though this relates to only a small minority of patients, the fact that a person may be forced to enter hospital or receive treatment makes any notion of free positive choice tenuous (see Chapter 10). Being excluded from employment in the main, psychiatric patients are also a group with very little 'buying power' and so they penetrate little into either of the boxes on the right of the figure. By the time we reach the top left box, the term 'consumer' hardly appears to be apposite at all.

In measuring satisfaction in the area of mental health, there appear to be a number of other differences between patients who use services for acute physical problems and those who receive psychiatric services:

1 *Contact with services for those with mental health problems is far more extensive than for most others who use the health and social services.* (Although they have this in common with some groups of physically disabled people.) Those who enter hospital for acute physical problems, such as appendicitis, are patients for a short time only, whether or not they experience their hospitalization as positive or negative. Thus, the quality of service and treatment does not have as many long-term consequences as for those who are psychiatric patients. The latter often spend many years of their lives in contact with the services and professionals.

2 *The consequences of being labelled 'ill' are often greater for a person who is given a psychiatric diagnosis.* For the majority of those with physical problems, the diagnosis itself is often only temporary and is often not stigmatizing. Since the diagnosis of a person as 'mentally ill' is done primarily on the basis of a judgement about a person's conduct, there is always a risk of invalidating their whole identity or sense of self. Again, certain physical disabilities (such as epilepsy) may carry with them stigma, and so the mental patient is not unique.

3 *There are social and economic consequences of contact with psychiatric services which apply much less often when acute medical services are used.* Those labelled as mentally ill are discriminated against by present and prospective employers and, as a result, are often subjected to a life of poverty. Educational opportunities are curtailed, family and intimate relationships affected and making social contact with people is fraught with difficulties. Again, some of these impediments to citizenship often apply to people with long-term physical disabilities.

Despite these differences between psychiatric and acute medical patients, let us look briefly at the literature which has included mental health service users within a discourse of being 'consumers' or 'clients', particularly in relation to 'quality assurance'.

Literature on psychiatric patient satisfaction and dissatisfaction

The emerging body of satisfaction research about mental health services has commonly adopted a needs-assessment approach. This has usually assessed patient satisfaction according to 'normative need'; that is need defined by an acknowledged expert (Bradshaw 1972; Prior 1989) and typically ascertained by means of standardized assessment tools. These approaches have been linked to the emphasis on 'quality assurance', which is a type of evaluation research which is concerned with patient satisfaction.

According to the WHO (1979), the aim of quality assurance is: '. . . to assure that each patient receives such a mix of diagnostic and therapeutic health services as is most likely to produce the optimal achievable health care outcome for that patient'. This form of evaluation of 'client need' focuses on the narrow measurement of the behaviour of the mental health client. Unlike the view of patients defined by psychopathology, this approach treats people as complete individuals in the sense that understanding is based on the everyday actions and language of individuals. However, this approach is still defined professionally, as this account of the observations of one quality assurance programme suggests:

> Once out of the client's hearing, however, the results of these inter-actions are often re-analysed in terms of a specific (and professionalised) linguistic framework. Thus, a game of ten-pin bowling is re-analysed in terms of 'motor skills'. A discussion about food is re-analysed in terms of coping skills. A lapse of memory is discussed in terms of a syndrome and a leisure time activity is analysed in terms of affective disorder. In fact client 'problems' are in many respects newly created through the application of behaviourist discourse to what are called 'activities of daily living'.
>
> (Prior 1991: 141–2)

In addition to this behaviourist approach, there is a small amount of research conducted from within statutory services which does not presume that mental health services are only there to do people good. Rather than 'normative need' this research has focused on 'felt need' (Bradshaw 1972). An early example of this was Mayer and Timms's (1970) work in which social workers were encouraged to take seriously the views expressed by clients. The work of Beresford and Croft (1986) also highlights the views of users of social services and emphasizes the need for genuine participation by users in research about services.

While professionally defined needs tend to focus on behaviour and the effectiveness of prescribed treatments, the 'felt need' evaluations tend to emphasize the material and social aspects of people's everyday lives. Kay and Legg (1986) found that the need to have a job was a high priority for those recently discharged from hospital. An example is a survey which examined the expressed needs of patients *vis-à-vis* their living arrangements and material and social support (Hatfield, Huxley and Hadi 1992). A sizeable minority of patients expressed dissatisfaction with their living arrangements. Those living in staffed accommodation were particularly critical and did not view their living situations as a result of their own positive choice. The survey also identified a 'substantial level of felt need for work'.

A more recent survey of discharged patients revealed a number of aspects about their quality of life in the community. These included their sense of vulnerability, the benefits of community care, an appreciation of the support of others, an awareness of the impact of scarce resources and disappointment about poor coordination between health and social services (MacDonald and Sheldon 1997).

Users as survivors

There has been some analysis of the users' views of services from those who do not work directly with people in service settings either as clinicians or as managers. The position of psychiatric users in a wider social context is the object of these analyses. Two perspectives can be identified in this regard. The first has adopted a phenomenological approach to understanding the social position of the mental patient. The second has tried to analyse the structural position of users as a social group within wider society. In particular there is an interest in users campaigning collectively as a 'new social movement' (see below).

The phenomenology of surviving the psychiatric system

An example of the expansion of the felt-need approach to users described earlier is provided by a phenomenological study. This is concerned with understanding the subjective meaning that people give to their experience of the social world. An example of this is the work of Barham and Hayward (1991), who made use of personal accounts of mental patients to explore their experiences of trying to live outside of hospital. The aim of this study was:

> To attempt to bring people with mental illness under the concept of personhood, required of us will be what Bernard Williams terms an 'effort at identification', in which the person 'should not be regarded as the surface to which a certain label can be applied, but one should try to see the world (including the label) from his point of view'.

In adopting this approach, their work takes us beyond the measuring of consumer satisfaction. Rather, the concern is with the mental patient's identity and social position in everyday life. The themes identified from the subjects themselves were:

- exclusion from participation in social life;
- burden, which 'refers to the cultural freight which agents are obliged to carry';
- reorientation, which refers to 'coping' with their vulnerabilities.

Everyday encounters reported by subjects suggested the continuing marginalization of people labelled as schizophrenic, as illustrated by this quote from one respondent who struck up a conversation in a pub:

I said I was schizophrenic and he said 'You don't want to tell people things like that, they might take you out and beat you up outside'. Anyway, I just got up and left because I didn't want any trouble.

(p. 16)

Participants in the study were also reluctant to enter or re-enter patienthood. Most wanted to establish their credibility as ordinary people with rights of citizenship, such as adequate employment and housing. The participants were only marginally more willing to be incorporated into community services than the old custodial regime. This suggests a fundamental questioning of the utility of services from the perspective of users themselves. Such a questioning is not acknowledged by the other two views (of patient and consumer) discussed earlier. Phenomenological analysis gives primacy to the individual experience of the patient in relation to the mental hospital or community. The wider collective role of mental health consumers, as a group within civil society, is also an aspect which is important in understanding the contemporary position of mental patients.

Survivors as a type of new social movement

The growth in the collective activities of mental health users over the last three decades has been noted by a number of commentators (Haafkens, Nijhof and van der Poel 1986; Burstow and Weitz 1988; Chamberlin 1988; Rogers and Pilgrim 1991; Crossley and Crossley 2001). During the 1970s, the Dutch and US survivors' movements gained national and State recognition. By 1977, 35 organizations were represented in the Netherlands. Organized mental patient pressure in the USA resulted in funding for research and for mental health services to be run exclusively by patients (Campbell and Schraiber 1989). From the 1980s onwards similar developments took place in the UK. User dissatisfaction reached such a point that, in terms of numbers and organizations, it constituted a mature 'new social movement'.

Social movements can be defined as loose networks of people that actively resist established dominant forms of power or pursue cultural or social change (Toch 1965). Tactics of civil disobedience which were built into a strategy for social change were typified in the non-violent movements led by Mahatma Gandhi and Martin Luther King. Social movements are characterized by mass mobilization (e.g. demonstrations) and for the most part act outside of formal organizations and bureaucratized pressure and charity groups. 'New' social movements can be distinguished conceptually from 'old' social movements in that they are further removed from the arena of production than the latter. Additionally, rather than seeking to defend existing social and property rights from erosion by the State, new social movements seek to establish new agendas and conquer new territory (Habermas 1981). Many, but not all are built upon a shared oppressed identity (e.g. the Women's Movement, Gay Liberation). Some are not built on a common identity but on a common cause (Animal Rights, the Ecology Movement).

Scott (1990) contrasts new social movements with the Labour (or workers') movement (the focus of the Marxian tradition in sociology). This movement has become a part of the political process through organized industrial action and negotiation (e.g. the TUC and the Labour Party). Its organization has become formalized or bureaucratized and its aims have been economic and political.

By contrast, the new social movements have mainly had social and cultural aims and have emphasized direct action and non-hierarchical forms of organization. Some social scientists have gone as far as arguing that the absorption of the Labour movement into the established political process, in capitalist society, leaves the new social movements as the only remaining radical challenge to the status quo (Marcuse 1964). The mental health service survivors' movement fits broadly conceptually within this new political pattern of radicalism. It is characterized by opposition to expert medical knowledge and a form of politics based on an identity derived from their mental health problems and contact with specialist services.

The growing activity within and around the health care arena has meant a greater focus by sociologists on typologies on Health Social Movements (HSMs) as a specific sub-typology of NSMs. Brown *et al.* (2004) have described three types of HSMs:

• health access movements;
• embodied health movements (EHM);
• constituency-based health movements.

In line with a traditional Weberian views of 'ideal types' these are not meant to be mutually exclusive but are likely to have cross-cutting characteristics. 'Access' has not been a key issue for the mental health service users' movement. Indeed, evading access to services, held in suspicion or contempt, has been noteworthy instead. Despite evidence of major inequalities in service provision operating in relation to a range of social groups with mental health problems, the failure of services to be seen as ameliorative and benevolent dissuades users from demands for service contact. Also, the coercive character of specialist services renders them as aversive. However, aspects of the two other typologies (EHMs and constituency based health movements) are evident. These challenge medical science and they emphasize the role of the patient's experience. EHMs in particular emphasize a common oppressed identity – a motif of the survivors' movement.

Sang (1989) has pointed out that the term 'advocacy' has been co-opted by professionals and is used loosely by them to include 'meeting clinical needs'. He distinguishes this professional discourse from two separate notions from service users themselves: citizen advocacy and self-advocacy. In the first of these, ordinary citizens (i.e. not professionals) form a relationship with a psychiatric patient to represent their interests as if they were their own. In the second case, psychiatric patients work together to represent their individual and collective interests independently of non-patients. Examples of self-advocacy since the 1980s in Britain are given in Box 11.1.

Survivors' groups have shared several concerns highlighted first by critical professionals during the 1960s (the so called 'anti-psychiatry' movement). While that critique was highly intellectual and came from professionals themselves, the more recent one has come from service users directly and is less theoretically oriented. Instead, practical direct action characterizes its form. However, the 'clinical' group described in the US clearly draws upon the

---

Box 11.1 **The emergence of the collective voice of the user: examples of direct action from the British survivors' movement after 1980**

Example 1:
In 1988, a campaign was launched by users in London to oppose changes being advocated by the Royal College of Psychiatrists to the Mental Health Act 1983. The proposed Community Treatment Order (CTOs) would have allowed doctors to treat patients in the community on a compulsory basis. This hostility to CTOs culminated in over a hundred users and their allies marching from Hyde Park to Belgrave Square. There, a wreath was laid at the steps of the Royal College of Psychiatrists, in honour of the deceased recipients of ECT and major tranquillizers. Speeches were made (including one from a Labour MP) and patients read poems critical of psychiatric treatment.

Example 2:
An organized opposition to the poster campaign, in the south of England, of SANE (Schizophrenia a National Emergency). This advertising campaign enjoyed the patronage of Prince Charles and the pop singer Sting. It was heavily financed by, amongst others, Rupert Murdoch and P&O ferries. The posters depicted psychiatric patients as frenziedly dangerous and called for a halt to the hospital closure programme. In response, London-based users' groups lobbied the Advertising Standards Authority about the offending posters.

Example 3:
The lobby of the then opposition (Labour Party) spokespeople in Parliament by a national network of 56 different users' groups. This network is dispersed throughout the country. The MPs agreed to meet the groups, to hear their complaints about existing services and their recommendations for changes in mental health policy.

Example 4:
In 2002 the NO Force movement organized a march through London which was attended by over three hundred people wishing to voice their opposition to government proposals to make it easier to detain people with a diagnosis of 'dangerous personality disorder' and compulsory treatment in the community.

---

therapeutic alternatives, which the 'anti-psychiatrists' themselves developed and advocated at an earlier point.

The mental health users' movement has emerged, and been transformed, from previously atomized voices of lone mental patients. The transformation has now led to a collective voice of shared resistance and demands for change. This has emerged as a result of a dialectical relation to wider public and collective movements, in turn connected to broader transformations in the social, economic and health arenas. The notion of 'habitus' has been used as a basis for understanding this transformation (Crossley and Crossley 2001). The notion combines the phenomenology (the survivors' personal experience) and historical features of social life. Thus, collective experience and action are viewed as being structured by the residue of previous experience and this 'habitus' in turn contributes to the further structuration of further experience and action.

From this perspective, the current activities and success of the survivors' movement can be related to the existence of audiences, relations of symbolic power and to the historical activity of service-user protest and resistance. Changes in the 'personal' voice of the mental patient changed significantly in the post-war period (Crossley and Crossley 2001). In the face of a discreditable identity of the mental patient, which prevailed in the 1950s and 60s, the Mental Patients Union in the 1970s and the Protection for the Rights of Mental Patients were concerned with 'pleas' to be assigned an authentic personal voice.

A shift to a more collectivized voice is clearly evident in the post-1980s period. Users' experiences are wedded now to broader social groupings and issues (e.g. gender and sexual abuse). The agenda of activism contributes explicitly to the discourse of political activism and resistance on the one hand and the development of alternative ways of managing madness on the other. The 'lived experience' and voice of users is combined in a way which produces an emancipatory form of dealing with mental suffering. This combination is evident for example in the way in which the Hearing Voices Network embraces and makes the connections between the social and the therapeutic:

> People who hear voices and their families and friends can gain greater benefits from de-stigmatising the experience, leading to a greater tolerance and understanding. This can be achieved through promoting more positive explanations, which give people a more positive framework for developing their own ways of coping and raising awareness about the experience in society as a whole.
>
> (www.hearing-voices.org.uk)

Users as providers

For some time services have been provided by users of services (Chamberlin 1977; Lindow 1994; Wallcraft 1996). User-led safe houses and drop-in day centres reflect the users' movement's priorities of voluntary relationships, alternatives to hospital admission, crisis intervention and personal support.

Between the diffuse self-care strategies and mutual support occurring spontaneously between patients in statutory services and funded user-led services, there is another layer of user involvement. In recent years, service providers have, to various degrees in different localities, sought the collaboration of users to support service developments. Minimally this has entailed surveys or consultation exercises about local-need identification (an extension of the role of user as consumer). It has also included: the formal acceptance by professional providers of innovations such as patients' councils; users being paid to train mental health staff (Crepaz-Keay, Binns and Wilson 1998) and users' and carers' groups being called upon to improve services in collaborative experiments in service development (Carpenter and Sbaraini 1997; Pilgrim and Waldron 1998).

User-led services have also introduced an alternative philosophical base to the management and treatment of mental health problems. At times this has had a feedback impact on traditional services. The Hearing Voices Network, informed by the work of Romme, works positively with people's experiences of hearing voices. Rather than attempting to obliterate the voices, as a traditional symptom-based approach might do, this user-led initiative attributes meaning to voice hearing. This offers alternative means of coping with voices that may at times cause their recipients distress.

The limits of the user as provider are essentially set by the willingness (or lack of it) to encroach upon the coercive social control role which professionals have traditionally taken. Professional norms have included State-delegated powers to detain and forcibly intervene in the lives of people who are socially deviant or incompetent (under the paternalistic guise of the 'treatment' of illness). Not only do user-led projects not include this function currently, because of the absence of legal powers, it is unlikely that they would want to accrue this traditional psychiatric professional service role, given that the main stimulus for the development of the service users' movement internationally was the civil libertarian objection to the coercive role of psychiatry in society. This point is made in a critical way by an academic psychiatric nurse:

> What matters here is that such services can show that they can provide safe and effective care to a high standard. The fact that all such services so far have had to institute rules that enable difficult people to be excluded indicates that such services are developing in a way that is supplementary rather than alternative to psychiatry.
>
> (Bowers 1998: 138)

While it is an open empirical question whether or not the vast array of user-led service experiments have *all* excluded 'difficult people', rather than a presumed 'fact', Bowers is probably correct in highlighting the tendency of user projects to eschew a coercive role and embrace voluntary relationships. However, what user-led projects do provide is an alternative to the readiness of psychiatry to coercively control those who are not 'difficult' (in the sense of being dangerous rule breakers) but who are harmlessly unintelligible to their fellows (e.g. voice hearers and those with inoffensive delusions).

Currently, psychiatrists regularly use their legal powers to remove the liberty of these types of patients – to be deemed to be mentally ill and without insight is sufficient for a forced psychiatric admission. User-led projects offer more benign alternatives to this group of people and in so doing provide a redefinition of who is difficult, by showing how this latter group can be helped where traditional services have failed.

A second criticism we would make of Bowers's position is that the lack of capacity (or willingness) of user projects to fully replace psychiatry's societal function also clarifies that function. In other words, at times some extreme rule breaking, such as sexual assault, violence or incorrigible madness, is simply beyond the capability of ordinary people to cope with and respond to safely, whether in domestic or public settings. In such circumstances, State-delegated social control is understandably invoked – 'something has to be done'. The police or psychiatry are called in then as part of a repressive State apparatus which is requested, respected and gratefully received by ordinary people who are *not* (or not deemed to be) the rule breakers in particular social crises (Coulter 1973). By stopping short of this role, user-led services clarify the embodied constitution of repressive social control enacted daily by the action of the police and mental health professionals.

The tension between advising, providing and campaigning

Over the last two decades the user movement has grown in numbers and developed a strong community of interest around shared beliefs and a coherent survivor discourse. Survivor groups have sought to assert both the legitimacy of experiential knowledge and their positions as citizens in the face of official responses, which have not always been supportive (Barnes 1999)

One development of the users' movement, which has converged with the interests of health service managers, is the development of user-led service innovations. For example, user-led services can be found in the voluntary sector in Britain and occasionally they are supported by statutory authorities. The large range of user-controlled facilities available in the USA is reviewed by Mowbray *et al.* (1997) This activity varies from the latent role of patients being self-caring and mutually supportive in professionally-led services and self-help groups, right through to funded projects which are managed and staffed by users themselves.

The growth in provision outside the mainstream has been responded to and incorporated by the State and service providers. Within mainstream health policy there has been a gradual shift from viewing users as patients to 'partners', in the design and delivery of services. The notion of 'expert by experience' has gained gradual acceptance and been established and implemented as part of mainstream health policy. This is encompassed in the 'recovery' model which has US origins but is being adopted as a strand within British mental health services.

User and patient involvement in the planning and delivery of adult mental health services has been increasingly promoted. There is some evidence that this has resulted in greater inclusivity and the dismantling of power differentials between users and professionals. Users have been able to position themselves as active citizens, not merely as individual consumers, by drawing on a broad range of networks (Bolzan and Gale 2002). These shifts suggest possibilities for greater inclusivity. However, barriers have also been noted. Despite the rhetoric of partnership and user involvement, which accompanies new policies, such as the coordination of care, there is an absence of a corresponding involvement of users (Rose *et al.* 2003). The practical implementation of government rhetoric about user involvement has been patchy – a mixture of local successes and failures.

User involvement for the most part remains in the gift of provider managers, in so far as they retain control over decision making and may expect users to address the organization-set agendas and conform to their management practices. Pressures to accommodate to the structure and assumptions of mental health services organizations have been interpreted as the need for organizations to adapt and for users to acquire new skills (Truman and Raine 2002). While users' involvement may have brought about changes in services and policies, the demands of the survivors' movement for improvements in the status and social conditions of people with mental health problems is still marginalized (Rutter *et al.* 2004).

A question remains over whether this incorporation of users within the structures of health service might undermine the strength of the very new social movement which facilitated the State response to increase user involvement in the first place. Smelser (1962), an early commentator on new social movements, noted that conservative interest groups might make concessions to the demands of social movements in order to defuse their more radical demands for social change. State incorporation and diversion into service structures may be another way to diffuse the strength of demand for changes in status and social inclusion in civil society.

Discussion

The four ways of viewing service users described in the second part of this chapter illustrate the construction of the mental patient from different vantage points. The first, of patient, has a narrow clinical conception of the user of services – as an extension or carrier of the mental illness he or she is deemed to be suffering. The conceptualization of the user as consumer defines the user of services as a whole person who has needs over and above those defined from a diagnostic viewpoint. This approach tends still to be professionally defined and is limited to the parameters of the provision and delivery of existing or achievable services. The third approach takes the expressed view of users as the main reference point of analysis, along with the collective structural position of mental patients within a wider social context. The fourth and most recent view of users is that they can be providers of care for other people with mental health problems.

The implications that stem from these conceptualizations are consequently different. The first accepts that professionally led services are most appropriate, given the paternalism that mental illness is deemed to necessitate. The second modifies this by recognizing the notion of the positive choice that the ideology of consumerism implies. The third position marks a departure from a professionally defined discourse because by giving a voice to user demands, professionally delivered services are brought into question or are rendered problematic. The fourth position opens up even more ambiguity by shifting care from the professional domain to that of the mutual care of patients.

The clinical conception points to a traditional therapist – patient relationship. Consumerism envisages a larger role for mental health users in health care. There is an implicit assumption that views and participation should be in relation to existing services, whether some of these are expanded or diminished as a result of feedback on the basis of 'felt need'. The survivor and provider views, in eschewing or distrusting professional interventions, emphasize that the fundamental needs of patients are for rights rather than specialized services. This would imply an increase in material and social resources, for example, improved access to housing and employment opportunities. A further requirement might be legislation aimed at ensuring that people with a psychiatric label are not discriminated against in civil society, along the lines of that already existing for race and sex.

These divergent implications of the four conceptions of the mental patient outlined earlier suggest that, rather than being neutral or value free, each is imbued with, or reflects, a set of competing interests and ideologies related to the three groups central to contemporary mental health services: clinicians, managers and users. The power of each of these interest groups interact to determine the types of priorities that come to prevail in the organization, distribution and delivery of services and resources to those with mental health problems in society. The interaction is also affected by media portrayals of psychiatric patients and by the influence of groups of their relatives. Thus, any social understanding of the role, status and credibility of people who use mental health services needs to be reached after an appraisal of the relative salience of a number of dynamic processes and disparate actors which surround and inscribe a set of identities upon them.

This chapter has highlighted some basic problems about defining who exactly is a user of mental health services. Although the term 'user' (in Britain) has become a new shorthand for 'psychiatric patient', we drew attention to the other parties being served and thus arguably 'using' these services. If a variety of parties use services then it is inevitable that they are a source of disappointment as the different interest groups often seek different ends. Both the relatives of psychiatric patients and patients themselves have become important social movements which have shaped the character of mental health services. The emergence of user-led mental health provision has also highlighted the shortcomings of professional work (from a patient perspective) and defined the social control role of psychiatry more clearly.

Questions

1 Describe the reasons for the rise of the mental health service users' movement.

2 Compare and contrast the expectations which patients and their relatives are likely to have about mental health services.

3 How do the mass media shape our views of psychiatric patients?

4 What have 'survivors' of the psychiatric system 'survived'?

5 What do user-led services tell us about mainstream mental health provision?

6 Why is the term 'carer' problematic in the field of mental health?

> **For discussion**
>
> If you were the relative of a person who became psychotic what would you
> want from services? Think about this question again but now as the patient.
> Compare and contrast both parts of the exercise.

Further reading

Crepaz-Keay, D., Binns, C. and Wilson, E. (1998) *Dancing With Angels: Involving
    Survivors in Mental Health Training*. London: CCETSW.
Crossley, N. (1998) Transforming the mental health field: the early history of
    the National Association of Mental Health. *Sociology of Health and Illness*,
    20(4): 458–88.
Mowbray, C.T., Moxley, D.P., Jasper, C.A. and Howell, L.L. (eds) (1997) *Con-
    sumers As Providers in Psychiatric Rehabilitation*. Columbia: International
    Association of Psycho-social Rehabilitation Services.
Pilgrim, D. and Waldron, L. (1998) User involvement in mental health service
    development: how far it can it go? *Journal of Mental Health*, 7(1): 95–104.
Rogers, A., Pilgrim, D. and Lacey, R. (1993) *Experiencing Psychiatry: Users' Views
    of Services*. Basingstoke: Macmillan.
Speed, E. (2002) Irish mental health social movements. *Irish Journal of Sociology*,
    11(2): 62–80.

References

Abbott, P. and Wallace, C. (eds) (1990) *The Sociology of the Caring Professions*. London: Falmer Press.

Abbotts, J. Williams, R., Sweeting, H. and West, P. (2001) Poor but healthy? The youngest generation of Irish Catholics in West Scotland. *Health Bulletin (Edinburgh)*, 59(6): 373–80.

Abel, B. (1988) *The British Legal Profession*. Oxford: Blackwell.

Abel, G., Becker, J., Mittleman, M. *et al.* (1987) Self-reported sex crimes of non-incarcerated paraphiliacs. *Journal of Interpersonal Violence*, 2(1): 3–25.

Abraham, J. and Sheppard, J. (1998) International comparative analysis and explanation in medical sociology: demystifying the Halcion anomaly. *Sociology*, 32(1): 141–62.

Abramson, M. (1972) The criminalisation of mentally disordered behaviour: possible side effects of a new mental health law. *Hospital and Community Psychiatry*, 23(3): 101–5.

Adorno, T.W., Frenkel-Brunswik, E., Levinson, D.J. and Sanford, R.N. (1950) *The Authoritarian Personality*. New York: Harper and Brothers.

Ahmad, W.I.U., Atkin, K. and Jones, L. (2002) (Re) constructing multiracial blackness: women's activism, difference and collective identity in Britain. *Social Science and Medicine*, 5(10): 1757–69.

Al-Issa, I. (1977) Social and cultural aspects of hallucinations. *Psychological Bulletin*, 84: 570–87.

Al-Issa, I. (1987) Gender roles in L. Diamant (ed.) *Male and Female Homosexuality: Psychological Approaches*. New York: Hemisphere.

Albrecht, G., Walker, V. and Levy, J. (1982) Social distance from the stigmatized: a test of two theories. *Social Science and Medicine*, 16: 1319–27.

Aldridge, D. (1997) *Suicide: The Tragedy of Hopelessness*. London: Jessica Kingsley.

Alemi, F., Mosavel, M., Stephens, R. *et al.* (1996) Electronic self-help and support groups. *Medical Care*, 34(10): 32–44.

Alexander, L.A. and Link, B.G. (2003) The impact of contact on stigmatizing attitudes toward people with mental illness. *Journal of Mental Health*, 12(3): 271–90.

Allison, T.R., Symmons, D.P., Brammah, T., Haynes, P., Rogers, A., Roxby, M. and Urwin, M. (2002) Musculoskeletal pain is more generalised among people from ethnic minorities than among white people in Greater Manchester. *Annals of Rheumatic Disorders*, 61(2): 151–6.

Allsop, J. (2002) Regulation and the medical profession in J. Allsop, and M. Saks, (eds) *Regulating the Health Professions*. London: SAGE.

Allsop, J. and Saks, M. (eds) (2002) *Regulating the Health Professions*. London: SAGE.

Almog, M., Curtis, S., Copeland, A. *et al.* (2004) Geographical variation in acute psychiatric admissions within New York City 1990–2000: growing inequalities in service use? *Social Science and Medicine*, 59(2): 361–76.

Althusser, L. (1971) *Lenin and Philosophy and Other Essays*. London: New Left Books.

Alzheimer's Disease Report (1992). London: Alzheimer's Disease Society.

American Psychiatric Association (APA) (1994) *Diagnostic and Statistical Manual of Mental Disorders*. Washington, DC: APA.

Aneschensel, C.S. and Succoff, S. (1996) The neighborhood context of mental health. *Journal of Health and Social Behavior*, 37: 293–311.

Angermeyer, M.C. and Schulze, B. (2001) Reinforcing stereotypes: how the focus on forensic cases in news reporting may influence public attitudes towards the mentally ill. *International Journal of Law and Psychiatry*, 24(4–5): 469–86.

Anthias, F. (1992) Connecting race and ethnic phenomena. *Sociology*, 26(3): 421–38.

Applebaum, P.S., Robbins, P.C. and Roth, L.H. (1999) A dimensional approach to delusions: comparisons across delusion type and diagnoses. *American Journal of Psychiatry*, 156: 1938–43.

Appelbaum, P.S., Robbins, P.C. and Monahan, J. (2000) Violence and delusions: data from the MacArthur Violence Risk Assessment Study. *American Journal of Psychiatry*, 157(4): 566–72.

Arber, S. and Ginn, J. (1991) *Gender and Later Life*. London: SAGE.

Armstrong, D. (1980) Madness and coping. *Sociology of Health and Illness*, 2(3): 393–413.

Armstrong, S. (2002) The emergence and implications of a mental health ethos in juvenile justice. *Sociology of Health and Illness*, 24: 599–620.

Atkinson, P. (1983) The reproduction of the professional community, in R. Dingwall and P. Lewis (eds) *The Sociology of the Professions*. London: Macmillan.

Audit Commission (1986) *Making a Reality of Community Care*. London: HMSO.

Audit Commission (1994) *Finding A Place: A Review of Mental Health Services For Adults*. London: HMSO.

Backett, K. and Davison, C. (1995) Lifecourses and life style – the social and cultural location of health behaviour. *Social Science and Medicine*, 40(5): 629–38.

Backett-Milburn, K., Cunningham-Burley, Davis, J. (2003) Contrasting lives, contrasting views? Understandings of health inequalities from children in differing social circumstances. *Social Science and Medicine*, 57(4): 613–23.

Badesha, J. and Horley, J. (2000) Self-construal among psychiatric outpatients: a test of the golden section. *British Journal of Medical Psychology*, 73(4): 547–51.

Baker, A.W. and Duncan, S.P. (1985) Child sexual abuse: a study of prevalence in Great Britain. *Child Abuse and Neglect*, 9: 457–67.

Baker, D. and Taylor, H. (1997) Inequality in health and health service use for mothers of young children. *Journal of Epidemiology and Community Health*, 51: 74–9.

Baker, M. and Menken, M. (2001) Time to abandon mental illness. *British Journal of Medicine*, 322: 937.

Baldwin, R.C., Anderson, D., Black, S., Evans, S., Jones, R., Wilson, K. and Iliffe S. (2003) Guideline for the management of late-life depression in primary care. *International Journal of Geriatric Psychiatry*, 18(9): 829–38.

Bannister, D. (1968) The logical requirements of research into schizophrenia. *British Journal of Psychiatry*, 114: 1088–97.

Bannister, D. and Fransella, F. (1970) *Inquiring Man*. Harmondsworth: Penguin.

Barbato, A., D'Avanzo, B., Rocca, G., Amatulli, A. and Lampugnani, D. (2004) A study of long-stay patients resettled in the community after closure of a psychiatric hospital in Italy. *Psychiatric Services*, 55(1): 839–50.

Barham, P. and Hayward, R. (1991) *From the Mental Patient to the Person*. London: Routledge.

Barker, C. and Pistrang, N. (2002) Psychotherapy and social support – integrating research on psychological helping. *Clinical Psychology Review*, 22(3): 361–79.

Barnes, C. and Mercer, G. (eds) (2004) *Implementing the Social Model of Disability: Theory and Research*. Leeds: Disability Press.

Barnes, M. (1999) Users as citizens: collective action and the local governance of welfare. *Social Policy and Administration*, 33(1): 73–90.

Barnes, M. and Maple, N. (1992) *Women and Mental Health: Challenging the Stereotypes*. Birmingham: Venture Press.

Barnes, M., Bowl, R. and Fisher, M. (1990) *Sectioned: Social Services and the 1983 Mental Health Act*. London: Routledge.

Barrett, M. and Roberts, H. (1978) Doctors and their patients, in H. Smart and B. Smart (eds) *Women, Sexuality and Social Control*. London: Routledge and Kegan Paul.

Bartley, M., Blane, D. and Davey-Smith, G. (1998) Beyond the Black Report. *Sociology of Health and Illness*, 20(5): 563–77.

Bartley, M., Davey-Smith, G. and Blane, D. (1997) Vital comparisons: the social construction of mortality measurement, in M.A. Elston (ed.) *The Sociology of Medical Science and Technology*. Oxford: Blackwell.

Barton, W.R. (1959) *Institutional Neurosis*. Bristol: Wright and Sons.

Baruch, G. and Treacher, A. (1978) *Psychiatry Observed*. London: Routledge and Kegan Paul.

Bassuk, E., Rubin, L. and Lauriat, A. (1984) Is homelessness a mental health problem? *American Journal of Psychiatry*, 141: 1546–50.

Bean, P. (1979) Psychiatrists' assessments of mental illness: a comparison of Thomas Scheff's approach to labelling theory. *British Journal of Psychiatry*, 135: 122–8.

Bean, P. (1980) *Admissions to Mental Hospital Compulsory*. Chichester: Wiley.

Bean, P. (1986) *Mental Disorder and Legal Control*. Cambridge: Cambridge University Press.

Bean, P., Bingley, W., Bynoe, I. *et al.* (1991) *Out of Harm's Way: MIND's Research Into Police and Psychiatric Action Under Section 136 of the Mental Health Act*. London: MIND.

Bebbington, P.E., Hurry, J. and Tennant, C. (1981) Psychiatric disorders in selected immigrant groups in Camberwell. *Social Psychiatry*, 16: 43–51.

Beck, A.T. (1970) Cognitive therapy: nature and relation to behaviour therapy. *Behaviour Therapy*, 1: 184–200.

Beck-Sander, A. (1998) Is insight into psychosis meaningful? *Journal of Mental Health*, 7(1): 25–34.

Beck, U. and Beck-Gersheim, E. (1995) *The Normal Chaos of Love*. Oxford: Polity Press.

Becker, J.V. (1988) The effects of child sexual abuse on adolescent sexual offenders, in G.E. Wyatt and G.J. Powell (eds) *Lasting Effects of Child Sexual Abuse*. Thousand Oaks, CA: SAGE.

Beliappa, J. (1991) *Illness or Distress? Alternative Models of Mental Health*. London: Confederation of Indian Organizations.

Bendalow, G. and Williams, S. (1998) *Emotions in Social Life: Critical Themes and Contemporary Issues*. London: Routledge.

Bentall, R.P. (2003) *Understanding Madness: Psychosis and Human Nature*. London: Penguin.

Bentall, R.P. (ed.) (1990) *Reconstructing Schizophrenia*. London: Routledge.

Bentall, R.P. and Pilgrim, D. (1993) Thomas Szasz, crazy talk and the myth of mental illness. *British Journal of Medical Psychology*, 66: 69–76.

Bentall, R.P. and Slade, P. (1985) Reality testing and auditory hallucinations: a signal detection analysis. *British Journal of Clinical Psychology*, 24: 159–69.

Bentall, R.P., Jackson, H. and Pilgrim, D. (1988) Abandoning the concept of schizophrenia: some implications of validity arguments for psychological research into psychotic phenomena. *British Journal of Clinical Psychology*, 27: 303–24.

Beresford, P. (2005) Developing self-defined social approaches to distress, in S. Ramon and J. Williams (eds) *Mental Health at the Crossroads: The Promise of the Psychosocial Approach*. London: Ashgate.

Beresford, P. and Croft, S. (1986) *Whose Welfare? Private Care or Public Service*. London: Lewis Cohen Urban Studies.

Bergin, A.E. (1971) The evaluation of therapeutic outcomes, in A.E. Bergin and S. Garfield (eds) *Handbook of Psychotherapy and Behavior Change*. New York: Wiley.

Bergin, A.E. and Lambert, M. (1978) The evaluation of therapeutic outcomes, in S. Garfield and A. Bergin (eds) *Handbook of Psychotherapy and Behavior Change*, 2nd edn. Chichester: Wiley.

Berrios, G.E.(1985) Obsessional disorders during the nineteenth century: terminological and classificatory issues, in W.F. Bynum, R. Porter and M. Shepherd (eds) *The Anatomy of Madness* (Volume 1). London: Tavistock.

Bhaskar, R. (1978) *A Realist Theory of Science*. New Jersey: Hassocks.

Bhaskar, R. (1989) *Reclaiming Reality*. London: Verso.

Bhui, K. and Bhugra, D. (2001) Transcultural psychiatry: some social and epidemiological research issues. *International Journal of Social Psychiatry*, 47(3): 1–9.

Bhui, K., Christie, Y. and Bhugra, D. (1995) The essential elements of culturally sensitive psychiatric services. *International Journal of Social Psychiatry*, 41(4): 242–56.

Bhui, K., Stansfeld, S., Hull, S., Preibe, S., Mole, T. and Feder, G. (2003) Ethnic variations in pathways to and use of specialist mental health services in the UK. *British Journal of Psychiatry*, 82: 105–16.

Biafora, F. (1995) Cross cultural perspectives on illness and wellness – implications for depression. *Journal of Social Distress and the Homeless*, 4(2): 105–29.

Bifulco, A. and Moran, A. (1998) *Wednesday's Child: Research into Women's Experience of Neglect and Abuse in Childhood and Adult Depression*. London: Routledge.

Bifulco, A., Harris, T.O. and Brown, G.W. (1992) Mourning or inadequate care? Re-examining the relationship of maternal loss in childhood with adult depression and anxiety. *Development and Psychopathology*, 4: 119–28.

Bion, W.R. (1959) *Experiences in Groups*. New York: Basic Books.

Blackburn, R. (1988) On moral judgements and personality disorders: the myth of psychopathic disorder re-visited. *British Journal of Psychiatry*, 153: 505–12.

Blaxter, M. (1990) *Health and Lifestyles*. London: Routledge.

Blaxter, M. (1997) Whose fault is it? People's own conceptions of the reasons for health inequalities. *Social Science and Medicine*, 44(6): 747–56.

Blumenthal, S. and Lavender, T. (2000) *Violence and Mental Disorder: A Critical Aid to the Assessment and Management of Risk*. London: Zito Trust.

Bolam, B., Murphy, S. and Gleeson, K. (2004) Individualisation and inequalities in health: a qualitative study of class identity and health. *Social Science and Medicine*, 59(7): 1355–65.

Bolton, P. (1984) Management of compulsorily admitted patients to a high security unit. *International Journal of Social Psychiatry*, 30: 77–84.

Bolzan, N. and Gale, F. (2002) The citizenship of excluded groups: challenging the consumerist agenda. *Social Policy and Administration*, 36(4): 363–75.

Bourdieu, P. (1997) The forms of capital, in J. Richardson (ed.) *Handbook of Theory and Research for the Sociology of Education*. New York: Greenwood Press.

Bowers, L. (1998) *The Social Nature of Mental Illness*. London: Routledge.

Bowl, R. (1996) Legislating for user involvement in the United Kingdom mental health services and the NHS and Community Care Act. *International Journal of Social Psychiatry*, 42(3): 165–80.

Bowlby, J. (1951) *Maternal Care and Mental Health*. Geneva: World Health Organization.

Boyle, M. (1991) *Schizophrenia: A Scientific Delusion*. London: Routledge.

Bracken, P. and Thomas, P. (2001) Post psychiatry: a new direction for mental health. *British Journal of Psychiatry*, 322: 724–7.

Bracken, P.J., Greenslade, L., Griffen, B. and Smyth, M. (1998) Mental health and ethnicity: an Irish dimension. *British Journal of Psychiatry*, 172: 103–5.

Bradshaw, J. (1972) The concept of social need. *New Society*, 3: 640–3.

Braginsky, B.M., Braginsky, D.D. and Ring, K. (1973) *Methods of Madness: The Mental Hospital as a Last Resort*. New York: Holt, Rinehart and Winston.

Braithwaite, J. (1989) *Crime, Shame and Reintegration*. Cambridge: Cambridge University Press.

Brakel, J., Parry, J. and Weiner, B. (1985) *The Mentally Disabled and the Law*. Chicago: American Bar Foundation.

Brayne, C. and Ames, D. (1988) The epidemiology of mental disorders in old age, in B. Gearing, M. Johnson and T. Heller (eds) *Mental Health Problems in Old Age*. London: Wiley.

Breeding, J. and Bauman, F. (2001) The ethics of informed parental consent to the psychiatric drugging of children. *Ethical Human Science Services*, 3(3): 175–88.

Breggin, P. (1993) *Toxic Psychiatry*. London: HarperCollins.

Breslau, N., Kessler, R.C., Chilcoat, H.D., *et al.* (1998) Trauma and post-traumatic stress disorder in the community – The 1996 Detroit Area Survey of Trauma. *Archives of General Psychiatry*, 55(7): 626–32.

Briere, J. and Runtz, M. (1987) Post-sexual abuse trauma: data implications for clinical practice. *Journal of Interpersonal Violence*, 2: 367–79.

Bright, R. (1997) *Wholeness in Later Life*. London: Jessica Kingsley Publishers.

Britten, N. (1991) Hospital consultants' views of their patients. *Sociology of Health and Illness*, 13(1): 83–97.

Broverman, D., Clarkson, F., Rosenkratz, P. *et al.* (1970) Sex role stereotypes and clinical judgements of mental health. *Journal of Consulting and Clinical Psychology*, 34: 1–7.

Brown, G.W. (1959) Experiences of discharged chronic schizophrenic patients in various types of living group. *Millbank Memorial Fund Quarterly*, 37: 105.

Brown, G.W. (1996) Onset and course of depressive disorders: summary of a research programme, in C. Mundt, M. Goldstein, K. Hahlweg and P. Fiedler (eds) *Interpersonal Factors in the Origin and Course of Affective Disorders*. London: Gaskell.

Brown, G.W. and Harris, T.O. (1978) *The Social Origins of Depression*. London: Tavistock.

Brown, G.W. and Moran, P.M. (1997) Single mothers, poverty and depression. *Psychological Medicine*, 27(1): 21–33.

Brown, G.W. and Wing, J.K. (1962) A comparative clinical and social survey of three mental hospitals. *The Sociological Review Monograph*, 5: 145–71.

Brown, G.W., Harris, T.O. and Bifulco, A. (1986) Long term effects of early loss of parent, in M. Rutter, C. Izard and P. Read (eds) *Depression in Childhood: Developmental Perspectives*. New York: Guilford Press.

Brown, G.W., Harris, T.O. and Hepworth, C. (1995) Loss, humiliation and entrapment among women developing depression: a patient and non-patient comparison. *Psychological Medicine*, 25: 7–21.

Brown, P. (1995) Naming and framing: the social construction of diagnosis and illness. *Journal of Health and Social Behaviour*, Extra Issue: 34–52.

Brown, P. and Funk, S.C. (1986) Tardive dyskinesia: barriers to the professional recognition of iatrogenic disease. *Journal of Health and Social Behaviour*, 27: 116–32.

Brown, P. and Zaverstoski, S. (2004) Social movements in health. *Sociology of Health and Illness*, 26(6): 679–94.

Browne, A. and Finklehor, D. (1986) Impact of child sexual abuse: a review of the research. *Psychological Bulletin*, 99: 66–77.

Browne, D. (1990) *Black People, Mental Health and the Courts*. London: NACRO.

Browning, C.R. and Cagney, K.A. (2003) Moving beyond poverty: neighborhood structure, social processes and health. *Journal of Health and Social Behavior*, 44(4): 552–71.

Bullough, V.L. (1987) The first clinicians, in L. Diamant (ed.) *Male and Female Homosexuality: Psychological Approaches*. New York: Hemisphere.

Burchell, B. (1992) Towards a social psychology of the labour market. *Journal of Occupational and Organisational Psychology*, 65: 345–54.

Burr, J. and Chapman, T. (2004) Contextualising experiences of depression in women from South Asian communities: a discursive approach. *Sociology of Health and Illness*, 26(4): 433–40.

Burrows, R., Bunton, R. and Nettleton, S. (1995) *The Sociology of Health Promotion: Critical Analyses of Consumption, Lifestyle and Risk.* London: Routledge.

Burstow, B. and Weitz, D. (eds) (1988) *Shrink Resistant: The Struggle Against Psychiatry in Canada.* Vancouver: New Star.

Bury, M. (1986) Social constructionism and the development of medical sociology. *Sociology of Health and Illness*, 8: 137–69.

Bury, M. and Gabe, J. (1990) Hooked? Media responses to tranquillizer dependence, in P. Abbott and G. Payne (eds) *New Directions in the Sociology of Health.* London: Falmer Press.

Buss, A.H. (1966) *Psychopathology.* New York: Wiley.

Cahill, C., Llewelyn, S.P. and Pearson, C. (1991) Long term aspects of sexual abuse which occurred in childhood: a review. *British Journal of Clinical Psychology*, 30: 117–30.

Cameron, E. and Bernardes, J. (1998) Gender and disadvantage in health: men's health for a change. *Sociology of Health and Illness*, 20(5): 673–93.

Camp, D.L., Finlay, W.M.L. and Lyons, E. (2002) Is low self-esteem an inevitable consequence of stigma? An example from women with chronic mental health problems. *Social Science and Medicine*, 55(5): 823–34.

Campbell, J. and Schraiber, R. (1989) *In Pursuit of Wellness: The Well-being Project.* Sacramento: The California Department of Mental Health.

Campbell, S.M., Shield, T., Rogers, A. and Gask, L. (2004) How do stakeholder groups vary in Delphi technique about primary mental health care and what factors influence their ratings? *Quality and Safety in Health Care*, 13(6): 428–34.

Campbell, T. and Heginbotham, C. (1991*) Mental Illness, Prejudice, Discrimination and the Law.* Dartmouth: Aldershot.

Carchedi, G. (1975) On the economic identification of the new middle class. *Economy and Society*, 4(1): 1–85.

Carlezon, W.A. and Konradi, C. (2004) Understanding the neurobiological consequences of early exposure to psychotropic drugs: linking behavior to molecules. *Neuropharmacology*, 47(1): 47–60.

Carpenter, J. and Sbaraini, S. (1997) *Choice, Information and Dignity: Involving Users and Carers in Care Management in Mental Health.* London: Policy Press.

Carpenter, L. and Brockington, I. (1980) A study of mental illness in Asians, West Indians and Africans living in Manchester. *British Journal of Psychiatry*, 137: 201–5.

Carpenter, M. (1980) Asylum nursing before 1914: a chapter in the history of nursing, in C. Davies (ed.) *Re-writing Nursing History.* London: Croom Helm.

Carpenter, M. (2000) 'It's a small world': mental health policy under welfare capitalism since 1945. *Sociology of Health and Illness*, 22(5): 602–19.

Carrick, R., Mitchell, A., Powell, R.A. and Lloyd, K. (2004) The quest for well-being: A qualitative study of the experience of taking antipsychotic medication. *Psychology and Psychotherapy – Theory Research and Practice*, 77: 19–33.

Carstairs, G.M. and Kapur, R.C. (1976) *The Great Universe of Kota: Stress, Change and Mental Disorder in an Indian Village.* London: Hogarth Press.

Castel, F., Castel, R. and Lovell, A. (1979) *The Psychiatric Society.* New York: Columbia Free Press.

Castel, R. (1983) Moral treatment: mental therapy and social control in the nineteenth century, in S. Cohen and A. Scull (eds) *Social Control and the State.* Oxford: Basil Blackwell.

Chadwick, P. (1997) *Schizophrenia: the Positive Perspective.* London: Routledge.

Chamberlin, J. (1977) *On Our Own.* London: MIND.

Chen, E., Harrison, G. and Standen, P. (1991) Management of first episode psychotic illness in Afro-Caribbean patients. *British Journal of Psychiatry*, 158: 517–22.

Cheshire, K. and Pilgrim, D. (2004) *A Short Introduction to Clinical Psychology*. London: SAGE.

Chesler, P. (1972) *Women and Madness*. New York: Doubleday.

Ciompi, L. (1984) Is there really a schizophrenia? The long term course of psychotic phenomena. *British Journal of Psychiatry*, 145: 636–40.

Clare, A. (1974) Mental illness in the Irish emigrant. *Journal of the Irish Medical Association*, 67: 20–4.

Clare, A. (1976) *Psychiatry in Dissent*. London: Tavistock.

Clare, A. (1999) Psychiatry's future: psychological medicine or biological psychiatry? *Journal of Mental Health*, 8(2): 109–11.

Clausen, J.A. and Kohn, M.L. (1959) Relation of schizophrenia to the social structure of a small city, in B. Pasamanick (ed.) *Epidemiology of Mental Disorders*. Washington, DC: American Association for the Advancement of Science.

Cleckley, H. (1941) *The Mask of Sanity*. St Louis, MS: C.V. Mosby.

Clegg, S.R. (1990) *Modern Organisations*. London: SAGE.

Cochrane, R. (1977) Mental illness in immigrants to England and Wales: an analysis of mental hospital admissions 1971. *Social Psychiatry*, 12: 2–35.

Cochrane, R. (1983) *The Social Creation of Mental Illness*. London: Longman.

Cochrane, R. and Bal, S. (1989) Mental hospital admission rates of immigrants to England: a comparison of 1971 and 1981. *Social Psychiatry*, 24: 2–11.

Cohen, D. (1989) *Soviet Psychiatry*. London: Paladin.

Cohen, D. (1997) A critique of the use of neuroleptic drugs in psychiatry, in S. Fisher and R.P. Greenberg (eds) *From Placebo to Panacea*. New York: Wiley.

Cohen, D. and Prusak, L. (2001) *In Good Company: How Social Capital Makes Organizations Work*. Boston: Harvard Business School Press.

Cohen, D., McCubbin, M., Collin, J. and Perodeau, G. (2001) Medications as social phenomena. *Health*, 4: 441–69.

Cole, M.G. and Bellavance, F. (1997) Depression in elderly inpatients: a meta-analysis of outcomes. *Canadian Medical Association Journal*, 15(157): 1055–60.

Colletta, J. J. and Cullen, M. L. (2000) *Violent Conflict and the Transformation of Social Capital*. Washington, DC: International Bank for Reconstruction and Development/World Bank.

Colombo, T., Bendelow, G., Fulford, B. and Williams, S. (2003) Evaluating the influence of implicit models of mental disorder on processes of shared decisions making within community based multi-disciplinary teams. *Social Science and Medicine*, 56: 1557–70.

Commander, M.J., Cochrane, R, Sashidaran, S.P., Akilu, F. and Wildsmith, E. (1999) Mental health care for Asian, black and white patients with non-affective psychoses: pathways to the psychiatric hospital, in-patient and after-care. *Social Psychiatry and Psychiatric Epidemiology*, 32(9): 484–91.

Cooper, D. (1968) *Psychiatry and Anti-Psychiatry*. London: Tavistock.

Cooperstock, R. (1978) Sex differences in psychotropic drug use. *Social Science and Medicine*, 12: 179–86.

Cope, R. (1989) The compulsory detention of Afro-Caribbeans under the Mental Health Act. *New Community*, 15(3): 343–56.

Copeland, J., Dewey, M., Wodd, N. *et al.* (1987) Range of mental illness among the elderly in the community. *British Journal of Psychiatry*, 150: 815–23.

Corrigan, P.W. (1998) The impact of stigma on severe mental illness. *Cognitive and Behavioral Practice*, 5(2): 201–22.

Corrigan, P.W. (2002) Empowerment and serious mental illness: treatment partnerships and community opportunities. *Psychiatric Quarterly*, 73(3): 217–28.

Corrigan, P.W. and Mathews, A.K. (2003) Stigma and disclosure: implications for coming out of the closet. *Journal of Mental Health*, 12(3): 235–48.

Coulter, J. (1973) *Approaches to Insanity*. New York: Wiley.

Craib, I. (1989) *Psychoanalysis and Social Theory: The Limits of Sociology*. Hemel Hempstead: Harvester Wheatsheaf.

Craib, I. (1997) Social constructionism as a social psychosis. *Sociology*, 31(1): 1–15.

Craib, I. (1998) *Experiencing Identity*. London: SAGE.

Crawford, D. (1989) The future of clinical psychology; whither or wither? *Clinical Psychology Forum*, 20: 29–31.

Crawford, M.J., de Jonge, E., Freeman, G.K. and Weaver, T. (2004) Providing continuity of care for people with severe mental illness – a narrative review. *Social Psychiatry and Psychiatric Epidemiology*, 39(4): 265–72.

Crepaz-Keay, D., Binns, C. and Wilson, E. (1998) *Dancing With Angels: Involving Survivors in Mental Health Training*. London: CCETSW.

Crocetti, G., Spiro, H. and Siassi, I. (1974) *Contemporary Attitudes Towards Mental Illness* Pittsburgh, PA : University of Pittsburgh Press.

Crompton, R. (1987) Gender, status and professionalism. *Sociology*, 21(3): 413–28.

Crossley M.L. and Crossley, N. (2001) 'Patient' voices, social movements and the habitus: how psychiatric survivors 'speak out'. *Social Science and Medicine*, 52(10): 1477–89.

Crossley, N. (1998) Transforming the mental health field: the early history of the National Association of Mental Health. *Sociology of Health and Illness*, 20(4): 458–88.

Crow, T.J., MacMillan, J.F., Johnson, A.L. and Johnstone, E.C. (1986) The Northwick Park study of first episodes of schizophrenia II: a controlled trial of prophylactic neuroleptic treatment. *British Journal of Psychiatry*, 148: 120–7.

Cuffe, S.P., Waller, J.L., Cuccaro, M.L., Pumariega, A.J. and Garrison, C.Z. (1995) Race and gender differences in the treatment of psychiatric disorders in young adolescents. *Journal of the American Academy of Child and Adolescent Psychiatry*, 34(11): 1536–43.

Currer, C. (1986) Concepts of well- and ill-being: the case of Pathan mothers in Britain, in C. Currer and M. Stacey (eds) *Concepts of Health, Illness and Disease*. Leamington Spa: Berg.

Curtis, S. and Jones, I. (1998) Is there a place for geography in the analysis of health inequality? *Sociology of Health and Illness*, 20(5): 645–72.

Davey Smith, G., Bartley, M. and Blane, D. (1990) The Black Report on socio-economic inequalities in health 10 years on. *British Medical Journal*, 301: 373–7.

Davidhazar, D. and Wehlage, D. (1984) Can the client with chronic schizophrenia consent to nursing research? *Journal of Advanced Nursing*, 9: 381–90.

Davis, A., Llewellyn, S.P. and Parry, G. (1985) Women and mental health: a guide for the approved social worker, in E. Brook and A. Davis (eds) *Women, the Family and Social Work*. London: Tavistock.

Day, D.M. and Page, S. (1986) Portrayal of mental illnesses in Canadian newspapers. *Canadian Journal of Psychiatry*, 31: 813–17.

De Boer, F. (1991) Sex differences in the construction of mental health care problems. Paper presented at the British Sociological Association Medical Sociology Conference, York.

de la Cuesta, C. (1993) Fringe work: peripheral work in health visiting. *Sociology of Health and Illness*, 15(5): 665–82.

DeSwaan, A. (1990) *The Management of Normality*. London: Routledge.

Dean, G., Walsh, D., Downing, H. and Shelly, P. (1981) First admission of native-born and immigrants to psychiatric hospitals in South-East England 1976. *British Journal of Psychiatry*, 139: 506–12.

Dennis, D.L. and Monahan, J. (eds) (1996) *Coercion and Aggressive Community Treatment*. New York: Plenum Press.

Department of Health (1997) press release re IRG.

Department of Health (1998) *Our Healthier Nation*. London: Department of Health.

Department of Health (2000) *The NHS Plan*. London: Department of Health.

Department of Health (2002) *Developing Services for Carers and Families of People with Mental Illness*. London: Department of Health.

Department of Health (2004) *Draft Mental Health Bill*. London: Department of Health.

Department of Health/Home Office (1999) *National Service Framework for Mental Health*. London: Department of Health.

DHSS (1980) *Inequalities in Health: Report of a Working Group (The Black Report)*. London: HMSO.

DHSS (1988) *Community Care: Agenda for Action (The Griffiths Report)*. London: HMSO.

Diala, C., Muntaner, C., Walrath, C. Nickerson, K.J., LaVeist, T.A. and Leaf, P.J. (2000) Racial differences in attitudes towards professional mental health care and in the use of services. *American Journal of Orthopsychiatry*, 70(4): 455–64.

Diamont, L. (1987) *Male and Female Homosexuality: Psychological Approaches*. New York: Hemisphere.

Dimock, P.T. (1988) Adult males sexually abused as children; characteristics and implications for treatment. *Journal of Interpersonal Violence*, 3: 203–21.

Dingwall, R., Tanaka, H. and Minamikata, S. (1991) Images of parenthood in the United Kingdom and Japan. *Sociology*, 25(3): 423–46.

Dinos, S., Lyons, E. and Finlay, W.M. (2005) Does chronic illness place constraints on positive construction of identity? Temporal comparisons and self evaluations in people with schizophrenia. *Social Science and Medicine* (in press).

Dohrenwend, B.P. and Dohrenwend, B.S. (1977) Sex differences in mental illness: a reply to Gove and Tudor. *American Journal of Sociology*, 82: 1336–41.

Dohrenwend, B.P., Brice, P., Levar, I. *et al.* (1992) Socio-economic status and psychiatric disorders: the causation selection issue. *Science*, 255: 946–51.

Donat, J.G. (1988) Medicine and religion: on the physical and mental disorders that accompanied the Ulster Revival of 1859, in W.F. Bynum, R. Porter and M. Shepherd (eds) *The Anatomy of Madness* (Volume III). London: Tavistock.

Donnelly, M. (1983) *Managing the Mind*. London: Tavistock.

Donzelot, J. (1979) *The Policing of Families*. London: Hutchinson.

Dooley, D., Prause, J. and Ham-Rowbottom, K.A. (2000) Underemployment and depression: longitudinal relationships. *Journal of Health and Social Behavior*, 41: 421–36.

Dover, S. and McWilliam, C. (1992) Physical illness associated with depression in the elderly in community based and hospital patients. *Psychiatric Bulletin*, 16: 612–13.

Dowrick, C. (2004) *Beyond Depression: A New Approach to Understanding and Management*. Oxford: Oxford University Press.

Dowrick, C., May, R., Richardson, M. and Bundred, P. (1996) The biopsychosocial model of general practice: rhetoric or reality? *British Journal of General Practice*, 46: 105–7.

Dreitzel, H.P. (ed.) (1973) *Childhood and Socialization*. London: Macmillan.

Dudley, M., Cantor, C. and Demoore, G. (1996) Jumping the gun – firearms and the mental health of Australians. *Australian and New Zealand Journal of Psychiatry*, 3: 370–81.

Dunham, H. (1957) Methodology of sociological investigations of mental disorders. *Journal of Social Psychiatry*, 3: 7–17.

Dunham, H. (1964) Social class and schizophrenia. *American Journal of Orthopsychiatry*, 34: 634–46.

DYG Corporation (1990) *Public Attitudes Toward People with Chronic Mental Illness*. Elmsford, NY: DYG Corporation.

Edge D., Baker, D. and Rogers, A. (2004) Perinatal depression among Black Caribbean women. *Health & Social Care in the Community*, 12(5): 430–8.

Eichenbaum, L. and Orbach, S. (1982) *Outside In Inside Out*. Harmondsworth: Penguin.

Elias, N. (1978) *The Civilising Process*. Oxford: Blackwell.

Ellaway, A. and Macintyre, S. (2004) You are where you live. Evidence shows that where we live has a significant impact on our mental health. *Mental Health Today*: 33–5.

Ellaway, A., Anderson, A., and Macintyre, S. (1997) Does area of residence affect body size and shape? *International Journal of Obesity*, 21(4): 304–8.

Elliot, A. (1992) *Social Theory and Psychoanalysis in Transition*. Oxford: Blackwell.

Ellis, A. (1970) *The Essence of Rational Psychotherapy*. New York: Institute for Rational Living.

Emerson, R.M. and Pollner, M. (1975) Dirty work designations: their features and consequences in a psychiatric setting. *Social Problems*, 3: 243–54.

Engel, G.L. (1980) The clinical application of the biopsychosocial model. *American Journal of Psychiatry*, 137: 535–44.

English, B. and Ehrenreich, D. (1976) *Complaints and Disorders: The Sexual Politics of Sickness*. London: Writers and Readers Publishing Cooperative.

Ennis, B. and Emery, R. (1978) *The Rights of Mental Patients – An American Civil Liberties Union Handbook*. New York: Avon.

Estroff, S. and Zimmer, C. (1994) Social networks, social support and violence among persons with severe and persistent mental illness, in J. Monahan and H. Steadman (eds) *Violence and Mental Disorder: Developments in Risk Assessments*. Chicago: Chicago University Press.

Etzioni, A. (1996) The responsive community: A communitarian perspective. *American Sociological Review*, 61(1): 1–11.

Evans, G. (1992) Is Britain a class divided society? *Sociology*, 26(2): 233–58.

Eysenck, H.J. (1952) The effects of psychotherapy: an evaluation. *Journal of Consulting Psychology*, 16: 319–24.

Eysenck, H.J. (1955) Psychiatric diagnosis as a psychological and statistical problem. *Psychological Reports*, 1: 3–17.

Eysenck, H.J. (1975) *The Future of Psychiatry*. London: Methuen.

Fabrikant, B. (1974) The psychotherapist and the female patient: perceptions and change, in V. Franks and V. Burtle (eds) *Women in Therapy*. New York: Brunner Mazel.

Farina, A. and Felner, R.D. (1973) Employment interviewer reactions to former mental patients. *Journal of Abnormal Psychology*, 82: 268–72.

Faris, R.E.L. (1944) Ecological factors in human behavior, in R.E.L. Farris and H.W. Dunham (eds) *Mental Disorders in Urban Areas: An Ecological Study of Schizophrenia*. Chicago: Chicago University Press.

Faris, R.E.L. and Dunham, H.W. (1939) *Mental Disorders in Urban Areas*. Chicago: University of Chicago Press.

Faulkner, A. (1997) 'Strange bedfellows' in the laboratory of the NHS? An analysis of the new science of health technology assessment in the United Kingdom, in M.A. Elston (ed.) *The Sociology of Medical Science and Technology*. Oxford: Blackwell.

Felton, C., Stansty, P., Shern, D. *et al.* (1995) Consumers as peer specialists on intensive case management teams – impact on client outcomes. *Psychiatric Services*, 46(10): 1037–44.

Fennell, G., Phillipson, C. and Evers, H. (1988) *The Sociology of Old Age*. Milton Keynes: Open University Press.

Fennell, P. (1991) Diversion of mentally disordered offenders from custody. *Criminal Law Review*, 1: 333–48.

Fenton, S. and Sadiq, A. (1991) *Asian Women and Depression*. London: Commission for Racial Equality.

Fenton, S. and Sadiq-Sangster, A. (1996) Culture, relativism and mental distress. *Sociology of Health and Illness*, 18(1): 66–85.

Fernando, S. (1988) *Race and Culture in Psychiatry*. London: Routledge.

Fernando, S. (1995) *Mental Health in a Multi-Ethnic Society*. London: Routledge.

Fernando, S., Ndegwa, D. and Wilson, M. (1998) *Forensic Psychiatry, Race and Culture*. London: Routledge.

Field Institute (1984) *In Pursuit of Wellness: A Survey of California Adults*. Sacramento: California Department of Mental Health.

Finkelhor, D. (1979) *Sexually Victimized Children*. New York: Free Press.

Finkelhor, D. (1984) *Child Sexual Abuse: New Theory and Research*. New York: Free Press.

Finn, S.E., Bailey, M., Schultz, R.T. and Faber, R. (1990) Subjective utility ratings of neuroleptics in treating schizophrenia. *Psychological Medicine*, 20: 843–8.

Fisher, S. and Greenberg, R.P. (eds) (1997) *From Placebo to Panacea: Putting Psychiatric Drugs to the Test*. New York: Wiley.

Forbat, L. (2002) 'Tinged with bitterness': re-presenting stress in family care. *Disability and Society*, 17(7): 759–68.

Forbat, L. and Henderson, J. (2003) The professionalisation of informal carers, in C. Davies (ed.) *The Future of the Health Workforce*. Basingstoke: Palgrave.

Ford, G., Ecob, R., Hunt, K., Macintyre, S. and West, P. (1994) Patterns of class inequality in health through the life span. Class gradients at 15, 35, and 55 yrs in the West of Scotland. *Social Science and Medicine*, 39(8): 1037–50.

Forsythe, B. (1990) Mental and social diagnosis and the English Prison Commission 1914–1939. *Social Policy and Administration*, 24(3): 237–53.

Foucault, M. (1961) *Folie et deraison: histoire de la Folie à l'age classique*. Paris: Plon.

Foucault, M. (1965) *Madness and Civilisation*. New York: Random House.

Foucault, M. (1978) About the concept of the 'dangerous individual' in 19th century legal psychiatry. *International Journal of Law and Psychiatry*, 1: 1–18.

Foucault, M. (1980) Power/knowledge, in C. Gordon (ed.) Brighton: Harvester Press.

Foucault, M. (1981) *The History of Sexuality* (Vol. 1). Harmondsworth: Penguin.

Foucault, M. (1988) Technologies of the self, in L. Martin (ed.) *Technologies of the Self*. London: Tavistock.

Francis, E. (1989) Black people, dangerousness and psychiatric compulsion, in A. Brackx and C. Grimshaw (eds) *Mental Health Care in Crisis*. London: Pluto.

Francis, E., Pilgrim, D., Rogers, A. and Sashidaran, S. (1989) Race and 'schizophrenia': a reply to Ineichen. *New Community*, 17: 161–3.

Franks, C.M. (1993) Cognitive-behavioural assessment and therapy with adolescents. *Psychotherapy*, 30(4): 698–9.

Frederick, J. (1991) *Positive Thinking for Mental Health*. London: The Black Mental Health Group.

Freidson, E. (1970) *Profession of Medicine*. New York: Harper and Row.

Freud, S. (1920) Beyond the pleasure principle, in the *Standard Edition of the Complete Psychological Works of Sigmund Freud*, vol. 18. London: Hogarth Press.

Freud, S. (1930) *Civilisation and Its Discontents*. London: Hogarth Press.

Freund, P. (1988) Understanding socialised human nature. *Theory and Society*, 17: 839–64.

Fromm, E. (1942) *Fear of Freedom*. New York: Routledge and Kegan Paul.

Fromm, E. (1955) *The Sane Society*. New York: Holt, Rinehart and Winston.

Fromm, E. (1970) *The Crisis of Psychoanalysis*. Harmondsworth: Penguin.

Fryer, D. (1995) Labour market disadvantage, deprivation and mental health. *The Psychologist*, 8(6): 265–72.

Furnham, A. (1984) Lay conceptions of neuroticism. *Personality and Individual Difference*, 5(1): 95–103.

Gabe, J. and Bury, M. (1996) Halcion nights: a sociological account. *Sociology*, 30(3): 447–71.

Gabe, J. and Lipshitsz-Phillips, S. (1982) Evil necessity? The meaning of benzodiazepine use for women patients from one general practice. *Sociology of Health and Illness*, 4(2): 201–11.

Gabe, J. and Thorogood, N. (1986) Prescribed drug use and the management of everyday life: the experiences of black and white working class women. *Sociological Review*, 34: 737–72.

Gamarnikow, E. (1978) Sexual division of labour: the case of nursing, in A. Kuhn and A. Wolpe (eds) *Feminism and Materialism: Women and Modes of Production*. London: Routledge and Kegan Paul.

Gater, R., Amaddeo, F., Tansella, M., Jackson, G. and Goldberg, D. (1995) A comparison of community based care for schizophrenia in Verona and South Manchester. *British Journal of Psychiatry*, 166: 344–52.

Gearing, B., Johnson, M. and Heller, T. (eds) (1988) *Mental Health Problems in Old Age*. London: Wiley.

Gelder, M., Mayou, R. and Cowen, P. (2001) *Shorter Oxford Textbook of Psychiatry*. Oxford: Oxford University Press.

Gelinas, D. (1983) The persisting negative effects of incest. *Psychiatry*, 46: 312–32.

Gerard, D.L. and Houston, L.G. (1953) Family setting and the ecology of schizophrenia. *Psychiatric Quarterly*, 27: 90–101.

Gergen, K. (1985) The social construction movement in modern psychology. *American Psychologist*, 40: 266–75.

Giddens, A. (1992) *Sociology*. Cambridge: Polity Press.

Giddens, A. (1992) *The Transformation of Intimacy*. Cambridge: Polity Press.

Gilbert, P. (1992) *Depression: The Evolution of Powerlessness*. Hove: Lawrence Erlbaum.

Gilroy, P. (1987) *There Ain't No Black in the Union Jack*. London: Hutchinson.

Gittens, D. (1998) *Madness in Its Place*. London: Routledge.

Godfrey, M. and Wistow, G. (1997) The user perspective on managing for health outcomes: the case of mental health. *Health and Social Care in the Community*, 5(5): 325–32.

Goffman, E. (1955) On face work. *Psychiatry*, 18: 213–31.

Goffman, E. (1961) *Asylums*. New York: Anchor.

Goffman, E. (1963) *Stigma: Some Notes on the Management of Spoiled Identity*. Harmondsworth: Penguin.

Goffman, E. (1971) *Relations in Public*. Harmondsworth: Penguin.

Goldberg, D. and Huxley, P. (1980) *Mental Illness in the Community*. London: Tavistock.

Goldberg, D. and Morrison, S.L. (1963) Schizophrenia and social class. *British Journal of Psychiatry*, 109: 785–802.

Goldberg, D., Gater, R, Sartorius, N., Ustan, T.B., Piccinelli, M., Gureje, O. and Rutter, C. (1997) The validity of two versions of the GHQ in the WHO study of mental health in general health care. *Psychological Medicine*, 27: 191–7.

Goldberg, D., Sharp, D., Strathdee, G. *et al.* (1993) *Developing a Strategy for a Primary Care Focus for Mental Health Services for the People of Lambeth, Southwark and Lewisham*. London: Institute of Psychiatry.

Goldie, N. (1977) The division of labour among mental health professionals – a negotiated or an imposed order?, in M. Stacey and M. Reid (eds) *Health and the Division of Labour*. London: Croom Helm.

Goldie, N., Pilgrim, D. and Rogers, A. (1989) *Community Mental Health Centres: Policy and Practice*. London: Good Practices in Mental Health.

Goldsmith, H.F., Holzer, C.E. and Manderscheid, R.W. (1998) Neighborhood characteristics and mental illness. *Evaluation and Program Planning*, 21: 211–25.

Goldstein, B. and Rosselli, F. (2003) Etiological paradigms of depression: the relationship between perceived causes, empowerment, treatment preferences and stigma. *Journal of Mental Health*, 12(4): 551–64.

Goldthorpe, J.H. and Marshall, G. (1992) The promising future of class analysis: a response to recent critiques. *Sociology*, 26(3): 381–400.

Goode, W. (1957) Community within a community: the professions. *American Sociological Review*, xx(1): 194–200.

Gorbien, M.J., Bishop, J. and Beers, M.H. (1992) Iatrogenic illness in hospitalised elderly people. *Journal of American Geriatrics Society*, 40: 1031–47.

Gory, M.L., Ritchey, F.J., Ritchey, J. and Mullis, J. (1990) Depression among homeless people. *Journal of Health and Social Behavior*, 31: 87–101.

Gottesman, I.I. and Shields, J. (1972) *Schizophrenia and Genetics*. London: Academic Press.

Gough, I. (1979) *Political Economy of the Welfare State*. London: Macmillan.

Gould, A. (1981) The salaried middle class in the corporatist welfare state. *Policy and Politics*, 9(4): 401–8.

Gouldner, A.W. (1979) *The Future of Intellectuals and the Rise of the New Class*. London: Macmillan.

Gove, W. (1972) The relationship between sex roles, marital status and mental illness. *Social Forces*, 51: 33–44.

Gove, W.R. (1970) Societal reaction as an explanation of mental illness: an evaluation. *American Sociological Review*, 35: 873–84.

Gove, W.R. (1975) The labeling theory of mental illness: a reply to Scheff. *American Sociological Review*, 40: 242–8.

Gove, W.R. (1982) The current status of the labeling theory of mental illness, in W.R. Gove (ed.) *Deviance and Mental Illness*. Beverley Hills, CA: SAGE.

Gove, W.R. (1984) Gender differences in mental and physical illness: the effects of fixed roles and nurturant roles. *Social Science and Medicine*, 19(2): 77–91.

Gove, W.R. and Geerken, M. (1977) Response bias in surveys of mental health: an empirical investigation. *American Journal of Sociology*, 82: 1289–317.

Gove, W.R. and Tudor, J.F. (1972) Adult sex roles and mental illness. *American Journal of Sociology*, 78: 812–35.

Graetz, B. (1993) Health consequences of unemployment and employment: longitudinal evidence for young men and women. *Social Science and Medicine*, 36: 715–24.

Granovetter, M. (1973) The strength of weak ties. *American Journal of Sociology*, 78: 1360–80.

Gray, B. (2002) Working with families in Tower Hamlets: an evaluation of the Family Welfare Association's Family Support Services. *Health and Social Care in the Community*, 10(2):

Greenslade, L. (1992) White skin, white masks: psychological distress among the Irish in Britain, in P. O'Sullivan (ed.) *The Irish in the New Communities*. Leicester: Leicester University Press.

Greenwood, J.D. (1994) *Realism, Identity and Emotion: Reclaiming Social Psychology*. London: SAGE.

Grisso, T., Davis, J., Vesselinov, R. Appelbaum, P.S. and Monahan, J. (2000) Violent thoughts and violent behaviour following hospitalization for mental disorder. *Journal of Consulting and Clinical Psychology*, 68(3): 388–98.

Grob, G. (1973) *Mental Institutions in America: Social Policy to 1875*. New York: Free Press.

Groenewegen, P.P., Leufkens, H.G., Spreeuwenberg, P. and Worm, W. (1999) Neighbourhood characteristics and use of benzodiazepines in the Netherlands. *Social Science and Medicine*, 48(12): 1701–11.

Guidano, G.F. (1987) *Complexity of the Self*. New York: Guilford Press.

Gunn, J. (1978) *Psychiatric Aspects of Imprisonment*. London: Academic Press.

Gunnell, D., Middleton, N., Whitley, E., Dorling, D., Frankel, S. (2003) Why are suicide rates rising in young men but falling in the elderly? A time-series analysis of trends in England and Wales 1950–1998. *Social Science and Medicine*, 57(4): 595–611.

Guze, S.B. (1989) Biological psychiatry: is there any other kind? *Psychological Medicine*, 19: 315–23.

Haafkens, J., Nijhof, G. and van der Poel, E. (1986) Mental health care and the opposition movement in the Netherlands. *Social Science and Medicine*, 22: 185–92.

Habermas, J. (1972) *Knowledge and Human Interests*. London: Heinemann.

Habermas, J. (1975) *Legitimation Crisis*. Boston: Beacon Press.

Habermas, J. (1981) New social movements. *Telos*, 48: 33–7.

Habermas, J. (1987) *The Philosophical Discourse of Modernity*. Cambridge: Polity Press.

Habermas, J. (1989) The tasks of a critical theory of society, in S.E. Bronner and D.M. Kellner (eds) *Critical Theory and Society: A Reader*. London: Routledge.

Hamid, W. (1991) Homeless people and community care: an assessment of the needs of homeless people. Unpublished PhD Thesis. University of London.

Hammer, M. (1968) Influence of small social networks as factors on mental hospital admission, in S.P. Spitzer and N.K. Denzin (eds) *The Mental Patient*. New York: McGraw-Hill.

Hardt, R.H. and Feinhandler, S.J. (1959) Social class and mental hospital prognosis. *American Sociological Review*, 24: 815–21.

Hare, R. (1991) *The Hare Psychopathy Checklist–Revised*. Toronto: Multi-Health Systems.

Harrison, G., Owens, D., Holton, A. *et al.* (1988) A prospective study of severe mental disorder in Afro-Caribbean patients. *Psychological Medicine*, 11: 289–302.

Harvey, D. (1989) *The Condition of Post-modernity*. Oxford: Basil Blackwell.

Hatfield, B., Huxley, P. and Hadi, M. (1992) Accommodation and employment: a survey into the circumstances and expressed needs of the users of mental health services in a northern town. *British Journal of Social Work*, 22(4): 32–50.

Hayes, J. and Nutman, P. (1981) *Understanding the Unemployed*. London: Tavistock.

Hayes, S.C. (1998) Scientific practice guidelines in a political, economic and professional context in K.S. Dobson and K.D. Craig (eds) *Empirically Supported Therapies: Best Practice in Professional Psychology*. London: SAGE.

Hayward, P. and Bright, J.A. (1997) Stigma and mental illness: a review and critique. *Journal of Mental Health*, 6: 345–54.

Healy, D. (1997) *The Anti-Depressant Era*. London: Harvard University Press.

Hearn, J. (1982) Notes on patriarchy, professionalisation and the semi-professions. *Sociology*, 16(2): 184–202.

Heitman, E. (1996) The public's role in the evaluation of health care technology – the conflict over ECT. *International Journal of Technology Assessment in Health*, 12(4): 657–72.

Hemmenki, E. (1977) Polypharmacy among psychiatric patients. *Acta Psychiatrica Scandinavica*, 56: 347–56.

Hemsi, L. (1967) Psychiatric morbidity of West Indian immigrants. *Social Psychiatry*, 2: 95–100.

Hensing, G., Alexanderson, K., Allebeck, P. and Bjurulf, P. (1996) Sick leave due to psychiatric disorder. *British Journal of Psychiatry*, 169: 740–6.

Hiday, V. (1995) The social context of mental illness and violence. *Journal of Health and Social Behavior*, 36: 122–37.

Hirsch, S.R. (1986) Clinical treatment of schizophrenia, in P.B. Bradley and S.R. Hirsch (eds) *The Psychopharmacology and Treatment of Schizophrenia*. Oxford: Oxford University Press.

Hirst, P. and Woolley, P. (1982) *Social Relations and Human Attributes*. London: Tavistock.

Hitch, P. (1981) Immigration and mental health: local research and social explanations. *New Community*, 9: 256–62.

Hitch, P. and Clegg, P. (1980) Modes of referral of overseas immigrant and native-born first admissions to psychiatric hospital. *Social Science and Medicine*, 14A: 369–74.

Hochschild, A. (1979) Emotion work, feeling rules and social structure. *American Journal of Sociology*, 85: 551–75.

Hochschild, A. (1983) *The Managed Heart: The Commercialisation of Human Feeling*. Berkeley: University of California Press.

Hochstedler-Steury, E. (1991) Specifying 'criminalization' of the mentally disordered misdemeanants. *Journal of Criminal Law and Criminality*, 82 (Summer): 334–59.

Hoenig, J. and Hamilton, M. (1969) *The Desegregation of the Mentally Ill*. London: Routledge and Kegan Paul.

Hoggett, B. (1990) *Mental Health Law*. London: Sweet & Maxwell.

Holland, R. (1978) *Self and Social Context*. London: Macmillan.

Hollander, D. (1991) Homelessness and mental illness in developing countries, in M. Page and R. Powell (eds) *Homelessness and Mental Illness: The Dark Side of Community Care*. London: Concern Publications.

Hollingshead, A. and Redlich, R.C. (1958) *Social Class and Mental Illness*. New York: Wiley.

Horkheimer, M. (1931) Die gegenwärtige Lage der Sozialphilosophie und die Aufgaben eines Instituts für Sozialforschung. *Frankfurter Universitätsreden*, 37: 13–20.

Horsfall, J. (1997) Psychiatric nursing: epistemological contradictions. *Advances in Nursing Science*, 20(1): 56–65.

Horwitz, A. (1983) *The Social Control of Mental Illness*. New York: Academic Press.

Horwitz, A. (2002) *Creating Mental Illness*. Chicago: Chicago University Press.

Howells, J.G. and Guirguis, W.R. (1985) *The Family and Schizophrenia*. New York: International Universities Press.

Huebner, D.M., Rebchook, G.M. and Kegeles, S.M. (2004) Experiences of harassment, discrimination and physical violence among young gay and bi-sexual men. *American Journal of Public Health*, 94(7): 1200–3.

Hughes, E. (1971) *The Sociological Eye: Selected Papers*. Chicago: Aldine Atherton.

Humphrey, M. and Haward, L. (1981) Sex differences in recruitment to clinical psychology. *Bulletin of the British Psychological Society*, 34: 413–14.

Hunt, S. (1990) Emotional distress and bad housing. *Health and Hygiene*, 11: 72–9.

Huxley, P. (1990) *Effective Community Mental Health Services*. Aldershot: Avebury.

Hydle, I. (1993) Abuse and neglect of the elderly – a Nordic perspective. *Scandinavian Journal of Social Medicine*, 2(2): 126–8.

Hyndman, S.J. (1990) Housing, dampness and health among British Bengalis in East London. *Social Science and Medicine*, 30: 131–41.

Illich, I. (1977a) *Limits to Medicine*. Harmondsworth: Penguin.

Illich, I. (1977b) Disabling professions, in I. Illich, I.K. Zola, J. McKnight *et al.* (eds) *Disabling Professions*. London: Marion Boyars.

Illsley, R. (1986) Social class, selection and class differences in relation to stillbirths and infant deaths. *British Medical Journal*, 229: 1520–4.

Ineichen, B. (1987) The mental health of Asians in Britain: a research note. *New Community*, 4: 1–2.

Ingleby, D. (1983) Mental health and social order, in S. Cohen and A. Scull (eds) *Social Control and the State*. Oxford: Blackwell.

Ingleby, D. (ed.) (1981) *Critical Psychiatry*. Harmondsworth: Penguin.

Jackson, P.B. (2004) Role sequencing: does order matter for mental health? *Journal of Health and Social Behaviour*, 45(2): 132–54.

Jacobs, H. (1991) The battle for inpatient care, in M. Page and R. Powell (eds) *Homelessness and Mental Illness: The Dark Side of Community Care*. London: Concern Publications.

Jacoby, R. (1975) *Social Amnesia: A Critique of Contemporary Psychology from Adler to Laing*. Boston: Beacon Press.

Jahoda, M. (1958) *Current Concepts of Positive Mental Health*. New York: Basic Books.

James, A. and Prout, A. (1990) *The Social Construction of Childhood*. London: Routledge.

James, N. (1989) Emotional labour: skill and work in the social regulation of feelings. *Sociological Review*, 37: 15–42.

Jamison, K.R. (1993) *Touched with Fire: Manic-Depressive Illness and the Artistic Temperament*. New York: Free Press.

Jamison, K.R. (1998) Stigma of manic depression: a psychologist's experience. *The Lancet*, 352: 1060.

Jefferys, M. (ed.) (1989) *Growing Old in the Twentieth Century*. London: Routledge.

Jehu, D. (ed.) (1995) *Patients As Victims*. London: Wiley.

Jenkins, J.H. and Karno, M. (1992) The meaning of expressed emotion: theoretical issues raised by cross-national research. *American Journal of Psychiatry*, 149: 9–21.

Jenkins, R., Griffiths, S., Wylie, I. *et al.* (eds) (1994) *The Prevention of Suicide*. London: HMSO.

Jodelet, D. (1991) *Madness and Social Representations*. London: Harvester Wheatsheaf.

Johnell, K., Merlo, J., Lynch, J. and Blennow, G. (2004) Neighbourhood social participation and women's use of anxiolytic-hypnotic drugs: a multilevel analysis. *Journal of Epidemiology and Community Health*, 58(1): 59–64.

Johns, L.C., Nazroo, J., Bebbington, P. and Kuipers, E. (2002) Occurrence of hallucinatory experiences in a community sample and ethnic variations. *British Journal of Psychiatry*, 180: 174–8.

Johnson, T. (1977) The professions in the class structure, in R. Scase (ed.) *Industrial Society: Class, Cleavage and Control*. London: Allen and Unwin.

Johnstone, L. (1993) Family management in 'schizophrenia': its assumptions and contradictions. *Journal of Mental Health*, 2: 255–69.

Jones, A. (1997) High psychiatric morbidity amongst Irish immigrants: an epistemological analysis. Unpublished PhD Thesis. Open University.

Jones, E.E., Farina, A., Hastorf, A.H., Markus, H., Miller, D.T. and Scott, R.A. (1984) *Social Stigma: The Psychology of Marked Relationships*. New York: Freeman.

Jones, G. and Berry, M. (1986) Regional secure units: the emerging picture, in G. Edwards (ed.) *Current Issues in Clinical Psychology*, 4. London: Plenum Press.

Jones, K. (1960) *Mental Health and Social Policy 1845–1959*. London: Routledge and Kegan Paul.

Jones, K. (1962) Review. *Sociological Review*, 8: 343–4.

Jones, L. and Cochrane, R. (1981) Stereotypes of mental illness: a test of the labelling hypothesis. *International Journal of Social Psychiatry*, 27: 99–107.

Jones, R. (1991) *Mental Health Act Manual*. London: Sweet & Maxwell.

Junginger, J. (1995) Command hallucinations and the predictions of dangerousness. *Psychiatric Services*, 46: 911–14.

Kai, J. and Crosland, A. (2001) Perspectives of people with enduring mental ill health from a community-based qualitative study. *British Journal of General Practice*, 51(11): 112–22.

Kaltiala-Heino, R., Marttunen, M., Rantanen, P. and Rimpela, M. (2003) Early puberty is associated with mental health problems in middle adolescence. *Social Science and Medicine*, 57(6): 1055–64.

Kaplan, M.S. and Marks, G. (1995) Appraisal of health risks: the roles of masculinity, femininity and sex. *Sociology of Health and Illness*, 17(2): 206–21.

Karlsen, S. and Nazroo, J. (2004) Fear of racism and health. *Journal of Epidemiology and Community Health*, 58: 1017–18.

Karon, B.P. and VandenBos, G.R. (1981) *Psychotherapy of Schizophrenia: The Treatment of Choice*. New York: Jason Aronson.

Kasl, S.V., Rodriguez, E. and Lasch, K.E. (1998) The impact of unemployment on health and well-being in B.P. Dohrenwend (ed.) *Adversity, Stress and Psychopathology*. Oxford: Oxford University Press.

Kawachi, I. and Berkman, L.F. (2001) Social ties and mental health. *Journal of Urban Health*, 78: 458–67.

Kay, A. and Legg, C. (1986) *Discharged into the Community*. London: Good Practices in Mental Health.

Kay, D., Beamish, P. and Roth, M. (1964) Old age mental disorders in Newcastle upon Tyne, part 1, a study of prevalence. *British Journal of Psychiatry*, 110: 146–8.

Kazdin, A.E., Stolar, M.J. and Marciano, P.L. (1995) Risk factors for dropping out of treatment among white and black families. *Journal of Family Psychology*, 9(4): 402–17.

Kellam, A.M.P. (1987) The neuroleptic syndrome, so called: a survey of the world literature. *British Journal of Psychiatry*, 150: 752–9.

Kenny, V. (1985) The post-colonial personality. *Crane Bag*, 9: 70–8.

Kilian, R., Lindenbach, I., Lobig, U., Uhle, M., Petscheleit, A. and Angermeyer, M.C. (2003) Indicators of empowerment and disempowerment in the subjective evaluation of the psychiatric treatment process by persons with severe and persistent mental illness: a qualitative and quantitative analysis. *Social Science and Medicine*, 57(6): 1127–42.

King, M., McKeown, E., Warner, J., Ramsay, A., Johnson, K., Cort, C., Wright, L., Blizard, R. and Davidson, O. (2003) Mental health and quality of life of gay men and lesbians in England and Wales: controlled, cross-sectional study. *British Journal of Psychiatry*, 183: 552–8.

Kirk, S.A. (1974) The impact of labeling on rejection of the mentally ill: an experimental study. *Journal of Health and Social Behaviour*, 15: 108–17.

Kirmayer, L.J. and Young, A. (1998) Culture and somatization: Clinical, epidemiological, and ethnographic perspectives. *Psychosomatic Medicine*, 60(4): 420–30.

Kitwood, T. (1988) The contribution of psychology to the understanding of senile dementia, in B. Gearing, M. Johnson and T. Heller (eds) *Mental Health Problems in Old Age*. London: Wiley.

Kitwood, T. and Bredin, K. (1992) Towards a theory of dementia care: personhood and well-being. *Ageing and Society*, 10: 177–96.

Klassen, D. and O'Connor, W. (1987) Predicting violence in mental patients: cross-validation of an actuarial scale. Paper presented at the annual meeting of the American Public Health Association.

Klatte, E., Liscomb, W., Rozynko, V. and Pught, L. (1969) Changing the legal status of mental hospital patients. *Hospital and Community Psychiatry*, 20: 199–202.

Kleinman, A. (1986) Some uses and misuses of the social sciences in medicine, in D.W. Fiske and R.A. Shweder (eds) *Metatheory and Social Science*. Chicago: Chicago University Press.

Kleinman, A. (1988) *Rethinking Psychiatry*. New York: Free Press.

Kobak, J. (1997) A computer-administered telephone interview to identify mental disorders. *Journal of the American Medical Association*, 278(11): 905–10.

Koenig, H.G., Larson, D.B. and Weaver, A. (1998) Research on religion and serious mental illness. *New Dimensions for Mental Health Services*, 80: 81–95.

Koffman, J., Fulop, N.J., Pashley, D. and Coleman, K. (1997) Ethnicity and the use of psychiatric beds: a one day survey in North and South Thames regions. *British Journal of Psychiatry*, 171: 238–41.

Kovel, J. (1988) *The Radical Spirit: Essays on Psychoanalysis and Society*. London: Free Association Press.

Krause, I.B. (1989) Sinking heart: a Punjabi communication of distress. *Social Science and Medicine*, 29(4): 563–7.

Kubie, S. (1954) The fundamental nature of the distinction between normality and neurosis. *Psychoanalytical Quarterly*, 23: 167–204.

Lacey, R. (1991) *The Complete Guide to Psychiatric Drugs*. London: Ebury Press.

Laing, R.D. (1959) *The Divided Self*. London: Tavistock.

Laing, R.D. (1967) *The Politics of Experience and the Bird of Paradise*. Harmondsworth: Penguin.

Laing, R.D. and Esterson, A. (1964) *Sanity, Madness and the Family*. Harmondsworth: Penguin.

Lambert, M.J. and Bergin, A.E. (1983) Therapist characteristics and their contribution to psychotherapy outcome, in C.E. Walker (ed.) *The Handbook of Clinical Psychology Vol I*. Homewood, CA: Dow Jones-Irwin.

Langer, T.S. and Michael, S.T. (1963) *Life Stress and Mental Health*. Glencoe: Free Press.

Lapouse, R., Monk, M. and Terris, W. (1956) The drift hypothesis and socio-economic differentials in schizophrenia. *American Journal of Public Health*, 46: 968–86.

Lasch, C. (1978) *The Culture of Narcissism*. New York: Norton.

Lashmar, P. (1995) Feel bad factor. *New Statesman and Society*, 9 June: 55–7.

Latour, B. (1987) *Science in Action: How to Follow Scientists and Engineers Through Society*. Cambridge, MA: Harvard University Press.

Law, J. (1992) Notes on the theory of the actor-network: ordering, strategy and heterogeneity. *Systems Practice*, 5: 379–93.

Lebow, J. (1982) Consumer satisfaction with mental health treatment. *Psychological Bulletin*, 91(2): 244–59.

Lees, S. (1997) How lay is lay? Chinese students' perceptions of anorexia nervosa in Hong Kong. *Social Science and Medicine*, 44(4): 491–502.

Lefley, H.P. (ed.) (1996) *Family Caregiving in Mental Illness*. London: SAGE.

Leifer, M., Kilbane, T., Jacobsen, T. and Grossman, G. (2004) A three-generational study of transmission of risk for sexual abuse. *Journal of Clinical Child and Adolescent Psychology*, 33(4): 662–72.

Lelliott, P. and Quirk, A. (2004) What is life like on acute psychiatric wards? *Current Opinion in Psychiatry*, 17(4): 297–310.

Lelliott, P., Audini B. and Duffett, R. (2001) Survey of patients from an inner-London health authority in medium secure psychiatric care. *British Journal of Psychiatry*, 178: 62–6.

Lemert, E. (1974) Beyond reach: the social reaction to deviance. *Social Problems*, 21: 457–67.

Lidz, C., Meisel, A., Zerubavel, E. *et al.* (1984) *Informed Consent: A Study of Decision Making in Psychiatry*. London: Guilford.

Lindow, V. (1994) *Self-help Alternatives to Mental Health Services*. London: MIND Publications.

Link, B. (2000) The stigma process: re-conceiving the definition of stigma. Paper presented at the American Public Health Association.

Link, B. and Phelan, J. (1995) Social conditions as fundamental causes of disease. *Journal of Health and Social Behaviour*, No SISI: 80–94.

Link, B.G., Andrews, H.A. and Cullen, F.T. (1992) The violent and illegal behavior of mental health patients reconsidered. *American Sociological Review*, 57: 275–92.

Littlewood, R. and Cross, S. (1980) Ethnic minorities and psychiatric services. *Sociology of Health and Illness*, 2: 194–201.

Littlewood, R. and Lipsedge, M. (1982) *Aliens and Alienists*. Harmondsworth: Penguin.

Lochner, K., Kawachi, I. and Kennedy, B.P. (1999) Social capital: a guide to its measurement. *Health and Place*, 5: 259–70.

Longo, R. (1982) Sexual learning and experiences among adolescent sexual offenders. *International Journal of Offender Therapy and Comparative Criminology*, 26: 235–41.

Lorant, V., Deliege, D., Eaton, W., Robert, A. and Ansseau, M. (2003) Socio-economic inequalities in depression: a meta-analysis. *American Journal of Epidemiology*, 157: 98–112.

Lowenthal, M. (1965) Antecedents of isolation and mental illness in old age. *Archives of General Psychiatry*, 12: 245–54.

Lundqvist, G., Hansson, K. and Svedin, C.G. (2004) The influence of childhood sexual abuse factors on women's health. *Nordic Journal of Psychiatry*, 58(5): 395–401.

Lupton, D. (1998) *The Emotional Self*. London: SAGE.

Lynch, D., Tamburrino, M. and Nagel, R. (1997) Telephone counselling for patients with minor depression: preliminary findings in a family practice setting. *Journal of Family Practice*, 44(3): 293–8.

Lyons, M. (1996) C. Wright Mills meets Prozac: the relevance of 'social emotion' to the sociology of health and illness, in V. James and J. Gabe (eds) *Health and the Sociology of Health and Illness Monograph*: 55–88.

MacDonald, G. and Sheldon, B. (1997) Community care services for the mentally ill: consumers' views. *International Journal of Social Psychiatry*, 43(1): 35–55.

Macintyre, S., Ellaway, A. and Cummins, S. (2002). Place effects on health: how can we conceptualise, operationalise and measure them. *Social Science and Medicine*, 55(1): 125–39.

Macintyre, S., MacIver, S. and Sooman, A. (1993) Area, class and health: should we be focusing on places or people? *Journal of Social Policy*, 22: 213–34.

MacLachlan, M. (1997) *Culture and Health*. London: Wiley.

Main, T. (1946) The hospital as a therapeutic institution. *Bulletin of the Menninger Clinic*, 10: 64–71.

Maloy, K. (1992) *Critiquing the Empirical Evidence: Does Involuntary Outpatient Commitment Work?* Washington, DC: Mental Health Policy Center.

Mann, A.H., Graham, N. and Ashby, D. (1984) Psychiatric illness in residential homes for the elderly: a survey in one London borough. *Age and Ageing*, 113: 257–65.

Manning, N. (1989) *The Therapeutic Community Movement: Charisma and Routinization*. London: Routledge.

Manning, N. (2002) Actor networks, policy networks and personality disorder. *Sociology of Health and Illness*, 24(5): 644–66.

Manthorpe, J. (1994) The family and informal care, in N. Malin (ed.) *Implementing Community Care*. Buckingham: Open University Press.

Marcuse, H. (1964) *One Dimensional Man*. London: Routledge and Kegan Paul.

Markham, D. (2003) Attitudes towards patients with a diagnosis of 'borderline personality disorder': social rejection and dangerousness. *Journal of Mental Health*, 12(6): 595–612.

Marks, I.M. (1987) *Fears, Phobias and Rituals*. Oxford: Oxford University Press.

Marshall, R. (1990) The genetics of schizophrenia: axiom or hypothesis?, in R.P. Bentall (ed.) *Reconstructing Schizophrenia*. London: Routledge.

Martin, J.P. (1985) *Hospitals in Trouble*. Oxford: Blackwell.

Marzillier, J. and Hall, J. (1987) *What Is Clinical Psychology?* Oxford: Oxford Medical Publications.

Masson, J. (1985) *The Assault on Truth: Freud's Suppression of the Seduction Theory*. Harmondsworth: Penguin.

Masson, J. (1988a) *A Dark Science: Women, Sexuality and Psychiatry in the Nineteenth Century*. New York: Noonday Press.

Masson, J. (1988b) *Against Therapy*. London: HarperCollins.

Masson, J. (1990) *Final Analysis*. London: HarperCollins.

Maule, M., Milne, J. and Williamson, J. (1984) Mental illness and physical health in older people. *Age and Ageing*, 13: 349–56.

Mayall, B. (1998) Towards a sociology of child health. *Sociology of Health and Illness*, 20(3): 269–88.

Mayer-Gross, W., Slater, E. and Roth, M. (1954) *Clinical Psychiatry*. London: Cassell.

Mayer, J. and Timms, N. (1970) *The Client Speaks*. London: Routledge and Kegan Paul.

McAndrew, S. and Warne, T. (2004) Ignoring the evidence dictating practice: sexual orientation, suicidality and the dichotomy of the mental health nurse. *Journal of Mental Health Nursing*, 11(4): 428–34.

McGovern, D. and Cope, R. (1987) The compulsory detention of males of different ethnic groups with special reference to offender patients. *British Journal of Psychiatry*, 150: 505–12.

McGuire, J. (ed.) (1995) *What Works? Reducing Re-offending, Guidelines for Research and Practice*. London: Wiley.

Mclean, C., Campbell, C. and Cornish, F. (2004) Social capital, participation and the perpetuation of health inequalities: obstacles to African-Caribbean participation in 'partnerships' to improve mental health. *Ethnic Health*, 9(4): 313–35.

McLeod, J.D., Pescosolido, B.A., Takeuchi, D.T. and Falkenberg White, T. (2004) Public attitudes toward the use of psychiatric medications for children. *Journal of Health and Social Behavior*, 45(1): 53–67.

McLoone, P. (1996) Suicide and deprivation in Scotland. *British Medical Journal*, 312: 543–4.

McQueen, C. and Henwood, K. (2002) Young men in 'crisis': attending to the language of teenage boys' distress. *Social Science and Medicine*, 55(9): 1493–1509.

Medawar, C. (1992) *Power and Dependence*. London: Social Audit.

Meltzer, H., Gill, B. and Pettigrew, M. (1994) *The Prevalence of Psychiatric Morbidity Among Adults Aged 16–64 Living in Private Households*. OPCS Surveys of Psychiatric Morbidity in Great Britain. London: HMSO.

Mercer, K. (1986) Racism and transcultural psychiatry, in P. Miller and N. Rose (eds) *The Power of Psychiatry*. Cambridge: Polity Press.

Metzl, J.M. and Angel, J. (2004) Assessing the impact of SSRI antidepressants on popular notions of women's depressive illness. *Social Science and Medicine*, 58(3): 577–84.

Meyer, J.E. (1988) The fate of the mentally ill in Germany during the Third Reich. *Psychological Medicine*, 18: 575–81.

Mheen, H., Stronks, K. and Mackenbach, J. (1998) A life course perspective on socio-economic inequalities in health. *Sociology of Health and Illness*, 20(5): 754–77.

Miller, P. (1986) Critiques of psychiatry and critical sociologies of madness, in P. Miller and N. Rose (eds) *The Power of Psychiatry*. Cambridge: Polity Press.

Miller, P. and Rose, N. (1988) The Tavistock programme: the government of subjectivity and social life. *Sociology*, 22(2): 171–92.

Milligan, C., Gatrell, A. and Bingley, A. (2004) 'Cultivating health': therapeutic landscapes and older people in northern England. *Social Science and Medicine*, 58(9): 1781–93.

Milliren, J.W. (1977) Some contingencies affecting the utilisation of tranquillisers in the long term care of the elderly. *Journal of Health and Social Behaviour*, 18: 206–11.

Mills, E. (1962) *Living with Mental Illness*. London: Institute of Community Studies/ Routledge and Kegan Paul.

Milne, D, McAnaney, A., Pollinger, B., Bateman, K. and Fewster, E. (2004) Analysis of the forms, functions and facilitation of social support in one English county: a way for professionals to improve the quality of health care. *International Journal of Health Care Quality Assurance*, 17(6): 294–301.

MIND (2004) *Ward Watch Report*. London: MIND

Mitchell, J. (1974) *Psychoanalysis and Feminism*. Harmondsworth: Penguin.

Mitchell, P.B., Slade, T. and Andrews, G. (2004) Twelve-month prevalence and disability of DSM-IV bipolar disorder in an Australian general population survey. *Psychological Medicine*, 34(5): 777–85.

Mohan, D., Murray, K., Taylor, P. and Stead, P. (1997) Developments in the use of regional secure unit beds over a 12-year period. *Journal of Forensic Psychiatry*, 2: 321–35.

Monahan, J. (1973) The psychiatrization of criminal behaviour: a reply. *Hospital and Community Psychiatry*, 24(2): 105–7.

Monahan, J. (1992) Mental disorder and violent behaviour perceptions and evidence. *American Psychologist*, 47(4): 511–21.

Monahan, J. and Steadman, H.J. (eds) (1994) *Violence and Mental Disorder: Developments in Risk Assessment*. Chicago: Chicago University Press.

Moncrieff, J. and Crawford, M.J. (2001) British psychiatry in the 20th century – observations from a psychiatric journal. *Social Science and Medicine*, 53(3): 349–56.

Morgan, C., Mallett, R., Hutchinson, G. and Leff, J. (2004) Negative pathways to psychiatric care and ethnicity: the bridge between social science and psychiatry. *Social Science and Medicine*, 58(4): 739–52.

Morgan, H.G. (1994) *Suicide Prevention: The Assessment and Management of Suicide Risk*. Cambridge: Anglia University.

Morris, R.G., Morris, L.W. and Britton, P.G. (1988) Factors affecting the emotional well-being of the care-givers of dementia sufferers. *British Journal of Psychiatry*, 152: 147–56.

Mowbray, C.T., Moxley, D.P., Jasper, C.A. and Howell, L.L. (eds) (1997) *Consumers As Providers in Psychiatric Rehabilitation*. Columbia: International Association of Psychosocial Rehabilitation Services.

Mulvany, J. (2000) Disability, impairment or illness? The relevance of the social model of disability to the study of mental disorder. *Sociology of Health and Illness*, 22(5): 582–601.

Muntaner, C., Lynch, J. and Smith, G.D. (2001) Social capital, disorganized communities and the third way: understanding the retreat from structural inequalities in epidemiology and public health. *International Journal of Health Services*, 31(2): 213–37.

Murphy, E. (1982) Social origins of depression in old age. *British Journal of Psychiatry*, 141: 135–42.

Murphy, E. (1988) Prevention of depression and suicide, in B. Gearing, M. Johnson and T. Heller (eds) *Mental Health Problems in Old Age*. London: Wiley.

Myers, J. (1974) Social class, life events and psychiatric symptoms: a longitudinal study, in B.S. Dohrenwend and B.P. Dohrenwend (eds) *Stressful Life Events: Their Nature and Effects*. New York: Wiley.

Myers, J. (1975) Life events, social integration and psychiatric symptomatology. *Journal of Health and Social Behavior*, 16: 121–7.

Nairn, R., Coverdale, J. and Claasen, D. (2001) From source material to news story in New Zealand print media: a prospective study of stigmatizing processes in depicting mental illness. *Australian and New Zealand Journal of Psychiatry*, 35(5): 654–59.

Navarro, V. (1979) *Medicine Under Capitalism*. New York: Prodist.

Nazroo, J. (1995) Uncovering gender differences in the use of marital violence: the effect of methodology. *Sociology*, 29(3): 475–9.

Nazroo, J. (1997) *Ethnicity and Mental Health*. London: Policy Studies Institute.

Nazroo, J. (1998) Genetic, cultural or socio-economic vulnerability? Explaining ethnic inequalities in health. *Sociology of Health and Illness*, 20(5): 710–30.

Nazroo, J.Y., Edwards, A.C. and Brown, G.W. (1998) Gender differences in the prevalence of depression: artifact, alternative disorders, biology or roles? *Sociology of Health and Illness*, 20(3): 3112–330.

Nazroo J.Y. and Karlsen S. (2003) More about ethnic identity from the British National Survey of Ethnic Minorities, patterns of identity among ethnic minority people: diversity and commonality. *Ethnic and Racial Studies*, 26(5): 902–30.

Nettleton, S. and Burrows, R. (1998) Mortgage debt, insecure home ownership and health: an exploratory study. *Sociology of Health and Illness*, 20(5): 731–53.

Newton, J. (1988) *Preventing Mental Illness*. London: Routledge.

Noble, L.M., Douglas, B.C. and Newman, S.P. (2001) What do patients expect of psychiatric services? A systematic and critical review of empirical studies. *Social Science and Medicine*, 52(7): 985–98.

Noble, P. and Rodger, S. (1989) Violence by psychiatric in-patients. *British Journal of Psychiatry*, 155: 384–90.

Norris, M. (1984) *Integration of Special Hospital Patients into the Community*. Aldershot: Gower.

North, C.S., Thompson, S.J., Polio, D.E., Ricci, D.A. and Smith, E.M. (1997) A diagnostic comparison of homeless and non-homeless patients in an urban mental health clinic. *Social Psychiatry and Psychiatric Epidemiology*, 32(4): 236–40.

O'Mahony, P. and Delanty, G. (1998) *Rethinking Irish History: Nationalism, Identity and Ideology*. Basingstoke: Macmillan.

Odell, S.M. and Commander, M.J. (2000) Risk factors for homelessness among people with psychotic disorders. *Social Psychiatry and Psychiatric Epidemiology*, 35: 9–11.

Offe, C. (1984) *Contradictions of the Welfare State*. London: Hutchinson.

Olson, M. and Pincus, H. (1994) Use of benzodiazepines in the community. *Archives of Internal Medicine*, 154(11): 1235–40.

Olsen, M. and Pincus, H. (1994) Outpatient psychotherapy in the US patterns of utilization. *American Journal of Psychiatry*, 51(9): 1289–94.

Olstead, R. (2002) Contesting the text: Canadian media depictions of the conflation of mental illness and criminality. *Sociology of Health and Illness*, 24(5): 621–43.

Onyett, S. (1994) *Community Mental Health Teams*. London: Avebury.

Oppenheimer, M. (1975) The proletarianisation of the professional. *Sociological Review Monograph*, 20.

Orbell, S., Hopkins, N. and Gillies, B. (1993) Measuring the impact of informal care. *Journal of Community and Applied Social Psychology*, 3: 149–63.

Ostamo, A. and Lonnqvist, J. (1992) Parasuicide rates by gender in Helsinki, 1988–91. Poster paper at Joint Conference of the British Sociological Association Medical Sociology Group and the European Society of Medical Sociology, Edinburgh.

Padgett, D.K., Patrick, C., Burns, B.J. and Schlesinger, H.J. (1994) Women and out-patient mental health services: use by black, Hispanic and white women in a nationally insured population. *Journal of Mental Health Administration*, 21(4): 347–60.

Page, M. and Powell, R. (eds) (1991) *Homelessness and Mental Illness: The Dark Side of Community Care*. London: Concern Publications.

Pahl, R.E. (1993) Does class analysis without class theory have a promising future? A reply to Goldthorpe and Marshall. *Sociology*, 27(2): 253–8.

Parker, I., Georgaca, E., Harper, D., McLaughlin, T. and Stowell-Smith, M. (1995) *Deconstructing Psychopathology*. London: SAGE.

Parkhouse, J. (1991) *Doctors' Careers: Aims and Experiences of Medical Graduates*. London: Routledge.

Parkman, S., Davies, S., Leese, M., Phelan, M. and Thornicroft, G. (1997) Ethnic differences in satisfaction with mental health services among representative people with psychosis in South London: PRiSM Study 4. *British Journal of Psychiatry*, 171: 260–4.

Parry, N. and Parry, G. (1977) Professionalism and unionism: aspects of class conflicts in the National Health Service. *Sociological Review*, 25(4): 823–40.

Parsons, T. (1939) The professions and the social structure. *Social Forces*, 17: 457–67.

Parsons, T. (1951) *The Social System*. Glencoe, IL: Free Press.

Paveza, G.J., Cohen, J.G., Eisdorfer, C. *et al.* (1992) Severe family violence and Alzheimer's Disease: prevalence and risk factors. *Gerontologist*, 32(4): 493–7.

Pearson, V. (1995) Goods on which one loses: women and mental health in China. *Social Science and Medicine*, 41(8): 1159–73.

Peay, J. (1989) *Tribunals on Trial: A Study of Decision-making under the Mental Health Act 1983*. Oxford: Oxford University Press.

Pelfrene, E., Vlerick, P., Moreau, M., Mak, R.P., Kornitzer, M. and De Backer, G. (2004) Use of benzodiazepine drugs and perceived job stress in a cohort of working men and women in Belgium. Results from the BELSTRESS-study. *Social Science and Medicine*, 59: 433–42.

Perring, C., Twigg, J. and Atkin, J. (1990) *Families Caring for People Diagnosed as Mentally Ill: The Literature Re-examined*. London: Social Policy Research Unit.

Perrow, C. (1965) Hospitals: technology, structure and goals, in J.G. March (ed.) *Handbook of Organisations*. Chicago: Rand McNally.

Pescosolido, B.A. and Wright, E.R. (2004) The view from two worlds: the convergence of social network reports between mental health clients and their ties. *Social Science and Medicine*, 58(9): 1795–1806.

Phillips, D. (1968) Social class and psychological disturbance: the influence of positive and negative experiences. *Social Psychiatry*, 3: 41–6.

Philo, G., Secker, J., Platt, S. *et al.* (1996) Media images of mental distress, in T. Heller *et al.* (eds) *Mental Health Matters: A Reader*. Basingstoke: Macmillan.

Pilger, J. (1989) *A Secret Country*. London: Vantage.

Pilgrim, D. (1988) Psychotherapy in special hospitals: a case of failure to thrive. *Free Associations*, 7: 11–26.

Pilgrim, D. (1992) Psychotherapy and political evasions, in W. Dryden and C. Feltham (eds) *Psychotherapy and its Discontents*. Milton Keynes: Open University Press.

Pilgrim, D. (1997a) *Psychotherapy and Society*. London: SAGE.

Pilgrim, D. (1997b) Some reflections on 'quality' and 'mental health'. *Journal of Mental Health*, 6(6): 567–76.

Pilgrim, D. (1998) Medical sociology and psychoanalysis: a rejoinder to Lupton. *Sociology of Health and Illness*, 20(4): 537–44.

Pilgrim, D. (2000) The real problem for post-modernism. *Journal of Family Therapy*, 22(1): 6–23.

Pilgrim, D. (2001) Disordered personalities and disordered concepts. *Journal of Mental Health*, 10(3): 253–66.

Pilgrim, D. (2002a) The biopsychosocial model in Anglo-American psychiatry: past present and future? *Journal of Mental Health*, 11(6): 585–94.

Pilgrim, D. (2002b) The emergence of clinical psychology as a profession, in J. Allsop and M. Saks (eds) *Regulating the Health Professions*. London: SAGE.

Pilgrim, D. and Bentall, R.P. (1999) The medicalisation of misery: a critical realist analysis of the concept of depression. *Journal of Mental Health*, 8(3): 261–74.

Pilgrim, D. and Guinan, P. (1999) From mitigation to culpability: rethinking the evidence about therapist sexual abuse. *European Journal of Counselling, Psychotherapy and Health*, 2(2): 153–68.

Pilgrim, D. and May, C. (1998) Social scientists and the British National Health Service. *Social Sciences in Health*, 4(1): 42–54.

Pilgrim, D. and Rogers, A. (1994) Something old, something new . . . sociology and the organisation of psychiatry. *Sociology*, 28(2): 521–38.

Pilgrim, D. and Rogers, A. (1997) A confined agenda? Guest editorial. *Journal of Mental Health*, 6(6): 539–42.

Pilgrim, D. and Rogers, A. (2003) Mental disorder and violence: an empirical picture in context. *Journal of Mental Health*, 12(1): 7–18.

Pilgrim, D. and Treacher, A. (1992) *Clinical Psychology Observed*. London: Routledge.

Pilgrim, D. and Waldron, L. (1998) User involvement in mental health service development: how far can it go? *Journal of Mental Health*, 7(1): 95–104.

Pilgrim, D., Rogers, A., Clarke, S. and Clark, W. (1997) Entering psychological treatment: decision-making factors for GPs and service users. *Journal of Interprofessional Care*, 11(3): 313–23.

Pillemer, K.A. and Finkelhor, D. (1988) The prevalence of elder abuse: a random sample survey. *Gerontologist*, 28: 51–7.

Pitt, B. (1988) Characteristics of depression in the elderly, in B. Gearing, M. Johnson and T. Heller (eds) *Mental Health Problems in Old Age*. London: Wiley.

Platt, S. (1984) Unemployment and suicidal behaviour: a review of the literature. *Social Science and Medicine*, 39: 93–115.

Pols, J. (2001) Enforcing patients' rights or improving care: the interference of two modes of doing good in mental health care. *Sociology of Health and Illness*, 25(4): 325–47.

Portes, A. (1998) Social capital: its origins and application in modern sociology. *Annual Review of Sociology*, 24: 1–24.

Post, F. (1969) The relationship to physical health of the affective illnesses in the elderly. Eighth International Congress of Gerontology Proceedings, Washington, DC.

Potier, M. (1992) *Evidence recorded by the Report of the Committee of Inquiry About Complaints at Ashworth Hospital*. London: HMSO.

Power, C., Matthews, S. and Manor, O. (1996) Inequalities in self-related health in the 1958 birth cohort – lifetime social circumstances or social mobility? *British Medical Journal*, 313: 449–53.

Power, C., Stansfeld, S.A., Mathews, S., Manor, O. and Hope, S. (2002) Childhood and adulthood risk factors for socio-economic differentials in psychological distress: evidence from the 1958 British birth cohort. *Social Science and Medicine*, 55(11): 1989–2004.

Price, D. (2002) Legal aspects of the regulation of the health professions, in J. Allsop and M. Saks (eds) *Regulating the Health Professions*. London: SAGE.

Prior, L. (1989) Evaluation research and quality assurance, in J. Gubrium and D. Silverman (eds) *The Politics of Field Research*. London: SAGE.

Prior, L. (1991) Mind, body and behaviour: theorisations of madness and the organisation of therapy. *Sociology*, 25(3): 403–22.

Pritchard, J. (1835) *A Treatise on Insanity and Other Disorders Affecting the Mind*. London: Sherwood, Gilbert and Piper.

Putnam, R. (2000) *Bowling Alone*. New York: Touchstone.

Quirk, A. and Lelliott, P. (2001) What do we know about life on acute psychiatric wards in the UK? A review of the research evidence. *Social Science and Medicine*, 53(12): 1565–74.

Rabkin, J. (1979) Criminal behavior of discharged psychiatric patients: a critical review of the research. *Psychological Bulletin*, 86: 1–27.

Rachman, S. (1971) *The Effects of Psychotherapy*. Oxford: Pergamon Press.

Ramon, S. (1983) The Mental Health (Amendment) Act 1982: reform or cosmetics? *Critical Social Policy*, 3(1): 38–53.

Ramon, S. (1985) *Psychiatry in Britain: Meaning and Policy*. London: Gower.

Ramon, S. (1986) The category of psychopathy: its professional and social context in Britain, in P. Miller and N. Rose (eds) *The Power of Psychiatry*. Cambridge: Polity Press.

Ramon, S. (1988) Introduction, in S. Ramon and M.G. Giannichedda (eds) *Psychiatry in Transition: The British and Italian*. Cambridge: Polity Press.

Ranger, C. (1989) Race, culture and 'cannabis psychosis': the role of social factors in the construction of a disease category. *New Community*, 15(3): 357–69.

Reading, R. and Reynolds, S. (2001) Debt, social disadvantage and maternal depression. *Social Science and Medicine*, 53(4): 441–53.

Redley, M. (2003) Towards a new perspective on deliberate self harm in an area of multiple deprivation. *Sociology of Health and Illness*, 25(4): 348–73.

Regier, D., Boyd, J., Burke, J. *et al.* (1988) Prevalence of mental disorders in the United States. *Archives of General Psychiatry*, 45: 977–85.

Reich, W. (1933/1975) *The Mass Psychology of Fascism*. London: Pelican.

Reich, W. (1942) *The Function of the Orgasm*. New York: Noonday Press.

Reiner, R. (1986) *The Politics of the Police*. London: Harvester Wheatsheaf.

Rhodes, A. and Goering, P. (1994) Gender differences in the use of outpatient mental health services. *Journal of Mental Health Administration*, 21(4): 338–46.

Richards, B. (ed.) (1984) *Capitalism and Infancy*. London: Free Associations.

Richards, D. (2004) Self-help: empowering service users or aiding cash strapped mental health services? *Journal of Mental Health*, 13(2): 117–25.

Richards, D.A., Lovell, K. and McEvoy, P. (2003) Access and effectiveness in psychological therapies: self-help as a routine health technology. *Health and Social Care in the Community*, 11(2): 175–82.

Rickwood, D.J. and Braithwaite, V.A. (1994) Social psychological factors affecting help seeking for emotional problems. *Social Science and Medicine*, 39(4): 563–72.

Ritzer, G. (1995) *The McDonaldization of Society*. London: SAGE.

Ritzer, G. (1997) *The McDonaldization Thesis*. London: SAGE.

Roberts, R., O'Connor, T., Dunn, J. and Golding J. (2004) The effects of child sexual abuse in later family life mental health, parenting and adjustment of offspring. *Child Abuse and Neglect*, 28(5): 535–45.

Rogers, A. (1990) Policing mental disorder: controversies, myths and realities. *Social Policy and Administration*, 24(3): 226–37.

Rogers, A. (1993a) Coercion and voluntary admissions: an examination of psychiatric patients' views. *Behavioural Sciences and the Law*, 11: 259–67.

Rogers, A. (1993b) Police and psychiatrists: a case of professional dominance. *Social Policy and Administration*, 27(1): 33–45.

Rogers, A. and Pilgrim, D. (1989) Citizenship and mental health. *Critical Social Policy*, 26: 25–32.

Rogers, A. and Pilgrim, D. (1991) 'Pulling down churches': accounting for the British mental health users' movement. *Sociology of Health and Illness*, 13(2): 129–48.

Rogers, A. and Pilgrim, D. (1996) *Mental Health Policy in Britain*. London: Macmillan.

Rogers, A. and Pilgrim, D. (1997) The contribution of lay knowledge to the understanding and promotion of mental health. *Journal of Mental Health*, 6(1): 23–35.

Rogers, A. and Pilgrim, D. (2003) *Mental Health and Inequality*. Basingstoke: Palgrave Macmillan.

Rogers, A., Day, J., Williams, B. *et al.* (1998) The meaning and management of medication: perspectives of patients with a diagnosis of schizophrenia. *Social Science and Medicine*, 47(9): 1313–23.

Rogers, A., Hassell, K. and Nicolaas, G. (1999) *Demanding Patients?* Buckingham: Open University Press.

Rogers, A., Pilgrim, D. and Lacey, R. (1993) *Experiencing Psychiatry: Users' Views of Services*. London: Macmillan.

Rogers, C.M. and Terry, T. (1984) Clinical interventions with boy victims of sexual abuse, in I. Stuart and J. Greer (eds) *Victims of Sexual Aggression*. New York: Van Nostrand Reinhold.

Romme, M. and Escher, S. (1993) *Accepting Voices*. London: Mind.

Rooke-Mathews, S. and Lindow, V. (1997) *A Survivors' Guide to Working in Mental Health Services*. London: Mind/Joseph Rowntree.

Rose, D. (1998) Television madness and community care. *Journal of Applied Community Social Psychology*, 8: 213–28.

Rose, D., Wykes, T., Leese, M., Bindman, J. and Fleischmann, P. (2003) Patients' perspectives on electroconvulsive therapy: systematic review. *British Medical Journal*, 326: 1363–5.

Rose, N. (1986) Law, rights and psychiatry, in P. Miller and N. Rose (eds) *The Power of Psychiatry*. Cambridge: Polity Press.

Rose, N. (1990) *Governing the Soul*. London: Routledge.

Rosen, G. (1968) *Madness in Society*. New York: Harper.

Rosen, G. (1979) The evolution of scientific medicine, in H. Freeman, S. Levine and L. Reeder (eds) *Handbook of Medical Sociology*. Englewood Cliffs, NJ: Prentice-Hall.

Ross, C. (2000) Neighborhood disadvantage and adult depression. *Journal of Health and Social Behavior*, 41: 177–87.

Ross, C., Mirowsky, J. and Pribesh, S. (2001) Powerlessness and the amplification of threat: neighbourhood disadvantage, disorder and mistrust *American Sociological Review*, 66: 568–91.

Roth, M. (1973) Psychiatry and its critics. *British Journal of Psychiatry*, 122: 174–6.

Rothman, D. (1971) *The Discovery of the Asylum: Social Order and Disorder in the New Republic*. Boston: Little Brown.

Rothman, D. (1983) Social control: the uses and abuses of the concept in the history of incarceration, in S. Cohen and A. Scull (eds) *Social Control and the State*. Oxford: Basil Blackwell.

Rowe, R., Tilbury, F., Rapley, M. and O'Ferrall, I. (2003) 'About a year before the breakdown I was having symptoms': sadness, pathology and the Australian newspaper media. *Sociology of Health and Illness*, 25(6): 680–96.

Royal College of Psychiatrists (1995) *The ECT Handbook* (Council Report 39). London: Royal College of Psychiatrists.

Royal College of Psychiatrists (Scottish Division) (1973) *The Future of Psychiatric Services in Scotland*. London: Royal College of Psychiatrists.

Runciman, W.G. (1990) How many classes are there in contemporary British society? *Sociology*, 24(3): 377–96.

Ruskin, P.E., Silves-Aylaiiau, M., Kling, M.A., Reed, S.A., Bradshaw, D.O., Nebel, J.R., Barrett, D., Knowles, F. and Huaber, P. (2004) Treatment outcomes in depression: comparison of remote treatment through telepsychiatry in inpatient treatment. *American Journal of Psychiatry*, 161(8): 1471–6.

Russell, D. (1983) The incidence and prevalence of intrafamilial sexual abuse of female children. *Child Abuse and Neglect*, 7: 133–45.

Rutter, D., Manley, C, Weaver T, *et al.* (2004) Patients or partners? Case studies of user involvement in the planning and delivery of adult mental health services in London. *Social Science and Medicine*, 58(10): 1973–84.

Rwegellera, G.G.C. (1977) Psychiatric morbidity among West Africans and West Indians living in London. *Psychological Medicine*, 7: 317–29.

Ryle, A. (1990) *Cognitive-Analytical Therapy: Active Participation in Change*. Chichester: Wiley.

Sainsbury Centre (1998) *Acute Problems: A Survey of the Quality of Care in Acute Psychiatric Wards* London: Sainsbury Centre for Mental Health.

Saks, M. (1983) Removing the blinkers? A critique of recent contributions to the sociology of the professions. *The Sociological Review*, 33: 1–21.

Saks, M. (ed.) (1992) *Alternative Medicine in Britain*. Oxford: Clarendon Press.

Samson, C. (1992) Confusing symbolic events with realities: the case of Community Mental Health in the USA. Paper presented at the BSA Medical Sociology Group and European Society of Medical Sociology, Edinburgh.

Samson, C. (1995) The fracturing of medical dominance in British psychiatry. *Sociology of Health and Illness*, 17(2): 245–68.

Sang, B. (1989) The independent voice of advocacy, in A. Brackx and C. Grimshaw (eds) *Mental Health Care in Crisis*. London: Pluto Press.

Sartre, J.-P. (1963) *Search for a Method*. New York: Knopf.

Sashidharan, S.P. (1986) Ideology and politics in transcultural psychiatry, in J.L. Cox (ed.) *Transcultural Psychiatry*. London: Croom Helm.

Sashidharan, S.P. (1993) Afro-Caribbeans and schizophrenia: the ethnic vulnerability hypothesis re-examined. *International Review of Psychiatry*, 5: 129–44.

Sayce, L. (1989) Community Mental Health Centres – rhetoric or reality?, in A. Brackx and C. Grimshaw (eds) *Mental Health Care in Crisis*. London: Pluto.

Sayce, L. (2000) *From Psychiatric Patient to Citizen: Overcoming Discrimination and Social Exclusion*. Basingstoke: Macmillan.

Scambler, A. (1998) Gender, health and the feminist debate on post-modernism, in G. Scambler and P. Higgs (eds) *Modernity, Medicine and Health*. London: Routledge.

Scambler, A., Scambler, G. and Craig, D. (1981) Kinship and friendship networks and women's demand for primary care. *Journal of the Royal College of General Practitioners*, 26: 746–50.

Scheff, T. (1966) *Being Mentally Ill: A Sociological Theory*. Chicago: Aldine.

Scheper-Hughes, N. (1979) *Saints, Scholars and Schizophrenics*. Berkeley: University of California Press.

Schnitzer, P.K. (1996) 'They don't come in': stories told, lessons taught about poor families and therapy. *American Journal of Orthopsychiatry*, 66(4): 572–82.

Schoener, G.R. and Lupker, E.L. (1996) Boundaries in group settings: ethical and practical issues, in B. DeChant (ed.) *Women and Group Psychotherapy*. New York: Guilford Press.

Scott, A. (1990) *Ideology and the New Social Movements*. London: Unwin Hyman.

Scott, M.B. and Lyman, S.M. (1968) Accounts. *American Journal of Sociology*, 33: 12–18.

Scott, R.D. (1973) The treatment barrier, part 1. *British Journal of Medical Psychology*, 46: 45–53.

Scull, A. (1977) *Decarceration: Community Treatment and the Deviant – A Radical View*. Englewood Cliffs, NJ: Prentice-Hall.

Scull, A. (1979) *Museums of Madness*. Harmondsworth: Penguin.

Secker, J. and Harding, C. (2002) African and African-Caribbean users' perceptions of inpatient services. *Journal of Mental Health Nursing*, 9(2): 161–7.

Secker, J. and Harding, C. (2002) Users' perceptions of an African and Caribbean mental health resource centre. *Health and Social Care in the Community*, 10(4): 270–6.

Sedgwick, P. (1982) *Psychopolitics*. London: Pluto Press.

Seligman, M.E.P. (1975) *Helplessness: On Depression, Development and Death*. San Francisco: Freeman.

Sennett, R. and Cobb, J. (1973) *The Hidden Injuries of Class*. New York: Knopf.

Shaw, C.M., Creed, F., Tomenson, B., Riste, L. and Cruikshank, J.K. (1999) Prevalence of anxiety and depressive illness and help seeking behaviour in African-Caribbeans and white Europeans: two phase general population survey. *British Medical Journal*, 318: 302–6.

Shaw, M., Dorling, D. and Brimblecombe, D. (1998) Changing the map: health in Britain 1951–1991. *Sociology of Health and Illness*, 20(5): 694–709.

Sheppard, M. (1990) Social work and psychiatric nursing, in P. Abbott and C. Wallace (eds) *The Sociology of the Caring Professions*. London: Falmer Press.

Sheppard, M. (1991) General practice, social work and mental health sections: the social control of women. *British Journal of Social Work*, 21: 663–83.

Shorter, E. (1998) *A History of Psychiatry: From the Era of the Asylum to the Age of Prozac*. Chichester: Wiley.

Sieff, E.M. (2003) Media frames of mental illnesses: the potential impact of negative frames. *Journal of Mental Health*, 12(3): 259–69.

Silver, E., Mulvey, E. and Monahan, J. (1999) Assessing violence risk among discharged psychiatric patients: an ecological approach. *Law and Human Behavior*, 23(2): 237–47.

Sjostrom, S. (1997) *Party or Patient? Discursive Practices Relating to Coercion in Psychiatric and Legal Settings*. Borea: Spinettstraket.

Skeem, J.L., Monahan, J. and Mulvey, E.P. (2002) Psychopathy, treatment involvement and subsequent violence amongst civil psychiatric patients. *Law and Human Behaviour*, 26(3): 577–603.

Skultans, V. (2003) From damaged nerves to masked depression, inevitability and hope in Latvian psychiatric narratives. *Social Science and Medicine*, 56(12): 2421–31.

Slater, P. (1977) *Origin and Significance of the Frankfurt School*. London: Routledge.

Sleath, B. and Shih, Y.C.T. (2003) Sociological influences on antidepressant prescribing. *Social Science and Medicine*, 56(6): 1335–44.

Smail, D. (1987) *Taking Care*. London: Dent.

Smail, D. (1996) *Getting By Without Psychotherapy*. London: HarperCollins.

Smaje, C. (1996) The ethnic patterning of health: new directions for theory and research. *Sociology of Health and Illness*, 18(2): 139–71.

Smelser, N. (1962) *A Theory of Collective Action*. New York: Free Press.

Snow, D., Baker, S., Anderson, L. and Martin, M. (1986) The myth of pervasive mental illness amongst the homeless. *Social Problems*, 33: 407–23.

Snowden, J. and Donnelly, M. (1986) A study of depression in nursing homes. *Journal of Psychiatric Research*, 20: 327–33.

Soskis, D.A. (1978) Schizophrenia and medical inpatients as informed drug consumers. *Archives of General Psychiatry*, 35: 645–7.

Soyka, M. (2000) Substance misuse, psychiatric disorder and violent and disturbed behaviour. *British Journal of Psychiatry*, 176: 345–50.

Spagnoli, A., Foresti, G., MacDonald, A. and Williams, P. (1986) Dementia and depression in Italian geriatric institutions. *International Journal of Geriatric Psychiatry*, 1: 15–23.

Spector, M. and Kitsuse, J. (1977) *Constructing Social Problems*. Menlo Park, CA: Cummings.

Speed, E. (2002) Irish mental health social movements. *Irish Journal of Sociology*, 11(2): 62–80.

Spitzer, R.L. (2003) Can some gay men and lesbians change their sexual orientation? 200 participants reporting a change from homosexual to heterosexual orientation. *Archives of Sexual Behaviour*, 32(5): 403–17.

Sproston, K. and Nazroo, J. (2002) *Ethnic Minority Psychiatric Illness Rates in the Community*. London: HMSO.

Srole, L., Langer, T.S., Michael, S.T. *et al.* (1962) *Mental Health in the Metropolis: The Midtown Manhattan Study*. New York: McGraw-Hill.

Stansfeld, S.A., Head, J., Fuhrer, R., Wardle, J. and Cattell, V. (2003) Social inequalities in depressive symptoms and physical functioning in the Whitehall II study: exploring a common cause explanation. *Journal of Epidemiology and Community Health*, 57: 361–7.

Steadman, H.J., Mulvey, E.P., Monahan, J. *et al.* (1998) Violence by people discharged from acute psychiatric inpatient facilities and by others in the same neighbourhoods. *Archives of General Psychiatry*, 55: 393–401.

Stein, J., Golding, J., Seigel, J. *et al.* (1988) Long term psychological sequelae of child sexual abuse: the Los Angeles epidemiologic catchment area study, in G.E. Wyatt and G.J. Powell (eds) *Lasting Effects of Child Sexual Abuse*. Thousand Oaks, CA: SAGE.

Stein, L. (1957) 'Social class' gradient in schizophrenia. *British Journal of Preventative and Social Medicine*, 11: 181–95.

Stevenson, P. (1992) *Evidence Cited in Report of the Committee of Inquiry Into Complaints About Ashworth Hospital* London: HMSO.

Stone, M. (1985) Shellshock and the psychologists, in W.F. Bynum, R. Porter and M. Shepherd (eds) *The Anatomy of Madness*, Vol. 2. London: Tavistock.

Sudbury, J. (2001) African-Caribbean interactions with mental health services in the UK: experiences and expectations of exclusion as (re)productive of health inequalities. *Ethnic and Racial Studies*, 24(1): 29–49.

Swanson, J. *et al.* (1990) Violence and psychiatric disorder in the community: evidence from the epidemiological catchment area surveys. *Hospital and Community Psychiatry*, 41: 761–70.

Swartz, M.S. *et al.* (1998) Taking the wrong drugs: the role of substance use and medication non-compliance in violence among severely mentally ill individuals. *Social Psychiatry and Psychiatric Epidemiology*, 33: 75–80.

Sweeting, H. and Gillhooly, M. (1997) Dementia and the phenomenon of social death. *Sociology of Health and Illness*, 19(1): 93–117.

Sweeting, H. and West, B. (1995) Family health in adolescence: a role for culture in the health inequalities debate. *Social Science and Medicine*, 40(2): 163–75.

Szasz, T.S. (1961) The uses of naming and the origin of the myth of mental illness. *American Psychologist*, 16: 59–65.

Szasz, T.S. (1963) *Law, Liberty and Psychiatry*. New York: Macmillan.

Szasz, T.S. (1971) *The Manufacture of Madness*. London: Routledge and Kegan Paul.

Szasz, T.S. (1992) Crazy talk: thought disorder or psychiatric arrogance? *British Journal of Medical Psychology*, 65: 38–44.

Taylor, P.J. (1985) Motives for offending among violent psychotic men. *British Journal of Psychiatry*, 147: 491–8.

Teasdale, K. (1987) Stigma and psychiatric day care. *Journal of Advanced Nursing*, 12: 339–46.

Tedeschi, J.T. and Reiss, M. (1981) Verbal strategies in impression management, in C. Antaki (ed.) *The Psychology of Ordinary Explanations of Social Behaviour*. London: Academic Press.

Teeson, M., Hodder, T. and Buhrich, N. (2000) Substance use disorders among homeless people in inner Syndey. *Social Psychiatry and Psychiatric Epidemiology*, 35(10): 451–6.

Thoits, P.A. (1985) Self-labeling processes in mental illness: the role of emotional deviance. *American Journal of Sociology*, 91: 221–49.

Thompson, A., Shaw, M., Harrison, G., Davidson, H., Gunnell, D. and Veue, J. (2004) Patterns of hospital admission for adult psychiatric illness in England: analysis of hospital episode statistics data. *British Journal of Psychiatry*, 185: 334–41.

Tietze, C., Lemkau, P. and Cooper, M. (1941) Schizophrenia, manic depressive psychosis and socio-economic status. *American Journal of Sociology*, 47: 167–75.

Toch, H. (1965) *The Social Psychology of Social Movements*. New York: Bobbs Merrill.

Tolmac, J. and Hodes, M. (2004) Ethnic variation among adolescent in-patients with psychotic disorders. *British Journal of Psychiatry*, 184: 428–31.

Toro, P.A. (1998) Homelessness, in A.S. Bellack and M. Hersen (eds) *Comprehensive Clinical Psychology* (Vol 9). New York: Pergamon.

Townsend, P. (1981) The structured dependency of the elderly: a creation of social policy in the twentieth century. *Ageing and Society*, 1: 1–28.

Trent, D.R. and Reed, C.A. (eds) (1997) *Promotion of Mental Health*. London: Ashgate.

Truman, C. and Raine, P. (2002) Experience and meaning of user involvement: some explorations from a community mental health project. *Health and Social Care in the Community*, 10(3): 136–43.

Tseng, W.-S. (2003) *Clinician's Guide to Cultural Psychiatry*. New York: Academic Press.

Tuckett, D. (1976) The organisation of hospitals, in D. Tuckett (ed.) *An Introduction to Medical Sociology*. London: Tavistock.

Turner, B.S. (1986) *Equality*. London: Tavistock.

Turner, B.S. (1987) *Medical Power and Social Knowledge*. London: SAGE.

Turner, B.S. (1990) The inter-disciplinary curriculum: from social medicine to post-modernism. *Sociology of Health and Illness*, 12(1): 1–23.

Tyrer, P. (1987) Benefits and risks of benzodiazepines. *Proceedings of the Royal Society of Medicine*, 114: 7–11.

Tyrer, P. (2000) *Personality Disorders: Diagnosis, Management and Course*. Oxford: Butterworth-Heinemann.

Unger, R. (1984) *Passion: An Essay on Personality*. New York: Free Press.

Ussher, J. (1994) Women and madness – a voice in the dark of women's despair. *Feminism and Psychology*, 4(2): 288–92.

Van Hoeken, D., Lucas, A.R. and Hoek, H.W. (1998) Epidemiology, in H.W. Hoek, J.L. Treasure and M.A. Kazman (eds) *Neurobiology in the Treatment of Eating Disorders*. Chichester: Wiley.

Wahl, O.F. (1995) *Medic Madness: Public Images of Mental Illness*. New Brunswick, NJ: Rutgers University Press.

Wahl, O.F. (2000) Obsessive-compulsive disorder in popular magazines. *Community Mental Health Journal*, 36(3): 307–12.

Waldron, I. (1977) Increased prescribing of Valium, Librium and other drugs – an example of economic and social factors in the practice of medicine. *International Journal of Health Services*, 7: 41–7.

Walker, A. (1980) The social creation of poverty and dependency in old age. *Journal of Social Policy*, 9: 49–75.

Wallcraft, J. (1996) Some models of asylum and help in times of crisis, in D. Tomlinson and J. Carrier (eds) *Asylum in the Community*. London: Routledge.

Walters, V. (1993) Stress, anxiety and depression – women's accounts of their health problems. *Social Science and Medicine*, 36(4): 393–402.

Warner, R. (1985) *Recovery from Schizophrenia: Psychiatry and Political Economy*. London: Routledge.

Warner, R. (2003) How much of the burden of schizophrenia is alleviated by treatment? *British Journal of Psychiatry*, 183: 375–6.

Warren, F. and Dolan, B. (2001) *Perspectives on Henderson Hospital*. Sutton: Henderson Hospital.

Watkins, T.R. and Callicutt, J.W. (1997) Self-help and advocacy groups in mental health, in T.R. Watkins and J.W. Callicutt (eds) *Mental Health Policy and Practice*. London: SAGE.

Watters, C. (1996) Representations of Asians' mental health in psychiatry, in C. Samson and N. South (eds) *The Social Construction of Social Policy*. London: Macmillan.

Weich, S. and Lewis, G. (1998) Poverty, unemployment and common mental health disorders: population based cohort study. *British Medical Journal*, 317: 115–19.

Weinberg, S.K. (1960) Social psychological aspects of schizophrenia, in J. Appleby (ed.) *Chronic Schizophrenia*. Glencoe, IL: Free Press.

Wells, J. (1998) Severe mental illness, statutory supervision and mental health nursing in the United Kingdom: meeting the challenge. *Journal of Advanced Nursing*, 27(4): 698–706.

Wenger, G.C. (1989) Support networks in old age: constructing a typology, in M. Jeffries (ed.) *Growing Old in the Twentieth Century*. London: Routledge.

West, P. and Sweeting, H. (2004) Evidence on equalization in health in youth from the West of Scotland. *Social Science and Medicine*, 59(1): 13–27.

Westergaard, J. (1992) About and beyond the underclass: some notes on influence of social climate on British sociology today. BSA Presidential Address. *Sociology*, 26: 575–87.

Westermeyer, J. and Kroll, J. (1978) Violence and mental illness in a peasant society: characteristics of violent behaviours and 'folk' use of restraints. *British Journal of Psychiatry*, 133: 529–41.

White, S. (1996) Regulating mental health and motherhood in contemporary welfare services. *Critical Social Policy*, 16: 67–94.

Whitely, J. (1955) 'Down and out in London' – mental illness in the lower social groups. *The Lancet*, 1: 529–41.

Whittington, C., Kendall, T., Fonagy, P., Cottrell, D., Cotgrove, A. and Boddington, E. (2004) Selective serotonin reuptake inhibitors in childhood depression: systematic review of published versus unpublished data. *The Lancet*, 24: 1341–5.

Whitton, A., Warner, R. and Appleby, L. (1996) The pathway to care in post-natal depression: women's attitudes to post-natal depression and its treatment. *British Journal of General Practice*, 46(408): 427–8.

Wiggins, R.D., Schofield, P., Sacker, A., Head, J. and Bartley, M. (2004) Social position and minor psychiatric morbidity over time in the British Household Panel Survey 1991–1998. *Journal of Epidemiology and Community Health*, 58(9): 779–84.

Wilkinson, R.G. (1996) *Unhealthy Societies: The Afflictions of Inequality*. London: Routledge.

Williams, P., Tarnopolosky, A., Hand, D. and Sheperd, M. (1986) Minor psychiatric morbidity and general practice consultations: the West London Survey. *Psychological Medicine Monograph*, Supplement: 9–14.

Williams, S.J. (1995) Theorising class, health and lifestyles: can Bourdieu help us? *Sociology of Health and Illness*, 17(5): 577–604.

Williams, S.J. (1998) Capitalising on emotions? Rethinking the inequalities in health debate. *Sociology*, 32(1): 121–40.

Wilson, C., Nairn, R., Coverdale, J. and Panapa, A. (1999) Constructing mental illness as dangerous: a pilot study. *Australian and New Zealand Journal of Psychiatry*, 33(2): 240–7.

Wilson, W.P. (1998) Religion and psychosis, in H. Koenig (ed.) *Handbook of Religion and Mental Health*. San Diego, CA: Academic Press.

Wing, J.K. (1962) Institutionalism in mental hospitals. *British Journal of Social and Clinical Psychology*, 1: 38–51.

Wing, J.K. (1978) *Reasoning about Madness*. Oxford: Oxford University Press.

Wing, J.K. and Freudenberg, R.K. (1961) The response of severely ill chronic schizophrenic patients to social stimulation. *American Journal of Psychiatry*, 118: 311–13.

Winnicott, D.W. (1958) *Collected Works*. London: Hogarth Press.

Witz, A. (1990) *Professions and Patriarchy*. London: Routledge.

Woolfe, J. and Tumin, S. (1990) *Prison Disturbances 1990 (The Tumin Report)*. London: HMSO, Cmnd 1456.

Woolgar, S. and Pawluch, D. (1985) Ontological gerrymandering: the anatomy of social problems' explanations. *Social Problems*, 32: 214–27.

World Health Organization (1979) *Schizophrenia: An International Follow-Up Study*. Chichester: Wiley.

World Health Organization (1986) *Ottawa Charter for Health Promotion*. Ottawa: WHO.

World Health Organization (1992) *The ICD-10 Classification of Mental and Behavioural Disorders*. Geneva: WHO.

World Health Organization (2001) *The World Health Report*. Geneva: WHO.

Wright, E.R., Gronfein, W.P. and Owens, T.J. (2000) Deinstitutionalization, social rejection, and the self-esteem of former mental patients. *Journal of Health and Social Behaviour*, 41(1): 68–90.

Wrong, D.H. (1961) The over-socialised conception of man in modern sociology. *American Sociological Review*, 26(2): 183–93.

Wyatt, G.E. and Powell, G.J. (eds) (1988) *Lasting Effects of Child Sexual Abuse*. Thousand Oaks. CA: SAGE.

Yates, A. (1970) *Behaviour Therapy*. New York: Wiley.

Ziersch, A.M., Baum, F.E., MacDougall, C. and Putland, C. (2005) Neighbourhood life and social capital: the implications for health. *Social Science and Medicine*, 60(1): 71–86.

Zimmerman, F.J., Christakis, D.A. and Vander Stoep, A. (2004) Tinker, tailor, soldier, patient: work attributes and depression disparities among young adults. *Social Science and Medicine*, 58(10): 1889–901.

Index

THE ART AND SCIENCE OF MENTAL HEALTH NURSING
A TEXTBOOK OF PRINCIPLES AND PRACTICE

Ian Norman and Iain Ryrie

Norman and Ryrie provide an integrative account of the discipline that accommodates many origins, influences and practices. I feel sure this book will be of considerable benefit to undergraduate nursing students and to qualified nurses engaged in professional development activities. I also believe the book is necessary reading for those who train our nursing workforce.
Andrew McCulloch, Chief Executive, The Mental Health Foundation

- What are the foundations of mental health nursing as a practice discipline?
- What interventions do mental health nurses draw upon?
- How can mental health nurses engage clients as partners in care and promote their recovery?

Mental health nursing is an art and a science; concerned with both the therapeutic relationship between nurse and client and the skills required for evidence-based practice. Nurses need to find ways of integrating both these elements to meet service users' demands and policy directives for mental health services.

This book provides an integrative account of mental health nursing, which incorporates its knowledge base and the practical skills required by nurses to meet the demands of national healthcare policy and service users' expectations.

Pedagogy to support readers includes chapter overviews and summary points, questions for reflection, annotated bibliographies, and fascinating case studies and service users' views to illustrate everyday clinical situations.

The Art and Science of Mental Health Nursing is essential reading for students, post-qualification mental health nurses and nurse lecturers.

Contributors
Peter Ashton, Robin Basu, Geoff Brennan, Daniel Bressington, Alison Carolan, Joe Curran, Jacqueline Curthroys, Philip Fennell, Richard Ford, Catherine Gamble, Lina Gega, Richard Gray, Kevin Gournay, Susan Gurney, Simon Houghton, John Keady, Cheryl Kipping, Steve Morgan, Ian Norman, Ian Noonan, Kingsley Norton, Steve Onyett, Leah Ousley, Shaun Parsons, Rachel Perkins, Hagen Rampes, Julie Repper, Paul Rogers, Iain Ryrie, Susan Sookoo, Marc Thurgood, Gill Todd, Janet Treasure, Keith Tudor, Andrew Wetherell, Phil Woods.

Contents
*Contributors – Preface – Foreword – **Part 1: Foundations** – The origins and expression of psychological distress – Mental health promotion – Mental health nursing: origins and orientations – The policy and service context for mental health nursing – Rehabilitation and recovery – Law and ethics of mental health nursing – **Part 2: Interventions** – Assessment and care planning – Assessing and managing risk – The therapeutic milieu – Psychosocial interventions – Pharmacological interventions and electro-convulsive therapy – Complementary and alternative therapies – **Part 3: Applications** – The person with a perceptual disorder – The person with a mood disorder – The person with an anxiety disorder – The person with an eating disorder – The person who misuses drugs or alcohol – Mental health problems in childhood and adolescence – The older person with dementia or other mental health problems – The person who uses forensic mental health services – The person with a personality disorder – **Part 4: Core Procedures** – Engaging clients in their care and treatment – Problems, goals and care planning – Behavioural techniques – Cognitive techniques – Medication management to concordance – Therapeutic management of aggression and violence – Therapeutic management of attempted suicide and self-harm – **Part 5: Future Directions** – Functional teams and whole systems – Reflections – Index.*

872pp   0 335 21242 5 (Paperback)   0 335 21588 2 (Hardback)

RESEARCH METHODS IN HEALTH
INVESTIGATING HEALTH AND HEALTH SERVICES

Ann Bowling

Praise for the first edition of *Research Methods in Health*:

> . . . a brilliantly clear documentation of different philosophies, approaches and methods of research about health and services. Laid out in an accessible and manageable way, it covers an enormous amount of material without sacrificing thoroughness . . . I would recommend it to a broad readership.
>
> *MIDIRS Midwifery Digest*

> . . . This major research textbook is as good as an introduction to the field as you are likely to find.
>
> *The International Journal of Social Psychiatry*

> . . . an easy to read book with excellent background information on the theory and practice of research. A summary of main points, key terms and recommended reading follows each chapter and there is a useful glossary of terms at the end of the book for quick reference . . . I particularly liked the checklists when undertaking literature reviews and writing research proposals.
>
> *British Journal of Health Care Management*

This new edition of Ann Bowling's well-known and highly respected text has been thoroughly revised and updated to reflect key methodological developments in health research. It is a comprehensive, easy to read guide to the range of methods used to study and evaluate health and health services. It describes the concepts and methods used by the main disciplines involved in health research, including: demography, epidemiology, health economics, psychology and sociology.

The research methods described cover the assessment of health needs, morbidity and mortality trends and rates, costing health services, sampling for survey research, cross-sectional and longitudinal survey design, experimental methods and techniques of group assignment, questionnaire design, interviewing techniques, coding and analysis of quantitative data, methods and analysis of qualitative observational studies, and types of unstructured interviewing.

With new material on topics such as cluster randomization, utility analyses, patients' preferences, and perception of risk, the text is aimed at students and researchers of health and health services. It has also been designed for health professionals and policy makers who have responsibility for applying research findings in practice, and who need to know how to judge the value of that research.

Contents
Part one: Investigating health services and health: the scope of research – Part two: The philosophy, theory and practice of research – Part three: Quantitative research: sampling and research methods – Part four: The tools of quantitative research – Part five: Qualitative and combined research methods, and their analysis – Index.

512pp   0 335 20643 3 (Paperback)   0 335 20644 1 (Hardback)

PUBLIC HEALTH FOR THE 21st CENTURY
NEW PERSPECTIVES ON POLICY, PARTICIPATION AND PRACTICE

Judy Orme, Jane Powell, Pat Taylor, Tony Harrison and Melanie Grey (eds)

This book explores the meaning of the 'new' public health within current debates, and the policy changes that are reshaping the context for public health. It moves away from public health medicine to a multidisciplinary approach to public health concerns. This book asks:

* Why is a multidisciplinary approach to public health important and where is its future?
* What is the nature of the new multidisciplinary public health?
* How can multidisciplinary public health professionals move towards an evidence-informed public health practice?

With analysis and reflection upon public health history theories, research and practice, *Public Health for the 21st Century* engages advanced undergraduate and graduate students, trainees and professionals across a broad range of disciplines.

Contributors
Gill Barrett, Jack Dowie, David Evans, Colin Fudge, Alison Gilchrist, Melanie Grey, Tony Harrison, Stuart Hashagen, David J. Hunter, Stuart McClean, Chris Miller, Jennie Naidoo, Judy Orme, Stephen Peckham, Jon Pollock, Jane Powell, Joyshri Sarangi, Gabriel Scally, Murray Stewart, Pat Taylor.

Contents
*Notes on contributors – Foreword – Acknowledgements – Introduction – **Part One: Policy for 21st century public health** – Public health policy – Public health meets modernization – Public health: a vision for the future – **Part Two: Participation and partnerships in 21st century public health** – Who are the partners in public health? – Capacity and capability in public health – Public health and primary care – Protecting the public's health – The lay contribution to public health – Community development and networking for health – **Part Three: Major contemporary themes in public health** – New directions in tackling inequalities in health – Neighbourhood renewal and regeneration – Implementing sustainable futures in cities – Globalization and health – **Part Four: Evidence and evaluation in 21st century public health** – Evidence-based multidisciplinary public health – Health economics and public health – Frameworks for measuring community health and well being – Health impact: its estimation, assessment and analysis – Glossary – References – Index.*

368pp   0 335 21193 3 (Paperback)   0 335 21194 1 (Hardback)

HANDBOOK OF HEALTH RESEARCH METHODS
INVESTIGATION, MEASUREMENT AND ANALYSIS

Ann Bowling and Shah Ebrahim

- Which research method should I use to evaluate services?
- How do I design a questionnaire?
- How do I conduct a systematic review of research?

This handbook helps researchers to plan, carry out, and analyse health research, and evaluate the quality of research studies. The book takes a multidisciplinary approach to enable researchers from different disciplines to work side by side in the investigation of population health, the evaluation of health care, and in health care delivery.

Handbook of Health Research Methods is an essential tool for researchers and postgraduate students taking masters courses, or undertaking doctoral programmes, in health services evaluation, health sciences, health management, public health, nursing, sociology, biology, medicine and epidemiology. However, the book also appeals to health professionals who wish to broaden their knowledge of research methods in order to make effective policy and practice decisions.

Contributors

Joy Adamson, Geraldine Barrett, Jane P. Biddulph, Ann Bowling, Sara Brookes, Jackie Brown, Simon Carter, Michel P. Coleman, Paul Cullinan, George Davey Smith, Paul Dieppe, Jenny Donovan, Craig Duncan, Shah Ebrahim, Vikki Entwistle, Clare Harries, Lesley Henderson, Kelvyn Jones, Olga Kostopoulou, Sarah J. Lewis, Richard Martin, Martin McKee, Graham Moon, Ellen Nolte, Alan O'Rourke, Ann Oakley, Tim Peters, Tina Ramkalawan, Caroline Sanders, Mary Shaw, Andrew Steptoe, Jonathan Sterne, Anne Stiggelbout, S.V. Subramanian, Kate Tilling, Liz Twigg, Suzanne Wait.

Ann Bowling is Professor of Health Services Research in the Department of Primary Care and Population Sciences at University College London, and has a part secondment to the MRC Health Services Research Collaboration, University of Bristol. Her other publications with Open University Press include: *Measuring Disease* (2001), *Research Methods in Health* (2002) and *Measuring Health* (2004).

Contents

Section 1: Introduction – Introduction: Research on health and health care – Describing and evaluating health systems – *Section 2: Multidisciplinary methods of investigation* – Evidence based health care: Systematic reviews – Critical appraisal – Features and designs of randomised and non-randomised controlled trials and non-randomised experimental designs – Epidemiological study designs in health care research and evaluation – Finding and using secondary data on the health and health care of populations – Quantitative social science: The survey – Approaches to qualitative data collection in social science – Combined qualitative and quantitative designs – Design and analysis of social intervention studies in health research – Area-based studies and the evaluation of multilevel influences on health outcomes – Mathematical models in health care – Economic evaluation of health care – *Section 3: Multidisciplinary research measurement* – Psychological approaches to measuring and modelling clinical decision making – Approaches to measuring patients' decision making – Techniques of questionnaire design – Measuring health outcomes from the patient's perspective – Genetics, health and population genetics research – Tools of psychosocial biology and health care research – *Section 4: Data analysis* – Key issues in the statistical analysis of quantitative data in research on health and health services – Key issues in the analysis of qualitative data on health services research – *Section 5: Essential issues to consider when conducting research* – Involving service users in health services research – Ethical and political issues in the conduct of research – Training for research – General glossary – General further reading – Index.

640pp   0 335 21460 6 (Paperback)   0 335 21461 4 (Hardback)

DISPUTING DOCTORS
THE SOCIO-LEGAL DYNAMICS OF COMPLAINTS ABOUT MEDICAL CARE

Linda Mulcahy

- What are patient experiences of making complaints against doctors and what do they seek to achieve?
- How do doctors and managers respond to complaints and what do their responses reveal about the implicit tensions in the doctor–patient relationship?
- What is the significance of the increasing incidence of disputes for approaches to the delivery of medical care?

This book looks at the dynamics of doctor–patient disputes. Reflecting on fifteen years of empirical research in the NHS it considers the contexts in which these disputes arise, the different ways in which the parties construct disputing narratives and moral identities in the course of making and defending their claims, and the extent to which existing systems for resolving disputes are sensitive to their needs.

This publication is timely. Since the 1970s there has been an increasing amount of concern about the rise in complaints and medical negligence claims made by patients and their relatives. Based on research with patients, relatives, doctors and NHS managers, the book analyses how they perceive these disputes and what they seek to achieve by holding each other to account.

Disputing Doctors is valuable reading for all students, researchers and academics working in the fields of the sociology of health and illness, socio-legal studies, law and medicine, medical sociology, nursing and health policy.

Contents
Introduction – All the president's men: the relationships between the state, the medical profession and doctor–patient disputes – An inspector calls: the policy context – The phantom menace?: looking at the relationship between medical mishaps, complaints and negligence claims – Forever amber?: looking at disputes with doctors from the perspective of the complainant – From fear to fraternity?: Doctors' reactions to being called to account – Devil and the deep: mediating differences between doctors and patients – A new hope: concluding thoughts – Bibliography – Index.

160pp   0 335 20260 8 (Paperback)

COMMUNITY MENTAL HEALTH NURSING AND DEMENTIA CARE
PRACTICE PERSPECTIVES

John Keady, Charlotte L. Clarke and Trevor Adams

A rounded account of Community Mental Health Nurses' practice in dementia care has been long overdue. This is the first book to focus on the role of Community Mental Health Nurses in their highly valued work with both people with dementia and their families.

This book:

- Explores the complexity and diversity of Community Mental Health Nurse work
- Captures perspectives from along the trajectory of dementia
- Identifies assessment and intervention approaches
- Discusses an emerging evidence base for implications in practice

Contributions to this collection of essays and articles are drawn from Community Mental Health Nurse practitioners and researchers at the forefront of their fields.

It is key reading for practitioners, researchers, students, managers and policy makers in the field of community mental health nursing and/or dementia care.

Contributors
Trevor Adams, Peter Ashton, Gill Boardman, Angela Carradice, Chris Clark, Charlotte L. Clarke, Jan Dewing, Sue Hahn, Mark Holman, John Keady, Kath Lowery, Jill Manthorpe, Cathy Mawhinney, Anne Mason, Paul McCloskey, Anne McKinley, Linda Miller, Gordon Mitchell, Elinor Moore, Michelle Murray, Mike Nolan, Peter Nolan, Tracy Packer, Sean Page, Marilla Pugh, Helen Pusey, Assumpta Ryan, Alison Soliman, Vicki Traynor, Dot Weaks, Heather Wilkinson.

Contents

320pp   0 335 21142 9 (Paperback)   0 335 21143 7 (Hardback)

Create
Excellent Video

PETER UTZ

PTR Prentice Hall
Englewood Cliffs, New Jersey 07632

Library of Congress Cataloging-in-Publication Data

UTZ, PETER.
    Create excellent video / by Peter Utz.

    Includes bibliographical references and index.
    ISBN 0-13-547142-7
    1. Home video systems. I. Title.
 TK9960.U8782 1990   90–46552
 778.59′9—dc20   CIP

Editorial/production supervision
  and interior design: BARBARA MARTTINE
Cover design: BEN SANTORA
Cover photo: Courtesy of Magnavox
Manufacturing buyer: KELLY BEHR/SUSAN BRUNKE

This book is also published under the title
MAKING GREAT VIDEO.

The publisher offers discounts on this book when ordered
in bulk quantities. For more information, write:

Special Sales/College Marketing
Prentice-Hall, Inc.
College Technical and Reference Division
Englewood Cliffs, New Jersey 07632

Printed in the United States of America

10 9 8 7

ISBN   0-13-547142-7

Prentice-Hall International (UK) Limited, *London*
Prentice-Hall of Australia Pty. Limited, *Sydney*
Prentice-Hall Canada Inc., *Toronto*
Prentice-Hall Hispanoamericana, S. A., *Mexico*
Prentice-Hall of India Private Limited, *New Delhi*
Prentice-Hall of Japan, Inc., *Tokyo*
Simon & Schuster Asia Pte. Ltd., *Singapore*
Editora Prentice-Hall do Brasil, Ltda., *Rio de Janeiro*